Diplomacy with a Difference:
The Commonwealth Office of
High Commissioner, 1880–2006

Diplomatic Studies

Series Editor

Jan Melissen

Netherlands Institute of International Relations 'Clingendael'

VOLUME 1

Diplomacy with a Difference: The Commonwealth Office of High Commissioner, 1880–2006

By

Lorna Lloyd

MARTINUS
NIJHOFF
PUBLISHERS

LEIDEN • BOSTON
2007

On the cover: Her Majesty the Queen and the Papua New Guinea High Commissioner to Britain, Ms. Jean Kekedo, 16 July 2002. Ms. Kekedo is presenting the Queen with a portrait to commemorate her 50th year on the throne by the Papua New Guinea artist, Laben John. Photo 1598725, Empics.

This book is printed on acid-free paper.

ISSN 1872-8863
ISBN 978 90 04 15497 1

PRINTED IN THE NETHERLANDS

to

Alan

CONTENTS

ACKNOWLEDGEMENTS

This book was made possible thanks to a Leverhulme Fellowship, a Canadian Faculty Research Award, and several semesters' research leave from Keele University. I am most appreciative of this support.

I gladly acknowledge the expert assistance provided by the staff of the following archives and libraries: Cape Town Archives; Cape Town University Archives (especially Ms. Lesley Hart); Churchill Archives Centre (especially Ms. Sandra Marsh); Congleton Public Library; the Irish National Archives (especially Mr. Tom Gilsenan); Keele University Library; the National Archives of Canada (especially Ms. Paulette Dozois and Ms. Marey Gregory); the Institute for Contemporary History, Orange Free State (especially Mrs. Esta Jones); the South African High Commission, London; the South African National Archives Repository, Pretoria; and The National Archives in Kew. I thank them for permission to quote from documents in their possession, and Sir Leonard Allison for permission to quote from his interview for the British Diplomatic Oral History Programme.

At Keele, Profs. Hidemi Suganami and John Horton were encouragingly supportive and helpful, especially in the matter of research leave, and, as always, Mrs. Sarah Gomersall went above and beyond the call of duty in making life easier. Those who lent support, answered queries, provided information, agreed to interviews, shared the fruits of their knowledge and experience, and gave helpful advice include: Dr. Colin Aikman, Dr. Philip Alexander, the late Lord Alport, Prof. David Armstrong, Prof. James Barber, Dr. John Barratt, Mr. John Becker, the late Lord Beloff, Sir Nicholas Bayne, Mr. Scott Bennett, Prof. Jacob Bercovitch, Mr. Glyn Berry, Mr. Michael Berry, Mr. Norman and Mrs. Eve Best, Mr. Jacques Bilodeau, Mr. J.S.F. Botha, Mr. Bill Bowden, Mr. Mark Brady, Mr. Bruce M. Brown, Mr. Gordon Brown, Mr. Peter Bursey, Mr. Frank Callanan, Mr. Harry and Mrs. Pamela Carter, Dr. Peter Catterall, Mr. Pieter Coetzee, the late Sir William Dale, Mr. Louis Delvoie, Miss Allison Derrett, Dr. Greg Donaghy, Mr. Richard and Mrs. Anna Dorman, Prof. Margaret Doxey, the Hon. K.D.S. Durr, the Hon. Fredrik S. Eaton O.C., Miss Eleanor Emery, Prof. Ronan Fanning, the late Sir Robin Fearn, Dr. Kent Fedorowich, Sir Anthony Figgis, Mr. Brand Fourie, the Hon. Royce Frith Q.C., the late Mr. Douglas and

Mrs. Dorothy Gageby, the late Lord Gillmore, Dr. Bülent Gökay, Prof. Erik Goldstein, H.E. Dr. Richard Grant, Mr. and Mrs. John Hadwen, Mrs. Susan Halls, Mr. Bryce Harland, Dr. Peter Henshaw, Dr. John Hilliker, Dr. Ann Hughes, Ms. Vivien Hughes, Mr. Alan Hunt, Dr. Michael Kennedy, Dr. Deborah Lavin, Prof. J.J. Lee, the late Lady Llewellyn Davies, Mr. E. Anton Loubser, Ms. Penny Loveridge, Dr. Donal Lowry, the Hon. Donald S. Macdonald, Dr. Hector Mackenzie, the Hon. Roy MacLaren, Mr. Len Marder, Sir Peter Marshall, Sir Humphrey Maud, Miss Rosaleen McGovern, Mr. Russ McKinney, Dr. Deidre McMahon, the Hon. Roy McMurtry QC, Prof. Jan Melissen, Mr. Arthur Menzies, Dr. Greg Mills, Sir Patrick Moberly, Dr. Steven Morewood, Ms. Sally Morphet, Prof. Marie Muller, Mr. C.J. Muller, the late Dr. Fred Nash, Prof. Peter Neary, Dr. George Ntamark, Prof. Eunan O'Halpin, Prof. Rosemary O'Kane, Prof. Ritchie Ovendale, Mr. John Oxley, Dr. Helen Parr, Ms. Jenny Partridge, Mr. Bill Peters, Mr. Gregory Quinn, Mr. Andrew Renton-Green, Mr. Gordon Robertson, Mr. Ben Rogers, Mr. Jeremy B. Shearar, Mr. Nicholas Sims, Dr. Simon Smith, Mr. Donald Sole, Prof. Jack Spence, Mr. Si and Mrs. Mary Taylor, Dr. Gerard Torsney, Mr. Sidney van Heeren, Mr. Albert van Niekerk, Sir Robert Wade-Gery, H.E. Mr. Ronald M. Sanders, Mr. J.H. Warren, Sir James Weatherall, Dr. Kobus Wessels, H.E. Mr. Sarath Kusum Wickremsinghe, Prof. Bob Wolfe, Dr. Denis Worrall, Dr. Bill Young, Mr. Tariq Zameer, and other informants who wished to remain anonymous, including a number of very helpful officials in several countries. I thank them all warmly.

In addition, I owe special thanks to the following people who assisted me much more than I could reasonably expect, and to whom this acknowledgement barely begins to convey my gratitude: Sir Brian Barder, who swiftly, expertly, and authoritatively responded to e-mails, corrected errors, and made valuable comments; Lady Barder, who let me read her interesting and useful paper on 'Early British Diplomatic Representation in Australia'; Mr. Kenneth East, who, during the course of our happy friendship, considerably improved my overall understanding of, and feel for, the subject; Prof. Geoff Berridge, who lent support and encouragement throughout; Col. Ned and the late Mrs. Betty Doyle, who were most hospitable and always helpful; Mr. Geoff Murray, who gave generously of his time and let me have access to his papers and unpublished memoirs; Mr. H. Basil and Mrs. Elizabeth Robinson, Prof. Norman Hillmer, and Prof. David and Mrs. Joan Farr, who were very kind and generous not just in respect of my research, but in every way; Prof. W. David McIntyre, who was similarly helpful in respect of both the Commonwealth and New Zealand; and Profs. Berridge and James, who allowed me to quote freely from their *Dictionary of Diplomacy* (London: Palgrave Macmillan, 2nd edition, 2003). Drs. David Tothill and Radziah Abdul Rahim freely shared their knowledge as well as material gathered in the course of their own research (on South Africa and Australia, and on Commonwealth consular relations respectively). To have acknowledged each and every instance of their assistance would have produced copiously littered footnotes. I want, though, to put on record that they were both exceedingly helpful: they considerably assisted my understanding of certain aspects of the book and tracked down otherwise elusive information.

All mistakes are, of course, my own.

I am further indebted to Mr. Gwyn and Mrs. Jan James, Mr. Egon and Mrs. Eileen Taska, and Mr. Terry and Mrs. Tricia Knight who looked after Zoë while I was doing research overseas. Eileen and Ms. Sally Gillman also provided unstinting moral support.

I am also grateful to Dr. Arthur Koedam at Brill for taking on my book, and to Mr. Hylke Faber and Ms. Caroline van Erp, my editors, for their efficiency, supportiveness, and helpfulness.

Last, but very far from least, Alan James encouraged me to pursue my interest in this subject and was always optimistic about what I was doing. He acted as research assistant in all the archives, assisted with interviews, provided stimulating and cheerful company, gave excellent advice on all aspects of the book, and was a keen critic of each draft. He also kept me going when I felt desperate and never complained about the book's huge demands and the extent to which it overshadowed our lives. Accordingly, I dedicate this book to Alan with deep gratitude and affection.

Lorna Lloyd
Congleton
20 January 2007

NOTE ON NOMENCLATURE

The United Kingdom of Great Britain and Northern Ireland is referred to as 'Britain'.

In accordance with official terminology, 'secretary' (often as part of a term) is variously used. Sometimes it refers to a government minister, as in Britain's and Canada's use of 'secretary of state'; sometimes the most senior official—the 'official head'—of a government ministry, as in Britain's use of 'permanent under-secretary' and Canada's of 'under-secretary'; and once it was used for the second most senior member of high commissions.

The Irish Free State, by Article 4 of the 1937 Constitution, changed its name to '*Eire*, or, in the English language, *Ireland*'. In post-1937 references, this book uses 'Ireland'. It should be noted, however, that between 1937 and 1949 Britain always used 'Eire'; and after Britain's Republic of Ireland Act of the latter year, she used 'Republic of Ireland' or 'Irish Republic' until the end of the twentieth century.

For the sake of stylistic convenience this book consistently uses what was once regarded as a grave solecism: 'high commission' rather than 'office of the high commissioner'. When 'high commission' began creeping in, in the early 1960s, it was regarded as a 'bastard term'[1] and 'a misuse of the language'.[2] High commissioners were in charge of offices, not commissions. However, by the end of the decade, convenience had won out.

---

[1] Norman Robertson (Canadian DEA under-secretary) in 1963, quoted in personal communication.

[2] Charles Ritchie (Canadian HC, London) telegram 5133, 22 October 1968, NAC, RG25, 11015, 22-6-8, part 3.

NOTE ON CITATIONS AND ABBREVIATIONS

The bibliography contains full details of all the works cited in footnotes. Works are cited by the names of authors and dates of publication alone unless they might be confused with other cited works.

Unless otherwise specified, telegrams and letters from high commissions and embassies are to the relevant department in the sending state. The recipient is identified only when a communication is personal or sent to a prime minister who does not also hold the external/foreign affairs portfolio.

All interviews and correspondence were conducted on the basis that names would not be divulged.

The following abbreviations are used for documentary sources:

BDEE	*British Documents on the End of Empire*
1945–1951 (with part)	Ronald Hyam (ed.) (1992), *The Labour Government and the End of Empire 1945–1951.*
1951–1957 (with part)	David Goldsworthy (ed.) (1994), *The Conservative Government and the End of Empire 1951–1957.*
Ghana (with part)	Richard Rathbone (ed.) (1992).
1957–1964 (with part)	Ronald Hyam and Wm Roger Louis (eds.) (2000), *The Conservative Government and the End of Empire 1957–1964* .
1964–1971 (with part)	S.R. Ashton and Wm Roger Louis (eds.) (2004), *East of Suez and the Commonwealth 1964–71.*
BL	London: The British Library
BUL	Birmingham: Birmingham University Library
DAFP (with volume number)	*Documents on Australian Foreign Policy 1939–1947.*
DCER (with volume number)	*Documents on Canadian External Relations.*
DCBO	*Dictionary of Canadian Biography Online.*
DIFP (with volume number)	*Documents on Irish Foreign Policy.*

DOHP	Cambridge: Churchill College, Churchill Archives Centre, British Diplomatic Oral History Programme.
INA	Dublin: Irish National Archives.
INCH	Bloemfontein: Institute for Contemporary History, University of the Orange Free State.
IOR	London: India Office Records.
NAC	Ottawa: National Archives of Canada. To avoid cumbersome footnotes, Canadian documents have been cited as follows: record group, microfilm reel number (if any), volume number, file number. Thus NAC, RG25 D1, T-1802, 792, 436 refers to record group RG25 D1, microfilm number T-1802, volume 792, file 436.
SAA	Pretoria: National Archives Repository of South Africa.
TNA	Kew: The National Archives: Public Record Office.
UCT	Cape Town: University of Cape Town Libraries.

Other abbreviations used in citations; those marked with an asterisk are also used in the main text:

AHC	Acting High Commissioner
AUS	Assistant Under-Secretary (third most senior rank of British officials—after the creation in 1925 of the position of Deputy Under-Secretary)
CDA *a.i.*	*Chargé d'affaires ad interim*
CO*	Colonial Office
CRO*	Commonwealth Relations Office
DEA*	Department of External Affairs
DFA*	Department of Foreign Affairs
DHC*	Deputy High Commissioner (second most senior member of some High Commissions)
DO*	Dominions Office
DUS	Deputy Under-Secretary (second most senior official)

FCO*	Foreign and Commonwealth Office
FO*	Foreign Office
HC	High Commissioner
HCO	High Commissioner's Office
MEA*	Minister for External Affairs
MFA*	Minister for Foreign Affairs
PM	Prime Minister
PMM	Prime Ministers' Meeting
PUS*	Permanent Under-Secretary (the senior official in some British government departments)
SDEA*	Secretary, Department of External Affairs (the senior official)
UK	United Kingdom

INTRODUCTION

The essence of diplomacy is communication. It is the means whereby sovereign states—notional persons—communicate with other states through their human representatives. Being notional they, like all such entities, can do so in no other way. And as virtually no state finds it practical or desirable either to live like a hermit or to engage externally in nothing but unannounced and undiscussed war, there is a universal imperative on states to engage in diplomacy. Hence it is a fundamental and ever-present element on the international scene. Martin Wight describes it as 'the master-institution of international relations'; and Alan James contends that it is one of the three basic requirements for the existence of an international society of states—the others (both of which bear on diplomacy) being an entrance requirement (sovereignty) and rules (international law).[1]

Traditionally, the primary mode for the conduct of diplomacy has been through residential missions. Those called embassies are headed by ambassadors, who are heads of mission of the first class; legations (a more or less extinct category) are headed by ministers, who fall into the second class; and heads of mission called *chargés d'affaires* make up the third. (Nowadays the latter are almost always temporary heads, which is indicated by the addition of '*ad interim*' to their title.) However, as hinted in the 1961 Vienna Convention on Diplomatic Relations, the use of one of these titles is not mandatory. In Article 14.1(a), which specifies the first class of heads of mission, the phrase 'ambassadors or nuncios accredited to Heads of State' is followed by the words 'and other heads of mission of equivalent rank'. This, among other things, acknowledged the fact that as between the member states of the Commonwealth, heads of missions were termed 'high commissioners', the missions they headed being 'high commissions'.

A. The Office of High Commissioner

The office of high commissioner dates from the latter part of the nineteenth century. That was when, just over a decade after one of Britain's

---

[1] See James (1993) 94–6.

colonies of settlement was designated as a 'dominion', it was agreed that her representative in London should be called 'high commissioner'. Later dominions followed suit. For quite a while these entities remained non-sovereign. However, although it was far from generally recognized at the time, they were embarked on what could later be seen as an inescapable, if somewhat erratic, voyage towards sovereignty. But surprisingly, on the face of it, even after they became unambiguously sovereign the heads of the resident missions which they exchanged with each other continued to be called high commissioners; and this practice has been followed by all subsequent Commonwealth members.[2]

The evolution of the office of high commissioner falls into eight distinctive but sometimes overlapping phases. The first, from 1880 to the outbreak in 1914 of the First World War, saw the emergence of the office of high commissioner. Canada had become a dominion in 1867, and her wish to elevate the level of her representation in London resulted in the appointment of a Canadian high commissioner in 1880. When, in the early years of the twentieth century Australia, New Zealand, and South Africa achieved dominion status, they soon followed the Canadian example—and in the case of New Zealand actually did so two years before becoming a dominion. From the first all these high commissioners had what could fairly convincingly be seen as a diplomatic role.

The second phase, from 1914 until the late 1930s, saw the consolidation of the office. The position of high commissioners in London was enhanced as they gained the same privileges (but not the same immunities) as foreign diplomats, saw an improvement in their status, and engaged in more duties of a typically diplomatic kind. But although they benefited from the intimate Commonwealth relationship, their role was also limited by the existence of other channels of communication between Commonwealth states, the familial nature of intra-Commonwealth relations, and the unwillingness of most of their prime ministers to grant them a full ambassadorial role. However, the office of high commissioner received a boost from some reciprocal appointments by Britain to dominion capitals. Britain had not been keen to make them, but was obliged so to act when some of the dominions—the ranks of

[2] The title 'high commissioner' has also been used in a variety of other international contexts: see Appendix 5, and Lloyd (2000) 47–9. But its Commonwealth use is by a considerable margin the most long-lasting and prominent.

which had, since 1922, included the Irish Free State[3]—ceased using their governors-general as the channel of communication with the London government. This meant that messages from Britain to those dominions had to find a different route.

The third phase, from the late 1930s to the mid-1940s, was marked by noticeable discontent on account of high commissioners having a lower status than ambassadors. One causal factor here was the opportunity given the dominions by the 1931 Statute of Westminster to advance (as Britain saw it) or regularize (as some of them saw it) their formal position to that of sovereign statehood. Canada, South Africa, and the Irish Fee State did so post-haste (Australia and New Zealand only followed suit in 1942 and 1947 respectively). Spurred on by this development, the Irish and South Africans, as part of an already ongoing campaign to be seen by the rest of the world as fully independent of Britain, called for the adoption of 'normal' diplomatic titles and procedures within the Commonwealth. They were unsuccessful. The Second World War (1939–45), however, acted as a significant agent of change. It clarified the dominions' genuine independence of Britain, and was the occasion of their manifest coming of age as international actors. Those who regarded the office of high commissioner as demeaning, and wanted to turn its holders into ambassadors, returned to the fray with greater vigour. Ireland (a neutral state during the War, which offered a telling indication of her independence) led the way, but South Africa was often in the same camp. There was also much moaning by some high commissioners about their status, and complaints about having to deal with Britain through a dedicated Whitehall[4] department, the Dominions Office,[5] rather than the Foreign Office.

Matters came to a head during the years 1946 to 1948, which make up the fourth phase of the high commissioner story. Discussions about

[3] It should be noted that Newfoundland was a dominion until 1934, when she came under direct rule, but her participation in international relations was minimal. References to 'the dominions' in this book do not therefore include Newfoundland. The date on which Newfoundland (a self-governing colony since 1855) became a dominion is obscure. Although her premier attended the 1902 Imperial Conference, he was said to have been 'only there by courtesy, as he was himself almost painfully aware'. In 1907 it was decided to adopt the title 'self-governing dominion' for all the self-governing colonies: Amery quoted in Tyler (1967) 417 n. 1; Roberts-Wray (1966) 17.

[4] A term which refers to the British government, after the London street on which some government offices are located.

[5] The Commonwealth Relations Office as of July 1947.

the office were first held in Ottawa, and then at the 1948 Commonwealth Prime Ministers' Meeting in London. No agreement could be found about a way forward, so it was accepted that the semantic *status quo* should for the time being continue. But it was also agreed—and without this the office might not have survived—that high commissioners should have equal status with ambassadors. It was only half a loaf, but an important one.

Almost immediately, however, it looked as though the office of high commissioner was doomed. India, which had with Pakistan gained independence as a dominion in 1947, was determined on becoming a republic. As the Commonwealth's constitutional theory then stood, it seemed that this would necessitate her departure from the 'family'. But there was an urgent desire on the part of other members, particularly Britain, to prevent that, and India was readily cooperative. A suitable constitutional device to achieve this end was found. However, almost to the day of her assumption of republican status in January 1950, India was insisting that she should exchange ambassadors with other Commonwealth countries, and in that case it seemed impossible as a practical matter that the others should, among themselves, continue to exchange high commissioners. Then India relented. The office was saved. Also during the late 1940s to the early 1950s (and in one respect as a direct outcome of the Indian issue) high commissioners were placed, in almost all Commonwealth capitals, on the same formal footing as foreign diplomats: they gained diplomatic immunities, the right to become *doyen* (or dean) of the diplomatic corps (except in London, where this did not happen for another 20 years) and, on appointment, were routinely furnished with credentials of a diplomatic or a roughly diplomatic kind. The years making up this fifth phase were crucial, in that they saw high commissioners achieving substantive equality with ambassadors. Also during this period, Ireland formally quit the Commonwealth (in 1949), but Britain's dealings with Ireland continued to be through the Commonwealth Relations Office, reflecting the fact that Ireland was not regarded as a foreign state. It was an odd arrangement that satisfied Ireland well—and continued until the disappearance of the Commonwealth Office in 1968.[6]

The sixth phase, from the early 1950s to the mid-1960s, was a time

[6] In 1966 the Commonwealth Relations and Colonial Offices merged to form the Commonwealth Office.

when high commissioners had the best of both worlds—and were 'ambassadors plus'. Not only did they enjoy virtually all the rights and privileges of foreign diplomats, but they also benefited from the continuing closeness of Commonwealth states, the regard in which they all held that organization, and the emphasis of some of its older members on developing links with newly-decolonised members. In consequence, short shrift was given to a mid-1950s suggestion that high commissioners might be turned into ambassadors. And at the 1961 UN conference which negotiated the Vienna Convention on Diplomatic Relations, all the Commonwealth members worked together to ensure that the office of high commissioner was acknowledged as existing alongside and in the same category as that of ambassador.

The seventh phase, from the early 1960s to the mid-1970s, saw the office of high commissioner beginning to lose its advantages. It was falling into conformity with the 'normal' diplomatic pattern, perhaps partly because the number of states in the Commonwealth increased sharply. In any event, the Commonwealth relationship began to weaken. One expression of this was the move towards consular relations within the group. Hitherto this had been deemed unnecessary, on the ground that individuals from Commonwealth states could turn for their needs to the governments of the states they were visiting. These years also saw the Whitehall department dedicated to relations with Commonwealth states being merged with the Foreign Office; the lessening utility of meetings of high commissioners; and, at the end of the 1960s, an Australian suggestion that high commissioners be turned into ambassadors. The Australians did not feel strongly enough to push very hard, but they prompted the British to make a careful evaluation of the office. In contrast to only a few years earlier, Britain found that she had no strong feelings about its retention, but that, on balance, the advantages outweighed its disadvantages.

The ongoing survival of the office since the mid-1970s (its eighth, and final, phase) is probably because the just-mentioned British attitude has found fairly general acceptance within the Commonwealth throughout the period. There is now scant difference between being an ambassador and a high commissioner, and it makes very little difference to the conduct of diplomacy. However, sometimes it is marginally advantageous to be a high commissioner, and in London, at least, many high commissioners cherish their office and believe themselves advantaged. Furthermore, Queen Elizabeth II, as Head of the Commonwealth (but now head of state of only a fairly small minority of its members), has always been a very Commonwealth-minded monarch. More specifically, she has been solicitous of high commissioners, and now and then her private words in defence of the office have been important in ensuring its survival into the twenty-first century.

B. High Commissioners and Diplomacy

In the traditional practice of international relations the right to despatch 'diplomatic' missions is confined to independent, sovereign states, and it is only to such missions and their members that 'diplomatic' law automatically applies. As sovereignty, in the sense of eligibility for membership in international society, connotes constitutional independence, none of the dominions can be said to have enjoyed this status prior to the 1930s. They were part of the British Empire, and hence subject to its constitutional arrangements. This suggests that their pre-sovereign representation abroad should not be designated as diplomatic. Such a suggestion is bolstered by the fact that because high commissioners represented governments sharing the same King rather than foreign heads of state, they were not accorded diplomatic status. And, lacking such status, they could not be members of the diplomatic corps. Nor were these disadvantages (as many saw them) automatically removed with the ending of the imperial relationship. Not until the early 1950s were high commissioners fully enclosed within the diplomatic fold. Only then, too, did they, in their communications with their receiving states, start as a matter of course to use the elaborate—some might say stilted—vocabulary which was orthodox in diplomatic circles (whilst, however, retaining a measure of undiplomatic informality which reflected their special relationship).

On the other hand there can be no doubt that the main purposes for which high commissioners began to be appointed were essentially the same as those expressed in diplomatic appointments: to represent the interests of the sending entity in the receiving one, and more particularly to provide a reliable and secure channel of communication between the two. And, as in the diplomatic world, these purposes were thought to be best served through the representative's residence, usually for some years, in the capital of the receiving entity. It also emerged from the very beginning of the high commissioner experience that those so honoured were susceptible to precisely the kind of sensitivities about personal treatment, language, and protocol which are from time to time manifest in the diplomatic context. Thus the first Canadian high commissioner, Sir Alexander Galt, believed that only membership of the diplomatic corps would have ensured 'proper respect' in the London circles in which he moved.[7] Professor Smiddy, the Irish Free State's high commissioner at the end of the 1920s, protested vigorously about 'people of no status or diplomatic importance or rank' having been placed higher than him at a dinner. He had, he felt, no option but to leave the room rather than sit at the end of a table.[8] References to the imperial-sounding 'His Majesty's Government', the 'British' Empire, and the 'British' Commonwealth caused contention from 1926 onwards, not least with the Irish, South Africans, and Canadians. As late as the mid-1950s, two British ambassadors at Lisbon caused offence by claiming that, as 'the only direct personal representative of the Crown', they were entitled to precedence over other Commonwealth ambassadors.[9] In a similar vein, much time and energy was expended on discussions about the titles of intra-Commonwealth envoys: hence the mountain of memoranda about the office of high commissioner in the 1930s and 1940s.

There are also reasons of a somewhat different kind for suggesting that the role of high commissioner can, at least from a relatively early date, be judged to be diplomatic. These stem from the fact that during the 1920s and 1930s all the dominions were engaged, before they became sovereign, in what were unquestionably diplomatic contexts. Some of this activity was consequential upon Australia, Canada, New Zealand, and South Africa having been made, in 1919, founder members of the League of Nations, and the Irish Free State becoming a member in 1923.[10] In this capacity their delegations participated in the meetings of the League Assembly in Geneva, alongside those of all the other member states. Moreover, three of the dominions—the Irish Free State, Canada, and South Africa—appointed permanent missions to the League in, respectively, 1923, 1924, and 1929. Like all such missions,

---

[7] Galt-Macdonald, 13 March 1881, quoted in Farr (1955) 268 and Skilling (1945) 97.

[8] Kiernan (secretary Irish HCO)-secretary of the Association of Electrical and Allied Manufacturers, 22 November 1929, INA, DFA, Embassy London, Box 1–14, file 3.

[9] Hon. W.F.T. Turgeon (Irish ambassador, Lisbon), no. 105, 31 May 1954; no. 446, 22 October 1956, NAC, RG25, 8196, 7753-A-40, part 2.1.

[10] India, which was not a dominion, was also a League member.

they were accorded diplomatic status by the receiving state.[11] In the light of these developments it would be strange if the concurrent activity of high commissioners was deemed not to be diplomatic.

Then, too, and more strikingly, four of the dominions made straightforward diplomatic appointments before they accepted the Statute of Westminster and obtained sovereignty. The Irish Free State was the first to do so, and indeed in 1920—two years before the Free State's creation—its unrecognized predecessor had purported to appoint a minister to Washington. His presence was only formally acknowledged by the United States in 1924. Further Irish legations were opened in Paris, Berlin, Tokyo, and the Holy See in 1929. Canada, meanwhile, had opened a legation in Washington in 1927, and in the next year took the King's breath away by deciding to establish legations at Paris and Tokyo.[12] In 1929 South Africa followed suit at The Hague, Rome, and Washington. Australia opened legations in Washington and Tokyo in 1940, and in Chungking a year later. No question was—or, indeed, could hardly be—raised about the diplomatic status of these missions and their members. Furthermore, as between Britain and the dominions it had been established by the end of the 1920s that the latter were alone responsible for their diplomatic appointments, and that their heads of mission were not subordinate to the British head of mission in the relevant capital—although, as has been mentioned, not all British ambassadors took this on board. Given, therefore, that a lot of undeniably diplomatic activity was being conducted by the dominions, it would be odd to assert that, because of their technically non-sovereign status, the entirely comparable work then being done by their high commissioners fell outside the diplomatic realm.

The apparent inconsistencies which existed during this period of no less than 30 years are at least partly explained by the way in which the constitutional position of the dominions evolved within the British Empire. Change tended to occur almost imperceptibly; there was often more than one view about what had occurred, or even whether anything had occurred at all; and the attitudes of Britain and the several dominions towards the significance of what was perceived as having gone on were often varied, sometimes widely so. The situation reflected

[11] Each mission had a different name, none of them being called a 'permanent mission'. Canada chose not to regard her mission as 'diplomatic', but it was so treated in Geneva.

[12] Nicolson (1952) 471 n.

Britain's lack of a written constitution, her markedly pragmatic disposition, and her suspicion of theory—as well as, at the political level, her reluctance to encourage a weakening of imperial ties. It was exemplified in a remark which was made about the 1926 Balfour Report by the British statesman whose name it bears. The Report, endorsed by the Imperial Conference of that year, stated that the dominions were 'autonomous communities within the British Empire, equal in status, in no way subordinate to one another in any aspect of their domestic or internal affairs, though united by a common allegiance to the Crown, and freely associated as members of the British Commonwealth of Nations'.[13] On the face of it this was momentous announcement. Yet Balfour said that there was nothing new in it: it was just a re-expression of 'phrases' which had long been 'tossed around'.[14] Others, however, were less easily satisfied, and the exact import of the phrases remained a matter for argument. Even after further discussion resulted, five years later, in the Statute of Westminster—which was designed to bring all legal ambiguities to an end—doubt remained as to whether the dominions had to march in step with Britain when the latter was at war.[15] And, as has been noted, two of the dominions—Australia and New Zealand—were in no hurry at all to take advantage of the Statute's terms. Unlike decolonisation after the Second World War, the grant to the dominions of political and legal independence did not occur at a stroke. Far from it.

Because of the complications and confusions of these developments, there is no obvious single date from which the activity of high commissioners can be designated as unambiguously 'diplomatic'. There are substantial problems with the choice of any year between 1880, when the first such appointment was made, and 1948, when it was decided that high commissioners should have the same status as ambassadors. That leaves just those two years. Given that by 1948 the dominions

---

[13] Quoted in Mansergh (1969) 233. The quoted words are often referred to as the 'Balfour Declaration'. Balfour's name is also always so linked with another, 1917, document in which Britain's support for the setting up of a national home for the Jews in Palestine was memorably enunciated.

[14] Quoted in Garner (1978) 174. See also Balfour-Sir George Foster, 4 May 1927, BM, Balfour papers, Add MSS 49697.

[15] However, this doubt was sometimes treated rather dismissively in London. In 1939 a member of the Dominions Office minuted, 'The King has declared war on Germany & that should be good enough for the whole Commonwealth': F.H. Cledbury (?), 29 September 1939, TNA, FO 372/3319.

had for some time been represented not just in Britain, but also at the League of Nations and in some individual states with whom their interests overlapped, the choice of that year would seem unduly fastidious. It would convey the wrong message about what high commissioners had long been doing. To favour 1880, on the other hand, might seem a little presumptuous. It was made very clear to the lone high commissioner who then entered the scene that he was set apart from the superior diplomats. And it was a couple of decades before an expansion occurred in the ranks of such officers. But from the start the office of high commissioner was diplomatic in character, if not in form. What then evolved was for a long while a distinctive imperial/Commonwealth communications system, the procedures and content of which at any moment reflected and symbolised the extent and character of relations between Britain and the dominions. It makes good sense to call it 'Commonwealth diplomacy' (and it was not the only anomaly in the diplomatic system).[16] Accordingly, in this book the term 'diplomatic' will be applied to all instances of high commissioner activity.

* * *

Today intra-Commonwealth[17] diplomacy is practically indistinguishable from the 'normal' sort, making the former's distinctive diplomatic terminology little more than quaint. But it took getting on for a hundred years for Commonwealth interchanges and the associated office of high commissioner to reach this condition. For most of that period the British Empire's idiosyncratic diplomatic system ran alongside, but outside, the established system, and towards the mid-twentieth century did so rather jerkily, as the members of the group evinced varying enthusiasm for assimilation into the orthodox scheme. However, the purposes and procedures of what was going on among Britain and the dominions were always recognizably a reflection of the larger pattern, and substantive—although not semantic—parity between the two was eventually decreed. Then there was something in the nature

[16] Iceland had diplomatic representation in Copenhagen in the inter-war years, when she shared a sovereign with Denmark; and in 1929 'the several states of the German Reich [we]re represented in one another by diplomatists, though the states have a mere scintilla of international personality as a relic from the past when they enjoyed a greater measure of independence under the imperial constitution': Keith (1929) 483.

[17] In this book the term 'Commonwealth' refers to Britain, the dominions and India after the First World War, and the territories that gained independence after the Second World War and chose to retain their association with this grouping.

of an Indian summer for the Commonwealth, in which its diplomats basked. In keeping with the character of such occidental seasons, it did not last long. Except in certain by no means unimportant but largely uncontentious areas, the Commonwealth's allure gradually lessened, leaving the title of 'high commissioner' standing like a prominent but lonely reminder of different times—a symbol of what was once a proud and significant edifice. The history of that office has its own intrinsic interest. But additionally it reveals much about the evolution and internal upsets of the British Empire at the height of its power, its translation into the Commonwealth, and the latter's experience as a political phenomenon of halting but inexorable decline.

CHAPTER ONE

BEGINNINGS, 1880–1914

A. Colonial Representation in London

Some of the colonies to which British people had emigrated were represented in London from an early date. Initially, this was mostly by means of 'colonial agents', who were charged with encouraging and supervising further emigration. One such was Benjamin Franklin, the Philadelphia publisher, public man, and scientist who helped draft the 1776 American Declaration of Independence. He was the Pennsylvania Assembly's representative for 16 years (1757–62, 1764–75), and during the second period also acted in this capacity for several other American colonies.[1] Nova Scotia was likewise represented (at least intermittently) from 1762.[2] At about the same time, Britain began appointing 'crown agents' to deal with the receipt of treasury money for colonies and, later, with the commercial and financial business of colonies acquired in the Napoleonic wars. Most were retired or serving Colonial Office (CO) clerks who treated their additional positions as sinecures, and the colonies often complained about them. As they were also regarded as having insufficient work to justify their salaries, the system was overhauled in 1833. All agents were dismissed apart from two CO clerks who gave up all their other responsibilities to become full-time administrative 'joint agents-general for the [crown] colonies' (later 'crown agents'). However, the standard of service fell as the two agents aged and took up outside directorships. In consequence, from the late 1850s colonies that had become self-governing[3] began dispensing with the services of

[1] He was appointed colonial agent for Georgia in 1768, New Jersey in 1769, and Massachusetts in 1770.

[2] David Farr communication.

[3] The move towards self-government within the then Empire began in 1841 when Upper and Lower Canada were united as 'Canada'. The new territory was given an executive council, legislative council, and house of assembly. From 1848 ministers were required to have the confidence of the Assembly or resign. In the domestic affairs of such colonies, the Crown retained only the right of veto on legislation and had no control over public officers other than the governor.

crown agents and appointing their own agents-general in London.[4] By the early 1870s, all the (then) Australian states and New Zealand had done so. After the Canadian colonies united into a confederation in 1867, a Canadian 'general resident agent and superintendent of colonization' (1874–76)[5] was belatedly and briefly appointed. By acting as their governments' mouthpieces and promoting the colonies' interests (particularly in respect of emigration and trade matters), such representatives were engaged in 'semi-diplomatic' activities.[6]

For example, the Queensland agent-general claimed in 1871 that Britain's colonial secretary had 'encouraged' agents-general to 'accept a diplomatic and confidential position as regards himself'.[7] In the 1880s, New Zealand's anxiety about Franco-German policies in the Pacific led it to use Sir Francis Dillon Bell, its educated, urbane, and sophisticated agent-general, 'to present the colonial viewpoint continuously in London'. Thanks to a 'combination of circumstance and personality', Bell became 'a key figure in the development of policy'. He frequently discussed the Pacific with politicians and civil servants, and spoke to French ministers in Paris and German diplomats in London. He also formed with his Australian counterparts a 'concert' which, while not always harmonious, nonetheless proved 'an effective pressure group'. In this way 'the Australasian representatives began to assume a clear diplomatic function'.[8] More generally, the role and status of all agents-general were enhanced.

Thus, in 1883 agents-general gained the right of direct access to the colonial secretary. And the CO began to use agents-general as a supplementary channel of communication for routine business. Formally-speaking all official communications between London and the colonies

[4] See Sunderland (2004) 1–5. The first agent-general was sent by South Australia in 1858, two years after an act granting it self-government. Other agents-general included Victoria (1868), Queensland (1869), New Zealand (1871), New South Wales (1871), the Cape Colony (1882), Tasmania (1885), Nova Scotia (1885), New Brunswick (1887), Western Australia (1892), Natal (1893), British Columbia (1901), Prince Edward Island (1902), Transvaal (1906), Ontario (1908), the Orange River Colony (1908), Quebec (1911, although an agency had been established in 1908), and Alberta (during the First World War and again after 1927).

[5] After 1880 Canada's provinces re-established separate agents, later elevating them to agents-general. The Australian states retained their agents-general after federation.

[6] Attard (1991) 15.

[7] Dalziel (1975) 75.

[8] *Ibid.*, 95, 96, 112.

had to go through the latters' governors (or governors-general), who represented both the imperial government and the Queen.[9] However, agents-general offered a convenient alternative to the unsatisfactorily cumbersome and slow gubernatorial channel, especially when urgent matters arose during a governor(-general)'s absence. Moreover, the colonies found that this practice gave them a means of making their voices felt directly on issues about which they felt strongly. Taking note of this development, *The Times* said in 1883 that, '[b]y imperceptible degrees', the agents-general had

> assumed diplomatic functions, they have risen from Consuls and Envoys and have become the mouthpieces of their Governments for political as well as business purposes....it is now...time that the Agents-General should enjoy the *status* of accredited representatives of their Governments....By a process which we are powerless to check or control they have come to be the only channel through which the Imperial government can obtain authentic knowledge of the aims and wishes of a colonial one, and it ought, therefore, to be our aim to give them every facility for discharging their functions. The Governor...is no longer capable of conveying what the colony has to say to us....It requires an envoy of its own, and we should be foolish indeed to hamper his action by any kind of pedantic adherence to out-worn theory.[10]

The CO and governors(-general) were far from ready to relinquish their constitutional powers. Nevertheless, in 1885 a former permanent under-secretary (the senior official) of the CO noted approvingly that agents-general had been 'cordially accepted and studiously raised in dignity and influence' by an imperial government that seemed intent on giving them 'relatively to the Colonial Minister, a status analogous to that which is held by the representatives of foreign States...in relation to the Minister for Foreign Affairs'.[11]

---

[9] Within the colonies, British authority lay with the governor, who could veto colonial legislation or reserve it for the sovereign's pleasure, at which stage it could be vetoed it on the advice of British ministers. Dominion governments had no right of access to the Crown, and did not even have the right to communicate directly with the British prime minister. All official communications between London and the colonies had to go through the governor(-general).

The province of Upper Canada had a governor-general from 1838 and Canada had a governor-general from confederation in 1867; Australia and South Africa acquired governors-general when they became dominions; New Zealand retained a governor until 1917 when the office was 'upgraded' to governor-general.

[10] 18 January 1883, quoted in Dalziel (1975) 88.

[11] Lord Blachford (PUS CO, 1860–71), 19 January 1885, quoted in Farr (1955) 254.

These developments were a significant inroad into an inter-imperial network based on superiority and subordination. As Dalziel has pointed out,

> the type of agent that emerged in the closing decades of the nineteenth century was a new phenomenon for whom a special status had to be worked out. He was not, in the strict sense of the word, a diplomat, for this would have denied the nature of the relationship that existed between colonial and mother country. Nevertheless, it is clear that his role, if not his status, was becoming that of a diplomat. He voiced the colonial viewpoint to the Colonial Office and to other departments of the imperial government; he was included in discussions on matters of common concern; he was regarded as a legitimate source of information on the country he represented; he had begun to represent his government at international gatherings and he attended official courts of the crown as did diplomats and ambassadors.[12]

The imperial set-up was fraying.

B. The Emergence of the Office of High Commissioner

Meanwhile, the new 'dominion of Canada'[13] had taken a crucial step in establishing the right of a self-governing territory to have a form of diplomatic representation in London.

In 1869, two years after confederation, the Liberal prime minister, Sir John A. Macdonald, decided that an agent who focused on emigration work and had only minimal political responsibilities did not adequately meet Canada's needs. But neither was an agent-general eminent enough. However, Macdonald's close friend and former finance minister, Sir John Rose, had moved to London as an investment banker, and was willing to represent Canada's interests in an unpaid and unofficial capacity.[14] At his own request, Rose had not been appointed as an agent. Instead, Macdonald 'accredited' him to the British government 'as a gentleman

---

[12] Dalziel (1975) 171.

[13] The name was chosen because the foreign secretary, Lord Stanley, feared a 'Kingdom of Canada' might offend American sensibilities: McNaught (1988) 130.

[14] Canada had had a somewhat disastrous experience with a British MP acting as agent-general during 1874–6 when Alexander Mackenzie was prime minister. Mackenzie made the appointment 'privately (and apparently rather frivolously)' but constant friction with Ottawa, combined with the need to economise, led to the downsizing and downgrading of the office and this prompted the agent's resignation in 1876: Farr (1955) 255.

possessing the confidence of the Canadian government with whom Her Majesty's Government may properly communicate on Canadian affairs'.[15] Thanks to his 'good judgement, tact and impeccable social standing', Rose became 'the most valued spokesman for the self-governing colonies in London'.[16] The CO and prime minister frequently consulted him, and his wide-ranging work touched on almost every substantive aspect of Anglo-Canadian relations. He also enjoyed the trust of Canada's next, Conservative, government (1873–78), which gave him the title 'financial commissioner'. Rose's invaluable service 'at the centre of the transformation' of the Anglo-Canadian relationship 'from a colonial to a political one and from an administrative to a diplomatic character'[17] led directly to the emergence of the office of high commissioner.

On becoming prime minister for a second time in 1878, Macdonald determined to establish Anglo-Canadian relations on a more efficient and equal basis. He needed more than Rose's part-time services and wanted a full-time 'resident minister to London with diplomatic or semi-diplomatic status'.[18] Without someone to engage in 'the fullest and most frank exchange of views with Her Majesty's Government' there was a danger 'of a feeling of indifference, if not of actual antagonism and irritation, on both sides'. Macdonald therefore proposed to appoint a 'quasi-diplomatic' representative who would enjoy the 'social advantages of such a rank and position'.[19] He accepted that such an official would need a title other than one of those customarily used in diplomacy. But it needed to be indicative of the importance and dignity of the office. Accordingly he proposed 'resident minister'.

The CO accepted that Anglo-Canadian relations were becoming more 'diplomatic' and less 'colonial',[20] and agreed with the Foreign Office (FO) that it would be useful to have a high-ranking Canadian official in London. However, since Canada was a subordinate part of

---

[15] Report of the Privy Council of Canada, 2 October 1869, quoted in *ibid.*, 256.

[16] David Farr communication, 15 June 1998.

[17] *Ibid.*

[18] Riddell (ed.) (1962) xxxii.

[19] Macdonald, Tilley and Tupper memorandum, 20 August 1879, quoted in Farr (1955) 257, 258.

[20] In 1868 a senior CO official said Britain had come to treat Canada 'pretty nearly as an independent country', and in 1870 Lord Carnarvon (colonial secretary) described Britain's relations with Canada as 'political rather than colonial': Elliot-Taylor, 26 June 1868; Carnarvon, 22 July 1870, quoted in Farr (1955) 299, 309.

the British empire, the colonial secretary insisted that her representative could have neither diplomatic status nor the right to negotiate directly with foreign powers:[21]

> the relations of such a person with Her Majesty's Government would not be correctly defined as being of a diplomatic character, and while Her Majesty's Government would readily accord to him the status in every way worthy of his important functions, his position would necessarily be more analogous to that of an officer in the home service, than to that of a Minister at a Foreign Court.[22]

Thus he would have to conduct his business through the CO and would need the foreign secretary's approval to participate in commercial discussions. He could not be called 'minister' since that was a recognised diplomatic title. The title 'commissioner' was thought suitable. However, since Macdonald firmly believed that Anglo-Canadian relations were now 'quasi-diplomatic',[23] he wanted the prefix 'high', partly to ensure that foreign governments appreciated the stature of his representative. As the representative of 'an auxiliary kingdom', the high commissioner was to enjoy 'the full prestige' of a resident minister; and 'so far as is consistent with our position of a dependency of the Empire', Macdonald wanted the high commissioner to play a diplomatic role and 'keep at once a position among the Corps Diplomatique'.[24]

[21] Macdonald wanted his envoy to have this right and to be 'duly accredited to foreign governments'. Before confederation, the Canadian provinces had participated unofficially in trade negotiations with Washington, and in 1865 the FO had instructed the British minister at Washington 'to co-operate and act in concert with the Dominion Government' although 'the primary duty of initiating and prosecuting the negotiations' lay with Canada: Rose memorandum quoted in Hall (1937) 235. In 1871 Macdonald represented Canada on a British commission negotiating a treaty to settle outstanding differences with the United States (including ones touching on important Canadian interests), the only pre-1914 political treaty where the Canadian representative was armed with 'full powers' (although in practice Britain retained control).

Colonial delegates also attended technical conferences such as that leading to the creation of the General Postal Union in 1874, and in 1883 Canada was, for the first time, represented at a (monetary) conference in her own right. At a submarine cable conference Canada's representative occasionally differed openly with the British delegation. However, Canada's representatives were always part of British delegations, and treaties had to be submitted through the FO for approval and signed by British ambassadors as well as Canadian representatives: Hilliker (1990) 19.

[22] Sir Michael Hicks-Beach (colonial secretary)-Marquess of Lorne (Canada's governor-general), 1 November 1879, quoted in Farr (1955) 260.

[23] Canadian government to British government, 1879, quoted in Skilling (1945) 93.

[24] Macdonald in Canadian House of Commons, 29 April 1880, quoted in Farr (1955) 263–4.

After some grumbling about Canadian grandiloquence and CO misgivings about other colonies wanting to emulate Canada, Britain agreed to the title. However she rejected Macdonald's notion that the high commissioner should be a member of the diplomatic corps, although promising to accord him 'a status in every way worthy of his important functions'.[25] In 1880 Sir Alexander Galt, one of the architects of confederation and Macdonald's first finance minister, was appointed high commissioner of Canada in London, and charged with four principal functions: promoting emigration; handling Canadian financial affairs in London; assisting in commercial negotiations; and generally promoting and safeguarding Canadian interests. Interestingly, when referring to this new office Macdonald was wont to use the term 'ambassador' rather than high commissioner (as did some other eminent Canadians).[26]

C. Early High Commissioners and the Establishment of the Office

Galt, like Rose, was close to Macdonald and 'the Dominion's most experienced diplomat'. However, in London he was a 'virtual failure'.[27] This was partly because he was out of sympathy with Britain's ruling Liberal party (he undiplomatically joined the Carlton Club, bastion of the Conservative opposition); his relationship with the colonial secretary was 'distinctly cool';[28] his heath was poor; he felt ill-placed socially and financially; he had an undiplomatic 'penchant for publicly revealing every notion he entertained';[29] and he resented the way 'these "arrogant insulars" turn up their noses' at colonials.[30] No doubt it was galling for an eminent person to discover that 'in London he did not count for more

[25] Hicks-Beach—Lorne 1 November 1879, quoted in Department of External Affairs (DEA) memorandum, 'High Commissioners: Title and Status. Historical Summary', 25 January 1947, NAC, RG25, 2942, 3011-A-40.

[26] Skilling (1945) 93. The high commissioner was to act on instructions from Ottawa, but Macdonald told Galt's successor, Tupper, that once they had been received it was for him 'as our Ambassador to urge the adoption of our views on the Home Government with all your power': Macdonald-Tupper, 16 February 1886, quoted in Skilling (1945) 100. Tupper does not appear to have completely refrained from taking initiatives.

[27] Farr (1955) 262, 268.

[28] *Ibid.*, 268.

[29] Jean-Pierre Kesteman in *DCBO.*

[30] Galt-Macdonald, 13 March 1881, quoted in Farr (1955) 268 and Skilling (1945) 97.

than an ant or silkworm'.[31] And like some later high commissioners, he was unable effortlessly to meld into England's snobbish, upper-class society.[32] But he attributed part of his discomfort to being excluded from the diplomatic corps, and believed that membership of it would compel the British to treat him with 'proper respect'.[33]

However, as had been made clear at the time of his appointment, that was not possible. Diplomats represent foreign heads of state whereas Galt was one of Queen Victoria's subjects and represented one of her governments. In consequence, his position differed from that of heads of foreign missions in many ways. First, it had been unnecessary to seek *agrément* (acceptance of a diplomatic appointment) before Galt was sent to the imperial capital. Second, he could not be accredited in the usual diplomatic way, as the Queen could not accredit a diplomat from herself to herself, a factor that was considered very important.[34] Third, Canada's subordinate constitutional status meant that Galt could not fulfil the ambassadorial function of serving as the official channel of communication. As has been mentioned, official correspondence (as opposed to unofficial, private letters that flowed between the high commissioner and prime minister) had to be channelled through the governor-general and colonial secretary, and the CO wanted to keep it that way. As the permanent under-secretary of the CO put it in 1911: 'the Governor is appointed by His Majesty's Government and is in constant touch with Ministers.... the Governor is our own man and for the purpose of getting at the people with whom we want to deal is in every way a better instrument' than the high commissioner.[35]

Fourth, Galt could not have diplomatic immunity for that was based not on statutes but on international law and practice, and as Canada was not foreign, her relations with Britain were not governed by inter-

---

[31] Malcolm Lindsay Shepherd memoirs, National Archives of Australia, A1632 1part2, digital page 125.

[32] Later complaints included the 'unfailing' 'Englishness of the English'; England's intense nationalism; her 'insufferable . . . air of superiority'; and her 'intolerable' '"tranquil consciousness of effortless superiority"': Loring Christie quoted in Granatstein (1982) 68; General Hertzog quoted in Millin (1950) 138; and Mackenzie King diary, 14 May 1929, http://king.collectionscanada.ca.

[33] Galt-Macdonald, quoted in Skilling (1945) 97.

[34] Until 1945 British constitutional theory maintained that just as the sovereign was one person, so was the crown juridically indivisible.

[35] Henry Lambert minute, 2 December 1911, quoted in Attard (1991) 41. In fact, Canada's first two high commissioners exchanged much personal correspondence with the prime minister.

national law.[36] Fifth, Galt was denied the diplomatic privileges, such as exemptions from import duty, that keep down the running costs of missions and constitute one of perks of diplomatic life. Sixth, he was denied a private presentation to Queen Victoria and refused diplomatic precedence, since he would then have outranked practically everyone else. Hence Galt felt personally humiliated at court where he was excluded from the diplomatic corps and treated as an ordinary subject.[37] Seventh, unlike foreign diplomats who could deal only with the FO, the high commissioner had the right of direct access to every Whitehall department except the FO.

Yet although the office of high commissioner was clearly not that of an ambassador or minister, it had obvious diplomatic elements and has been regarded as having achieved '*de facto* diplomatic status' by the end of the century.[38] This was partly because Galt's successors were eminent and had the financial wherewithal and social graces to withstand London's social and gustatory challenges in the years before 1914.[39]

In particular, Galt's successor, Sir Charles Tupper (1883–87, 1888–96), elevated the office and made it indispensable. A man of considerable

---

[36] Until 1914 Britain held firm to the principle enunciated by Sir John Harding, the Queen's advocate, in May 1860: 'The Colonies are integral portions of the Queen's Dominions, more especially for all International purposes': Smith (1932) 49–50. 'The immunities enjoyed by foreign diplomats in the United Kingdom do not rest upon statutes but upon international law and practice. The only statute bearing on the matter is one passed in the reign of Queen Anne.... This statute did not purport to confer immunity but only referred to its existence, and its main effect was to provide penalties for persons who might be tempted to prosecute their claims against persons entitled to immunity': Diplomatic Immunities (Commonwealth Countries and Republic of Ireland) Bill, brief for second reading debate, November 1951, TNA, DO35/2226.

[37] Ambassadors were near the top of England and Wales' lengthy table of precedence as traditionally and by courtesy they yielded only to royal highnesses. Ministers (heading legations) were not far behind. Galt was quietly (and in a personal rather than official capacity) included about halfway down the list, and Galt was also given personal *entrée* to royal ceremonial occasions such as *Levées* and Drawing rooms (as were his Canadian successors). (These events were held, respectively, in the morning and afternoon, and were occasions when important personages were introduced at Court.) Galt's successor was, moreover, given a private audience with Queen Victoria soon after arriving. In 1911 King George V extended the privilege of *entrée* to the high commissioners from the other dominions, and also accorded them a fairly prominent position on the floor of the House of Lords, on the right of the throne. But none of this made up for the perceived slights which were consequential upon high commissioners not being treated as members of the diplomatic corps—a situation which continued until the middle of the twentieth century.

[38] Farr (1955) 269.

[39] Attard records several Australian comments about needing the capacity to cope with big dinners: (1991) 64–6.

ability, standing and personal qualities, he engaged in 'highly political activities' in London[40] and was *de facto* a Canadian cabinet minister (he also proceeded directly from the high commissionership to become, briefly, prime minister). He therefore spoke with more authority than most ambassadors and ministers and enjoyed excellent contacts in all the right quarters, making the most of his right of direct access everywhere in Whitehall other than the FO. Moving in high social circles, Tupper was constantly in touch with the colonial secretary, but he also had access to the prime minister and the foreign secretary. On occasion, he acted jointly with the representatives of the Australasian and South African colonies, 'among whom he was inevitably the *doyen*'.[41] According to Macdonald, he was 'on several occasions... dealt with as a quasi member of the *corps diplomatique*'[42] and colonial ministers began consulting high commissioners in the manner of 'diplomatic agents'.[43] '[H]is was no mean influence'.[44] Together with Lord Strathcona and Mount Royal (1896–1914) (who until 1900 was Sir Donald Smith), he 'raised the prestige of the office to a level of "ambassadorial importance"'.[45]

This kind of imperial development ran counter to a powerful sentiment in Britain in favour of imperial federation.[46] Federalists suggested high commissioners should develop in alternative directions and become resident cabinet ministers sitting on an imperial council. However, as Hancock points out, such federalist proposals only served to disclose and highlight the 'intense national attachments' which were developing in Canada (and elsewhere).[47] This guaranteed that nothing would come of centralising proposals, although it was years before the impossibility of the federal dream was fully accepted in Britain.[48] What, in fact, was

---

[40] M. McKenzie memorandum, 'Status of High Commissioner for Canada in the UK', 3 May 1957, NAC, 6371, 3011-A-40, part 3.

[41] Skilling (1945) 99.

[42] Macdonald-Lord Stanley (Canada's governor-general), 15 August 1890, quoted in Skilling (1945) 100 and Farr (1955) 269.

[43] Quoted in Skilling (1945) 99.

[44] Skilling (1945) 99.

[45] Farr (1955) 269. See also Skilling (1945) 84 & 104; Dalziel (1975) 112.

[46] According to Hancock, for forty years from the early 1870s onwards 'imperial federation continued to be urged as the only satisfactory solution of the imperial problem': Hancock (1937) 31.

[47] *Ibid.*, 32, 44.

[48] Thus in 1932 *The Times* saw Stanley Bruce's appointment as resident minister as a welcome experiment. 'One effect', it said, 'is the possibility of the abolition of the High Commissioner's office and the substitution for it of representation on the lines of Mr.

emerging was a *sui generis* diplomatic system within the empire, which pointed towards imperial fragmentation. It became 'a matter of course'[49] in the early twentieth century for the other dominions which were then created to appoint high commissioners: New Zealand did so in 1905, the Commonwealth of Australia in 1910, the Union of South Africa in 1911, Newfoundland in 1918, and the Irish Free State in 1922.[50] To these dominions, the high commissionership was 'a necessary corollary to the advanced status of self-governing communities'.[51] As New Zealand's prime minister saw it, his country would now be represented by 'a diplomat... in close touch with the Colonial Office, British statesmen and people, and at the same time financial and commercial representative, ambassador, and courtier... the eyes, ears, and voice of the New Zealand government in Great Britain'.[52]

However, it should be noted that dominion status was not the *condition sine qua non* for the appointment of a high commissioner. Constitutional development within the British empire never marched to a single tune. Thus New Zealand appointed a high commissioner two years before becoming a dominion; and after the First World War both India (a 'jewel' in the empire but unambiguously subordinate) and the self-governing colony of Southern Rhodesia were allowed to appoint high commissioners—although their position in London was comparable only to that of the agents-general sent by Australian states.[53] Nor was the appointment of a high commissioner automatic. Political instability and a heavy legislative load are said to have been responsible for

Bruce's temporary post.... If the working of the experiment justifies the change it may be adopted as a permanent system, in which case the High Commissionership would be abolished and Australia would in future be represented in London by a Cabinet Minister who, as himself a member of the Australian Government, would be able to speak for that Government with full knowledge and authority. The experiment is at least worth making.... The residence in London of a member of the Commonwealth Government cannot fail to make it very much easier for the Governments of Great Britain and of Australia to understand one another's problems, and it should facilitate their cooperation in every field of their activity': 11 February 1932.

[49] Attard (1991) 25.

[50] Newfoundland came under direct British control in 1934 and replaced her high commissioner with a trade commissioner who confined himself to commercial matters.

[51] Attard (1991) 25.

[52] Seddon announcing the decision to appoint a high commissioner, quoted in Dalziel (1975) 167, and W. David McIntyre communication, 22 September 1998.

[53] The 1919 Government of India Act allowed the governor-general (the viceroy), with the approval of Britain's secretary of state for India, to appoint a high commissioner for India. This he did in 1920.

an Australian high commissioner not being appointed until nine years after the grant of dominion status, during which time both Melbourne[54] and London felt the want of someone able to conduct routine business efficiently and economically on behalf of the Australian Commonwealth as a whole.[55] Meanwhile, the agents-general of Australia's constituent states pursued their parochial interests and provincial rivalries.[56]

D. Conclusion

By the late nineteenth and early twentieth centuries the British colonies were steadily moving from a subordinate position towards a relationship of equality with the motherland. This was exemplified in the emergence of a new 'network of contacts'[57] of a diplomatic sort, seen first in the raised status of colonial agents-general and then in the creation of the office of high commissioner. It was a disturbing development for Britain, but she was able to insist on the status of high commissioners being different from that of heads of foreign diplomatic missions. After a faltering start, high commissioners quickly revealed their potential as additional and valuable channels of communication between the dominions and London. There was still some way to go before they were used to the full, and even longer before they secured diplomatic status. But by 1914, when the First World War led to a transformation in the international standing of the dominions and their relationship with Britain, the office of high commissioner had been firmly established.

[54] Melbourne was the federal capital until 1927.

[55] Attard (1991) 60. Australia appointed a high commissioner in 1910.

[56] The opening of a small interim office headed by an 'official representative of the Commonwealth [of Australia] in London' was not enough for Australia's needs as the official representative lacked weight and was fiercely resented by the agents-general.

[57] Stanley Baldwin quoted in Hancock (1937) 30.

CHAPTER TWO

CONSOLIDATION, 1914–LATE 1930s

A. The Growing Stature of the Dominions: Their Entry into International Relations and the Question of Constitutional Change

The First World War changed the imperial relationship and led to a period of 'quiet ferment' in the development of the Commonwealth.[1] Before the War, the sovereignty of the King and the British Parliament over the whole Empire was unimpaired; the dominions had no say in imperial foreign policy (even on matters of direct concern); and when Britain declared war in 1914 the dominions were automatically at war. By 1939 the dominions were independent international actors, three of them were sovereign states,[2] and they took their own decisions about entering the Second World War, with Ireland choosing to remain neutral.

Thanks to the dominions' contribution to the war effort and their increased assertiveness regarding their own, individual, interests, Britain promised in 1915 to consult them about the terms of peace. This promise was repeated in 1917, when an Imperial War Cabinet and an Imperial War Conference were created. The first gave the dominions a say in the conduct of the war; the second an opportunity to discuss intra-imperial affairs. At the same time, the dominions were declared 'autonomous' members of an 'Imperial Commonwealth'. Thereafter, 'Commonwealth' was increasingly used, and in 1921 it became 'a new, official designation of the Empire'. In addition, Britain promised the dominions 'continuous consultation' and 'an adequate voice in foreign policy and foreign relations'.[3] What, precisely, this meant was not stated; it was to be worked out at a special post-war constitutional conference.

---

[1] See Lloyd (2003) 279–303.

[2] On sovereignty, see James (1986) *passim*.

[3] Hancock (1937) 54 and Cmd. 8566 (1917) quoted in *ibid.* 54 n. 2, 64. As a member of the Imperial War Conference and 'an important part' of the Commonwealth, India, too, was in receipt of these promises.

However, by 1921 the pace of constitutional development was deemed to have rendered such a conference unnecessary.

Meanwhile, vociferous dominion demands had prompted the British prime minister, David Lloyd George, to arrange for their representatives to attend the Paris Peace Conference as part of a 'British Empire' delegation. Signing the peace treaties confirmed the dominions' international status, as did founder membership of the League of Nations, International Labour Organisation (ILO), and Permanent Court of International Justice.[4] Within a few years they had successfully asserted their right to act independently in international relations in the following ways: to send and receive legations; to negotiate and sign treaties; to enjoy all the rights of League membership, including eligibility for election to its Council; to receive separate invitations to conferences; and, seemingly (inasmuch as they did not sign the 1925 Locarno Treaties), to remain at peace when Britain was at war. Furthermore, although they promised to consult on matters of common concern, a common view was not to be assumed. All this was before the dominions had achieved either the right to sovereign statehood or the capacity to participate very actively in international relations.

The dominions were therefore a puzzling phenomenon. Moreover, the uncertainty regarding their formal position was fostered and accentuated by two political factors. On the one hand, most dominions were unclear about the precise international status which they sought; nor did they agree about the speed at which they should travel to whatever destination might lie at the end of the constitutional road along which they were straggling. Thus they never presented Britain with anything remotely resembling a united front on questions about the status of their representatives within and without the emerging Commonwealth.

On the other hand, most dominions were keen to assert their formal equality with Britain. The mother country was not outrightly obstructionist. She made concessions, while trying to discourage decisive steps and avoid anything that could be seen as diluting the dominions' position within the Empire/Commonwealth. Even the striking Balfour Declaration that emerged from the 1926 Imperial Conference was quite convincingly regarded in Britain not as a hard-won dominion victory but as doing little more than endorse the established constitutional situation.

---

[4] Although India was not within sight of dominion status, she also became a member of these organisations.

Nonetheless, it was important in confirming that the dominions were 'autonomous Communities . . . equal in status, in no way subordinate one to the other in any aspect of their dominion or external affairs, though united by a common allegiance to the Crown, and freely associated as members of the British Commonwealth of Nations'. That each was clearly 'the master of its own destiny. . . . subject to no compulsion whatever'[5] was underlined by terminological changes: 'imperial government' was dropped; Britain should no longer speak as if the King's only government and parliament was in London; and 'British Empire' was not to be used in treaties and at the League of Nations. At the 1930 Imperial Conference, some dominions even insisted that 'His Britannic Majesty' could be used only in respect of Britain.[6]

By 1931 it was possible for Britain's Parliament to embody the Balfour Declaration in legislative form, in the shape of the Statute of Westminster. It gave the dominions the opportunity to claim formal sovereignty. But it did not solve all the constitutional problems. Canada, the Irish Free State, and South Africa immediately accepted the Statute; but Australia and New Zealand expressly requested that the Statute should not be applied to them (only changing their minds in 1942 and 1947 respectively). And so far as all the dominions were concerned, there remained (at least in Britain's eyes) the imperial doctrine of *inter-se*. It held that shared allegiance to the King meant that intra-Commonwealth relations were of a special, non-foreign nature and were not governed by international law. The doctrine was a valuable constitutional device, protecting key features of the Commonwealth during this transitional period.[7] However, it was not well-understood, and two dominions—the Irish Free State[8] and South Africa—vigorously rejected it. Not until 1939, when Ireland opted for neutrality, was there complete clarification

[5] 'Report of Inter-Imperial Relations Committee', *Imperial Conference, 1926. Summary of Proceedings*, Cmd. 2768.

[6] See Percy Koppel (FO)-law officers, 15 May 1931, TNA, U407/14/750, FO834/40. A member of the Australian High Commission 'enjoyed persuading—without much difficulty—the Russian Embassy [at London] to insert in Valsov's Commission [as first Soviet minister at Canberra] the phrase "*His Britannic Majesty's* Commonwealth of Australia"': Stirling (1974) 289.

[7] For example, it protected preferential trading tariffs, the common nationality of Commonwealth citizens (thus exempting them from treatment as aliens in any part of the empire), and the diplomatic unity of the empire. This last consideration meant that that Britain could, on occasion, speak as if the Commonwealth were a single diplomatic unit, and the dominions could use British diplomatic representatives.

[8] In 1937 the name was changed to Ireland.

of the key point that part of the King's realms (however tenuous, as in Ireland's case) could remain at peace when the rest were at war.

Another step forward in the early 1930s was the acquisition by the Irish Free State and South Africa of their own Great Seals (that is the seal affixed to certain documents signed by the sovereign, such as royal proclamations, and, in respect of external relations, the issue of full powers and instruments of ratification). They were only to be used on the advice of the two governments concerned.[9] Canada, which had had her own Great Seal since 1869, began using it on all Canadian instruments in the 1930s. (Australia only followed suit in 1955 and New Zealand—calling it simply a Seal—in 1977.)

Britain, the antipodean dominions, and Buckingham Palace[10] all worried about where these changes would lead. In 1926 the Lord Chancellor stomped out of the Imperial Conference 'saying he was not going to be a party to the breaking up of the British Empire'.[11] The Foreign Office (FO) and the Labour prime minister, Ramsay MacDonald, spoke of the disruption of the diplomatic unity of the Empire leading to 'disaster' and 'chaos'.[12] The King, too, had 'feelings of no little anxiety as to the continued unity of the empire'.[13] Britain did not find it easy to come to terms with changing realities by relinquishing archaic notions of superiority and recognising that dominions were not there to do her bidding. Lloyd George had already caused huge offence by taking dominion military support for granted at the outset of the 1922 Near East (Chanak) crisis; at the 1924 and 1929 League Assemblies, Ramsay MacDonald was brusque with dominion delegates and made them feel as if they were back at school; and as late as 1936 the Conservative prime minister, Stanley Baldwin, was 'a trifle surprised and shocked'

---

[9] Britain would have liked the Great Seal of the Realm to be regarded as a Commonwealth seal. When DO officials discussed this with the Lord Chancellor, 'Lord Sankey, who was a tall man, put his hand on [E.J.] Harding's [PUS] shoulder, and said, "My dear boy, if they want to break away, they'll break away, and you won't stop them with Seals or anything else"': Dixon memoirs, 42.

[10] The British sovereign's London residence, often spoken of simply as 'the Palace'.

[11] D.B. MacRae-J.W. Dafoe, 21 November 1926 quoted in Cook (1965) 61.

[12] Koppel memorandum, 1926 quoted in Hillmer (1981) 65; MacDonald-Robert Cecil, 7 August 1930, BL, Cecil papers, Add MSS 51081.

[13] Nicolson (1952) 485. In 1930 the King had for the first time found his wishes overridden—over the appointment of an Australian governor-general. Hence the announcement 'icily' did not refer to the King being pleased to make the appointment: Garner (1978) 66–7; Nicolson (1952) 477–82.

to learn that the King's other prime ministers were as much concerned as him with the abdication, and entitled to offer counsel on it.[14] A high commissioner sent to Ottawa in 1938 'had mighty little idea when [he] arrived, of what it means to be a Dominion'.[15]

B. The Enhanced Standing of High Commissioners in London

Naturally these developments affected the standing of high commissioners. The First World War has been described as 'a forcing-house'[16] for dominion representatives, whose status was additionally enhanced by Canada's decision to upgrade her wartime representation to cabinet minister. During the post-war years their office was further consolidated and enhanced. Five developments require note.

1. *The Importance of the Office*

The importance of the high commissionership was underlined by the continuing appointment to it of men of stature. Frequently they came from the ranks of former prime ministers, senior cabinet ministers, or prominent businessmen, reflecting the importance of relations with London—the focal point of the dominions' external relations. Apart from the Irish Free State, the dominions thought it essential that such a blue-riband appointment should be an eminent public figure. This ruled out officials (and there was in any case a lack of trained and experienced officers in the dominions' embryonic Departments of External Affairs [DEAs]),[17] and the post had no appeal for still-ambitious politicians. (Australia also thought businessmen lacked appropriate experience.) Hence the high commissionership often went to those who had already

[14] MacDonald (1969) 124.

[15] Sir Gerald Campbell quoted in Garner (1978) 46 n. After establishing that the official who had been sent to open the first Canadian legation at Tokyo 'could speak a more or less intelligible form of English', the British ambassador's wife 'bombarded' him with 'inquiries as to why Canada should be opening diplomatic offices abroad, especially in Japan. "Quite unnecessary, you know; we don't mind looking after things for you, and, of course, we have had a long experience. So silly of you".' The first secretary's wife, who had been 'wondering if you would be wearing spurs and a cowboy hats,' was surprised to find he had written a book: Keenleyside (1981) 269.

[16] E.A. Walker quoted in Attard (1991) 116.

[17] The dominions had no accredited heads of mission outside London until 1924.

made their mark in politics, which underlined the importance of the office to the sending government.

The office also went to people to whom prime ministers were politically indebted and whom they wanted to reward. For example, Sir George Reid had already (in 1908) been given the high commissionership for standing down as leader of Australia's Free Trade Party, and in 1922 Canada's Mackenzie King gave it to his close friend and financial benefactor, the self-made tea tycoon, Peter Larkin. Larkin also had the added advantage of being 'safe', as King (like South Africa's prime ministers) wanted to keep control over relations with Britain. On the other hand, some eminent appointees were gracefully being put out to pasture in London—such as cabinet ministers who had become liabilities; and others were dangerous political rivals who were being sent into exile, sometimes with felicitous outcomes. One such example was Stanley Bruce who became an international statesman in the 1930s and has been described as Australia's 'first and best diplomatist'.[18] South Africa, unusually, had several high commissioners who went on to hold senior government appointments, including, in 1929, a future foreign minister, Eric Louw.[19] And during turbulent times Australia followed Canada's earlier example of upgrading her representation to the level of a cabinet minister. For example, Bruce, whose first task was to encourage financial confidence in Australia, held the position of resident minister for a year from 1932 until October 1933, when he became high commissioner.[20] During the Second World War Churchill also recognised the advantages of 'political' high commissioners when he decided that British representation in Ottawa, Canberra, and Pretoria should 'be on cabinet level'.[21]

---

[18] Alfred Stirling, quoted in E.T. Williams and C.S. Nicholls (eds.) (1995) 158.

[19] One South African high commissioner who did not fall into this category but who immensely impressed King George V was Deneys Reitz. 'A wonderful record to fight against us in the Boer War and then to lead our troops in the next war,' said the King, who was cross when Hertzog refused to let him bestow an honour on Reitz: Clifford (1964) 169.

[20] Australia appointed two more resident ministers: J.A. Beasley from August to November 1946 when he became high commissioner; and E.J. Harrison (1950–51).

[21] Churchill-Smuts (South African PM), secret & personal, 12 February 1941, TNA, DO121/106. Sending Malcolm MacDonald to Ottawa was an inspired move. Mackenzie King had admired his father, the former prime minister, and was lonely. He came greatly to enjoy MacDonald's excellent, egalitarian personality. It was MacDonald who alerted Canadians to the US treating the northwest as its own backyard, and so impressed was King by MacDonald's paper on the subject that it became a Canadian government paper.

The appointment of senior people as high commissioners had several advantages. They were likely to be accorded quick and easy access, and the higher their standing the wider their *entrée* and acceptability. If they were close to their prime ministers, their messages home—especially personal letters—were likely to get through to the top and might influence policy. Meanwhile, what they said in London carried weight, and they could say it with the confidence and experience of people of their background. Such political clout was, perhaps, especially important at times of crisis and war, but there was always much to be said for a politician's ability to take, and assume responsibility for, quick decisions. Indeed, when in the thick of hectic developments in London, such high commissioners occasionally took policy decisions without always consulting or informing home.

2. *An Expanding Work Load*

Meanwhile, the workload of high commissioners had increased, focusing on those matters that were the stuff of bilateral relations with Britain: finance, trade, emigration, war debts, loans, and agricultural matters. For example, Australia's Major-General Ryrie (1927–32) concentrated on 'men, money and markets'[22] and W.J. Jordan (1935–51) 'felt that his job was to sell New Zealand mutton and butter'.[23] It has sometimes been suggested that this emphasis distinguished high commissioners from diplomats proper, reflecting the then current assumption that real diplomats concentrated on political issues and did not sully themselves with economic questions. But from the perspective of the twenty-first century, early intra-Commonwealth diplomacy has a rather modern flavour, as nowadays trade is one of the most important of diplomacy's expanded tasks, accounting 'for a considerable portion of the cost of any major nation's diplomatic service'.[24]

Conferencing was another task that took up a fair amount of time for high commissioners, it often being very convenient for their governments to send them to, say, meetings of the League of Nations in Geneva. In addition to annual meetings of the Assembly and periodic meetings of

[22] Attard (1991) 209. In 1939 the high commission was 'still almost entirely concerned' with commercial and financial matters: W.R. Hodgson (SDEA) memorandum, 'Australian high commissioner, Canada', 13 September 1939, *DAFP* 2, 233, http://www.info.dfat.gov.au/info/historical/HistDocs.nsf/.

[23] Nicholls (1961) 383.

[24] Phillips (1995) 60.

the Council (after 1927 there was always a dominion representative on the Council), there were yearly meetings of the ILO and—for Australia, New Zealand and South Africa—the Permanent Mandates Commission. On top of this, there were conferences on reparations (1924 and 1929) and naval disarmament (1927). By the end of the decade, the burden of normal work combined with being outside Britain for, on average, a third of the year was almost too much for Ryrie.

3. *The Growing Diplomatic Character of the Office*

A third way in which the office of high commissioner was enhanced resulted from Irish-South African efforts to emphasise its diplomatic character. Their high commissioners and governments, but especially the latter, were inclined to regard the office in a diplomatic light, to use it as the channel of communication with the British government and to emphasise diplomatic procedures. Britain was forced to respond and, although she would not yield on principles, she occasionally made significant concessions. In this way some distinctions were broken down without much argument.

In fact, the most important restriction on high commissioners playing a diplomatic role—the use of the governor-general as the formal channel of communication between the dominions and London—had been threatened as early as the end of the First World War. In 1918 the feisty and abrasive Australian prime minister, Billy Hughes, demanded the right to bypass not only governors-general but also the CO, and deal directly with British ministers, including the prime minister. Governors-general protested, some vehemently, but especially as for all practical purposes Hughes and the Canadian prime minister were already corresponding with Lloyd George, Britain felt obliged to recognise that Hughes had a point. In 1918 the Imperial War Conference therefore resolved that dominion prime ministers had the right of such direct communication in circumstances deemed special by them. An important formal step forward had been taken. It was taken even further in 1931 when the Irish Free State successfully claimed for her ministers the right of direct access to the sovereign. Her minister for external affairs, Patrick McGilligan swiftly availed himself of this right, but McGilligan envisaged that it would usually be the high commissioner who approached the King and, in so doing, obtain 'a special position of dignity'.[25] South Africa followed the Irish example.

---

[25] DEA-CRO, no. 233, 12 September 1930, INA, DFA, S6009/1. In practice

A little earlier, in 1928, South Africa's prime minister, General Hertzog (1924–39), had told the dominions secretary, Leo Amery (1924–29), that he wanted his high commissioner to have diplomatic status and perhaps a diplomatic title, such as 'High Commissioner . . . and Diplomatic Representative'.[26] Amery said on the one hand that this would be 'liable to cause misconception of free open and intimate relations and co-operation which are attribute of Empire';[27] and on the other that the title of high commissioner already had significant standing.[28] Hertzog disagreed. But although his high commissioner continued complaining about his title and, specifically, that it made foreigners think he was part of British delegations to international conferences—so causing him 'great discomfiture'[29]—Hertzog ceased pushing in that direction. Instead, he concentrated on establishing the diplomatic character of the office as a practical matter, without directly challenging Britain.

In March 1929 Hertzog obtained the governor-general's approval for the high commissioner to be given 'additional duties', including 'the care of the interests of the Union in the United Kingdom in as full and ample a manner as . . . an Envoy Extraordinary and Minister Plenipotentiary'.[30] Eric Louw, the newly-arrived high commissioner (for whom Hertzog sought retrospective *agrément*, saying the process of appointing a high commissioner should be the same as for heads of legation), regarded himself 'as function[ing] in all respects as Minister Plenipotentiary', reporting 'officially *only* to the [South African] Minister of External Affairs'.[31] In 1930 Hertzog declared that Louw's successor, Charles te Water, ranked higher than any other South African head

most submissions were made through governors-general. Berriedale Keith had said it would be a 'constitutional monstrosity' for the King to act on the advice of dominion ministers; the King's private secretary objected; and the King remarked to McGilligan that 'he always knew that the British Constitution was elastic and added "aren't we stretching it a bit far these days"?': Nicolson (1952) 487; Garner (1978) 65; Costello address to the Canadian Bar Association, 1 September 1948, INA, DFA, London Embassy, F100/5/6.

[26] Draft minute, 6 November 1928, SAA, BTS, 43/4, vol. 1; Dixon minute, July 1948, TNA, DO35/3203.

[27] Smit (South African HC, 1925–29) telegram, 21 December 1928; Smit-MEA, 28 December 1928, SAA, BTS, 43/4, vol. 2.

[28] See Amery-Clifford, telegram 1, 4 January 1929, SAA, BTS, 43/4, vol. 2.

[29] Te Water (South African HC, 1929–39)-Hertzog, 31 March 1932, SAA, BTS, 43/4 vol. 2. See also Smit-Hertzog, 28 December 1928, SAA, BTS, 43/4 vol. 2.

[30] This would, however, be 'without prejudice to the existing system of direct communication': Hertzog minute 785 for governor-general, March 1929, P.M.12/10, SAA, BTS, 43/4, vol. 2.

[31] Smiddy-Louw interview, 5 April 1929, INA, DFA, Embassy London, Box 1–14, file 3.

of mission; and at the Imperial Conference warned of the 'imperative necessity' of rejecting 'every theory or doctrine, no matter how ancient or venerable' that conflicted with equal rights, privileges and freedom.[32] Within a couple of years his high commissioner described his functions as having undergone 'a profound change'. From being a channel for conducting 'business and administrative activities', he had become his government's 'mouthpiece' and was 'regularly' used for 'diplomatic and political work'.[33]

By the mid-1930s te Water's 'diplomatic' stature had been underlined in several further ways. His second-in-command was a political secretary (rather than a Treasury official).[34] He was (like his Irish counterpart) dealing with the London missions of states in which the Union was unrepresented;[35] and he had become the channel of communication 'in all matters of importance' with Pretoria.[36] (Also, although he hated socialising, te Water cultivated close relations with the foreign secretary as a means of emphasising his engagement in 'diplomatic work'.) When the question of a change of title was resurrected in 1937, Hertzog saw no need: Britain knew te Water was the Union's diplomatic representative, he performed the same tasks as heads of legations, and as a practical matter was in no way inferior to them. The same could be said of his fellow high commissioners.

4. *Winning Enhanced Status*

However, given human nature, the sensitivity of dominions to anything suggestive of colonial inferiority, and the importance of symbolism in diplomacy, it is unsurprising that high commissioners made complaints about their lack of diplomatic status. This was especially evident as regards *placement*. A number of letters were sent after formal dinners, reminding the organisers that high commissioners were not colonial nobodies, and on at least one occasion the Irish high commissioner walked out, having found himself seated below 'people of no status

[32] *Irish Independent*, 15 November 1930.

[33] Te Water Annual Report for 1932, February 1933, SAA, BTS 4/2/24/1, vol. 1.

[34] As there was no DEA when the office of high commissioner was established, the South African HC was originally made responsible to the Department of Finance. Only after South Africa left the Commonwealth in 1961 was South Africa House, London (where her High Commission/Embassy was located) transferred to the DFA: Nöthling (2005) 549.

[35] The FO agreed to this step forward in 1936.

[36] van Wyk (2005) 44, 47.

or diplomatic importance or rank'.[37] Also, as in Galt's day, there were many laments about the consequences of being beyond the diplomatic pale: that high commissioners were practically ignored by ambassadors and came well below the representatives of even small and unfriendly states in the table of precedence.[38] Additionally, it was 'always embarrassing' at Court that there was 'no special place assigned to us when presented to the King'.[39] Feelings of injustice were further fuelled by the denial of diplomatic privileges such as tax exemptions.

Dominion prime ministers acted on their representatives' complaints, and the position of high commissioners was raised at the 1923, 1926, and 1930 Imperial Conferences. As a result their status was from time to time advanced: they were granted diplomatic privileges; raised higher in the table of precedence; and permitted to wear diplomatic uniform (which had extra gold oakleaf embroidery on the chest and cuffs),[40] pass 'the Royal presence', and present their fellow countrymen to their majesties.[41] From at least the early 1920s they also had 'silver passes'—small circular silver plaques that 'special people' can present to the Metropolitan Police to facilitate journeys to official occasions such as state ceremonies. And they were received by the King on arrival and departure. But they could not have diplomatic status.[42]

[37] Kiernan (secretary, Irish HCO)-secretary, Association of Electrical and Allied Manufacturers, 22 November 1929, INA, DFA, Embassy London, Box 1–14, file 3. In 1930 the high commissioners united to tell the Royal Academy of Arts that unless they were given 'their proper place at the top table' they would boycott future dinners: Kiernan note, 12 March 1930; Dulanty (Irish HC)-DEA, 15 March 1930, INA, DFA London Embassy, Box 1–14, file 3.

[38] See Larkin-King, 3 December 1924, *DCER* 3, 46. In 1922 the marshal of the London diplomatic corps and the CO had also taken up the question of precedence, because of difficulties at state balls and banquets.

[39] Larkin (Canadian HC)-King, 2 November 1923, NAC, King papers, MG26, J1, vol. 95.

[40] A member of Canada's High Commission in London reported that for his duties at the 1937 Coronation he put together a coat which 'had enough gold braid on it for an ambassador' and an admiral's cocked hat. '[N]obody seemed to mind, not even His Majesty', he said: Pearson (1973) 116–7.

[41] This took effect in 1930 but Dulanty soon abandoned Palace receptions. Louw had boycotted them but te Water did not. At the 1930 London Naval Conference, the first item of business was whether the British prime minister should present Commonwealth delegates or whether this should be done by each chief dominion delegate. Britain wanted the first course, Canada wanted the second. 'The Canadian view prevailed; Dominion status was maintained': Pearson (1973) 82.

[42] This of course meant they did not enjoy diplomatic immunity and precedence. In the inter-war years, however, immunity was not an issue.

5. *Consultation, Information Gathering, and High Commissioners' Meetings*

As regards consultation and information gathering, the position of high commissioners markedly improved. In the early 1920s they gained the right to approach the FO (in addition to home departments). And in 1924 Austen Chamberlain, the foreign secretary, agreed to meet dominion representatives when they had instructions to seek a personal interview. But he did so grudgingly, expressing fears that anything that suggested high commissioners were 'ambassadors' would encourage 'separatist feeling' and threaten imperial unity.[43]

Nonetheless, once members of high commissions had gained admission to the FO, they were neither regarded as, nor treated like, foreigners. Doors were always open and officials were 'invariably kind and helpful'. 'I got on terms with some of them which enabled me to know almost as much about what was going on as they knew themselves', said Lester Pearson. 'They were my friends and they trusted me; hence they would let me see, without hesitation, many telegrams and despatches that came to their desks.... As a result, I was able to help my High Commissioner to keep informed on developments in foreign policy.'[44]

Advantageous access was accompanied by the creation, in 1925, of a dedicated Whitehall department, the Dominions Office (DO), which from 1926 onwards sent confidential FO prints and telegrams to high commissioners.[45] Unfortunately, at home the dominions were poorly placed to make much use of this first-class information. Mackenzie King was definitely interested in it. But in Wellington, for example, initially there was no-one to read and analyse incoming documents for the prime minister, and most of them were immediately consigned to the filing cabinet. Things improved, but only slightly, in 1926, with the appointment to the Prime Minister's Department of an imperial affairs officer. A decade later '[t]wo or three officials of high ability but unlimited range of responsibility struggled as best they could with the flood of overseas documentation'.[46] It also happened that since over-busy

---

[43] Chamberlain-Amery, 25 November 1924 in Wigley (1977) 233. Only in 1948 did high commissioners gain the right of direct access to the foreign secretary as well as to the FO.

[44] Pearson (1973) 108.

[45] Chamberlain protested strongly about Amery arranging this without consulting him first.

[46] Wood (1958) 51. New Zealand did not have a DEA until 1943. The ending

prime ministers sometimes delayed decision-making, permanent officials and even high commissioners sometimes took decisions in matters of ministerial importance.

After 1928 attendance at meetings of the Committee of Imperial Defence (CID) provided an occasional source of information for high commissioners. But Mackenzie King never let his high commissioner attend, and the other high commissioners were only welcome when the subject-matter was not particularly secret, had already been discussed by the Cabinet, and was of dominion interest. Even in the run-up to the 1939 war, the high commissioners' participation was very limited.

More important, and useful, were high commissioners' meetings. On returning to office in 1924, Amery thought it would be a good idea to develop an informal, pragmatic channel of communication with the dominions via their high commissioners. He said it was difficult in cablegrams to provide 'the proper "light and shade"' and he wanted high commissioners to 'communicate with their chiefs just as Ambassadors of other countries do'.[47] He therefore arranged an early meeting of high commissioners with Baldwin and Chamberlain. It was 'an unqualified success'.[48] The high commissioners were 'very pleased.... We went as far as we could without forcing the hands of the Dominion Governments by treating the Dominion High Commissioners as their diplomatic representatives.'[49] Other meetings followed.

However, when Mackenzie King learned what had passed, he denounced such 'conferences'.[50] His suspicions had been raised by renewed talk of the dominions appointing resident cabinet ministers in London, and by a British request for Canadian support over a crisis in Egypt. He believed Britain was making 'a determined effort' to create a kind of centralised, imperial council that would draw the dominions 'into all matters of [British] foreign policy regardless altogether of the extent of our interest'.[51] He accordingly demanded that Amery stop holding meetings and, for good measure, insisted that the role of his

of the abdication crisis was delayed by New Zealand's slowness in replying to Baldwin's request for views. '"They could not find out who Mrs. Simpson was," Baldwin recalled in 1947': Thorpe (1996) 66.

[47] Larkin-King, private, 13 March 1925, NAC, RG25, 4480, 50020–40, part 1.

[48] Amery-Chamberlain, 24 November 1924 in Attard (1991) 267.

[49] Amery diary, 18 November 1924 in Attard (1991) 267. Cf. McNeill (Irish HC)-FitzGerald (MEA), 17 November 1924, *DIFP* II, 369–70.

[50] Wigley (1977) 233.

[51] King-Larkin, 12 December 1924, quoted in *ibid.* 233.

high commissioner, Peter Larkin, must be limited to 'conveying messages' and proffering advice.[52]

It was true that international issues had been the foremost topic of discussion at high commissioners' meetings; and true, too, that Britain hoped to keep the Commonwealth diplomatically in step on important issues. But imperial affairs were not the only item on the agenda. Moreover, as Larkin pointed out, he could hardly refuse to attend an informal meeting with the prime minister, adding that he had been careful to avoid being manoeuvred into participating in some 'sort of central council of the different parts of the Empire'.[53] King was unmoved. Nor did he yield to Amery's pleas about 'the lack of any form of personal communication between us'. 'As between foreign countries every communication is really personal', Amery had said:

> either the Foreign Secretary here sees the Ambassador from the country he is dealing with, or asks our Ambassador to see the Foreign Minister of that country. All the communications are really by word of mouth and therefore capable of the amplification and explanation which can be secured by that method. On the other hand the communications between the British and Canadian Governments are entirely by cable or despatch with all the possibilities of misunderstanding which that involves.... it would make a great difference if you had someone at this end with whom we British Ministers could discuss matters freely.... I think I can speak for Austen Chamberlain equally, we should be only too glad to talk freely with the High Commissioner if you wished us to do so.[54]

However, Amery had to give way, and the meetings were abandoned. Amery did try, a few months' later, to revive his gatherings in the shape of 'at home' sessions (instead of briefings). But only a few were held. Another start was made after the 1926 Imperial Conference, but King again objected. Larkin dropped out of the meetings, which ceased in May 1927.

There is conflicting evidence about whether regular meetings were reintroduced while King was out of office from 1930 to 1935.[55] What

---

[52] King-Larkin, 15 December 1924, *DCER* 3, 377. This was in confirmation of Larkin's self-description of himself as 'practically a Minister or Ambassador, but with no powers other than to convey messages between the two Governments and on occasion—seeing the other side of the picture from that presented to you—to give opinions as to the wisdom of any particular course': Larkin-King, 3 December 1924, *DCER* 3, 46.

[53] Larkin-King, 30 December 1924, NAC, RG25, 4480, 50020–40, part 1.

[54] Amery-King, 13 March 1925, NAC, RG25, 3419, 1–1926/29.

[55] Hall says they were, and that this was suggested by R.B. Bennett (Canadian PM,

is sure is that when King was back in power, he reimposed the 'absurd inhibitions'[56] on his high commissioner, Vincent Massey. Nonetheless, Massey attended the meetings, which became frequent during the Abyssinian and Rhineland crises in 1935 and 1936, assuring King that he would jealously preserve Canadian autonomy. King rebuked Massey and the following spring forbade his attendance, repeating the well-worn reasons he had used a decade earlier. The new dominions secretary, Malcolm MacDonald, had no more success than Amery in reassuring King that the meetings simply supplemented the information given in telegrams and gave 'the "atmosphere" of a situation'.[57] After the Germans entered Prague in March 1939 King allowed Massey to attend, but only as a 'nervous eavesdropper'[58] who could not speak without special instructions. Meanwhile, Stanley Bruce of Australia was reluctant to speak when records were kept, the British did not always reveal the full facts, and high commissioners were not always satisfied. However, such meetings were a useful supplement to other machinery for keeping the dominions informed, and their informality suited everyone on the spot: they allowed freedom of expression and provided the model for what, in wartime, participants liked to think of as 'the junior war cabinet'.[59]

C. Limitations on High Commissioners as Diplomats

1. *Problems with Prime Ministers*

Mackenzie King's refusal to allow Larkin to attend Amery's meetings can to a considerable extent be explained by King's personality. King was a

---

1930–35). Attard says some were held during the Manchurian crisis but there was then a gap until J.H. Thomas (dominions secretary, 1931–35) revived them in July 1935: Hall (1971) 599, Attard (1991) 310.

[56] Massey (1963) 237.

[57] MacDonald-King in F.H. Soward, 'Canadian external policy 1946–1952', NAC, RG25, 3843, 36–1946/1. See also MacDonald memorandum, 'Imperial Co-operation', March 1944, enclosed in MacDonald-Cranborne (dominions secretary), 11 March 1944, secret & personal, TNA, DO121/68.

[58] Bissell (1986) 78. During the war, Massey 'showed surprising courage in coming to the meetings at all', sidling in separately from the other high commissioners, through a different door to avoid the press: Joe Garner in Stirling (1974) 432. But Massey did not dare appear in a published group photograph, and when the war ended he resorted to attending almost in secret: S.F. Waterson diary, 11 May 1940, Waterson papers, UCT; Nicholls (1961) 387.

[59] Massey in Edwards (1984) 115.

suspicious and undoubtedly difficult man who feared the impact on his high commissioner of 'sinister British influences' and 'the subtle social pressure of the London environment'.[60] The prim, aristocratic, 'over-educated',[61] and Anglophile Vincent Massey got aggravatingly under King's skin, and by 1935 formerly cordial relations between them had been replaced by prime ministerial impatience, inconsiderateness, and constant watchfulness. Hence King's determination to limit Massey's diplomatic role both in London and abroad. Hence, too, the deliberate squandering of first-class information and sources of information because King mistakenly believed that it came at the cost of dominion autonomy. 'We often felt', said Pearson, 'that we might as well have mailed a batch of local press clippings'.[62]

As a head of mission Massey was far from alone in being somewhat alienated from his sending government, but the chances of this were higher when, as with most high commissioners, they were political appointees. In fact, in 1917 one of the CO objections to using high commissioners as channels of communication was a well-founded belief that they did not always enjoy the confidence of their governments. The fixed, five-year term for Australian high commissioners made it almost inevitable that new prime ministers would inherit high commissioners of a different political persuasion. Sometimes the two were old rivals or political foes—Australia's Andrew Fisher (1916–21) was so estranged from his prime minister that he did not write to him. And some high commissioners were just not up to scratch. The New Zealander, Jordan, was a 'disastrous' member of the League of Nations Council. He brought ridicule on his country and the Commonwealth, seriously endangered peace by 'his irresponsible utterances', and was 'the worst possible advertisement for the democratic form of Government'. Among other things, he suggested that Spain should be put under League tutelage as a mandated territory![63]

---

[60] Massey diary, 17 June 1937 in Massey (1963) 242. Cf. Laurier quoted in Skilling (1945) 107.

[61] Stacey (1984) 125.

[62] Pearson (1973) 108–9.

[63] R. Stevenson minute, 20 October 1937, TNA, T14606/14606/384, FO372/3205. It was several weeks before the bibulous and not over-educated Canadian high commissioner, G. Howard Ferguson (1930–35), learned from British sources that he was expected to make reports to Ottawa. He had gone to England not 'to take care of Canadian affairs, but to mend and fix, change, reform and improve British affairs': *Toronto Daily Star*, 6 December 1930. Sir Alexander Cadogan (PUS, FO) described high commissioners in general as 'the most undependable busybodies' who probably

2. *Other Channels of Communication*

The high commissioners' role as channel of communications was also hindered by organisational weaknesses and the existence of other routes: high commissions were chronically understaffed,[64] and alternative channels were grounded in imperial practice. In consequence, until about 1950 Britain continued to regard high commissioners as only supplementary to the other channels of communication.

i. *Prime Minister to Prime Minister*

The 1926 Imperial Conference spoke of the right of dominion prime ministers to contact the British prime minister directly (which had been approved in 1918) as a not unusual means of communication. This had an obvious attraction to dominion prime ministers, and became an important feature of intra-Commonwealth diplomacy. After all, relations with Britain were exceedingly important, so it was natural for prime ministers to want to have them under their direct control. They also enjoyed being able to communicate confidentially with their opposite numbers and so knowing (or at least believing) they were assured of attention at the highest level. This was especially valuable in times of crisis or war, when speedy communication was needed, or for handling particularly important or delicate issues, such as the 1936 abdication crisis. It also allowed them to bypass high commissioners whenever they wanted.

Thus in 1926 Coates of New Zealand would only agree to his high commissioner 'being put in the position to convey a certain amount of supplementary information' if it did not interfere with direct communications between governments.[65] In 1930 Canada's Richard Bennett said

---

'really haven't enough work to do'. Bruce of Australia was 'bad' and the antipodeans spoke 'irresponsible rubbish': Cadogan diary, 13 September 1939 and 26 February 1941 in Dilks (ed.) (1971) 216, 359.

[64] Canada's disadvantages in dealing with well-staffed and highly-qualified Whitehall departments were increased by King's wasteful use of manpower. Lester Pearson was sent off to obtain ruins from the bombed House of Commons, and the Canadian High Commission in London was bombarded with messages 'on non-policy matters. Many of these seemed of no great significance but, because they came from the Prime Minister, had naturally to be given priority consideration.' One 'super-sealed double-enclosed letter . . . marked "Secret-Urgent-Most Immediate"' was a copy of a telegram of thanks sent by Prince Felix of Luxembourg to King on his departure from Canada: Pearson (1973) 146.

[65] Amery-Chamberlain, 23 December 1926, BUL, Austen Chamberlain papers, AC53/40.

Howard Ferguson 'was not a diplomat, for under the Convention [*sic*] of 1926 communications were from Prime Minister to Prime Minister'.[66] And Mackenzie King came up with two self-serving justifications. First, he strongly believed

> that any important communication between British Govt. should be direct in form of communication from Prime Minster to Prime Minster or between Secretary of State for Dominions and Secretary of State for External Affairs as has been customary in the past and should not be through High Commissioner. This is the only way in which we can possibly have opportunity required collectively to consider and state attitude and policy and which will ensure full responsibility of British as well as Canadian Government with respect to any statement of policy or position and avoid all possibility of misunderstanding as to what has been said or meant in any verbal communication.[67]

Second, King said direct prime ministerial communication was necessary 'because G.B. and Canada were not foreign countries to each other & the relations were such as to make it necessary for him to carry on important negotiations himself'. He knew 'this British crowd'; 'they wanted watching'.[68] A few years later South Africa's wartime high commissioner echoed the feelings of Canada's high commissioner. 'I'm getting used to being ignored', he wrote in his diary, 'but it doesn't become any pleasanter.'[69]

Easy prime ministerial communication was assisted by personal relationships built up during visits to London and at regular imperial conferences. The conferences considered issues of common interest, laid down the main lines of co-operation, and served as a means of sharing information. Their resolutions were in the nature of honourable undertakings on the part of governments that adopted them. Together with periodic visits and interchanges of officials, they nourished the special nature of the Commonwealth relationship—albeit at the cost of hindering the development of the office of high commissioner.

ii. *Government-to-Government*

Of course the prime ministerial channel was not used for everyday business, but neither were high commissioners. The normal channel for

---

[66] Quoted in British Commonwealth Relations Conference, draft agenda, section A, item 1, no. 2 (a) iv, NAC, RG25, 3434, 1–1–1–1933–1.

[67] King-Massey telegram 89, 14 March 1936 in *DCER* 6, 961.

[68] Massey diary, 17 June 1937 in Massey (1963) 242.

[69] Waterson diary, 3 August 1942 in van Wyk (2005) 54.

communications was government-to-government, that is, between the DO and the appropriate dominion department. In consequence, Britain regarded high commissioners as 'not in any sense the diplomatic representatives in the U.K. of their Government [*sic*] in the sense of being the sole or even the principal link between the British Cabinet and the Dominion Government'. Instead, she saw government-to-government communication as indicative of the intimacy of intra-Commonwealth relations 'as distinct from aloofness characteristic of diplomatic contact'.[70] But this meant that high commissioners sometimes had to wait 'in complete ignorance' for two or three days before finding out what their governments had said to Britain's.[71] It also relegated high commissioners to a secondary role: only being used 'when matters in question can be more conveniently dealt with informally or orally, or to supplement telegrams exchanged between Governments with points best conveyed informally or orally'.[72] This might have been useful when high commissioners were poor or distrusted, and later (for a while) it rendered interests sections unnecessary within the Commonwealth context.[73] But it hampered the growth of the office. Not until about 1950 did Britain recognise that high commissioners (especially her own) were a normal, and valuable, channel for communication and consultation.[74]

Britain's view did not go entirely unchallenged. It was never fully accepted by South Africa who, as has been seen, had long emphasised the diplomatic character of the office of high commissioner. In keeping with this approach Eric Louw complained to Hertzog several times in 1929 that his position would be untenable unless he became the primary channel of communication. After he left London he described

[70] Pethwick-Lawrence (secretary of state for India and Burma)—governor of Burma, personal, 12 March 1947, TNA, I.B.(47)40, CAB134/344. Dr Deidre McMahon kindly drew my attention to this document.

[71] Pacaud (secretary, Canadian HCO)-Skelton, personal, 2 April 1929, NAC, T-1803, RG25, D1, 792, 447.

[72] Pethwick-Lawrence—governor of Burma, 12 March 1947.

[73] It was usual to use the British head of mission as the channel for communications from Commonwealth to foreign states in which they were not represented. This was formalised by the 1930 Imperial Conference. The British also undertook consular work for unrepresented Commonwealth states and did so without payment, communicating directly with the Commonwealth government concerned.

[74] By 1953, when the bulk of correspondence went through high commissions, a member of the Commonwealth Service said it was a 'measure of the way in which our ideas have changed since 1947 that it should already strike me as strange that direct communication . . . should ever have been regarded as the *main* channel of correspondence': J.D. Murray (DHC Karachi)-A.F. Morley (head of Constitutional Department), 26 May 1953, TNA, DO35/5223.

direct communication as '"absurd, unhealthy and wrong": humiliating for the representative and running counter to the independent status claimed by the Union'.[75] This belief, together with some dissatisfaction with the DO, later resulted in a proposal for, in effect, the winding up of the latter.

The creation of the DO in 1925 could be seen as a tribute to the dominions. But Mackenzie King was not alone in seeing it as 'a glorified Colonial Office'.[76] A former official secretary of Australia House reportedly left London 'exceedingly bitter' against the DO, supposedly because 'all' DO officials 'had been trained in Colonial Office work, and... their attitude is to regard the Overseas Dominions to some extent as inferiors, carrying the Colonial Office official attitude into their work with the Dominions'.[77] Moreover, it came to South African ears that a 'very responsible' DO official regarded high commissioners as 'merely glorified "Trade Commissioners"'.[78]

Another source of dissatisfaction arose out of the DO's position as an intermediate department between the FO and high commissions, since it led to frustrating and irritating delays in transmitting information about international affairs from the former to the latter. 'Instead of rushing like a swiftly-running cataract', said Australia's Billy Hughes, the DO 'crawls like a half-baked centipede'.[79] During the 1936 Rhineland crisis, Massey fulminated that 'The machinery of the DO instead of keeping us in close touch with foreign crises at present seems somehow to provide an obstacle or rather delay in getting news which we could get and sometimes do receive informally from FO. What good purpose does the DO serve?'[80] There was also a troubling suggestion of inferior status in high commissioners not being able to deal directly with the FO.

Already, in 1929, Hertzog had been told by one of his advisers that 'As the State members of the British Commonwealth are sovereign entities under the common Crown there can be no impropriety in their

[75] Quoted in van Wyk (2005), 39.
[76] Te Water-Hertzog, 3 December 1936 in Tennyson (1982) 86.
[77] J. Kiernan (Irish Representative, Canberra)-F.H. Boland (SDEA), 9 December 1946, INA, DFA, Ottawa Embassy, D/30/1.
[78] Bodenstein *aide mémoire*, 'Communications Between our Department and Dominions Office', 15 February 1933, SAA, channels of communication—policy, BTS, 37/1P, vol. 1.
[79] Quoted in Garner (1978) 139.
[80] Diary, March 1936 in Massey (1963) 236.

having diplomatic and political relations with each other.'[81] Now, in 1937, when South Africa was pushing Canada to receive a diplomatic envoy, the 'sinister'[82] Dr. H.D.J. Bodenstein, secretary of external affairs (SDEA, the senior DEA official), who enjoyed remarkable latitude of action, proposed that the Imperial Conference be asked to agree that high commissioners should be used in the same manner as ambassadors (so that all their dealings would be with the FO), and that they should be assimilated into the diplomatic corps. This, of course, implied the demise of the DO, and Bodenstein was partly motivated because he thought the DO still had a CO mentality. He also thought such a change would reflect the extent of dealings with London on 'external affairs'; emphasise the dominions' 'status as sovereign independent states' 'on the same footing as foreign countries'; and remove FO ignorance about the dominions' feelings and views.[83]

Britain's feathers were ruffled. An inter-departmental committee objected that Bodenstein's proposal was inappropriate, unnecessary and based on ignorance. He had, it was suggested, exaggerated the extent of foreign issues arising in relations with Britain and had unacceptably blurred foreign and intra-Commonwealth relations. Nor was it for South Africa to tell Britain how to conduct her business. It was not true that the FO and DO only communicated 'by means of "ad hoc written communications"'. There was close and constant co-operation between them, and whenever practicable the foreign secretary was brought into close contact with high commissioners. The DO was, moreover, a busy department and played a valuable co-ordinating role. And it would be

[81] F. van den Heever (DEA professional adviser, international law) memorandum, 'The Status of the Representative of His Majesty's Government in the Union with His Majesty's Government in Great Britain', 24 June 1929, P.M. 12/10, SAA, BTS, 43/4, vol. 2.

[82] The British disliked and distrusted Bodenstein so much that Malcolm MacDonald thought 'his removal from his present post is one of the most important changes required in the British Commonwealth': MacDonald-Clark, private & personal, 22 February 1937, Clark Papers, UCT, BC81 Cb15. 'It is no exaggeration to say that on constitutional questions and matters affecting imperial relations Bodenstein *is* the Government.' It was 'a tragedy that he should be where he is': Clark-Harding, 8 March 1937, Clark Papers, UCT, BC81 Ca5.

[83] See te Water-CRO, 26 November 1936, TNA, T17362/6518/384, FO372/3163; te Water-Hertzog, 3 December 1936 in Tennyson (1982) 86; Bodenstein memorandum, 'Change in Channel of Communication between the United Kingdom Government and the Governments of the Dominions', 14 January 1937, SAA, Channels of Communication—Policy, BTS 37/1P, vol. 1; TNA, DO35/541/2; Clark (British HC)-Batterbee (AUS, DO), 6 January 1937, TNA, DO35/541/2.

impractical to add to the pressure on an over-burdened foreign secretary.[84] In the event, South Africa was dissuaded from raising the question, although she did not cease pursuing her diplomatic ambitions.

iii. *Liaison officers*

For most of the interwar period Australia (and, for a few years, New Zealand) had an additional means of engaging in direct prime ministerial or governmental communication with Britain, which occasionally left some high commissioners even further out in the cold. This extra channel was created in consequence of the Australian prime minister, Stanley Bruce, not getting on with his London representative. Bruce therefore, in 1924, persuaded his British counterpart to receive Richard Casey as his 'confidential personal correspondent on external affairs'[85]—a position which became informally known as that of 'liaison officer'. Casey was given a room in the Cabinet Office and had direct access to the cabinet secretary, to the foreign secretary, Austen Chamberlain (who told FO 'to help him in any way they can'),[86] and to the DO. He saw confidential FO, Cabinet, and Committee of Imperial Defence papers, and received daily copies of all telegrams exchanged between London and Melbourne (Australia's capital until 1927). There was only one restriction: he was not allowed possession of Cabinet minutes. As Bruce put it, Casey

> saw and knew everything that was going on, and the regular personal letters he used to write to me probably present the best picture that exists of the political and international situation at that time.... From the time Casey went to London... until... 1945, Australia was invariably better informed on international affairs, and had far more influence on the UK Government and its policy, than all the rest of the Empire put together.[87]

For financial reasons the post was abolished in 1931, but Bruce quietly arranged for it to be unofficially continued and in 1932 it was restored. There were, however, disadvantages in the arrangement. In addition to detracting from the office of high commissioner, it hindered Australia's

[84] Clark 'Memorandum on Bodenstein's Memorandum on Channel of Communication', 23 March 1937, TNA, DO35/541/2.

[85] Amery-King, 22 December 1924, NAC, RG25, 3419, 1–1926/29. See also Attard (1991) 185–6.

[86] Chamberlain memorandum, 29 December 1924 in Attard (1991) 264; Amery-King, 22 December 1924. However, Chamberlain expected Casey to seek a personal interview only when instructed.

[87] Quoted in Edwards (1965) 87.

emergence from Britain's shadow, fostering her Anglo-centric world view. (Casey regarded Australia's intimate relationship with Britain as more 'sensible' than the 'immature' posturing of Canada, South Africa, and the Irish Free State.)[88] Moreover, although Casey has been described as Bruce's 'informal and personal ambassador',[89] the relatively low status he and subsequent incumbents enjoyed and the virtually one-way flow of correspondence from them to Australia meant it was impractical for London to see them as able to speak confidently on behalf of their governments. Only New Zealand followed Australia, and that was very late (1936).[90] The attitude of the other dominions was summed up by the senior DEA official, Oscar Skelton, who contrasted Australia's cosying-up to Britain with Canada's 'entirely different idea of inter-Imperial relations'.[91]

D. The Decline of the Office of Governor-General and the Emergence of British High Commissioners

As mentioned above, by the early 1920s the role of governors-general as the dominions' channel of communication with Britain was already in decline. They remained, however, the representatives in the dominions not only of the sovereign but also of the British government. Clearly, for many formal acts the sovereign needed an on-the-spot representative for the efficient conduct of affairs. (The King was each dominion's head of state as well as Britain's.) But there was a growing question about the appropriateness of a British representative being armed, so it might seem from his title, with gubernatorial power in territories that saw themselves as autonomous. Territories, too, which were playing a growing part on the international stage. Something would have to give.

Matters came to a head in June 1926 when Canada's governor-general, Lord Byng, refused Mackenzie King's request to dissolve Parliament. At the Imperial Conference later that year, King successfully demanded the right to deprive the governor-general of what remained

[88] Hudson and Sharp (1988) 88.
[89] Hudson (1986) 170.
[90] An FO official had been seconded to the New Zealand Prime Minister's Office (1928–30) but the experiment was not repeated.
[91] Undated Skelton minute on Amery-King, 22 December 1924, NAC, RG25, 3419, 1-1926/30.

of his role as 'ambassador of the British Government'.[92] Only New Zealand and Newfoundland failed to take immediate advantage of this right, the other four governors-general losing not just this role but also the associated one of being the official channel of communication of the dominions with London.[93]

This decision revealed a 'serious weakness' in the inter-imperial network.[94] As Amery put it, Britain had been trying to do what she 'had never thought possible in regard to foreign Governments'. She had 'made no attempt to supplement the written by the spoken word. . . . in the Dominions, alone of all the countries in the world, there is nobody who can either represent the point of view of the British Government on matters of international interest or who is there to defend any British interest'.[95] The answer, as King suggested, was for Britain to send envoys to the dominions. '[T]he business transacted between the Governments of Britain and Canada was', he said, sufficiently large to be dealt with in the same manner as was employed in the case of foreign Governments, many of which were smaller than Canada. . . . he had in mind the establishment in the Empire of a sort of diplomatic representation such as existed in the rest of the world.'[96] This would also have the advantage of underlining dominion equality with Britain, providing a counterbalance to the influence of the USA's newly-appointed envoy to Canada, and leaving Anglo-Canadian relations firmly under King's control in Ottawa. Initially, King wanted a more elevated title than 'high commissioner' and to give Britain's envoy 'regular formal precedence' over the diplomatic corps. However, on this last point Amery demurred and King gave way.[97]

---

[92] Christie memorandum, 'The High Commissioner's Office', 11 May 1920 in *DCER* 3, 22. In fact, Byng already saw himself in practice as solely the representative of the King.

[93] Direct communication with the Irish government began on 1 May 1927, with the Canadian and South African governments in July 1927, and with Australia on 1 January 1928. Not until 1941 did New Zealand follow this path. Newfoundland's dominion status went into limbo in 1934.

[94] Chamberlain, Amery, and Balfour quoted in Hillmer (1979) 341.

[95] Amery (1927) 11–12.

[96] Committee on Inter-Imperial Relations, 4 November 1926, *DCER* 4, 130–1.

[97] Amery pointed out that Britain's administrative high commissioners in South Africa, Egypt, Iraq, and Sudan had significant status; also that such precedence could not be granted to British citizens without flouting diplomatic protocol. At this time Larkin changed his letter paper from 'High Commissioner *for* Canada' to 'High Commissioner *of* Canada', believing that it would emphasise the distinction between dominion envoys and the administrative high commissioners: Larkin-King, 4 November 1927, NAC, T-1803, RG25, D1, 792, 444.

In London, meanwhile, there was a marked lack of enthusiasm for the idea of a British high commissioner. The Cabinet thought the title was too high-flown, there were fears of encouraging separatism, and the Treasury objected to the expense. But the case could not be resisted. There was then a lengthy tussle (which had to be resolved by the prime minister, Stanley Baldwin) over whether the FO or DO should 'own' the high commissioner. The latter won[98] and in 1928 a distinguished public servant, Sir William Clark, became the first British high commissioner.[99] But not before there was some further fall-out. The governor-general was surprised and annoyed to learn that his consent was not needed for the appointment (it being a government-to-government

[98] The tussle revealed quite different views about the nature of the Commonwealth and Anglo-Dominion relations. The departments' views of the job may be summarised thus:

DO view	FO view
Covering all questions affecting both governments.	Should primarily deal with foreign policy.
DO man capable of conducting public relations and explaining Britain to Canadians.	Skilled diplomat required.
Accept Dominions' right to determine their own foreign policies.	Hope that closer contact will, to some extent, produce united foreign policy under British guidance.
Diplomatic career might produce habit of mind unsuitable for work in Dominions.	DO inexperienced and 'too prone to accommodate and coddle tiresome clients': Garner (1978) 38.

[99] The style '*British* high commissioner' reflected his distinction from ambassadors, as only those who held commissions or warrants from the King specifically appointing them to their posts (such as ambassadors) were entitled to the style 'His Majesty's . . .'

It was also the case that British high commissioners, not being diplomats, did not fly Britain's diplomatic flag (the Union flag with the royal arms in the centre surrounded by a green garland) at their residences and on their cars. Instead they flew the Union flag (popularly called the Union Jack). But because, in Australia, the governors (the Queen's representatives in each of Australia's constituent states) also flew the Union flag, the British high commissioner, in 1937, was permitted to use on his official car a Union flag defaced by a white circle in the middle with 'U.K.H.C.' on it in black. High commissioners in New Zealand (and also in the Federation of Rhodesia and Nyasaland) adopted the same car flag. However, the use of this flag was phased out in the 1950s. The 2000 version of a procedures manual issued by the FCO said that the Union flag was to be flown at posts in Commonwealth countries.

one). And King George V 'seemed genuinely puzzled' about the impact of British high commissioners. He hoped his governors-general would not be reduced to doing nothing more than 'opening bazaars, making pretty speeches etc'.[100]

In the beginning Clark and his staff did not recognise that their job was diplomatic rather than advisory. They also 'seemed to have rather exalted ideas as to the identity of their opposite numbers in the queer colony to which they had been temporarily exiled'.[101] Initially Clark addressed himself to the governor-general rather than the prime minister. And a junior official (on secondment from the FO) seemed to think he should advise Canadian ministers how to do their jobs. He was 'deeply hurt' when King not only complained about a 2.30 a.m. phone call, but 'didn't realize that he was merely offering to help him run the Canadian government'.[102] Then King 'had a real blowout' when told by Clark that Canada had (unwittingly) flouted diplomatic etiquette:

> we in Canada did not need to be told how to behave, we did not intend to be told by the Br. Frgn. Office, or his office.... we wished our representative to stand on his own feet... we would make our own mistakes if need be, but intended to hold to the equality of status basis in every particular.... this "tranquil consciousness of effortless superiority" on the part of Englishmen was intolerable ... I felt I could not contain the feeling of indignation at the way the High Comm'rs Office has been seeking to "keep tab" on us. It was a warm half hour.[103]

Afterwards King was 'properly contrite and distressed'.[104] And as it happened Clark was 'a considerable success', unlike his two successors (Sir Francis Floud and Sir Gerald Campbell) who were duds who did not read Canada well and whose relations with King were poor.[105]

At first none of the other dominions were interested in receiving a British high commissioner:

> [Bruce of Australia] said he would never want to see the man, as he would always prefer to act through his man at this end.... Coates is absolutely opposed to any form of liaison in New Zealand.... The position in South Africa is... peculiar.... there is obviously no room in South Africa for

[100] King diary, 11 October 1928, http://king.collectionscanada.ca.
[101] Keenleyside (1981) 249.
[102] *Ibid.*, 249–250.
[103] King diary, 14 May 1929, http://king.collectionscanada.ca.
[104] P. Mason (assistant secretary, British HCO) minute, 24 February 1939, TNA, DO127/38.
[105] Garner (1978) 41.

> another British High Commissioner representing the British point of view on other matters [besides the protectorates][106]. . . . Healy re-affirmed . . . his objection to the appointment of any British representative in Ireland . . . as likely to be regarded with suspicion. . . . Newfoundland do not want liaison at either end, and indeed have asked that the telegrams to them should be discontinued as an unnecessary expense.[107]

However, South Africa was already edging in the direction of receiving a high commissioner, and within a little more than a decade all but Newfoundland (no longer a dominion) had followed in Ottawa's footsteps.

As indicated above, there was already a high commissioner in South Africa, and had been since the mid-nineteenth century. That office was quite different from the one with which this book is concerned. It was attached to the governor-general's office in respect of his additional, quasi-diplomatic role in connection with certain neighbouring territories.[108] According to Bede Clifford (imperial secretary—the administrative head of that high commissioner's office), Hertzog affected to regard the high commissioner 'as the counterpart in the Union of his own High Commissioner in London'. Perhaps for this reason Hertzog would often stop to talk to Clifford on his evening walks home.[109] Clifford reported these conversations to London through the high commissioner, and this unusual South African-British channel of communication was for a while tacitly accepted by the British Government. However, after the 1926 Imperial Conference, Clifford was given the title, 'Representative

---

[106] I.e., Basutoland, Bechuanaland, and Swaziland—on which see immediately below.

[107] Amery-Chamberlain, 23 December 1926, BUL, Chamberlain papers, AC53/40.

[108] The office arose from a commission vested in the governor of the Cape Colony in 1846. The title passed after 1900 to the governor of the Transvaal and was then transferred to the governor-general of the Union in 1910. As well as having a 'quasi diplomatic role' in connection with the independent Dutch republics, the British governor was in 1854 given administrative powers and functions in respect of what later became the Rhodesias and the native administrations in Basutoland, the Bechuanaland Protectorate, and Swaziland. The high commissioner's powers over the administration of Southern Rhodesia lapsed when it gained responsible self-government in 1923, but until 1937 he retained certain powers and functions in respect of native administration in that territory. His functions in respect of Northern Rhodesia ceased in 1924 when the first governor was appointed and the British South Africa Company's administration was transferred to the Crown: Joint Research Department (Commonwealth Section), 'The use of the term "High Commissioner" in the Commonwealth', 13 April 1967, TNA, FCO68/449.

[109] Clifford's office in Brynterion was alongside the Prime Minister's house.

of the Government of the United Kingdom of Great Britain and Northern Ireland to the Union of South Africa'—an appointment which reflected Hertzog's refusal to receive anyone else as Britain's envoy, and his rejection of Amery's contention that Clifford was 'too junior'.[110]

Clifford's new position was 'somewhat nebulous' as it had never been officially announced and was not known to the outside world.[111] However, the arrangement benefited Britain since Clifford not only gained access to South Africa's intra-Commonwealth correspondence but also 'that with the rest of the World, should he ask for it—a privilege which . . . he does not hesitate to make use of'.[112] Partly because this was a 'most difficult period' in Anglo-South African relations,[113] Clifford was overworked and an FO official was assigned to help him. As the time for him to leave the Union drew near, Britain sought South Africa's agreement to establishing a post comparable to Clark's in Ottawa, and in so doing to separate the existing high commissionership for the native territories from the office of governor-general. Hertzog agreed. Thus when Clifford left in 1931 his work was taken over by the newly-appointed British high commissioner, Sir Herbert Stanley, who was given the additional, separate office of 'High Commissioner for Basutoland, the Bechuanaland Protectorate, and Swaziland'.[114] It was a challenging and difficult appointment, requiring the combined talents of a diplomat and colonial administrator. Hence the choice of Sir Herbert, a former imperial secretary in South Africa whose immediately previous job had been the governorship of Ceylon, the senior post in the Colonial Service.

In Australia there had been a lowly British government representative overseeing migration since 1925. In 1931 the newly-arrived representative was told to prepare for the arrival of a high commissioner towards the end of the year. However, because of 'the financial crisis',[115] Sir Geoffrey Whiskard was not named until August 1935 and he did not arrive until March 1936. New Zealand, who objected to

[110] Clifford (1964) 163, 164.

[111] W. Farrell memorandum, 'Status of High Commissioner', 27 October 1928, SAA, BTS, 43/4, vol. 1.

[112] *Ibid.* These rights were also enjoyed by Clark in Ottawa.

[113] Clifford (1964) 179.

[114] The offices had different precedence, uniform and staffs, and while one high commissioner was appointed by a letter from the dominions secretary, the other was appointed by the King and was answerable to the colonial secretary.

[115] MacDonald-Lyons quoted in Jane Barder manuscript.

what she regarded as the separatist wedge British high commissioners introduced into the empire, did not accept one until early 1939, when her governor-general finally relinquished his role as representative of the British government.

Although the Irish Free State had appointed a high commissioner to London in 1922, the year of her creation, British representation in Ireland was delayed because Dublin objected to the 'imperial history' of the title 'high commissioner'.[116] In addition, in the 1930s the long-serving Irish high commissioner, John Dulanty, discouraged Britain from making an appointment because he wanted to remain the only formal link between Britain and Ireland. The consequence was to give added weight to the role of the governor-general (until the introduction of the changes agreed at the 1926 Imperial Conference), and to the role of the Irish high commissioner in London who, in the 1930s, was the only channel of communication between the two governments. Britain was fortunate in the men Dublin sent. James McNeill (one of Dulanty's predecessors) was 'conspicuously successful'.[117] Dulanty (who had never actually lived in Ireland) was witty, gregarious, lovable, shrewd, knowledgeable and able; 'a man by whose conversation . . . no man was ever bored'; and he won and retained the confidence of both de Valera and Churchill.[118] Like Joseph Walshe, the Irish SDEA, Dulanty valued the Commonwealth connection, including access to some FO telegrams and (belatedly) confidential Committee of Imperial Defence communications. But in his 'position as go-between [Dulanty] offended procedural niceties at the Dominions Office, and officials there tended to keep him a trifle at arm's length as a result'.[119]

The lack of any Commonwealth representative in Dublin contributed to that capital's failure always to appreciate the extent to which the group was undergoing change. A senior Irish civil servant even believed that Ottawa only appointed a high commissioner to London after Dublin had done so! And the British, too, were disadvantaged by not having a high commissioner in Dublin, particularly as Ireland's governors-general were never suitable as sources of information. In the early 1930s the British trade commissioner in Dublin, William Peters, did a good job of political reporting for the DO. But he felt underused;

---

116 Garner (1978) 236.
117 'Commissioners and consuls', *The Irish Times*, 13 October 1928.
118 Mansergh (1958) 411 n. 2. See also McMahon (1984) 24–5.
119 McMahon (1984) 25.

his lowly status meant that his political advice carried little weight; and in any case he left in 1935.[120] Britain's inadequate knowledge of Irish affairs was to some extent alleviated by reading the communications exchanged between Ireland and the other dominions (which were routed through the DO). Sometimes she also intercepted, and decrypted, external telegrams sent by Ireland or by foreign missions in Dublin. But mostly she relied on the press, casual visitors to Ireland, members of the Anglo-Irish ascendancy, and supporters and members of the defeated *Cumann na nGaedheal* administration. Altogether it was not the most efficient way of gathering information. Thus, for example, British policymakers had scant knowledge or understanding of Eamon de Valera (President of the Executive Council 1932–37, *taoiseach* 1936–48). During the economic war with Ireland at the end of the 1930s, the British were said to have 'paid dearly for their ignorance of the Irish scene'.[121] In 1939 'the Director of Naval Intelligence, Admiral Godfrey, wrote regretfully: "I realise now that . . . we knew very little about Ireland or the Irish; had we known more we might have tackled the problem more effectively from the start."'[122] Not until the summer of 1939 was a British envoy sent to Dublin. As this was prompted by the approach of war and Irish manoeuvrings to do away with the office of high commissioner, it will be discussed in the next chapter.

[120] His strong urging for the appointment of 'a political representative with status and credentials' were dismissed in London on the grounds that 'the time was not yet ripe' and it 'would almost certainly give rise to false impressions': Batterbee and Harding minutes, 2 February and 28 November 1934, TNA, DO35/251/3.

[121] McMahon letter, 4 March 1999. 'Few British ministers had actually met de Valera, but most remembered Lloyd George's jokes that arguing with de Valera was like trying to catch a man on a merry-go-round or picking up mercury with a fork. . . . De Valera was an unwelcome nemesis in 1932, and to many British ministers and officials an unbalanced one, to judge from the frequent and unflattering references to his mental health. The words "lunatic", "visionary", "dreamer", "crank" . . . were sprinkled in letters, diaries and minutes. During the height of tension in the summer of 1932 the Dominions Office was actually mulling over the idea of using a doctor from Leopardstown Hospital in Dublin as an intermediary because he claimed that he had "the medical knowledge . . . essential for dealing with the psychological problem presented by Mr. de Valera's mind"': McMahon (1984) 30.

[122] McMahon (1984) 30.

E. South African and Irish Overtures to Canada, and the Despatch of a South African 'Accredited Representative'

Until the Second World War the dominions had been faint-hearted players on the international stage, as reflected in the smallness of their DEAs and diplomatic corps and their minimal representation in other states.[123] Partly for this reason, but also because of the importance to them of London and the Commonwealth relationship, their world view was largely obtained via London. Thus, for example, the difficult and alien General Hertzog looked to the Commonwealth as the 'the focus' of his 'personal diplomacy' as much as General Smuts (who was a Commonwealth man),[124] and it has been argued that until 1948 'the formation of major South African foreign policy was still largely in London'.[125] The fact was that the dominions had very

---

[123] This was particularly true of New Zealand which only began exchanging missions with foreign states in 1940 when she appointed a minister at Washington after the fall of France. After the war, Holland, the leader of the 1949 National Government, wanted to close the DEA and there was a 'lack of interest of New Zealand in their diplomatic representation abroad and even a feeling of criticism towards the increase of diplomatic representation in Wellington': Alfred Rive (Canadian HC)-Pearson (under-secretary) quoted in Norman Robertson-DEA, 16 January 1948, NAC, RG25, 2942, 3011-A-40; Harland (1992) 15.

Australia was hardly more forward. In 1937 she placed a counsellor in the British Embassy at Washington in 1937, and three years later she established a separate legation at Washington and opened one in Tokyo. There was no diplomatic corps in Canberra before a US minister arrived in 1940, and the Japanese and Netherlands ministers (who arrived in 1941 and 1942 respectively) mostly stayed in Melbourne.

'Domestic politics was the reason for the setting up of the South African department of foreign affairs and the opening of diplomatic and consular missions in the first place—to demonstrate the country's political independence of the United Kingdom. What was important was less the substance of the relationship these offices symbolised than the fact that they existed at all': Tothill (2000b). In 1939 South Africa had eight legations (USA, France, Germany, Belgium, Italy, the Netherlands, Sweden, and Portugal), three of them headed by non-resident ministers, and consulates-general in Hamburg, Lorenço Marques, and Buenos Aires. There were eight legations in the Union (USA, France, Belgium, Germany, Italy, Netherlands, Portugal, and Japan).

In 1939 Ireland had seven legations (USA, France, Germany, Belgium, Italy, Spain, and the Holy See), one headed by a non-resident minister; a consulate-general in New York; and consulates in Boston, Chicago and San Francisco. There were six legations in Dublin (USA, France, Belgium, Germany, Italy, and the Holy See). Canada, meanwhile, had established five legations (USA, France, Japan, Belgium, and the Netherlands), one with a non-resident head, and received four (USA, France, Belgium, and Japan).

[124] Geldenhuys (1984) 7.

[125] E.S. Munger in *ibid.*, 7.

few dealings with, or interest in, one another,[126] and not even much bilateral trade. Thus they hardly needed more than a handful of trade commissioners,[127] and in 1930 South Africa even thought that Canada did not take enough of her exports to warrant a full-time one. There was, however, a slight interest in exchanging missions for the sake of gesture politics. In 1928 Hertzog sought to save money and blur the distinction between Commonwealth and foreign relations by making a joint diplomatic appointment to Washington and Ottawa. He was surprised and annoyed to be rebuffed, Canada objecting to the insult to her dignity and the threat to the legal distinctiveness of the empire, as well as worrying that such an appointment might be thought to point towards North American integration!

Meanwhile, the Irish Free State had begun courting the senior dominion. In 1928 she intimated a wish for 'diplomatic representation' in Canada;[128] in 1931 she made an informal approach; and in 1934 she began actively pursuing an exchange of representatives as a prelude to all-round representation. London welcomed de Valera's suggestion, but Canada's Conservative prime minister, R.B. Bennett, prevaricated in the hope that he could first agree an exchange of high commissioners with Canberra. However, Australia thought an exchange was 'inopportune', as its priority was settling the appointment of a British high commissioner (which did not happen until 1936).[129] It was another six months before Skelton told Walshe that

> The Government was much interested in the proposal but between the upset of public business caused by Mr. Bennett's illness and the difficulty in deciding between conflicting considerations as to the best men to send, a definite reply was postponed and I am afraid on account of the

---

[126] As Duncan Hall put it, if the Commonwealth was a family, it was 'a family of an odd kind, hardly knowing each other, but only the Mother Country': quoted in Tothill (1998).

[127] In 1936 Canada had trade commissioners in London and Auckland (supplemented, in London, until 1936 by agents-general representing Quebec and British Columbia); Australia had six agents-general representing its individual states in London and trade commissioners in New York, Paris, Ottawa, Wellington, China, The Hague, Tokyo, and the Netherlands East Indies; New Zealand had trade commissioners in Sydney and Toronto; South Africa had trade commissioners in London, Montreal, and Nairobi; Newfoundland had a trade commissioner in London; and Britain had two trade commissioners in Montreal and one each in Toronto, Vancouver, Winnipeg, Sydney, Melbourne, Wellington, Cape Town, Durban, Johannesburg, and Dublin.

[128] See Keith (1929) 484.

[129] Joseph Lyons (Australian PM)-R.B. Bennett (Canadian PM), 13 February 1925, NAC, T-1762, RG25 D1, 753, 227.

> prorogation of the present Parliament it will not be possible to make provision for the High Commissionership this term.[130]

Walshe responded by expressing hope for 'an early exchange . . . with other Commonwealth countries, starting with Canada'.[131] King's return to power two months later made that unlikely. In 1937 King rejected DEA suggestions that Canada open high commissions in Australia, New Zealand, and South Africa, and a few more legations elsewhere (she already had legations at Washington, Paris, and Tokyo): 'Representation in any foreign country is almost certain to draw us into situations involving religious or other questions.'[132] Nonetheless, the question of exchanging high commissioners had become an 'ever-live topic'.[133]

That autumn (1937) the South Africans had begun working on King. Wanting to use diplomatic styles, but knowing King was content with current arrangements and disinclined to rock the Commonwealth boat, Hertzog pressed King to receive an 'accredited representative' (the title bestowed on South Africa's envoy to the League of Nations). When Canada queried the title, saying it would necessarily mean its holder had a lower status than a high commissioner, Bodenstein retorted that 'the term had been chosen out of respect for the feelings of the Canadian authorities'. South Africa really wanted to appoint a 'minister', so as to assimilate Commonwealth representatives with ordinary diplomatic heads of mission in the class below ambassadors, 'rather than an officer with so inferior a status as that of a High Commissioner' with its 'administrative' connotations.[134] But she was willing to settle for an 'accredited representative' with diplomatic status. There was, said Hertzog,

> nothing in the legal relations between the Union and Canada which would militate against, or stand in the way of, an exchange of properly designated diplomatic agents. . . . we do not see any reason why it should not be possible for the head of state of the Union to be represented in Canada

---

[130] Skelton-Walshe, 5 July 1935, NAC, RG25, 1711, 584–34.

[131] Extract from Walshe-Skelton, 28 August 1935, NAC, RG25, D1, T-1807, 802, 556, parts 1–2.

[132] King diary, 9 December 1937 quoted in Hilliker (1990) 189.

[133] Keith Officer (Australian counsellor, British Embassy Washington), 2 August 1939, *DAFP* II, 163.

[134] DEA memorandum, 'The Status of the Accredited Representative of the Union of South Africa', 26 January 1944, NAC, RG25, 2942, 3011-A-40; Norman Robertson (under-secretary)-Vincent Massey (Canadian HC, London), 7 July 1944, NAC, RG25, 2942, 3011-A-40.

> and to be accredited to the head of state of Canada. In deference to the position taken up by you . . . and not wishing to prejudice our position, we decided to choose the vague title [of accredited representative] . . . in the hope that it would be . . . acceptable. The main thing for us was establish contact with you all along the line, on a diplomatic basis. This . . . evaded the difficulty of having, at this stage, to raise with you pointedly the question whether the nature of the British Commonwealth allows of an exchange of diplomatic agents with titles commonly used.'[135]

King agreed to accept David de Waal Meyer (Hertzog's nephew and former South African trade commissioner in Canada) as an 'Accredited Representative', but refused him diplomatic status. Hertzog protested that there was 'no justification, either in law or in common sense, for perpetuation of such an unsatisfactory state of affairs'.[136] Meyer himself believed 'the only reason' for Ottawa's rebuff was to prevent him ranking above the British high commissioner.[137] But King refused to 'fall in with a novel proposal . . . which raised contentious questions of intra-Commonwealth relations'.[138] Meyer might 'discharge substantially the same functions' as a diplomat but his status, privileges and immunities were those of a high commissioner.[139] Nonetheless, when Meyer arrived in 1938, he described himself as 'the first diplomatic representative of one Dominion in another' and insisted that the British high commissioner was his junior![140] (The word 'diplomatic' was also prominent in his correspondence with the DEA.)

F. Conclusion

In the 1920s and early 1930s there were two significant developments affecting the office of high commissioner. First, the standing of high

[135] Bodenstein-Skelton, 26 February 1938 in Tennyson (1982) 88–9.

[136] Hertzog-King, 31 March 1938 in *ibid.*, 89.

[137] Meyer-Bodenstein, 26 February 1941, SAA, BTS, PM1/28/5 vol. 1.

[138] Hume Wrong (assistant under-secretary)-Burchell, personal, 24 October 1944, NAC, RG25, 2942, 3011-A-40.

[139] King-Hertzog, 29 March 1938 in DEA memorandum, 'The Status of the Accredited Representative of the Union of South Africa'.

[140] Holmes-Harding, 15 July 1939 in Tennyson (1982) 90. Accordingly, and despite Canada's clear view that Meyer had the status of a high commissioner, Meyer insisted that, in keeping with diplomatic practice, Sir Gerald Campbell should first call on him. Sir Gerald 'agreed not "to stand on any question of principle etc. in this matter"' and to make the first visit: Laurent Beaudry (assistant under-secretary) memorandum, 8 October 1938 in *ibid.*, 90.

commissioners rose as the dominions became international actors and won the right to sovereign statehood. And because of the importance of London to the dominions, the high commission in London was regarded as the most important resident mission; prime ministers even described high commissioners as having the highest rank in their fledgling diplomatic services. Second, Britain was impelled to begin sending high commissioners when governors-general ceased being representatives of the British government. In this way a Commonwealth overseas service was born and the DO began slowly to gain first-hand knowledge of the self-governing Empire.

Dominion prime ministers often paid tribute to the importance of the office of high commissioner by appointing eminent men, sometimes as an enticing and elevated means of removing them from domestic politics. This did not distinguish high commissioners from some other foreign heads of mission in major capitals. Nor did some high commissioners differ much from foreign heads of mission in finding their diplomatic role (as spokesman and trusted channel of communication) limited by presidential or prime ministerial distrust and jealousy. But chiefly the development of the office of high commissioner was restricted because prime ministers wanted to keep control not just of foreign policy but also of the most important aspect of their countries' external relations: dealings with the former imperial power.[141] And high commissioners also laboured under an extra disadvantage that was not shared by foreign envoys: the existence of additional, direct channels of communication (including liaison officers), and London's insistence until about 1950 that the normal channel of communication was not the high commissioner but government-to-government, via prime ministers or the DO. This caused frustration amongst high commissioners, and as the British themselves pointed out, contrasted sharply with the 'accepted diplomatic practice that Foreign Governments do not correspond with one another direct' but through their accredited representatives.[142]

[141] Hence Canada and South Africa combined the offices of prime minister and minister of external affairs until 1947 and 1948 respectively; New Zealand often combined them until 1990; Ireland combined them briefly in 1927 and from 1932 to 1948; but since 1932 Australia has usually kept them separate.

[142] Clifford-Hertzog conversation, 23 October 1928, P.M. 4/19, SAA, channels of communication-policy, BTS 37/1P, vol. 1. When the South Africans displayed an inclination to adopt the same approach in dealings with foreign states (by asking the British

As regards ongoing complaints about the high commissioners' 'sub-diplomatic status',[143] the precedence and privileges of high commissioners had been much improved by 1930 (by which time Britain felt she had gone as far as she could in her treatment of Commonwealth representatives, who had no standing in diplomatic law). Of course this did not prevent grumbling, and the first British high commissioner thought that it did not look well for him to be seated conspicuously lower than foreign envoys. (At a government dinner he was not even at the high table.)[144] On the other hand, Britain's envoys in South Africa had to insist on being treated differently from the diplomatic corps! When Hertzog tried to seat Clifford with foreign ministers at the opening of parliament, Clifford complained that it would give the impression that the South Africans had done so 'deliberately', in order

> to emphasise that Britain is just as foreign as any other country. The facts may be otherwise, but the *impression* will be the same. I am prepared to take precedence below the foreign ministers, but if I am to be put among them I shall not attend.[145]

Before turning to the rising tide of dissatisfaction with the status of the office of high commissioner, it is worth noting that from some points of view its unusual nature could be seen as advantageous. Thus for all the limitations placed on him, Vincent Massey thought he was better off being a high commissioner than he would have been if he were an ambassador and treated like a foreign envoy. His office had, he thought, the 'merit of great flexibility', of being 'much less bound by definite

---

ambassador at Lisbon to deliver a communication from Hertzog to the Portuguese foreign minister), Britain's representative, Clifford, gently pointed out that: 'It was the invariable rule that an ambassador receives his instructions from the Government which he represents, but it is left to him to decide the manner in which those instructions are communicated to the foreign Government concerned. To ask him to deliver a signed despatch to a member of the Government to which he is accredited eliminates him as the spokesman and representative of his own Government; suggests that he does not enjoy the confidence of that Government; damages the prestige of his post; relegates him to the position of a common messenger or postman and thus defeats the whole purpose of maintaining a highly qualified and expensive diplomatic service.'

[143] van Wyk (2005) 48.

[144] Garner (1978) 45.

[145] Clifford (1964) 173. The South Africans responded by seating Clifford 'above and apart from the foreign ministers'. Lord Harlech (British HC, 1941–44) allegedly did 'everything possible to prevent' British Commonwealth representatives being included in the Diplomatic List: Burchell-Robertson, 13 June 1944, NAC, RG25, 2942, 3011-A-40.

tradition than a purely diplomatic post and this lends great interest to the work'.[146] There was no point sacrificing such 'real advantages' as informal and direct access to officials and ministers 'in order to move up several places at table'.[147] But few high commissioners agreed.

---

146 Massey-A.J. Glazebrook, 23 March 1936 in Massey (1963) 228–9.

147 Holmes memorandum, 1 August 1944 in Tennyson (1982) 107–8. See also McGreer memorandum, 'Status and precedence of High Commissioners prior to 1948', 6 July 1956, NAC, RG25, 6371, 3011-A-40, part 3.

CHAPTER THREE

DISCONTENT, LATE 1930s–MID-1940s

In the inter-war years, the dominions' interest in international relations mostly revolved around their relationship with Britain. The more 'backward'—Australia and New Zealand—wanted to underline the strength of the imperial bond. The more 'advanced'—Canada, South Africa, and the Irish Free State/Ireland—wanted to assert their independence of Britain by becoming sovereign states and winning full recognition of their right to act independently on the world stage. The extent of this last endeavour was evident when, in 1939, each dominion made up its own mind about entering the War. Australia and New Zealand hastened after Britain; South Africa entered only after a change of prime minister; Canada delayed for almost a week; and Ireland remained neutral. During the War, the participating dominions deployed their military forces independently and were leading members of the victorious alliance. They also became much more active diplomatically and began playing a fuller international role; hence their Departments of External Affairs (DEAs) expanded and there was a mushrooming of foreign (i.e. non-Commonwealth) diplomatic missions to and from the dominions (several at ambassadorial level).[1] At the War's end there was no question that the dominions were 'fully sovereign states pursuing their own foreign policies in the light of their own interests'.[2] Moreover, especially

[1] In 1939 New Zealand neither sent nor received foreign diplomatic missions, and Australia had only a counsellor attached to the British Embassy at Washington. However, South Africa had eight legations accredited to foreign capitals, Canada five, and Ireland seven. In 1945 the position was:

	Canada	Australia	New Zealand	South Africa	Ireland
Embassies	9	–	–	–	–
Legations	7 (1 dual)	7	2	6	9 (1 dual)

Dual accreditation has been counted as two legations. Sources: Mansergh (1958a) Appendix D, Michael Kennedy, David Tothill and various documents.

[2] Mansergh (1948c) 130.

in comparison to the occupied states of Europe, the dominions were relatively significant. In 1938 Canada had referred to herself as one of the 'small Members' of the League;[3] by the early 1940s she was said to be 'the third most important country in the West' and, arguably, remained so until the mid-1950s.[4]

Additionally, by 1946 the Commonwealth was a close and accepted international association. Its intimate ties were much valued by all except Ireland; and it was, from the beginning, a recognised UN group, so giving the dominions a privileged opportunity to be elected to key UN organs.[5] It was 'taken seriously' by Britain's post-War Labour government and by her prime minister 'more than anyone'.[6] Quite apart from the not unimportant issue of sentiment, the Commonwealth was important in economic terms and could be useful in the developing Cold War and as a makeweight in Britain's relations with the superpowers.[7] This helps to explain the importance she attached to India staying in the Commonwealth after the transfer of power in August 1947, and the stress she placed on retaining outward and visible signs of Commonwealth membership, such as the office of high commissioner. But on this last matter it became increasingly evident that Britain was very much in a minority.

A. High Commissioners and High Commissioners' Meetings During the Second World War

As in 1914–18, wartime demands and the dominions' heightened stature on the world stage resulted in the increasing use of all high commissions. And in London there was an additional call on high commissioners' time: daily meetings (including some on Sundays) with Dominions Office (DO) ministers and its civil service head, the permanent under-secretary, lasted up to two or more hours. One observer described them

---

[3] Undated & unsigned draft notes, 'Canadian policy regarding League of Nations', c. 1938, NAC, T-1745, RG25 D1, 715, file 4, parts 1–5.

[4] Reid (1981) 14.

[5] Until the mid-1960s there was always (in addition to Britain) another Commonwealth representative on the UN Security Council, and the group of Commonwealth members was also allocated important positions in the General Assembly.

[6] Introduction, *BDEE 1945–51* I, lxvii. Attlee's 'chief governmental effort probably went into preserving and developing the Commonwealth': *ibid.*

[7] A term coined by W.T.R. Fox in 1944: Evans and Newham (1998) 522.

as having a 'practical character';[8] another says they were 'informal, secret, intimate, frank';[9] and one of the high commissioners (regarded as 'outstanding')[10] said they were 'an admirable demonstration of the family relationship'.[11]

However, the usefulness of these meetings was limited by two factors. The first was the personality, status, and ability of the ministerial head (secretary of state) of the DO. During the War years, none of the three holders of this office was uniformly impressive. The chronically unpunctual Viscount Caldecote was held in contempt, so it was not surprising that his 'meetings seldom achieved a temperature above tepid'.[12] Viscount Cranborne, Caldecote's successor, was admired and respected. He made high commissioners 'feel that we were significant parts of the war machine',[13] and his frank speaking lifted the meetings 'onto a different plane'.[14] But he was not a member of prime minister Winston Churchill's inner circle, did not know much of what was happening on the wider scene and, when he did, was often instructed not to reveal it. Clement Attlee, his successor, had authority as deputy prime minister. But he was uncommunicative and, according to a British high commissioner, was a 'rotten' dominions secretary who knew nothing about the dominions.[15]

Second, the meetings were limited inasmuch as they were intended only to convey information rather than obtain dominion views. Churchill had a very conservative view of the 'British Empire' (as he preferred to call the Commonwealth),[16] and 'no conception of the British Dominions

---

8 Hankey (1946) 154.

9 Garner (1978) 198.

10 *Ibid.* 199.

11 Vincent Massey (Canadian HC) quoted in Garner (1978) 200. The need to respond to the demands of war had ended many of the restrictions which Ottawa had imposed on Massey.

12 Garner (1978) 199. High commissioners 'stamped up and down while being kept waiting': Stirling (1974) 432.

13 Nicholls (1961) 382.

14 Garner (1978) 199.

15 Colville diary, 21 December 1942, in Colville (1987) 61. As Massey put it, talking to Attlee was 'a little like a conversation with a bronze Buddha except for the monosyllabic ejaculations which he utters occasionally': diary, 26 July 1943, quoted in Bissell (1986) 125.

16 However, being obliged to recognise changing anti-imperial attitudes, he unsuccessfully tried to popularise the phrase 'British Empire and Commonwealth'. The phrase appears in the communiqué of the 1944 Commonwealth Prime Minister's Conference but no other official document: Gordon Walker (1962) 191.

as separate entities'.[17] Thus he regarded high commissioners as 'mere postmen'[18] who should not be told very much. He sent bullying minutes to the DO complaining about secrets being told to dominion governments; instructed Cranborne 'not to scatter so much deadly and secret information over this very large circle';[19] and soon broke his 1944 promise to meet high commissioners every month.[20] The unsurprising result was much high commissioner grumbling about the meetings' lack of substantive content—even taxi drivers and shopkeepers seemed to possess information that had not officially been divulged to them.[21]

Still, if high commissioners were kept largely in the dark, so were cabinet ministers; and the formers' rather extravagant expectations about their meetings was a mark of the Commonwealth's intimacy. Moreover, it seems clear that the meetings were at least useful as a subsidiary source of information and as a means of ventilating sometimes very discontented views. Additionally, it was not true that the London high commissioners were always excluded from higher counsels. Moving freely between the DO and FO, at least some of them and their staff saw papers 'of the utmost confidentiality'.[22] (Moreover, FO officials were instructed that dominion prime ministers were to be given information on important matters 'either before or simultaneously with the United States and Soviet Governments but never later than those Governments except in very exceptional circumstances'.)[23] Also, after the United States entered the War, Commonwealth envoys met regularly in Washington at the British Embassy. During these reportedly very useful gatherings, it was possible to put dominion views not only to the British ambassador but also to Britain's very high ranking military representatives in the United States. As in London, the 'friendly family atmosphere' facilitated congenial and useful discussions:

> we learned much from pooling and exchanging views and gossip. We also told each other about our problems . . . [which were] nicely balanced between the stupidity and delays of our home offices and the confu-

[17] Robert Menzies (Australian PM), 28 May 1941, quoted in Thorne (1978) 63.
[18] Donald Sole letter, 25 May 1941, Sole manuscript, 49.
[19] Cross (1967) 57.
[20] Just two or three meetings took place, one in Churchill's bedroom.
[21] Garner (1978) 200–1.
[22] Dilks (1991) 9.
[23] Office circular 14, 31 May 1943, quoted in Stacey (1981) 367–9.

sions and difficulties of dealing with the government departments in Washington.[24]

And, reflecting the close Commonwealth relationship, it became customary for Churchill, when visiting Washington, to meet all Commonwealth heads of mission. On one occasion they gathered in the Cabinet Room of the White House.[25]

B. The Expansion of High Commissions

The pattern of great busyness in London was reflected in Britain's own high commissions. They gained military advisers (so-named to distinguish them from the 'fully diplomatic' *attachés*) and information sections; trade commissioners became more closely associated with them; and there was greater recognition of the need for staff to travel in the dominions to which they were posted. Only by working very long hours, neglecting some peace-time functions such as reporting, and doing a good deal of the routine work perfunctorily was it possible to get by.

Meanwhile, the War witnessed an appreciable increase in the number of high commissioners, as its outbreak precipitated their widespread exchange between the dominions. Most of them had relatively little to do, as there was not much by way of inter-dominion relations. But such exchanges constituted important symbolic demonstrations of war-time solidarity.

South Africa and Ireland had been first in the field by establishing missions in Canada before the outbreak of war, but the latter was soon very much in the lead by becoming, until the end of the 1940s, the only dominion to have a high commission in every Commonwealth capital. Moreover, as can be seen from the following table, she was for some time the only dominion in which every other Commonwealth member was represented:

[24] Pearson (1973) 218. He added, 'The British were less critical about their London masters than the rest of us', he added, 'but concentrated on how many and grievous were the mistakes of the Americans as "new boys"'.

[25] Churchill observed that the last time so many Britishers had met at the White House during a war they had burned it down: Pearson (1973) 228.

The growth of inter-dominion representation 1938–1946

From	To	Arrival of high commissioner/ representative[26]
South Africa	Canada	1938
Ireland	Canada	1939
	Australia	1946
Canada	Australia	1939
	Ireland	1940
	South Africa	1940
	New Zealand	1940
Australia	Canada	1940
	New Zealand	1943
	India	1943
	South Africa	1946
	Ireland	1946
New Zealand	Canada	1944
	Australia	1943

Canada made her first move on 11 September 1939, the day after entering the week-old War. Following adverse press comment about her delay in going to war, and amidst 'talk of Empire War Cabinets in London',[27] she announced she was going to appoint high commissioners to all the other dominions as a material contribution to wartime co-operation. Then Australia burst into representational activity, notwithstanding the unenthusiasm for it of her wartime Labor prime minster, John Curtin. (He thought the expense was unwarranted.) But her pugilistic and self-aggrandising external affairs minister, H.V. Evatt (1941–49), was of a different persuasion. He was determined to raise Australia's status and standing internationally, and extended his Department's 'tentacles . . . to embrace new activities'.[28] And he prevailed, so precipitating a rapid growth in the number of Australian missions.

[26] Where there is a date for presentation of credentials, this has been taken as the date of arrival.

[27] Skelton (under-secretary, DEA) memorandum, 4 October 1939, NAC, T-1802, RG25 D1, 791, 428.

[28] E.J. Williams (British HC, Canberra), no. 372, 30 July 1946, TNA, DO114/115.

The remaining three dominions took a narrower and more languid line about their representational needs. New Zealand, for example, only opened a high commission in Ottawa in 1942, and did not appoint a high commissioner for another two years.[29] Nor was she in a hurry to send anyone to Canberra. Not until 1943 did wartime needs convince her prime minister that such a move was necessary to improve the exchange of 'mutual information and for frank discussion in the utmost confidence' between the two Australasian states.[30] Ireland went no further than to open high commissions in Canada and Australia. And it was only in 1949 that South Africa reciprocated the 1946 appointment of an Australian high commissioner.

This rather spotty record says much about the lack of substance in most inter-dominion relationships.[31] During the War years 'virtually no business was transacted between Ottawa and Pretoria';[32] in 1942 Canada's high commissioner in Canberra had little to do beyond arranging aid; and being posted as Canada's high commissioner to

---

[29] She was not represented in Dublin until 1965 when her high commissioner in London was 'cross-accredited'. Relations with Dublin had, all along, been largely handled through the London High Commission. Only in 1996 did she open a resident mission in Pretoria.

[30] Peter Fraser (New Zealand PM)-John Curtin (Australian PM), cablegram 48, 20 February 1943, *DAFP* VI, 269. The imminent physical collapse through overwork of Carl Berendsen (head of the Prime Minister's Department, secretary for the Cook Islands, and war cabinet secretary) 'added almost as much to the urgency . . . as did policy divergences': McGibbon (1993) 3. Australia reciprocated nine months later.

[31] There was one exception to this situation, in that Canada's wartime high commissioners in Newfoundland were very hard worked, reflecting the fact that her relations with this territory were 'more varied, more important and more urgent' than with all the other dominions combined: Norman Robertson (under-secretary, DEA)-King, 15 July 1941, quoted in Hilliker (1990) 248.

In 1934 Newfoundland had reverted to a semi-colonial condition (under British tutelage) and she rejected an early exchange of representatives with Canada as being too expensive. However, Canada's wartime interests led her to send a high commissioner to Newfoundland in 1941. Hitherto there had been at least six different channels of communication but now 'all wartime matters between Canada and Newfoundland were dealt with though the [Canadian] high commissioner's office in St John's': Hilliker (1990) 247–8. But as one Canadian high commissioner wryly remarked, his title was 'something of a misnomer in a country where members of the Government . . . are only Commissioners . . . the title is too high-sounding and what status we have is more than we can support': Scott MacDonald-Escott Reid (about-to-be assistant under-secretary), 8 March 1947, NAC, RG 25, 4045, 10577–40 vol. 1. It might be added that the title was also a misnomer in that these high commissioners were not in the same category as the ones which are the focus of this book, in that they were not engaged in international diplomacy.

[32] Tennyson (1982) 101.

New Zealand was a kindly way of 'rounding out'[33] the career of Walter Riddell (who had angered his prime minister by proposing oil sanctions against Italy in 1935 and was reportedly 'of little use'[34] in Washington). Nonetheless, when dominions failed to send or replace high commissioners, there were hurt feelings: South Africa was unhappy in 1940 about Canada's slowness in sending someone to Pretoria, and Australia felt offended by South Africa's unenthusiasm for having a high commissioner in Canberra. The situation was not helped by the lack of solid work in wartime (and for some time afterwards) making high commissionerships unappealing to, and frustrating for, vigorous, able, and intelligent men.

C. Anglo-Irish Complications

Wartime solidarity was not the only reason for inter-dominion exchanges. The Commonwealth dissidents—South Africa and Ireland—had already opened missions in Ottawa before the War because they wanted to emphasise their countries' independent standing, and hoped to move the Commonwealth in the direction of 'normal' diplomatic practices. For this last reason, the question of title was at issue. Hence South Africa had succeeded in appointing not a high commissioner but an 'Accredited Representative' to Canada in 1938.[35] It was for the same reason that Britain ended up sending a 'Representative' to Dublin.

The Irish Free State had always been a Commonwealth anomaly. Dominion status was 'psychologically alien' to the Irish.[36] It had been imposed against a background of civil war and partition, and accepted only because, as Michael Collins put it, it 'gave freedom to achieve freedom'.[37] A decade later, in 1932, Eamon de Valera won power and set about the task of fundamentally altering the Irish Free State's relationship to Britain and the Commonwealth. First he removed the monarchical trimmings by, *inter alia*, demoting the governor-general[38]

---

[33] Skelton memorandum, 16 December 1939, NAC, T-1802, RG25 D1, 791, 428.
[34] King diary, 5 November 1939, http://king.collectionscanada.ca/EN.
[35] See above, chapter 2, section E.
[36] Mansergh cited in McMahon (1984) 48.
[37] McIntyre (2002) 394.
[38] After a number of humiliating snubs, one governor-general received a compensatory lunch at Buckingham Palace. De Valera then went 'to great and tortuous lengths' to avoid replacing him, but ended up nominating Domhnall O'Buachalla (Donal

and removing the oath of allegiance to the King. Then he abolished common nationality.[39] And in 1936 he took advantage of the abdication crisis[40] to introduce a new Constitution (which came into force in 1937) which changed the English name of the state to 'Ireland' and on the face of it made Ireland a republic.[41] This was done by replacing the governor-general with a president (*uachtarán na hEireann*), and omitting any direct reference to the King in the Constitution. At the same time, the head of government ceased being called 'President of the Executive Council', instead adopting the ancient name '*taoiseach*' (meaning 'leader' or 'chief'). His powers were also extended to include, for example, the right to decide to call elections and dismiss ministers. But de Valera stopped short of describing Ireland as a republic[42] and left it up to Britain to determine the consequences for Ireland's membership of the Commonwealth (which he had no desire to leave).[43]

The rest of the Commonwealth fudged the issue, saying Ireland's position in the Commonwealth was fundamentally unaltered. This was possible because her 1936 External Relations Act (ERA) declared that as long as Ireland was associated with Britain and the dominions, and as long as those states recognised the King 'as the symbol of their co-operation' and enabled him to act on their behalf in diplomatic matters, he could continue to do likewise for her—always, of course, on the advice of her government.[44] This 'masterpiece of . . . hair-splitting'[45] meant that the King continued signing Ireland's international

Buckley), a provincial shopkeeper who had taken part in the 1916 Rising and had long been connected with the Irish language movement. O'Buachalla foreswore the viceregal lodge for a suburban house chosen by de Valera and confined himself to his formal duties, avoiding any ceremonial role: McMahon (1984) 63.

[39] The 1935 Nationality and Citizenship Act declared that Irish citizens were not also British subjects and rejected the idea of common nationality. British law continued to regard them as British subjects.

[40] In which the Irish Free State played no part.

[41] The Irish name was changed from *Saorstát Éireann* to *Éire*.

[42] Article 5 of the Constitution declared Ireland to be a 'sovereign, independent, democratic State'. Although he regarded his country as in external association with, rather than a full member of, the Commonwealth, political expediency dictated that de Valera should not spell this out in full.

[43] During the 1937 Imperial Conference (which he did not attend) de Valera said 'he wasn't leaving the Commonwealth; they'd have to chuck him out': McIntyre (2002) 20.

[44] It appears that not until his speech to the *Dáil* on 11 July 1945 did de Valera refer in public to Ireland being a 'republic' or to the King's role under the ERA: Massey, A. 305, 27 July 1945, NAC, 4480, 50021–40, part 1.

[45] McIntyre (1999) 195.

agreements, appointing her diplomatic and consular representatives (whose letters of credence and *exequaturs* were now in Irish),[46] and receiving the letters of credence and *exequaturs* of diplomats and consuls appointed to Dublin (which were opened by the president before being passed on—which led to some eyebrow raising at Buckingham Palace). In London, the Irish high commissioner, John Dulanty (1930–50), continued regularly attending high commissioners' meetings (despite feeling 'like a whore at a christening').[47] He also slipped into the DO on Sundays to see the more important telegrams and, with de Valera's tacit approval, continued on Armistice Day to lay official wreaths at London's cenotaph. However, in practice Britain recognised Ireland's *de facto* secession: ministers avoided referring to her as a dominion; during the War they spoke of Ireland's 'non-participation' rather than her neutrality (because of uncertainty about the constitutional aspects of the latter); and in 1939 they bowed to Ireland's wish to receive a British 'representative' rather than a 'high commissioner'.

Until then Britain had had no kind of diplomatic representation in Dublin. This was due to several factors. On Britain's side there was an allegedly dismissive attitude towards Ireland—she was seen as a kind of troublesome Isle of Wight;[48] also there was some political and official disinclination in London to try to get close to de Valera's government. On Ireland's side there was opposition from Dulanty, her high commissioner in London, who 'poured freezing water on the idea whenever it was mentioned to him by British officials because he relished the role of Mr Fixit, of being the only formal link between the two governments'.[49] Furthermore, members of both British and Irish government departments tended to contact their opposite numbers directly. And during the 1930s British high commissioners were still novel, reaching all the other Commonwealth members only in the second half of the decade.

---

[46] In October 1932 the King agreed to sign *exequaturs* and commissions of appointment in Irish if they were accompanied by an English-language version for the record: Liesching (PUS, CRO)-E. McCarthy (Australian DHC, London), 14 August 1953, TNA DO127/92. Names, too, were in their Irish form. When Patrick Cosgrave signed a letter to Mussolini as Liam MacCosgair, the Italians had to ask their consul in Dublin who he was: Lowry (2000) 189.

[47] Lowry (2000) 194.

[48] On the 'Isle of Wight syndrome' see Peck (1978) 18.

[49] Deidre McMahon letter, 4 March 1999.

Nonetheless, by 1936 both London and Dublin recognised the need for a resident British mission in Dublin. British Cabinet approval was obtained and the DO was discussing remuneration with the Treasury when plans were scuppered because the Free State refused to receive a 'high commissioner' and Britain refused to use the diplomatic style 'minister' or 'ambassador'. But the need for clear and efficient communication between London and Dublin in wartime, soon made it imperative to overcome this problem. First, however, de Valera wanted to exchange missions with Canada in order to emphasise Ireland's 'independence' of Britain.[50] Since Canada was anyway contemplating sending a high commissioner to Dublin, her prime minister, Mackenzie King, immediately agreed. And because Ireland wanted to follow 'normal' diplomatic practice, she sought, and received, Canada's approval for her nominee as high commissioner. He was John Hearne, the former External Affairs legal adviser, who arrived in Ottawa in August 1939 (bearing what was said to be 'the customary . . . letter of introduction').[51] King was then slow to reciprocate, partly because he considered Dublin a 'trivial' post,[52] and Dublin learned (through the British) that Canada did not plan to appoint anyone before the middle of 1940. The news 'very much upset' Joseph Walshe, the secretary of external affairs (the senior official), who 'begged' them not to tell de Valera.[53] However, as it turned out a Canadian high commissioner arrived in Dublin a little earlier, in March 1940.

Meanwhile, Anglo-Irish negotiations had again run aground on the question of titles. Ireland objected to 'high commissioner' because it had colonial overtones and implied 'administrative functions and the power to interfere' rather than diplomatic functions.[54] It would also raise domestic difficulties since it would constitute 'an appointment of a new and special character'.[55] Britain continued to resist de Valera's pressure to adopt the diplomatic style 'minister'. But wanting de Valera's goodwill and the most benevolent neutrality possible, and fearing a head-on

[50] King memorandum, 'Interview with Sir Gerald Campbell [British HC]', 4 March 1939, *DCER* 6, 64.
[51] *Ottawa Citizen*, 31 July 1939, based on report from Dublin.
[52] King diary, 5 July 1946, http://king.collectionscanada.ca.
[53] Liesching (AUS, DO) minute, 'The Early Appointment of a UK High Commissioner in Dublin', 5 July 1939, TNA, DO127/39.
[54] Draft Interim Report on the Status and Title of Commonwealth High Commissioners in London (first revision), July 1947, TNA, DO35/2186.
[55] Garner (1978) 237.

collision over wartime naval measures if Britain were unrepresented in Dublin, she offered the title 'representative'. De Valera agreed (as a temporary measure), but would not allow him to be called 'UK' Representative, since that might imply acceptance of the six Northern counties' incorporation into Britain. A compromise emerged. When Sir John Maffey took up his post in October 1939, he was styled 'British Representative' by Dublin and 'UK Representative' by London.[56]

Maffey, who had served with great distinction in the Indian North-West Frontier Province (where he became 'a sort of honorary Pathan')[57] and Sudan (where he was much loved and respected governor), was equally successful in Ireland. He richly earned his 1947 elevation to the peerage (as Lord Rugby) for his delicate and difficult work. According to Sir William Clark, who undertook an investigation into British representation in the dominions, Maffey's 'functions and accordingly his office' were 'not really comparable' with those of Britain's other four high commissioners since he was so closely and continuously in contact with the DO/CRO. However, Clark had no doubt about Maffey's diplomatic role: 'general representational functions in an unobtrusive form are important; there is a great deal of "contact" work of all sorts, and a great deal of purely "consular" work'.[58]

D. High Commissioner Woes: Canada and South Africa

In 1943, five years after Daniel de Waal Meyer had arrived in Canada as South Africa's 'Accredited Representative', his 'ambiguous and meaningless title'[59] gave rise to problems. His title was not recognised in certain South African financial legislation and, in consequence (a Union min-

---

[56] Interestingly, in 1969 Britain appointed a 'UK Representative to the Northern Ireland Government' (where the security situation was deteriorating badly). As Northern Ireland was part of Britain, the appointment was made by the Home Office; but the incumbent, and his successor, were from the Foreign Office: Peck (1978) 21–2.

[57] Gilbert Laithwaite, 'John Loader Maffey' in E.T. Williams & C.S. Nicholls (eds) (1995) 713.

[58] Sir William Clark, 'Report on UK Representation in the Dominions with Special Reference to Establishment and Accommodation Aspects', July/August 1947, TNA, DO35/2646 (Clark Report).

[59] John Holmes (special assistant to Robertson) note, 15 November 1944, NAC, RG25, 2942, 3011-A-40. All subsequent unreferenced footnotes in this chapter are taken from this NAC file.

ister told Parliament in 1943), Meyer lacked not only the title but also the rank of a high commissioner.[60] Canada, which had hitherto assumed that Meyer was a high commissioner in all but name, therefore asked the Union to raise Meyer to that status. Canada's high commissioner to South Africa, Charles Burchell (a not unbiased reporter since he keenly wanted to bear a diplomatic style), said that South Africa wanted to use 'minister' or 'ambassador', which was certainly true of her DEA officials and of General Hertzog's pre-war government. In 1938 this would have been too daring a move for Mackenzie King. However, when Canada's DEA pondered the matter in the last year of the War, it saw no objection in principle: if South Africa wanted to change the title, it was up to her; there was probably no significant problem in switching to diplomatic titles; and it made 'no real difference' to Canada since she would continue treating Meyer as a high commissioner.[61]

However, as Canada's under-secretary for external affairs (the most senior DEA official) explained, this was not the time to try to make a change: there were more important things to worry about; it would be difficult to reach a consensus on what the title should be; any talks would be bound to open up the question of Ireland's position within the Commonwealth; and it was not worth raising 'this thorny matter' on 'an issue of minor importance'.[62] Therefore, when Meyer left Canada in 1944 Canada pressed South Africa to appoint a representative with the title, as well as the rank, of high commissioner. South Africa complied (though almost a year passed before Dr. P.R. Viljoen arrived as such in September 1945).

Meanwhile, at the other end of the relationship, South Africa had seemingly been taking out her dissatisfaction with the office of high commissioner on the sole dominion representative of that species. Problems had begun as soon as the first Canadian high commissioner, Henri Laureys (1940–44), set foot in the Union. He found himself in a lonely, 'peculiar and unpleasant' position.[63] His office was not 'properly' understood and he had a 'low official rating',[64] being denied the

[60] The South Africans soon agreed to amend the legislation that had given rise to the difficulty.

[61] Holmes note, 15 November 1944.

[62] Robertson-Burchell, personal and confidential, 27 November 1944.

[63] Laureys, 16 December 1940, no. 79, NAC, RG25, 2942, 3011–40.

[64] Burchell-Read, 22 May 1945.

appropriate 'courtesies and consideration'[65] such as the diplomatic and railway privileges enjoyed by members of the British high commission. The British high commissioner (Sir Edward Harding, 1940–41) was 'cold and distant',[66] superior and 'aloof'.[67] The tiny diplomatic corps cold-shouldered him, and did not include him in joint birthday greetings to the King, special religious services, and state dinners. Ottawa told Laureys that he could not expect to be a member of the diplomatic corps but he should be treated appropriately. The difference between high commissioners and heads of legations was 'well recognized and should, in practice, give rise to no misunderstanding'.[68] Laureys remained unhappy. A year-and-a-half into his high commissionership his standing had still not been clearly established, and he was continuing to plague Ottawa with detailed questions about tax exemptions.

Laureys' successor, Charles Burchell (1944–45), claimed that personally he did not 'give a damn for protocol stuff'.[69] This is belied by his tedious chronicling of perceived discourtesies and insults. His complaints were not always justified but he had plenty of time to contemplate such matters. Moreover, after having been comparatively well-treated as high commissioner in Australia (1939–41) and Newfoundland (1941–44), it was unpleasant to discover he had become one of the 'Low Commissioners'.[70] For in South Africa, where his title carried a 'most unfortunate' colonial 'aroma', he was only a 'quasi-diplomat' with 'little, if any, official standing'.[71]

Although it was South Africa's policy 'to assimilate the position of Commonwealth representatives, as far as immunities, etc. went, to that of the diplomatic representatives of other countries',[72] Burchell felt poorly treated. In 1941 'everyone' had turned up to greet Lord Harlech, the new British high commissioner,[73] and the acting secretary

[65] Laureys, 31 March 1941, no. 32, NAC, RG25, 2942, 3011–40.
[66] Laureys, 16 December 1940, NAC, RG25, 2942, 3011–40.
[67] Garner (1978) 20.
[68] DEA-Laureys, 21 April 1941, no. 17, NAC, RG25, 2942, 3011–40.
[69] Burchell (Canadian HC, St. John's)-Pearson (under-secretary, DEA), personal & confidential, 29 December 1948, NAC, RG25, 6194-A-40, part 2.3.
[70] D'Arcy McGreer (Canadian HC, Pretoria)-Howard Measures quoting John Kearney (Canadian HC, Dublin, 1941–45), 27 July 1948, NAC, RG25, 2942, 3011–40.
[71] Burchell-Robertson, 8 January 1945, 7 February 1945, 13 June 1944.
[72] D.D. Forsyth (South African SDEA) reported in Robertson-Burchell, personal & confidential, 10 June 1944.
[73] Harlech-Cranborne (dominions secretary), 29 May 1941, TNA, DO121/107.

of external affairs turned out for his successor, Sir Evelyn Baring in 1944. But (in accordance with usual South African practice) neither Laureys nor Burchell was neither met on arrival. Nor did anyone from the DEA call on Burchell.[74] Like Laureys he was vexed about the denial of diplomatic privileges and other perks (especially as the British high commissioner enjoyed some of the latter), and he wanted diplomatic immunity which, he believed, was enjoyed by everyone in legations, 'right down to the office boy and household servants'![75]

Then there was his 'non-recognition' by the diplomatic corps,[76] an indifferent bunch of men who resented finding themselves in 'a most uninteresting post and more or less a dead end',[77] and who 'were always fussing about their status & this & that (most of them had nothing else to do!)'.[78] Not only that, the *doyen* was an exceedingly unpopular mischief-maker, 'a snob, a bounder and a butter-in'.[79] Being excluded from state dinners or given lower *placement* was 'very degrading to the good name and fame of Canada', especially given that Canada was helping to free 'the over-run countries such as Greece, Poland, Belgium and Holland'.[80] It also galling for Burchell to be 'put in back seats with church wardens'[81] at special services (such as the one following D-Day—the 1944 Allied invasion of France) and omitted from the list of those present. In the end, he preferred to absent himself rather than be humiliated.

But not only was Burchell's status lower than heads of foreign legations. He was 'miles below'[82] the British high commissioner. It was, said Burchell, 'perfectly absurd' for the South Africans to claim that Lord Harlech had 'the same standing and position' as him and that they were treated 'on the same footing'.[83] Part of the problem was that Harlech was also high commissioner for the Basutoland, Bechuanaland, and

---

[74] No-one from the DEA greeted Sir William Clark in 1935, and H.D.J. Bodenstein (SDEA) did not call on Clark.
[75] Burchell-Robertson, 30 January 1945.
[76] *Ibid.*, 13 June 1944
[77] McGreer-Measures, personal, 13 May 1947.
[78] Cecil Syers (AUS, DO) minute January 1947, TNA, DO35/3328.
[79] Harlech-Cranborne, secret & personal, 10 November 1943, TNA, DO121/107.
[80] Burchell-Pearson, personal & confidential, 29 December 1948, NAC, RG25, 6194-A-40, part 2.3.
[81] Burchell-Robertson, 13 June 1944.
[82] *Ibid.*
[83] Burchell-Robertson, personal & confidential, 8 July and 9 August 1944.

Swaziland Protectorates. In that capacity he had precedence immediately after the governor-general, and in practice the South Africans might not always have found it easy to distinguish between Harlech's two offices. But the consequence was that Burchell felt he was treated as an inferior, colonial representative. For example, the acting British high commissioner, Cecil Syers, was flown on a government plane to Durban for a military lunch where he was seated on the top table, close to Smuts, while his Canadian colleague sat 'at the far corner of a side table . . . [in] quite the lowest seat'. Then, at a postprandial 'thanksgiving cavalcade', Burchell had had to sit in an unreserved seat in the 'gods' while Syers sat next to Smuts on the centre platform from which Smuts spoke.[84]

Nor did it help that that the staunchly conservative Harlech came over to Burchell as somewhat humourless, tactless, and autocratic, leading to complaints about him being standoffish, superior, snooty, paternal, and (like Sir Ronald Cross, his British colleague in Australia) the wrong type of man for the job.[85] (By contrast the US minister described Harlech as being 'as outstanding among [resident diplomats] as his job was beyond theirs in range and complexity'.)[86] Burchell also said that Harlech fostered the impression that he was the only high commissioner, so that people thought Burchell's office was tagged on to Harlech's. When, however, Burchell was not being mistaken for Harlech's underling, he tended to be confused with trade commissioners[87] or expected to be engaged upon administrative, colonial-type tasks. He determined that instead of being 'neither fish, flesh nor fowl'[88] his successors should be 'on the same level'[89] as Britain's representative and admitted to the diplomatic corps.

This meant abolishing the 'misleading and confusing' title of 'high commissioner',[90] a step that Burchell had favoured even before he went to South Africa. It was one thing for Vincent Massey in London to want to keep the title, but it was increasingly inappropriate in South

[84] Burchell-Robertson, 9 August 1944.

[85] Smuts preferred doing business with the DHC, Roy Price, who was 'an exceedingly delightful little man': Colville diary, 21 June 1942 in Colville (1987) 55.

[86] Lincoln MacVeagh-President Roosevelt in 1942. Quoted in Tothill (1995).

[87] This was partly because one trade commissioner had made such a good impression.

[88] Burchell-Robertson, personal, 30 October 1944.

[89] Burchell-Robertson, personal, 27 October 1944.

[90] Burchell-Robertson, 13 June 1944.

Africa. 'I am going to have considerable difficulty unless and until you change the name of your representative to this country', he said. 'A High Commissioner for a Dominion . . . will always be regarded as a very minor satellite and will always be given a very inferior place to the United Kingdom High Commissioner . . . [rather than being] properly recognized, not only officially but unofficially'.[91]

As Massey pointed out, while the basic problem was Harlech's dual role in South Africa, the Union government could, if it chose, resolve most of Burchell's difficulties. But apparently it had no intention of doing so. Instead, it seemed by its treatment of Burchell to be 'trying to blackmail [Canada into] exchanging ambassadors'.[92] In addition, Burchell claimed that South Africa was showing displeasure with Ottawa by appointing as her high commissioner to Canada 'a ranking member of the Broederbond'[93] (Dr. P.R. Viljoen) and by (entirely properly) not seeking *agrément* for him. Yet it was not South Africa that Burchell blamed but 'the Canadian Government for not giving her representatives the proper official standing'.[94]

When Burchell's complaints had begun pouring in, Canada's head of protocol commented: 'These matters of prestige are troublesome & futile. . . . I hope Burchell won't be bitten by the bug that infected Laureys when he was there!'[95] While Burchell's position was 'obviously unsatisfactory', it was important

> to assess properly the reasons for the trouble. There seems no reason why our problems should not be solved by frank and friendly discussions with the South African and possibly other Commonwealth governments. Before we assimilate the position of our representatives in Commonwealth countries to those of the representatives of foreign countries, we should be careful that we do not sacrifice certain real advantages in order to move up several places at table. Mr. Massey has been quite emphatic that as High Commissioner he enjoys privileges of informal and direct approaches to United Kingdom officials which are not enjoyed by Ambassadors and Ministers.[96]

---

[91] Burchell-Robertson, 9 August 1944.

[92] Holmes handwritten, undated note for Robertson, 'Status of high commissioners in South Africa', 28 August 1944.

[93] Burchell-Robertson, 27 October 1944, quoted in Tennyson (1982) 105. Founded in 1918, the secretive and highly influential Broederbond promoted Afrikaner nationalism and the republican ideal. In 1944 Smuts banned civil servants from belonging to it.

[94] Burchell, no. 121, 8 July 1944.

[95] Measures note, 2 December 1944.

[96] Holmes note, 1 August 1944.

Ottawa advised Burchell to concentrate on piecemeal enhancement of his status. Then it sent soothing words about it taking 'a little time' to 'educate' the South Africans about 'the implications of the Statute of Westminster'.[97] And then, as the DEA grew weary of Burchell's woes, Norman Robertson (the under-secretary) in effect told Burchell to put up with it for the duration. In addition to the other objections to making a move at that time, it would be difficult to change only Burchell's title without also re-naming all the other high commissioners. This did not stop Burchell nagging, but Ottawa saw no need to do anything, especially as high commissioners in Ottawa seemed content with their lot.

This is not to say that Ottawa ignored the substance of Burchell's grievances. They were carefully considered. Some were dismissed as ill-founded (such as the claim that the title 'high commissioner' had intrinsic colonial connotations); others were 'trivial', had been 'rectified', or had been a '[m]atter for formal protest'. [98] In themselves the complained-of incidents were petty, but cumulatively they were 'quite serious'.[99] Burchell's position was 'humiliating',[100] and Canada made it clear both directly and indirectly (via the DO) that she would not permanently tolerate having her high commissioners treated less favourably than foreigners. Indeed, she concluded that there was much to be said for doing away with the office and the second class treatment of Canadians. But securing equality by turning high commissioners into ambassadors ran into the problem of how the King could accredit a head of mission to himself. Additionally, Britain would fiercely resist that step, and any intra-Commonwealth discussions would probably emphasise the 'diversity of opinion . . . not only as among the different Government [*sic.*], but as among the different Canadian High Commissioners, as well as representatives of other Commonwealth Governments in Ottawa'.[101] There might also be problems with provincial legislatures challenging Canadian legislation giving high commissioners ambassadorial status and privileges. And since Canada was the only dominion to

[97] Robertson-Burchell, 5 December 1944, NAC, RG25, 2942, 3011–40.

[98] Robertson marginal notes on Holmes note, 'Status of High Commissioners in South Africa', 28 August 1944.

[99] Hume Wrong (associate under-secretary, DEA) memorandum, 5 September 1944.

[100] Holmes note, 'Status of high commissioners in South Africa', 28 August 1944.

[101] John Read (legal adviser, DEA) draft despatch, 6 July 1945.

appoint ambassadors (as distinct from ministers), any exchanges with the other dominions would probably have to be at the lower diplomatic level. But it would hardly do to have 'an Ambassador in Lima and a Minister in Canberra'.[102] Thus while Canada was not always happy about the position, it would have to be tolerated for the time being.

E. The Standing of High Commissioners Elsewhere

It was not only in South Africa that diplomatic life was a source of high commissioner woe. The prospect of under-employment in small, provincial-feeling dominion capitals often had no appeal.[103] Wellington, for example, was said to lack culture and its inhabitants to suffer from 'deadening mental and spiritual insensibility'.[104] At the end of the 1940s it was asserted that Ottawa was insufficiently large 'to allow diplomatic life to be swallowed up in it' and that its small, mostly Anglophone elite had 'too much Oxbridge, and too many closed windows'.[105] Exclusion (everywhere) from the—often very moderately sized[106]—diplomatic corps continued to rankle, and a British government report recognised that not only was the inferior precedence of high commissioners unsatisfactory but also that dominion high commissioners could feel adversely affected by it.[107]

With their generally light workloads,[108] both high commissioners and foreign heads of legation had plenty of time to ruminate on matters

---

[102] Holmes note, 24 October 1944.

[103] Australia and the United States reportedly raised their legations to embassies to make the job in Canberra 'more attractive to men of high ability': *Sydney Morning Herald*, 17 January 1947.

[104] Sir Patrick Duff (British HC, Wellington)-Machtig (PUS, DO), personal, 20 June 1947, TNA, DO121/116. 'How comes it that a people enjoying material wellbeing to such an unusual degree', Duff wondered, 'are so noticeably deficient in vitality, aspiration, quality and inspiration and plod through existence under a solid blight of indifference and humourlessness'?

[105] Maryon Pearson quoted in English (1992) 9.

[106] The biggest dominion diplomatic corps was in Ottawa where, in 1942, there were ten legations. The smallest was in Wellington, where there were just two legations at the War's end. New Zealanders tended to be critical of, or see little reason for, a bigger diplomatic corps. One member of the government thought it was 'all right' for there to be a US legation, but every other state should make do with a consulate-general: Alfred Rive (Canadian HC, Wellington)-Pearson, 18 December 1947.

[107] Clark Report.

[108] This remained true well into the 1950s. See, for example, Carrington (1988) 123.

of protocol. In Wellington, the diplomatic corps' 'futile and petty'[109] displays of disdain for high commissioners were causing DEA officials to lose sleep. The main culprit was Armand Gazel, the (French) *doyen* (and 'a very nasty piece of work'),[110] who had 'no truck or trade with High Commissioners', whom he regarded as 'simply not-very-senior members . . . of an imperial civil service'.[111] He took every opportunity to decry them as 'an inferior species who might be mentioned in the same breath with, but after, consuls'.[112] Looking in a different direction, Gazel claimed to be on a par with the governor-general, Sir Cyril Newell, on the grounds that they both represented heads of state. Gazel's wife accordingly refused the customary curtsey to Newell, and the other ministers' wives followed suit. Newell, who hated Gazel, retaliated 'by giving Sir Patrick [Duff—the British high commissioner, 1945–49] special recognition whenever he can, such as at the ball where he singled [him] and Lady Duff out for special attention before he hobnobbed with the ministers'.[113] When Gazel left (for South Africa, where he made more mischief), his underemployed Belgian successor, who was 'notorious for . . . concerning himself unduly with tiny points of protocol and precedence', became 'a tiresome irritant'.[114]

Formally-speaking all high commissioners were in the same boat (except that in South Africa the dual-hatted British high commissioner received some special treatment). It might, therefore, be expected that Britain's high commissioners would have regarded their position as unsatisfactory. This seems to have been true of Duff in that the governor-general helped him avoid occasions where his lower precedence would be manifest.[115] But not only was the prestige of British high commissioners unaffected by their relatively lowly precedence, they had several advantages over their dominion counterparts. Most found plenty to do and were confident of their and their country's position. In Wellington, for example, Sir Harry Batterbee (1939–45) believed he

[109] N. Costar (British HCO, Wellington)-C.R. Price (a senior DO official), 9 January 1947, TNA, DO35/3203.
[110] Rive-Pearson, 27 December 1946.
[111] Rive, no. 72, 10 February 1949, NAC, RG25, 3997, 10062–40.
[112] Costar-Price, 9 January 1947.
[113] Rive-Pearson, 27 December 1946.
[114] Costar (AUS, CRO) minute, 4 November 1948, TNA, DO35/3204.
[115] If possible, Duff was not invited to the same functions as heads of legations, and Duff evaded 'all invitations . . . which would show him in precedence below any of the three ministers': Rive-Pearson, 27 December 1946.

possessed ambassadorial rank, and Duff was 'effulgent with the light from "Home"'.[116] And they enjoyed special treatment. An Australian governor-general largely ignored the diplomatic corps and 'completely ignored' all the high commissioners except Britain's.[117] New Zealand's governor-general and government regarded Duff as in effect the senior envoy in Wellington, and thought that as he represented the 'Home Government' he should be 'on a footing with Ministers of the Crown'[118] (which naturally induced resentment and complaints from his Canadian colleague). And the Dublin authorities did 'their utmost to accord Sir John [Maffey] a diplomatic status higher than that of his colleagues, or the heads of foreign Missions'.[119]

British high commissioners were also splendidly accommodated. In Canada, it was in Earnscliffe, the beautiful Victorian home of Canada's first prime minister.[120] In South Africa, Britain's high commissioner was

> singularly fortunate in his setting, which puts him in a category by himself as compared with the other High Commissioners and with the heads of diplomatic missioners [*sic.*]. In Pretoria . . . he alone has his residence in the quarter in Brynterion otherwise reserved for houses of Cabinet Ministers. . . . the situation of the house with the Union Jack flying over it in the middle of the area otherwise set apart for Government House, the Administrator's residence, and houses for Cabinet Ministers, cannot fail to be impressive. The location of the office in Cape Town is similarly unique. It stands in Parliament Street, the local Whitehall, which otherwise is almost wholly occupied by government offices, and faces Parliament Buildings and Government House. The High Commissioner also has a permanent residence in Cape Town, whereas his diplomatic colleagues have for the most part to sojourn in the Mount Nelson Hotel. . . . These . . . are all things that matter[121]

Of course, accommodation did not in itself induce respect. The USA had built 'a sumptuous embassy complete with chancery' in Australia,

[116] Rive-Pearson, 22 August 1947.
[117] Davis (Canadian HC, Canberra), no. 108, 8 January 1946, NAC, RG25, 5699, 4-G(s), part 2.
[118] Rive-Pearson, 18 December 1947.
[119] E.J. Garland (Canadian AHC, Dublin), no. 133, 14 November 1946, NAC, RG25, 2942, 3011.
[120] In later years it also had geographical advantages as it was very close to the prime ministerial residence that St Laurent had grudgingly agreed to purchase in 1951. Even more conveniently, in 1973 External Affairs was relocated next door, permitting ministers and deputy ministers to slip out to see the British high commissioner.
[121] W.H. Clark and M.E. Antrobus, 'Supplementary Report on United Kingdom Representation in the Dominions', January 1948, TNA, DO35/2646.

but little was heard of the American ambassador. On the other hand, the British high commissioner in New Zealand obviously enjoyed high public esteem, and he was 'in constant demand for public appearances of all kinds'; and in Ireland 'Lord Rugby's personality has been decisive'[122] in contributing to the regard in which he was held. In Melbourne (Australia's capital until 1927) there had been a tendency to regard a high commissioner as 'necessarily less important and less equipped' than a foreign diplomat.[123] But for the most part dominion high commissioners were satisfied and said they were well received—including Burchell's successors as Canadian high commissioner in South Africa and Australia, whose favourable reports belied Burchell's whinging. (One received 'the utmost courtesy and consideration by the South African authorities',[124] the other—who unlike Burchell enjoyed the happiest and friendliest relations with the British high commissioner—found the Australian government 'meticulous' in treating him much the same as his British counterpart.)[125] Except for the Irish high commissioner (who was good at finding problems), high commissioners in Ottawa seemed generally content and had 'no reason for complaint'.[126] Dublin ranked all Commonwealth envoys with the heads of legations and gave them diplomatic privileges and immunity, but tried to give members of the Commonwealth 'family' better treatment in practice by being 'markedly attentive' to high commissioners.[127] (This was assisted by the fact that Ireland had not formally established an order of precedence for diplomats.) Meanwhile, not only was the lower precedence of high commissioners seldom obvious in London, but

> a good deal more fuss is made over Commonwealth representatives by [Britain's] Government Hospitality Committee and by public and semi-public bodies, generally, than is made over any foreign representative,

---

[122] Clark Report.

[123] *Ibid.*

[124] McGreer-Measures, personal, 13 May 1947.

[125] Davis-Robertson, undated, received 9 August 1944, In so doing, the government laid itself open to recrimination from fully-fledged diplomats. In turn, Davis' successor, K.A. Greene (1947–49), not only 'receive[d] every consideration', he thought there was a 'tendency' 'to pay more attention to' high commissioners than to heads of legations: Greene-Pearson, 30 December 1947. Nor did Greene have many precedence problems; his only suffering was at official parties—although there being so few missions in Canberra he was never far down the line.

[126] Holmes note, 1 August 1944.

[127] Garland, no. 133, 14 November 1946.

> except the American Ambassador. . . . the questions of official style and precedence which our representatives in Canberra and Pretoria brought to our attention, and with which we are familiar in Ottawa . . . seem rather remote and of secondary importance here.[128]

F. Post-War Developments

Nonetheless, by the end of the Second World War there was a real head of steam behind demands that high commissioners should have equality with foreign diplomats, if not a change of title. And by then the time was ripe for change. Several factors contributed to this. First, Britain began to see faults in the Commonwealth's diplomatic set-up. On the one hand she was getting uneasy about the status of her representatives in the dominions. The appearance there of Soviet and American missions, and especially the often 'opulent' and 'lavish' character of the latter,[129] raised fears about British high commissioners being 'overshadowed' because of their 'anomalous' and 'relatively minor' position.[130] The arrival, too, of ex-enemy 'representatives' (the title given to the envoys of Italy, an ex-enemy state) aggravated matters for British high commissioners, as they found it hard to accept that they should rank lower than such people in tables of precedence. On the other hand, Britain's Foreign Office (FO), which had designs on British representation in the Commonwealth, was critical of high commissions, suggesting that they should be organised on the same lines as embassies and legations, and in particular that they should improve their arrangements for reporting on foreign policy. More generally, the FO contended that the job of representing Britain in a dominion was broadly similar to doing so in a foreign state.[131]

Second, the earlier laments of dominion high commissioners about their lowly status received added point as the dominions upgraded and enlarged their overseas representation. As late as 1941 Canada's Mackenzie King had spoken of maintaining 'a sense of true proportion in

---

[128] Robertson (Canadian HC, London 1946–49), telegram 2232, 20 November 1946.

[129] Clark Report.

[130] Editorial, 'Ambassadors within the Empire', *Melbourne Age*, 2 January 1947.

[131] The CRO insisted there were still differences, including that members of high commissions were not put to the same expenses as those who had a 'position in the diplomatic circle': W.A.B. Hamilton (AUS, CRO) minute, 14 November 1949, TNA, DO35/2647.

the eyes of the world in the beginnings of our diplomatic service'.[132] But on learning that there were no financial implications in following other states and raising legations to embassies, he overcame his fears about Canada's representatives getting swollen heads. In consequence, and also to remove doubts about Canada's status and 'mark . . . the emergence of Canada as a world power of major rank',[133] Canada began in 1943 to exchange ambassadors rather than ministers with certain foreign states. By 1945 Australia and South Africa, too, were exchanging ambassadors with third states. It was becoming increasingly 'ludicrous' that because of 'curious aspects of protocol',[134] the dominions' most senior envoys—in London—held so ostensibly humble an office as high commissioner. As even de Valera, the Irish *taoiseach*, reportedly said, it was

> strange that the representative in Great Britain of a great country like Canada should rank behind, say, the Minister from a small country like Chile—and stranger yet, that in Canada, the representative of a still greater nation like Great Britain should, as he put it—'play "second fiddle" to a Minister from Chile'.[135]

Third, and more generally, dominion unease about this matter reflected an important psychological shift in both official and unofficial attitudes. There was a rising national consciousness which fostered a desire to do away with what was becoming seen as a misunderstood 'vestigial remnant' of 'colonial subordination'.[136] It was suggested in the Canadian press that the title 'high commissioner' was 'a limitation of our sovereignty'.[137] And in Australia the low status of the office was seen as a diplomatic handicap. According to the *Melbourne Age*, representation abroad ought to be 'consistent with Australia's prestige and dignity as a Pacific power' and the dominions' status as 'nations in their own right. If they have risen to the full dignity of embassies in foreign lands, it seems only fitting that they should be similarly represented in the Mother Country.'[138]

---

[132] Canadian House of Commons, 25 February 1941, quoted in Meyer-Bodenstein, 26 February 1941, SAA, BTS, PM1/28/5, vol. 1.

[133] King-L. McCarthy (Canadian ambassador, Washington), 12 January 1944, quoted in Skilling (1945) 255–6.

[134] *Sydney Morning Herald*, 17 January 1947.

[135] Kearney, no. 13, 20 January 1945.

[136] Reid (1990) 166.

[137] *Le Devoir*, 27 January 1944, quoted in Skilling (1945) 131, n. 107.

[138] Editorial, 'Ambassadors within the Empire', *Melbourne Age*, 2 January 1947.

Interestingly, in view of her 'loyal' inter-war stance, this critical approach was especially marked in Australia, where a growingly assertive nationalism was more than personified in Labor's megalomaniacal H.V. Evatt. Evatt pushed Australia into an actively independent foreign policy; won himself a starring role at the UN; and reorganised, professionalized, and hugely expanded the DEA and Australian representation overseas. In the process he made many enemies.[139] His relations with Britain were at best brusque, and though he was 'a Commonwealth man', he enjoyed tweaking Britain's imperial tail, and he became a lesser member of the anti-high commissioner camp. Much to the disgust of the British High Commission in Canberra, he did not respect protocolaire distinctions between Commonwealth and foreign envoys—an acting high commissioner 'took very great exception to being classified as a member of the Diplomatic Corps' at a luncheon.[140] Moreover, he not only received a 'Minister Plenipotentiary Representative of Ireland in Australia' (as indicated in the next chapter) but also offered to exchange ministers with India to help her stay in the Commonwealth, it having been suggested that the title high commissioner was an obstacle to them.

Things on the 'high commissioner front' were coming to a head. Ireland took the lead.

1. *Ireland and Australia: 'an Ambassador, or a Minister or a What'?*[141]

Ireland wanted to get rid of the office of high commissioner. But, realising this was not immediately 'on', she—like South Africa at an earlier

[139] There are many testimonies to the dreadfulness of working with or under a man whom one DEA official described as 'evil': Frances Stuart quoted in David Tothill e-mail, 26 October 2000. One diplomat considered him 'the most frightful man in the world': Cadogan diary, 23 May 1945, quoted in Tothill (1995); another said that as President of the 1948 General Assembly, he 'established a record for pompous ineffectiveness': Egeland (1977) 145; a third that he 'has become insufferably megalomaniacal and irresponsible. . . . Like many Australians, he seems to regard Canadians as mealy-mouthed fence-sitters. . . . [and is] very jealous of any Canadian initiative or achievement': diary, 23 August 1946, in Charles Ritchie (1981) 8; a fourth told a friend, 'He has an ever widening circle of enemies': Dixon-Clyne, 21 May 1950, quoted in Ayres (2003) 200; and, finally, an observer of Australian public life thought 'One must go back to Shakespeare's Iago for so authentic a model of treachery and envy': Peter Ryan quoted in Tothill (1993).

[140] Davis-Robertson, no. 86, 11 December 1944, NAC, RG25, 5699, 4-G(s), part 2.

[141] Kiernan (Irish representative)-US ambassador conversation, 9 November 1946, INA, DFA, Secretary's Office, P 12/14(iii)a.

date—moved towards her goal in a piecemeal way. Already, in the late 1930s, she had started doing so by pressing, successfully, for Britain's representative (Maffey) to be so termed (although the *taoiseach* would have preferred a conventional diplomatic title). That was a step in the right direction, away from 'empty forms' and valueless 'relics of the past' that rendered cordial relationships 'impossible'.[142] Now, soon after the War, de Valera wanted the dominions also to agree to receive 'Representatives' and Australia swiftly agreed. Evatt had been interested in an exchange with Ireland for some time, as it had both political and personal appeal. He was of Irish descent, had championed Ireland's application for UN membership, and the establishment of direct relations would appeal to Irish Catholic voters.[143] In addition, he had reportedly been much exercised about the title high commissioner (although not to the extent of raising it in the Cabinet), and no doubt relished the opportunity to cock a snook at Britain and enhance his reputation for independent-mindedness. And so, in 1946, Dr. T.J. Kiernan, the former director of Irish broadcasting and minister to the Holy See, arrived in Canberra bearing from his minister of external affairs a 'letter of credence' which described Kiernan as 'Minister Plenipotentiary Representative of Ireland in Australia'. This was an amalgam of his personal rank (minister) and Maffey's title, but in practice he was 'generally known as the "Irish Minister"',[144] which was how regarded himself.[145] Thus he referred to the 'Irish Legation' and 'Irish Minister'; his personal card read '*Ministre Plenipotentiaire d'Irelande* with, underneath, in his own handwriting, 'Representative of Ireland in Australia';[146] he

---

[142] Seán MacBride (Irish MEA)-Philip Noel-Baker (commonwealth secretary) conversation, 16 June 1948, TNA, DO121/18.

[143] It was estimated that between a fifth and a third of Australia's population was of Irish Catholic descent.

[144] Boland (SDEA)-Irish heads of mission, 12 December 1946, INA, DFA, Ottawa Embassy, D/30/1; Greene-Pearson, 30 December 1947.

[145] Kiernan 'made clear' from the beginning that his mission 'was in no way different from a legation': General report of Canberra Legation from opening of mission, 10 October 1946 to 31 December 1947, INA, DFA, Embassy Canberra, Box 16–30.

[146] C.M. Croft (Canadian AHC, Canberra), no. 904, 23 October 1946. Using 'Ireland' instead of 'Éire' was a point of honour, and was seen by diplomats in Canberra as 'merely another instance of Ireland's habitual' efforts to irritate Britain (by seeming thereby to imply that Britain's rule over the six counties of Northern Ireland was illegitimate): O'Farrell (1980) 13; the Australian government took no notice, studiously using 'Éire' (though in 1946 the out-of-date 'Irish Free State' was used in her Diplomatic List).

rejected office space in a projected building for Commonwealth representatives in Canberra; insisted on dealing with the DEA (like foreign diplomats) rather than the Prime Minister's Office (to which high commissioners had the right of direct access); emphasised his 'foreignness' by having a bi-lingual letter-head; and had diplomatic plates on his car. Evatt himself always called Kiernan 'Mr. Minister'.[147]

This caused some bafflement. Washington asked its ambassador at Canberra to find out whether Kiernan was 'an Ambassador, or a Minister or a What'?;[148] and when Evatt was away his own 'bewildered'[149] officials carefully avoided using his terminology. This was very proper, for as the envoy of a Commonwealth country Kiernan had not been appointed to Australia as a diplomatic minister. What Canberra had done was simply to accept that that was his personal rank. This is clear from the Irish financial estimates, the Australian Diplomatic List, and from Kiernan being treated as the high commissioner of the youngest dominion.

Meanwhile, when Evatt refused Ireland's informal request that her man in Dublin should be given the title of 'Representative', the Irish DEA did not press, and orthodoxy prevailed when Australia neither sought *agrément* for W.J. Dignam's appointment as high commissioner nor provided a letter of introduction. The absence of the latter displeased the Irish. Form mattered much in Dublin, and even in relatively unimportant matters they went 'to incredible lengths'.[150] Thus, after arriving in Dublin in September 1946, Dignam spent several months in limbo. He told Canberra that only when he was furnished with 'at least a short formal letter of introduction'[151] for presentation at a formal ceremony at Dublin Castle would he be given the usual banquet for newly-arrived envoys—an occasion to which Ireland attached 'the greatest importance'.[152] With London warning Australia about serious constitutional issues and embarrassment to other Commonwealth members, Canberra refused to adopt this novel procedure. However, letters of introduction were not unknown, and Dignam begged for

[147] General report of Canberra Legation from opening of mission.
[148] Kiernan-US ambassador conversation, 9 November 1946.
[149] Croft, no. 904, 23 October 1946.
[150] J.A. Chapdelaine (Canadian AHC Dublin), no. 61, 29 March 1950, NAC, RG25, 50021–40, part 3.
[151] Dignam cablegram 619, 9 September 1946, *DAFP* X, 194.
[152] Cecil Syers (DUS, CRO) minute, 13 January 1949, TNA, DO35/4229.

one:[153] 'The Irish view is that members of the family, and Australia before any, are entitled at least to the same if not greater status and dignity *than* [*sic.*] an outsider.' Britain's objections 'exaggerate[d] the importance of outward formality and conflict[ed] with the more generally accepted Australian viewpoint that British Commonwealth links are not so fragile as to depend on abstention from or be endangered by [*sic.*] ceremony of this kind'.[154]

After a while Evatt acquiesced and provided Dignam with a letter introducing him as his 'Representative'. Dignam presented his 'Letter of Appointment' to the *taoiseach* in early December, but this was followed by 'a very informal' official lunch rather than a banquet—possibly because Dignam had complained a little too openly that that the Irish over-emphasised form rather than substance.[155]

This did not resolve all Irish-Australian problems. According to Kiernan, 'many years' of 'anti-Irish propaganda' and 'ridicule' had created in Australia a 'formidable wall of prejudice' against Ireland.[156] Imperialists and left-wingers alike had opposed the opening of the high commission in Dublin, and the opposition objected to the cost of representation in what they regarded as a minor state. They also thought it was an unnecessary piece of empire-building by the DEA. In addition, Kiernan believed that not only were Australia's senior officials 'almost all anti-Labor' and 'anti-Irish independence', but John Burton, the DEA secretary, was 'anti-Irish on sectarian grounds'.[157] (His father was president-general of the Methodist Church of Australasia.) Traditionalist DEA officials were also said to have been unhappy about Evatt's choice of Dignam—a Roman Catholic barrister of Irish descent, who was active in the Labor Party—to represent Australia in Dublin.

---

[153] In support of his plea, Dignam drew attention to the recently-deceased Canadian high commissioner's 'formal Letter of Credence' which was written on parchment and signed by the MEA and governor-general. However, the document was Mahoney's personal commission of appointment—a quite different document, which was never intended to be used in this way. The Irish appear not to have realised this, and hence were disappointed when the letter subsequently provided for Dignam was less handsome and not also signed by the governor-general: Garland, no. 133, 14 November 1946; Measures-Garland, no. 11, 25 January 1947.

[154] Dignam-Evatt cablegram 619, 9 September 1946, *DAFP* X, 194–5.

[155] Garland, no. 149, 5 December 1946.

[156] Irish Embassy, Canberra, 1949 Annual Report, INA, DFA, Embassy Canberra, Box 16–30, A/18/2.

[157] General report of Canberra Legation from opening of mission.

2. *Moving Forwards: Ireland and Canada*

In 1939, when Britain agreed that Maffey, her man in Dublin, should be styled 'Representative', de Valera tried to get Canada to do the same with Ireland's recently despatched high commissioner to Ottawa, Joseph Hearne. Ottawa said it was too late. Ireland accepted that, but made it clear she intended to obtain the 'complete assimilation of the status' of her representative to that of 'Minister Plenipotentiary in all other respects'.[158] In 1945, as the term of office of Canada's high commissioner in Dublin, Kearney, was drawing to a close, de Valera again said he wanted to use diplomatic titles, but did not press when Canada said the time was not ripe. However, when Kearney's successor died a few months after taking office, Ireland pushed hard for his replacement to be called 'Ambassador Representative of Canada in Ireland'.[159] She said the Commonwealth relationship was strained by the

> misguided effort to give it expression in forms which hark back to colonialisms and are therefore utterly inappropriate to facts of present free association. The title High Commissioner is such a form. It is a definitely colonial title and in practice its application to Commonwealth diplomatic representatives has effect of relegating them to a place lower in prestige and public estimation than non-Commonwealth representatives whereas the logic of the association is that they should have the special status of Ambassador. Whatever the position elsewhere these considerations have special force here in Dublin.[160]

Instead of arriving with 'no more official notice than that of a commercial traveller', Commonwealth envoys should be received 'with at least the same degree of ceremony and honour as non-Commonwealth representative viz. formal reception in Castle with mounted escort [*sic.*] exchange of speeches, salute and official dinner'.[161]

> It is really no argument to say that Ambassadors are never accredited otherwise than by heads of States [*sic.*] and that any other method of accrediting Ambassadors would be anomalous. The whole Commonwealth itself is an anomaly, and, indeed, there is no greater anomaly

[158] Irish *aide-mémoire*, handed to DEA on 29 December 1939, *DCER 7*, 8.
[159] Hearne-Pearson, 2 November 1946, INA, DFA, Ottawa Embassy, D/30/1.
[160] DEA-Hearne telegram 67, 26 October 1946, INA, DFA, Ottawa Embassy, D/30/1.
[161] DEA-Hearne telegram 68, 26 October 1946, INA, DFA, Ottawa Embassy, D/30/1.

> known in history of political institutions than the arrangement under which this republic maintains its special relationship with the British Commonwealth.[162]

Canada was willing to meet Ireland half-way. She in effect asked for *agrément* and, ignoring British pressure, prepared an embellished letter which 'did not mention the word "credence" [or diplomatic relations], but [wa]s a rough approximation of the letter' de Valera had recently provided for Kiernan, her high commissioner to Australia.[163] But although Mackenzie King 'did not like the expression "High Commissioner"',[164] he was under pressure from Britain to retain the title, and would not drop it without wider Commonwealth discussion. Since that would delay five or six other diplomatic appointments, and Ireland was evidently not going to insist on her request, Canada adopted the quicker and easier course. She appointed a high commissioner to Dublin, and King asked (in November 1946) for Commonwealth talks on the status and title of high commissioner.[165]

The Irish were 'delighted, and perhaps surprised' that, when making this call, King emphasised the equality of high commissioners and ambassadors; and they believed that his reference to the title being not 'completely satisfactory' indicated a disposition 'to abolish the term'.[166] But Ireland's high commissioner in Ottawa, Hearne (who 'displayed inordinate resentment and annoyance' at not knowing about King's announcement before Dublin was told),[167] judged shrewdly when he told Dublin that King was

> first and last a Commonwealth and Empire man, is against bilateral developments, and . . . wants to tie us into the Commonwealth. . . . he now emerges as the sponsor of a proposal to remove another anomaly. The publicity is all his own. But how far he will be prepared to go . . . is another question. If the issue is not to be smothered with constitutional and legal considerations that no longer affect us as they do . . . the other countries . . . we would have to clear the ground for discussion and practically settle the point before any conference meets. Your method of dealing with each Government separately is the better way.[168]

---

[162] Boland-Hearne, 20 December 1946, INA, DFA, Ottawa Embassy, D/30/1.
[163] Pearson-Alphonse Turgeon (Canadian HC, Dublin), 23 December 1946, *DCER* 12, 1488–9.
[164] Hearne-Boland, 12 November 1946, INA, DFA, Ottawa Embassy, D/30/1.
[165] See King-Garland, telegram 76, 8 November 1946, *DCER* 12, 1493–4.
[166] Boland-all missions, 12 December 1946, INA, DFA, Ottawa Embassy D/30/1.
[167] Pearson-Robertson, telegram 1942, 8 November 1946.
[168] Hearne-Boland, 12 November 1946, INA, DFA, Ottawa Embassy, D/30/1.

Certainly, while he was in London in November 1947, King said he wanted to 'hasten slowly'[169] and 'did not want High Commissioners to get too big for their boots'.[170] But once he had raised the subject it was clear that elsewhere in the Commonwealth there was considerable support for turning high commissioners into ambassadors, and doing so sooner rather than later.

G. Deputy High Commissioners

A notable wartime development was the emergence of deputy high commissioners (DHCs)—a by-product of Churchill's practice of appointing cabinet ministers to Washington and the dominions. Ostensibly, Churchill claimed that ministerial-level appointments were needed because 'so much statecraft is required in our representatives' that they needed to have had parliamentary experience 'of the forces which move and change Governments'.[171] But overseas posts were also useful for disposing of politicians who were out of favour and with whom he was exasperated. According to John Colville, Churchill's assistant private secretary, 'There was quite a bit of "my language fails, go out and govern New South Wales" in the despatch of Hoare to Madrid, Cross to Canberra, Malcolm MacDonald to Canada, Dorman-Smith to Burma, and even Lord Halifax to Washington.'[172] (The despatch of Harlech to South Africa was an exception.) Ronald Cross, (Australia 1941–46), for example, was a Chamberlainite (Churchill had been deeply critical of Chamberlain's pre-War administration in Britain), and was also widely regarded and treated as a political failure. And Malcolm MacDonald (Canada 1941–46) was 'rat-poison' to Churchill because, as Dominions Secretary, he had in 1938 negotiated the renunciation of Britain's rights in certain Irish ports.[173]

---

[169] Sir John Stephenson (DUS, CRO) note, 'The Status of High Commissioners', c. 26 May 1948, TNA, DO35/3203.

[170] Patrick Gordon Walker (Parliamentary under-secretary, CRO) minute, 24 November 1947, TNA, DO35/3203.

[171] Churchill-Cranborne (dominions secretary) personal minute, 7 May 1944, M.636/4, DO 121/108.

[172] Colville (1986) 515.

[173] Alexander Cadogan (PUS, FO) diary, 18 December 1940 in Dilks (ed.) (1971) 341. Under the 1938 Anglo-Irish Agreement Britain withdrew her forces from the ports (and their defence facilities) of Cobh, Berehaven, and Lough Swilly in return for a one-off payment of £10 million. (These rights had been accorded in the 1921

Nonetheless, the office of high commissioner was elevated by the appointment of cabinet ministers to it, and strengthened by the appointment of senior officials (of assistant under-secretary rank) as DHCs to look after the office side of things and provide administrative back up. When, at the War's end, the Commonwealth Service again provided most high commissioners, the title DHC survived and came to be used in all British high commissions, and in time, most Commonwealth members adopted the title (but were selective in using it).[174] Not all DHCs were given work worthy of their rank,[175] but many came to play more than an internal administrative role, becoming the high commissioner's deputy in every diplomatic sense.[176] Hence the office came to be seen as having a certain cachet,[177] and career foreign service officers sometimes found it a relief in London to be able to concentrate on the 'nitty gritty', leaving the pomp and ceremony to the high commissioner. As a former DHC in London put it, he had 'seen so many ceremonies, eaten so much bad food, and worn so many uncomfortable clothes', he was glad to be out of it and to be able to concentrate on 'the serious diplomatic work'.[178]

Treaty which gave dominion status to the Irish Free State.) Churchill felt passionately about this 'numbing loss', which he equated with withdrawal from Gibraltar or Malta: Garner (1978) 234. Knowing Churchill's feelings, Mackenzie King took great pleasure in (deservedly) praising MacDonald whenever his name came up in discussion.

[174] By 1945 Australia and India had adopted the title in London; by the mid-1950s two more of the seven high commissions in London had DHCs (South Africa and Ceylon); and by 1960 there was a DHC in almost all. Thereafter the number of DHCs began declining. In 1967 Britain decided to discontinue using the title in Commonwealth capitals 'unless there were good reasons to the contrary' (but this decision seems to have been barely implemented): 'Nomenclature at UK Posts and Outposts in other Commonwealth Countries', 9 May 1972, TNA, FCO 68/449. For the position at 'outposts', see Chapter 7, Section A.1, and also Section A.2.iii.

[175] By 1949 South Africa's high commissioner in London had obtained a suitably senior DEA official, C.H. Torrance, to serve as 'Secretary and DHC'. Egeland had hoped Torrance would 'assist me in the many routine matters, especially in the increasingly important diplomatic and representational spheres', but Torrance's administrative work left him little time to attend to political matters: Egeland (1977) 200.

[176] When Eric Louw took charge of South Africa's DEA in 1955, he decided 'to administer the London office as an Embassy' and to turn the DHC into a 'minister counsellor': Nöthling (2005) 547. This was 'in order to give [him] the requisite status both in diplomatic circles and within the office itself': Liesching (British HC, Pretoria)-Gilbert Laithwaite (PUS, CRO), personal and confidential, 25 August 1956, TNA, DO35/5015.

[177] Hence, perhaps, the number of requests by South African diplomats who wanted to become DHCs when South Africa returned to the Commonwealth in 1994.

[178] Interview.

H. Conclusion

From the late 1930s there was a rising tide of dissatisfaction with the office of high commissioner. This was because of a number of interrelated factors, beginning with the growth in he political stature of the dominions. By 1945 they had become not insignificant members of the victorious alliance[179] and were playing an active and useful role in international relations. In addition, the rise in the number of high commissioners combined with the Irish-South African campaign against the office (which, in the Union, made life uncomfortable for two Canadian high commissioners) heightened sensitivity to, and complaints about, perceived second-class treatment. It also led, in three cases, to the title 'representative' or 'minister plenipotentiary representative' being substituted for high commissioner (although the receiving states treated them as if they were high commissioners). This, in turn, led DEAs to examine their attitudes towards the title and, in so doing, they decided there was much to be said for switching to normal diplomatic styles. As will be seen in the next chapter, the problem of the King receiving envoys from himself remained a major difficulty in the way of such a move but, like the whole notion of Commonwealth representatives being outside the diplomatic fold, was given increasingly short shrift. There was, it is true, a close attachment in certain quarters to the sixty-six-year-old office of high commissioner, so that when Mackenzie King called for discussions about it there were some stout sorties in its defence. But before long the general view was that the office was doomed.

179 Excluding, of course, Ireland, which had been neutral.

CHAPTER FOUR

EQUAL STATUS, 1946–1948

When, in November 1946, the Canadian prime minister, Mackenzie King, called for talks on the office of high commissioner, Britain launched a 'diversionary attack'[1] on what she perceived to be its incumbents' 'weakest flank': she suggested that 'all troubles will be over' if they were given the title 'excellency'.[2] Apart from Ireland, who was already addressing high commissioners in this way, none of the dominions welcomed Britain's move. Until recently, only their governors-general (together with the British high commissioner for Bechuanaland, Basutoland, and Swaziland) had been so styled. The arrival of an American ambassador in Ottawa at the end of 1943 had led to Canada's speedy adoption of what had by then become the common practice of bestowing 'excellency' not only on ambassadors but also on lower-ranking ministers plenipotentiary (who headed legations).[3] But she was reluctant to have any more excellencies in Ottawa. Also, like Australia, she thought Britain's proposal did not address the fundamental problem of the status of high commissioners, and was unlikely to remove confusion about the nature of the office. New Zealand said it 'would detract in the minds of the public in the Dominions from the significance' of using this title for the governor-general.[4] Nor did South Africa like the suggestion. The British high commissioner there 'only rarely' functioned in his gubernatorial capacity[5] (and was therefore seldom called 'excellency'); the Union had not followed the fashion of addressing heads

[1] Lester Pearson (under-secretary, DEA)-Norman Robertson (Canadian HC, London), 28 November 1946, *DCER* 12, 1496.

[2] CRO circular telegram 465, 19 November 1946, NAC, RG25, 2942, 3011-A-40.

[3] See 'Styles Accorded to Foreign Representatives in Canada, 1927 to 1945', Annex B to Arnold Heeney (assistant under-secretary, DEA) memorandum, 'Designation of High Commissioners as "His Excellency"', 9 November 1950, NAC, RG25, 6194, 3011-A-40 (part 2.3). In response to pressure from heads of legations, Britain began addressing them as 'excellency' in 1940.

[4] New Zealand telegram 12, 20 January 1947, TNA, DO35/3328.

[5] G. Heaton Nicholls (South African HC)-Viscount Addison (dominions secretary), 3 January 1947, TNA, DO35/3328.

of legations as 'excellencies'; and she was not disposed to change her existing practice.

Meanwhile, Britain put much effort into trying to get Lester Pearson, the official at the head of Canada's Department of External Affairs (DEA) (the under-secretary for external affairs), to see things her way. There were several reasons for this. Canada's views carried weight; in terms of international awareness and experience she was the most sophisticated dominion; and Britain's policymakers knew Pearson well. But Britain did not get far with Pearson, as he and many of his officials were in favour of turning high commissioners into ambassadors. However, they were held in check by both domestic and Commonwealth considerations. Not least of the former was the position of their prime minister, Mackenzie King, who favoured some change but wanted to move slowly and was worried about high commissioners getting 'out of their place'.[6] On a wider front, Canada did not wish to provoke needless controversy between the conservative British and the radical Irish. Since agreement would be difficult, and awkward clashes might occur, Pearson hoped to be able to restrict discussion at the forthcoming talks to 'the merits of certain common sense changes of style and precedence'.[7]

A. Discussions in Ottawa

Britain would have liked the talks to have been held in London. But the Irish preferred Ottawa since Pearson's views were 'sound as far as they go'. When 'we have swallowed the camel of neutrality' Pearson had said to Britain's high commissioner (referring to Ireland's position during the Second World War), 'why should we strain at the gnat of Minister Plenipotentiary?'[8] The South Africans, too, thought Ottawa preferable to London, as did Canada herself. As her high commissioner in London, Norman Robertson, pointed out:

> In London, the Diplomatic Corps is large and loosely organized. Occasions when relative precedence of Commonwealth and foreign diplomatic

[6] Patrick Gordon Walker (parliamentary under-secretary, CRO) 16 December 1947, TNA, DO35/3203.
[7] Charles Ritchie (head of First Political Division) memorandum, 'Official Title of Commonwealth Representatives', 27 November 1946, *DCER* 12, 1497–8.
[8] John Hearne (Irish HC)-F. Boland (SDEA), 12 November 1946, INA, DFA, Ottawa Embassy, D/30/1.

> representatives might hit the eye and provoke comment appear to be fairly infrequent. Furthermore, a good deal more fuss is made over Commonwealth representatives . . . generally, than is made over any foreign representative, except the American Ambassador. For these reasons, the questions of official style and precedence which our representatives in Canberra and Pretoria brought to our attention, and with which we are familiar in Ottawa, are bound [in London] to seem rather remote and of secondary importance here.
>
> Another consideration . . . is that the Dominions Office, which would handle United Kingdom participation in such a meeting, is, on grounds of general policy, disposed to stress and maintain the badges which distinguish intra-Commonwealth representatives from diplomatic representatives generally. This means that they would be quite prepared to raise the precedence of Commonwealth representatives relative to the general table of precedence, and would probably be prepared to use another style than 'High Commissioner', if agreement could be reached on the question of nomenclature . . . On the other hand, they would, I believe, be quite firmly opposed to our policy of gradually assimilating the style and status of Commonwealth representatives to those enjoyed by diplomatic representatives of other countries.
>
> I have no doubt that our practice of encouraging the assimilation of diplomatic representatives into a single category is wise, but I doubt very much whether it would receive general endorsement in the Commonwealth at this time, certainly not at a Commonwealth meeting in London.
>
> The prime minister has raised the general question in a form which has attracted a good deal of press attention over here. His statement will probably stimulate some more thinking and discussion about these questions, precedence and official styles, which might make it easier to reach general agreement in a year or two. I would, therefore, be inclined to let things simmer a little longer before formally proposing a Commonwealth meeting to discuss the matter.[9]

Especially as Canada had raised the matter, she had some claim to make the running. So Ottawa it was. And Pearson followed Robertson's advice to approach the matter in a preliminary and informal way. Because all Commonwealth members were represented in Ottawa, instead of seeking ministerial-level talks he arranged two meetings with the resident high commissioners in the early months of 1947.

First, however, in mid-January the British high commissioner, Sir Alexander Clutterbuck (1946–52), held a 'pre-meeting' with his fellow high commissioners to exchange personal views. Only he and the Irish high commissioner, John Hearne (1939–49), knew their government's

[9] Robertson telegram 2232, 20 November 1946, NAC, RG25, 2942, 3011-A-40. On second thoughts, he suggested Dublin might be better than Ottawa.

views, and only the latter was keen on diplomatic titles. Accordingly, Hearne made little headway when he argued that 'high commissioner' was unsuitable as its 'colonial history and association obscured the character of our relations' and 'derogated . . . from the diplomatic status' of Commonwealth representatives. Mackenzie King, was (Hearne reported) 'definitely opposed' to merging high commissioners with the diplomatic corps, and David Wilson of New Zealand (1944–47) and P.R. Viljoen of South Africa (1945–49) 'rather liked' being high commissioners. Commonwealth representatives 'should be differentiated in some way from representatives of foreign countries,' Viljoen was reported to have said. 'We were all Commonwealth people . . . The friends of Commonwealth countries were the other Commonwealth countries.' Wilson suggested dropping 'high': 'commissioner' was 'a good word' on its own.[10] But Viljoen, like Clutterbuck, thought high commissioners had either to be that or ambassadors. There was no alternative. Moreover, since Wilson and Viljoen were evidently concerned with their personal prestige and social standing, and wanted ambassadorial status (albeit without the title), a way had to be found of satisfying this wish. Otherwise, said Clutterbuck, it was 'virtually inevitable' that high commissioners would become ambassadors and members of the diplomatic corps.[11]

At the first of Pearson's meetings with the high commissioners just under two weeks later Clutterbuck, hoping to deflect any tendency to move in an ambassadorial direction, said that the 'crux of the problem was not title but status'. On this he made the 'personal suggestion' that for purposes of precedence high commissioners might be listed together with ambassadors, which would surmount the problem of their 'inferior' status.[12] He also suggested that high commissioners should become 'excellencies'. Only the New Zealand acting high commissioner, Robert Firth, was in a position to express his government's views. This was that the title should be retained but that high commissioners should

[10] Hearne-Boland, 16 January 1947, INA, DFA, Ottawa Embassy, D/30/1. The new Australian high commissioner, Frank Forde, had not yet reached Ottawa and Clutterbuck had not invited the Australian AHC. Clutterbuck expected Forde to take the same line as Viljoen and Wilson.

[11] Clutterbuck-Eric Machtig (PUS, CRO), telegram 74, secret & personal, 21 January 1947, TNA, DO35/3203.

[12] Escott Reid (about-to-be assistant under-secretary DEA) memorandum, 'Informal Discussion of Title and Status of High Commissioners on 27 January 1947', NAC, RG25, 2942, 3011-A-40. Clutterbuck's suggestion turned out to be the saving of the office, but not before huge quantities of time and effort had gone into considering the alternatives.

become full members of the diplomatic corps and rank with them in order of appointment, which was also Viljoen's personal view. The newly-arrived Australian high commissioner, Frank Forde, could go no further than say the subject was under consideration in Canberra and that he, personally, thought there should be an improvement in the status of high commissioners. On the other side, Hearne put the Irish argument that the title was 'misleading and disliked', and that high commissioners should become fully-fledged ambassadors. Pearson, for Canada, hesitantly agreed with Hearne. But he was unwilling 'to go the whole way' with him as he thought there would be strong 'political opposition' to such a change in 'certain quarters'.[13] Nonetheless, Canada was, from Ireland's point of view, moving in the right direction: she had decided that the procedure for appointing high commissioners should approximate, as far as possible, to appointments to foreign states, and had begun giving notice of appointments and providing letters of introduction that were similar to letters of credence.

By the end of the hour-and-a-half-long meeting only two things had been agreed. First, that no-one could think of a satisfactory alternative to 'high commissioner'; and, second, that although it would be difficult to work out how to do it, high commissioners had to be put on a 'proper footing' of equality of status with ambassadors.[14] In Hearne's view, 'the most likely result' would be 'a new type of High Commissioner'.[15]

Just under two months later, in March, Pearson called a second meeting. At its outset Forde announced that his minister for external affairs, H.V. Evatt, was insistent that so important a matter could only be discussed by prime ministers, and accordingly refused to give even a tentative indication of Australia's views. Everyone else thought it would be absurd to abandon purely exploratory talks aimed at facilitating a prime ministerial decision, so the meeting continued. But the ensuing sixty minutes achieved little, although it appeared that New Zealand had joined the Irish camp. In a 'surprisingly "progressive"'[16] move, she said she was agreeable to using diplomatic titles and ranking Commonwealth envoys with ambassadors; saw 'no insuperable difficulty'[17] about issuing credentials; and was not opposed to high commissioners having

[13] Hearne-Boland, 29 January 1947, INA, DFA, Ottawa Embassy, D/30/1.
[14] Viljoen-D.D. Forsyth (SDEA), 17 January 1947, SAA, BTS, 180/3.
[15] Hearne-Boland, 29 January 1947.
[16] Clutterbuck telegram 303, 24 March 1947, TNA, DO35/3328.
[17] Hearne-Boland, 22 March 1947, INA, DFA, Ottawa Embassy, D/30/1.

diplomatic immunity. And Pearson came out in favour of switching to ambassador by agreement, though his government was still 'committed to nothing'.[18] But neither Hearne nor Viljoen had heard from their governments, leaving the former with nothing to add to what he had said before, and the latter unable to give any indication of his government's policy. (In fact, South Africa's prime minister, Field-Marshal Smuts, shared Evatt's view that this was a matter to be dealt with by prime ministers.) As for Clutterbuck, who just visited London, he was, Hearne said, in his best '"full of difficulty" mood'.[19] He explained confidentially that the Dominions Office (DO) was exploring the possibility of giving high commissioners ambassadorial precedence, without, however, listing them with the ambassadors. But he also said there was 'a good deal of "mystification" about the whole thing in London. There were Home Office views, and views of the Lord Chancellor's Office, and of other offices and there was a general fear that any changes of long established customs, precedence, and so on, would lead to all sorts of confusion'.[20] He himself thought his frankness and personal support for raising the precedence of high commissioners was appreciated by the other high commissioners, who were impatient of 'outworn constitutional niceties'.[21] Hearne told Dublin that 'no one cared much how it was to be done. The question was how *could* it be done?'[22]

Thus it became accepted that the status of high commissioners should be discussed at the next Prime Ministers' Meeting, which would meet in London in October 1948. The balance was shifting in favour of 'ambassador' as against 'high commissioner', but the outcome was still uncertain. And in 1948 the views of another three, new dominions—India, Pakistan, and Ceylon—would have to be taken into account.

B. Dominion Views of the Office

As Canada's Department of External Affairs (DEA) saw it, the basic problem was that high commissioners lacked diplomatic immunity and had 'considerably lower' precedence than diplomats, whereas they ought

[18] *Ibid.*
[19] *Ibid.*
[20] *Ibid.*
[21] Clutterbuck-Sir John Stephenson (DUS) telegram 678, secret and personal, 29 July 1947, TNA, DO35/3203.
[22] Hearne-Boland, 22 March 1947.

to be treated as considerately as foreigners and rank with ambassadors.[23] One solution was to change the title. There were three arguments for doing this: the title's alleged colonial overtones; its ambiguity (inasmuch as it was also bestowed on Britain's representatives who held high executive functions in territories such as Palestine); and because high commissioners were frequently confused with non-diplomatic trade commissioners. If diplomatic titles were to be avoided, there was 'much to be said' for 'representative'.[24] It might be more suitable for Canada's first appointment to India, South Africa would not object, and Australia could hardly do so (having already received one from Ireland). But as it was not a recognised diplomatic title its adoption would still, presumably, leave high commissioners in the same inferior position. However, giving high commissioners legal equality with foreign heads of mission by raising them to ambassadors met with three difficulties.

First there was the old problem of the King being unable to accredit someone to himself. Canada thought this was surmountable. After all, in the inter-war years, when Iceland and Denmark shared a common sovereign, Reykjavik had had diplomatic representation in Copenhagen.[25] In other contexts, too, people who hold two offices can write to themselves in their different capacities.[26] And if it proved impossible to overcome the argument that an ambassador must be accredited by and to a head of state, 'that mystical institution the Crown'[27] should be able to find a way round the problem. The King might, for example, simply be informed of nominations and asked to issue an instrument

[23] DEA memorandum, 'Status and Title of High Commissioners', 28 July 1948, NAC, RG25, 2942, 3011-A-40.

[24] Pearson memorandum, 30 October 1946, *DCER* 12, 1490, 1489. The prime minister agreed.

[25] Under the Danish-Icelandic Act of Union of 1918, the two sovereign states shared the same King, who appointed an Icelandic minister to Copenhagen. Initially Iceland's minister was not accredited to the King and not considered a member of the diplomatic corps. He was given diplomatic status in 1934, but was required to abstain the *décanat*.

[26] At the beginning of the twentieth century, when the governor of a British colony who was also its General Officer Commanding was faced with a civil-military dispute, he used to 'sit down and write a letter to the G.O.C., carry it into the next room, put on a sword, and sit down and write a reply': C.W. Dixon (constitutional adviser) minute, 15 November 1962, TNA, DO161/145.

[27] Hume Wrong (Canadian ambassador, Washington) in an informal letter quoted in DEA memorandum, 'High Commissioners: Title and Status. Current Problems', 1947, INA, DFA, Ottawa Embassy, D/30/1.

of appointment having the effect of letters of credence. Alternatively, the governor-general or the secretary of state for external affairs might issue letters of credence.[28] The second problem was that exchanging ambassadors would probably be too drastic for Mackenzie King and 'might result in unnecessary domestic controversy'.[29] And, third, it would be difficult to obtain unanimity and any discussions might give rise to argumentation on points of principle.

In Australia, too, there was 'increasing pressure' to treat Commonwealth representatives on a par with ambassadors, which was underlined by 'an interesting and well-informed' editorial on the 'inferior status' of high commissioners and their title's 'anachronistic "colonial" connotations'.[30] Although the subject was said to have 'greatly exercised' Evatt,[31] it was also reported that the government attached little importance to it. High commissioners were well treated in Canberra, but opinion was divided about whether they should be treated even better. The young and dynamic official who headed the DEA, John Burton, thought high commissioners should be straightforwardly translated into ambassadors. His Minister, Evatt, thought high commissioners should be senior to all foreign representatives. And Ben Chifley, the prime minister and Treasurer, thought the British high commissioner should always be regarded as the senior high commissioner. Since Chifley was willing to overrule Evatt on matters that interested him, had a 'pronounced' sympathy for Britain,[32] and, in discussions with Britain's cabinet secretary, expressed agreement 'on all the matters they discussed, including the status of High Commissioners',[33] there was a good chance of Chifley's view prevailing.

New Zealand's prime minister and minister for external affairs, Peter Fraser, was 'scornful of the whole subject' and initially refused to take

---

[28] There might, however, be problems about the governor-general addressing them to another governor-general, and it was 'even more doubtful' whether he could so address the King himself (as would be required if he were to issue letters for a Canadian ambassador to Britain): A.J. Pick (Commonwealth Division) memorandum, 8 March 1951, NAC, RG25, 4045, 10566-40, 1.

[29] Pearson memorandum, 31 January 1947, NAC, RG25, 2942, 3011-A-40.

[30] W.C. Hankinson (British AHC, Canberra)-C.R. Price (a senior official) 8 January 1947, TNA, DO35/3203; Editorial, 'Ambassadors within the empire', *Melbourne Age*, 2 January 1947.

[31] Hearne-Boland, 29 January 1947.

[32] Edwards (1984) 173.

[33] Greene (Canadian HC, Canberra)-Pearson, top secret, for Pearson only, 30 August 1948, NAC, RG25, 2942, 3011-A-40.

any interest in it.[34] New Zealand was, he said, happy with a title that had 'come to have such a splendid significance in Dominions'.[35] Precedence was, however, important in New Zealand and, providing high commissioners would not outrank government ministers, Fraser and his advisers favoured raising high commissioners to at least ambassadorial level (if not higher) so as to dash the pretensions of the troublesome diplomatic corps. Furthermore, New Zealand's DEA wanted high commissioners to carry credentials and enjoy full diplomatic rights, including immunity.

Until Ireland withdrew from discussions following the *taoiseach's* announcement (in September 1948) that she would become a republic and therefore (necessarily—as it was then thought) quit the Commonwealth, her attitude was clear and unyielding. She was uninterested in any 'extraneous or antiquated constitutional considerations', such as higher precedence. Nor did she want to continue sidestepping the issue by using the title 'representative'. Her policy was to abolish the outdated office of high commissioner; 'to give frank and full expression in the form and manner of our diplomatic representation to the existing juridical character of our relations';[36] and to establish 'that Eire is in relation to the United Kingdom a foreign country'.[37] As a DEA memorandum put it,

> the title 'High Commissioner' is obsolete and anomalous. It suggests executive rather than representative functions. It harps [*sic.*] back to the era of colonialism and suggests undesirable and misleading implications as to the nature of the relations between Ireland and the States of the Commonwealth.... and vice versa, by leaving the officials concerned without any clearly recognisable diplomatic rank and dignity, [and] tends to place them on a lower plane than representatives of other countries.... [T]here is an irrefutable case for changing the title... and for designating the officials concerned by a title which would make clear, by reference to established practice, their character as diplomatic representatives of the highest rank.... [who] occupy a position of special dignity and importance and... this object would be best secured

---

[34] Alfred Rive (Canadian HC) telegram 14, 14 January 1947, NAC, RG25, 2942, 3011-A-40.

[35] This was 'despite its wider use for example, in Palestine, South African protectorates and in certain international spheres': New Zealand telegram 12, 20 January 1947, TNA, DO35/3328.

[36] Hearne-Boland, 29 January 1947.

[37] Dixon-Rugby (British representative) conversation, 9 August 1948, TNA, DO35/3203.

> by attributing to them the rank and title of Ambassador.... [R]elations between Ireland and the States of the British Commonwealth ... would be strengthened by a change which could only serve to signalise the importance attached to them.[38]

South Africa was at first ambivalent. Her earlier radical attitude had mellowed under Smuts—so much so that John Dulanty, the Irish high commissioner in London, told his South African counterpart that 'when I read General Smuts' speeches and heard your broadcasts I said to myself "those fellows have been nobbled by the British"'.[39] Attitudes in the press were mixed. But the former Nationalist prime minister, General Hertzog (1924–39), the DEA, and the vast majority of South Africa's high commissioners had all along wanted diplomatic titles, or at least diplomatic precedence, and this was the DEA's line in 1947. Furthermore, in what was to prove a fateful change, the National Party (or Nationalists) won power in June 1948. The new government found it

> difficult to reconcile the inferior status of High Commissioners vis-à-vis foreign representatives with the position of the different Commonwealth states as full-fledged members of the international community. There was ... little justification for an arrangement which seemed to imply that Commonwealth States were not equal in status to foreign countries. Moreover ... it was inconsistent that Union representatives should occupy an inferior position in those countries with which the Union maintained the most intimate relations. Similarly it was surely illogical that Ministers Plenipotentiary in the Union should outrank the representatives of the Commonwealth—the entity with which the Union was most closely associated in international affairs.[40]

But as to the policy implications of that position South Africa was in a fix. Until then ministers plenipotentiary were the highest-ranking diplomatic envoys to and from the Union, and she wanted it to stay that way. But while heads of legation came relatively high in South Africa's table of precedence, they came relatively low in Britain's table, and even

---

[38] Irish memorandum, 18 August 1948, enclosed in Seán MacBride (MEA)-Rugby, 20 August 1948, TNA, DO35/3203, PREM8/1333.

[39] Mansergh (1958) 411–2, n. 2.

[40] DEA directive for Eric Louw (minister of mining and economic development, South African delegate to PMM-1948) 'Status of High Commissioners', sent to Louw on 2 October 1948, SAA, BTS, 180/3; BTS, 79/2 vol. 2. DEA directives on Commonwealth relations 'differ[ed] very little in broad essentials from what we would have prepared for a United Party Minister': letter, 4 October 1948, quoted in Sole manuscript, 126.

lower in Canada's. This would not do. But if high commissioners were given ambassadorial status, and South Africa fell into line, she could hardly continue to refuse to let France and the United States upgrade their legations to embassies. But if she did not fall into line, and offered high commissioners ministerial standing, the other dominions would probably reciprocate, which would mean not only that South Africa's high commissioners would have low precedence, but also that they would always be outranked by the other high commissioners. That would not do either. She therefore decided to bite the bullet. Eric Louw (who was to represent the Nationalist government at the Meeting) was instructed that if no one else raised the subject he was to call for diplomatic titles, and hence equality of status with foreign envoys.

Interestingly, South Africa's desire to use diplomatic titles was not accompanied by a desire to deal with Britain through the Foreign Office (FO)—which had been keenly sought before the War and was strongly urged by her former high commissioner, Charles te Water (1929–39). This was not because South Africa thought the Commonwealth Relations Office (CRO) (the July 1947 successor to the Dominions and India Offices)[41] an improvement on the DO. Nor did it reflect her attitude to the Commonwealth. It was because the Union recognised she was better off being one of a small group of states dealing with the CRO and having the right to talk to any government minister and deal with other departments, including the FO, than being one of a much larger group whose sole channel of communication was through the FO. Accordingly, she contended that using diplomatic designations should not mean having to deal exclusively with the FO, since the terminological change 'would hardly affect the special relationship which exists between the Commonwealth nations'.[42]

As to the three additional members welcomed into the Commonwealth in August 1947 and February 1948, the high commissioners in London of Pakistan and Ceylon very much wanted to have the title and status of ambassador. India appeared to side with Ireland and Canada. At the end of 1947 Sir Girja Bajpai (the senior official in the Ministry of External Affairs), who was working on plans to rank high commissioners

---

[41] It 'was to have been the Commonwealth Affairs Office but someone at the last minute realised "affairs" had other implications': Sir Richard Best interview of Sir Harold Smedley, 22 May 1997, CAC, DOHP, 23.

[42] Commonwealth Conference, London, October 11th 1948, 'Machinery for Consultation between Commonwealth Governments', SAA, BTS 79/2, vol. 2.

with ambassadors or ministers on a reciprocal basis, 'made the usual remark' about the absurdity of an ambassador from a small state like Afghanistan appearing 'to be more highly esteemed than a High Commissioner from any dominion'.[43] And her ambassador at Washington cordially welcomed the idea of putting high commissioners on the same level as ambassadors, and using ordinary diplomatic titles.

In the dominions, therefore, it seemed that while the title of high commissioner was in some places still appreciated, there was also a fair amount of hostility towards it; and on all sides it was thought indefensible that the existing lowly status of Commonwealth representatives should continue.

C. Britain's Deliberations

Meanwhile, in London minds were being concentrated. Quite apart from the concerns being expressed by the dominions, the issue was receiving some public notice. Early in 1946, a former foreign secretary was supported in the House of Lords when he argued the need to improve the status of 'our most important Ambassadors in the whole world'—that is, the high commissioners.[44] The significance of Mackenzie King's November 1946 call for discussions on the matter was noted by *The Times*.[45] The following month a major enquiry was set up, under Britain's first high commissioner, Sir William Clark, to examine the internal organisation of high commissions, which prompted the *Manchester Guardian* to argue that they were 'in all essentials Embassies of the first rank' and should be 'accorded that status'.[46] This received widespread attention.[47] And within the government much concern was being expressed about the position of Britain's representative in soon-to-be-independent India.

---

[43] S. Morley Scott (Canadian AHC, New Delhi), no. 218, 22 December 1947, NAC, RG25, 2942, 3011-A-40.

[44] Viscount Templewood (formerly Sir Samuel Hoare) in Vincent Massey (Canadian HC, London), 8 April 1946, *DCER* 12, 1240; House of Lords, *Debs*., 23 January 1946. There were also complaints about Britain's slowness in replacing high commissioners. This was thought to suggest that she did not regard high commissions as important posts: *Ibid*. The worst delay was in Australia. Cross left in June 1945 and his successor was announced in July 1946.

[45] 8 November 1946.

[46] 'The Dominions', *Manchester Guardian*, 28 December 1946.

[47] Newspapers in Australia and New Zealand were among those who took note of it. See editorial, 'Ambassadors within the Empire', *Melbourne Age*, 2 January 1947; N. Costar (official secretary British HCO, Wellington)-Price, 9 January 1947, TNA, DO35/3203.

Both the prime minister, Clement Attlee, and the foreign secretary, Ernest Bevin, attached great importance to the independence of India, a development which was little short of momentous in terms of both British and imperial politics, and they wanted to ensure that Britain's interests there were well protected. However, the pre-independence position was that high commissioners came well down in the local table of precedence, whereas ambassadors would be given the second-highest place. In response to the concern which this elicited, it was allowed on the eve of independence that high commissioners could be raised—but to no higher a place than one between the provincial governors and the chief justice. And this for the representative of the former imperial power in India, where considerable consequence was attributed to outward expressions of rank! The British high commissioner in India pleaded for something to be done, and his dominion counterparts did likewise in communications that struck an unusually wounded note. Thus Canada's high commissioner said that for once it would be untrue 'to say that it is only the dignity of my country and not my own personal feelings which are involved'. He felt personally humiliated and considerably disadvantaged, and spent 'a good deal of time' trying to explain 'why a country of Canada's international status should be represented by a person holding a lower rank than representatives of countries having a similar or less influential international status.... It may be due to the heat of Delhi or because my well of patience is too shallow, but I find it increasingly difficult to display good humour in my replies'.[48] Britain's high commissioner in Pakistan was similarly aggrieved. At Bevin's suggestion, Britain's high commissioners on the subcontinent were transferred to the top diplomatic grade (hitherto reserved for the head of the Foreign Office and the heads of mission at Washington, Paris, Cairo, Moscow, and Nanking); and in 1948 the commonwealth secretary proposed that Britain's new high commissioner to India should also receive the highest salary of any British head of mission.[49] But the heads of the FO and CRO were agreed that the situation was still 'intolerable',[50] and Attlee echoed them, observing that

---

[48] John D. Kearney (Canadian HC), no. 145, 12 May 1948, NAC, RG25, 2942, 3011-A-40.

[49] S. Morley Scott (Canadian DHC, New Delhi)-R.A. MacKay (head of Commonwealth Division) 23 September 1948, NAC, RG25, 2942, 3011-A-40.

[50] Bevin (foreign secretary) reported in Perminter (South African HCO, London), 19 March 1948, quoted in Tothill (1995); Philip Noel-Baker (commonwealth secretary) minute for Attlee, 37/48, 28 June 1948, TNA, DO121/19.

it was 'invidious and practically disadvantageous'.[51] But this meant that the whole high commissioner question had to be addressed.

In considering what might be done, Britain was throughout guided by a determination that nothing must detract from the 'idea'[52] of Commonwealth membership. This necessitated the maintenance of some kind of outward and visible distinction between Commonwealth and foreign envoys. Yet dominion opinion seemed to be moving strongly in the opposite direction, and even the Clark enquiry supported that thrust by contending that the job of representing Britain was much the same in all states. There was, said the Clark report, 'a certain lack of realism' about trying to retain the old Commonwealth conception of a distinctive family relationship.[53] How was everyone to be satisfied? The problem had four loosely-linked aspects: legal immunity; appointment and accreditation; title and style; and status and precedence.

To an age which often identifies immunity from the legal processes of the receiving state as one of the principal features of diplomatic life, it may appear strange that the matter was so little mentioned in the many 1940s disquisitions on the shortcomings of the office of high commissioner. The lack of any real pressure for it was probably because infringements of the law were uncommon, and administrative action was taken to put high commission staff as far as possible in the same position as foreign diplomats. This meant that, in Britain, for example, it was normal not to prosecute the former for alleged offences of a criminal kind. This pragmatic approach also avoided the undesirable prospect of formally discriminating in favour of a very small group of British subjects. For, until the late 1940s, high commissioners—*all* high commissioners—and their staffs enjoyed that status. (Immunity

---

[51] Attlee minute for Chuter Ede (home secretary), 14 July 1948, PREM8/1333.

[52] Lord Chamberlain's Office (signature illegible)-Price, 3 January 1947, TNA, DO35/3203.

[53] 'Report on UK Representation in the Dominions with Special Reference to Establishment and Accommodation Aspects', July/August 1947, TNA, DO35/2646. Clark also recommended that the members of a high commission, other than its head, should be given normal diplomatic titles instead of the existing diverse confusing and occasionally inconvenient nomenclatures. Thus in Canada, Australia, and South Africa the senior member of the British high commissioner's staff was styled deputy high commissioner, in New Zealand he was official secretary, and in Ireland principal secretary. In addition, in Britain's High Commission in Canada there was a senior secretary and some assistant secretaries; in Australia an official secretary and an assistant secretary or an assistant official secretary; in New Zealand an official secretary and an assistant secretary; in South Africa a political secretary and assistant secretaries; and in Ireland an assistant secretary who was usually described as a private secretary.

for diplomats—i.e. foreigners—was just about tolerable.) Thus initially Britain was not at all disposed to raise the subject.

However, three developments encouraged the CRO, with FO support, to advance the case for high commissioners to be granted immunity. In the first place, Britain was tacitly moving towards accepting the concept of the divisibility of the Crown, which would enable Commonwealth high commissioners to be deemed the representatives of their own (albeit not foreign) sovereigns. Second, it had been agreed in early 1947 that Britain and the dominions would each establish local criteria for citizenship (so that while remaining 'British subjects' Canadians, for example, would also be Canadian citizens). Accordingly, high commission staff at the level which was elsewhere termed 'diplomatic' would not, in the normal way, be British citizens. This, too, would ease the grant of immunity. Third, and most immediately of all, in April 1948 there was a court case involving the senior South African trade commissioner whose piano-playing daughter disturbed the neighbours by practising at all hours. He could not be 'administratively' helped by the government (the Crown not being a party—for this was a civil, not a criminal matter), and his plea of diplomatic immunity was (properly) unsupported by the FO. Since a junior American consular official had recently claimed immunity, and Union high commissioners had always tended to claim diplomatic status, the CRO had feared South Africa might make an issue of it. This did not happen, as South Africa's DEA refused, in the particular circumstances, to press for her official to be given privileged treatment. But other cases of a similar kind might follow. To officials in the CRO and the FO, immunity seemed the answer. But they were unable to overcome ministerial objections that that was a step too far in the direction of assimilating high commissioners with ambassadors.

This last concern was also evident in British discussions about the appointment and accreditation of Commonwealth representatives. Diplomatic-type formalities, such as *agrément* (the formal agreement of the receiving state to accept a named individual as the sending state's head of mission), were frowned on. A change of head could continue to be arranged either by the departing officer giving his hosts a 'more or less formal notification' of it, or by the latter simply asking the outgoing head who was going to succeed him.[54] A high commissioner could,

[54] Price-A.F. Morley (Burma Office), 3 October 1947, TNA, DO35/3203.

it was thought, be appointed by the King as the representative of one of his governments to another. But there could be no question of someone appointed in this way being given letters of credence, or anything approximating to them. These were letters from the sending state's head of state to his counterpart in the receiving state—'Sir My Brother'—asking the latter (to use typical wording) to give 'entire credence to all that [X] shall have occasion to communicate to you in my name'. Within the Commonwealth this would be an 'apparent absurdity', in that the King would be writing to himself; it would make the monarch 'look ridiculous'.[55]

On the issue of title and style, the British were relaxed about high commissioners being given the style of 'excellency'. But over the title of 'ambassador' they continued to choke: it would be as a deplorable dilution of the Commonwealth's distinctiveness. At first the problem's resolution was thought to lie in finding an ambassadorial-sounding alternative. No one could come up with anything suitable. 'Commonwealth Ambassador' was disliked and would make little headway in the dominions. 'Minister of State' or 'Resident Minister' would not do: in Britain such phraseology had political connotations and was therefore unsuitable for officials (Britain not being in the habit of appointing Cabinet ministers as heads of mission).[56] 'Envoy' was 'too "foreign"',[57] and 'Resident Representative' was 'not . . . nice'.[58] 'His Excellency the Representative and Envoy' was scarcely better. 'Envoy-General' was a possibility, but was unenthusiastically received. 'His Majesty's Representative' might suit Britain, but hardly the less monarchically-minded members of the Commonwealth. In desperation, Britain wondered about 'Ambassador-at-Large'.

As the fruitlessness of the search became increasingly obvious, Britain's attachment to the existing title grew correspondingly, and she hoped that in the absence of agreement on an alternative the rest of the Commonwealth might agree to live with it. Moreover, the British public's attachment to established terminology and constitutional forms

---

[55] Stephenson minute and Machtig minute thereon, 9 April 1947, TNA, DO35/3203.

[56] Winston Churchill's wartime appointment of the Australian politician and diplomat, Richard Casey, as British 'Minister of State' resident in the Middle East, with a seat in the War Cabinet (1942–44), was an exception.

[57] Chifley quoted in C.R. Price (British AHC, Canberra) telegram 539, 18 August 1948, TNA, DO35/3203.

[58] Lord Chamberlain's Office-Price, 3 January 1947.

which emphasised the close Commonwealth relationship had been revealed during recent discussion about the British Nationality Act, so that was another reason for sticking to 'high commissioner'. Britain had also begun worrying whether an alteration in this respect would have repercussions on the position of the Crown and on preferential Commonwealth tariffs. Accordingly, she came to think that it would probably be best if attention could be diverted from the question of a change of title, and instead just focus on the importance of heightening the status and precedence of its holders.

There was general agreement in Britain, as elsewhere, that in these respects the position of high commissioners should be improved. Indeed, this was now seen as the only way of averting the serious threat of them being turned into ambassadors and/or becoming members of the local diplomatic corps. But the crucial question was how much their status should be improved, and at whose expense? It was, moreover, a question which was complicated on account of each of the dominions having her own table of precedence, which meant that a change that would be satisfactory in London could not be straightforwardly replicated elsewhere.

The question was referred to an interdepartmental committee of senior officials under the chairmanship of Sir Edward Bridges (secretary to the Treasury).[59] In Britain ambassadors ranked immediately after the sovereign and other royal highnesses, whereas high commissioners came way down the list. They should not, it was thought, be promoted to the ambassadorial level, which would put them above the high officers of state (a group of seven which included Britain's two Anglican archbishops and the prime minister). But nor, a majority felt, should ambassadors (of whom there were now 28) remain above the high officers. Instead, they should be placed immediately below them (after the lord privy seal), which was also the position recommended for high commissioners. It was thought that high commissioners and ambassadors should continue to be treated as separate groups, so as to

[59] It included DUS-level representatives from the Cabinet Office, FO, DO/CRO, Burma Office, Home Office, and CO. Much of what follows relies on the committee's two reports (which in essentials do not much differ): 'Draft Interim Report on the Status and Title of Commonwealth High Commissioners in London', (first revise), July 1947, TNA, DO35/2186; and 'Report on the Status and Title of Commonwealth High Commissioners in London', December 1947, TNA, PREM8/1333; and also draft memorandum, 'Precedence of High Commissioners in London', 31 July 1947, TNA, DO35/3203.

preserve the conception of the Commonwealth's representatives forming a single body with its own order of precedence (whereby high commissioners were ranked according to the seniority in the Commonwealth of the country they represented). As to which of the groups should come first, the committee's Interim Report came out openly in favour of the high commissioners; in its second, final Report a majority said, in effect, the same thing. It was suggested that this was not as offensive to ambassadors as it might seem, for four reasons. First, ambassadors, not being British subjects, did not formally appear in the correct version of Britain's table of precedence, but were covered in a footnote to it. This could be quietly amended. Second (although this was not said explicitly), the change could be fudged by the new footnote positioning ambassadors in exactly the position which would be occupied in the table by high commissioners. (The scope which this offered for confusion was illustrated by Clutterbuck interpreting the proposal to mean that ambassadors would come above high commissioners.)[60] Third, where high commissioners and ambassadors appeared as groups, things could be arranged so as 'not to suggest that either group ranks above the other'. And, fourth, where members of the two groups were present as individuals, as at banquets and similar occasions, 'there would be no difficulty in adopting the system already in practice here whereby High Commissioners are "interleaved" with foreign Ambassadors, United Kingdom Cabinet Ministers and other distinguished persons. This is a well-established principle.'[61]

None of this suited the FO. It said that giving a British national (a high commissioner) 'precedence before a *foreign* personage representing the ruler of his country' would flout 'a long-established rule of international courtesy'—and not just international: Britain's 'foreign guests' were, like lunch or dinner guests at a country house, entitled to enter and leave rooms before family members. In a shrewd blow it argued that to accept the recommendation would mean 'virtually admitting that [high commissioners] are not members of the family'.[62] The foreign

[60] See Machtig-Clutterbuck, secret and personal, 15 August & 29 September 1947, and Clutterbuck-Machtig, secret and personal, 20 August 1947, TNA, DO35/2186, DO35/3203.

[61] Machtig-Clutterbuck, secret and personal, 29 September 1947. The points were also made in the reports of the Committee of Officials.

[62] Draft memorandum, 'Precedence of High Commissioners in London'.

secretary, however, chose not to press these, or other, 'obsolete'[63] FO objections on the prime minister, who was advised that the proposed changes were appropriate, good for the Commonwealth, and necessary if Britain were to avoid high commissioners becoming ambassadors. Attlee was convinced. The 'present lowly position' of high commissioners had long been 'a source of irritation'; and there were 'practical difficulties' in treating 'representatives of major States such as Canada and Australia on a lower level than the Ministers of petty independent foreign States'.[64] In preparation for the Prime Ministers' Meeting these ideas were now circulated to the dominions, and were discussed with the cabinet secretary, Sir Norman Brook, when he visited three of the old dominions (Canada, New Zealand, and Australia) in August and September 1948 to convey Britain's view about the future constitutional relationship between independent members of the Commonwealth.

Attlee's telegram to his dominion counterparts setting out the proposed changes to Britain's table of precedence had included the rather casual suggestion that 'As to visiting Commonwealth Ministers I think they might rank with their opposite numbers in the U.K. Government'.[65] However, those opposite numbers all came below the salt—that is, below the ambassadors and high commissioners posted in London. The prospect of a dominion government minister being outranked by an official—his high commissioner—aroused something not far short of outrage in the old Commonwealth. In New Zealand, where there was a feeling 'that the Holy Ghost descended on a man as soon as he was elected by popular vote',[66] it was thought that even members of

[63] Stephenson note for Noel-Baker, 'The Status of High Commissioners', 26 May 1948, TNA, DO35/3203.

[64] Attlee minute for Chuter Ede, 14 July 1948. This was in response to a complaint from the home secretary, 'who ha[d] a good deal of personal interest in these matters, quite apart from his official concern', and was 'a little unhappy' that his prerogative of taking the King's pleasure on questions of precedence had been seemingly usurped because of an 'accidental oversight' excluding him from committee discussions. He objected that the proposed changes raised 'a number of most delicate issues' that should not be considered in isolation, and did not want high commissioners to outrank secretaries of state. Attlee ruled in favour of making 'the least possible change to effect the purpose in view': L. Helsby (principal private secretary to the prime minister) minute for Attlee, 21 July 1948; Ede minute for Attlee, 12 July 1948; Attlee minute for Ede, 14 July 1948, TNA, PREM8/1333.

[65] Attlee circular telegram to dominion prime ministers, 4 August 1948, TNA, PREM8/1333.

[66] Rive-Pearson, 12 August 1948, NAC, RG25, 2942, 3011-A-40.

parliament would refuse to suffer such an indignity. Britain backtracked, and told the prime ministers in London that in any new arrangements visiting cabinet ministers would be placed above their high commissioners. Attlee had also expressed the hope that if Britain altered the ranking of high commissioners in the suggested way, the dominions would accord similar treatment to Britain's high commissioners. This, too, raised some eyebrows, given the relatively high place which was being proposed for high commissioners in Britain, and the variations between the dominions' tables of precedence. For this, and another, reason Britain suggested that the implementation of any changes in precedence should be nationally handled as each member saw fit.

That other reason arose out of Britain's proposal that in giving high commissioners equal status with ambassadors, they should be treated as 'separate groups but both [*sic.*] on a footing of equality'.[67] It was felt in some dominions that this would create 'considerable difficulty'[68]—and understandably so as it was by no means obvious how precedence could be happily arranged when the representatives were present in groups. As to Britain's suggestion that where they were present as individuals they could be interleaved with ambassadors, this too elicited objections. Canberra was divided; Dublin was not interested; there would be difficulties in Pretoria; and it would not work in Ottawa and Wellington (and in the latter it would not even be understood). As Clutterbuck put it: interleaving 'might work all right in the U.K., where ... except on formal occasions—Ambassadors and high commissioners do not often run across each other', but not in a small capital like Ottawa 'where we meet almost every day at some official or social function or at private luncheons or dinners. Some definite order, which everyone knows ... is essential if friction is to be avoided'. Clearly interleaving had no future in other capitals.[69]

Nonetheless, the good news for Britain was that there was a warm welcome on all sides for her central proposal that high commissioners should have equal status with ambassadors. It was widely suggested that in implementing this high commissioners and ambassadors should be

[67] Attlee circular telegram, 4 August 1948.

[68] Brook report on visit to dominions, CRO Print, May 1950, TNA, DO35/3204.

[69] Clutterbuck-Machtig, secret and personal, 20 August 1947. And see Noel-Baker memorandum, 'Status of High Commissioners', September 1948, CR(48)7, TNA, CAB 134/118; Norman Brook (cabinet secretary) minute for Attlee, 'Status of High Commissioners', 6 October 1948, TNA, PREM8/1333.

seen as a single group, with individuals being accorded precedence in a national capital on the basis of their respective dates of appointment (the practice that was already followed in respect of ambassadors). This would mean ceasing to accord precedence, as among high commissioners, according to their state's seniority within the Commonwealth, and there were some doubts about whether high commissioners were capable of accepting the consequences without complaining. (The commonwealth secretary thought it would not make much difference to British high commissioners, as they would still be treated 'as the principal Commonwealth representative[s]'.)[70] But their states were aboard, and Britain now had at least a half-promising strategy for the Prime Ministers' Meeting. She circulated a revised version of her proposals, repeating her preference for two groups and interleaving, but saying it was up to each member to decide how to apply the principle of equal precedence for high commissioners. As to their title, she knew from Brook's trip (and other sources) that there was 'general dislike'[71] for it. But she would 'discourage' the idea that high commissioners should be called ambassadors, observing that she did 'not wish to make our High Commissioners abroad, or Commonwealth High Commissioners in London, look as much like "foreigners" as possible'; and hope that her belief that 'none of the suggestions for a new title will command universal support' would prove right, and result in agreement that 'the least evil is to leave the existing title unchanged'.[72]

D. The Prime Ministers' Meeting, 11–22 October 1948

The 1948 Prime Ministers' Meeting was, as usual, held in London and conducted on an informal basis, with no resolutions and no voting. It was notable for being the first that was attended by the leaders of the three newly-independent Asian members of the Commonwealth: India, Pakistan, and Ceylon.[73] It was also notable for Ireland's absence.

---

[70] Noel-Baker memorandum, 'Status of High Commissioners', September 1948.

[71] Brook report on visit to Dominions.

[72] Brook-Attlee, 16 October 1948, TNA, PREM8/1333.

[73] The paucity of their 'Old Commonwealth' counterparts was also noteworthy. South Africa and Australia were represented by Eric Louw (minister of mines and economic affairs) and H.V. Evatt (MEA); and while Mackenzie King was in London he missed the meetings on medical advice. Norman Robertson (Canadian HC) attended the meetings for a few days until St Laurent (MEA) could take over.

She had, it is true, not attended any Imperial Conferences since 1932 (though Dulanty had hovered on the fringe in 1937), but her absence had always been *ad hoc*,[74] and in 1948 the commonwealth secretary had intended to offer her an invitation. Then, on 7 September, the *taoiseach*, John Costello, suddenly announced that Ireland was going to remove her remaining link with the Crown (by repealing her External Relations Act) and, therefore (as was intended by Ireland and deemed automatic elsewhere), leave the Commonwealth. In this circumstance no invitation was issued—although the Irish version had it that an issued invitation was withdrawn.[75]

Ireland's absence probably had a big impact on the proceedings. It might have added to the cordiality of the discussion of defence, security, and economic development, on which the meeting focused and on which the participants' observations tended to be at a high, and hence agreeable, level of generality. It almost certainly contributed to the success of the meeting on the specific matter with which this book is concerned, the office of high commissioner. For she would undoubtedly have spoken powerfully against the title, having again emphasised as recently as August that she regarded the title as 'obsolete and anomalous'.[76] Without her, the 'ambassadorial camp' was significantly diminished. South Africa and Australia were still stoutly in it, insisting they would settle for nothing short of that title. They were joined by Pakistan and Ceylon. But Britain, New Zealand, and India wanted no change. (Nor did King George VI, who thought the suggestion 'wholly misconceived'.)[77] Canada thought that in the long run high commissioners should become ambassadors, but not now. Things were finely balanced.[78]

---

[74] During the War resort was had to a Canadian formula that Ireland would not be invited to wartime meetings: Massey, no. A.305, 27 July 1945, NAC, 4480, 50021–40, part 1.

[75] The official Irish version, as recounted to the Canadians, was of 'a rather tortuous chain of events' in which they had been invited and had accepted or were prepared to accept an invitation only to find it withdrawn at the last moment: Cf. Robertson (Paris)-Pearson telegram 12, top secret & personal, 20 September 1948; DEA memorandum, 'Participation of Ireland in Prime Ministers' Meeting', 24 September 1948, NAC, 4480, 50021–40, part 1. However, both Turgeon and Machtig said Rugby was at no time authorized to issue an invitation, and the latter said Dublin's account was neither correct nor completely candid.

[76] Memorandum on position of high commissioners, 18 August 1948, enclosed in MacBride-Rugby, 20 August 1948, INA, DFA, D/30/1, PREM 8/1333, NAC, RG25, 4481, 50023–40, part 1.

[77] Helsby minute for Attlee, 21 October 1948, TNA, PREM8/1333.

[78] Thus an official was wrong when he said a few months' later that there had been

As there was no immediate agreement, the meeting accepted South Africa's suggestion that a committee of high commissioners and officials should consider the subject and related matters. It noted six arguments in favour of a change to 'ambassador'. First, it would constitute 'a recognition of the sovereign and independent character of Commonwealth countries'. And, since it was abundantly clear by then that everyone agreed high commissioners should be on an equal footing with ambassadors, 'there was less reason for continuing to draw this distinction'. Second, ' "ambassador" was a well understood title carrying greater prestige than the title "High Commissioner" with its misleading associations, and was better understood by the public'. Third, there was 'rapidly ceasing' to be any difference in the functions discharged by high commissioners and ambassadors. Fourth, there was no 'difference in practice' between the relations Commonwealth states had with each other and with foreign states to whom they were close. Fifth, the change 'might be of real importance politically to Ceylon's international position', as at the United Nations the Soviet Union (when vetoing Ceylon's application for membership) had alleged, 'with some appearance of justification', that the Anglo-Ceylonese defence agreement meant that she 'was not really independent'.[79] And, sixth, adopting the title 'ambassador' 'would dispose of all difficulties in connection with the personal status and precedence of UK representatives'.

Five contrary arguments were noted. First, the title 'high commissioner' marked 'the family character, and the greater intimacy and in some respects informality' of Commonwealth relations. Second, it was a 'well-settled tradition' for ambassadors to represent a head of state, while high commissioners represented governments. Third, in practice the position of a high commissioner was different from that of an ambassador: 'his contacts both in nature and extent were closer [and] more intimate . . . Could it seriously be maintained that the ordinary Foreign Ambassador in a Commonwealth country bore anything like the same relation or was in the same intimate confidence as a United Kingdom representative?' Fourth, the 'functions of Ambassadors and High Commissioners were not necessarily identical'. And, fifth, 'any

a 'unanimous feeling against the term "High Commissioner" ': Turnbull minute, 12 July 1949, TNA, DO35/3212.

[79] J.S. Bennett (a senior CO official) notes for discussion, 5 July 1954 in *BDEE Ghana* II, 89.

misunderstandings' about 'the true position of High Commissioners' would not be removed by their being raised to the rank of ambassador.

The arguments in favour of a change secured the most support in the committee. But a minority was unpersuaded. Nor could a generally acceptable alternative title be found. The committee therefore sat on the fence, merely concluding that if a change were made it should be to 'ambassador'. This was not of much help to the prime ministers who, when they again discussed the matter, remained no less divided than before. They, too, therefore sat on the fence, accepting Canada's suggestion (which was also Britain's aim) that the title should be reconsidered at a later date. But they supported the committee's other recommendations, which included the very important one that 'High Commissioners should rank with Foreign Ambassadors for purposes of precedence'. The practical application of this principle was left for each member to decide, but the committee frowned fiercely on the idea of separate groups; said that high commissioners and ambassadors 'should take precedence in strict order and date of appointment' (which would make it unnecessary to devise a special system of interleaving); and that 'seniority of countries should be abandoned as a basis for precedence of High Commissioners *inter se*'. (Britain implicitly and Canada explicitly agreed thereby to give up their positions as first and second in Commonwealth rankings.) As to whether high commissioners should be granted the style of 'excellency', that too was left for individual action. The issue of whether high commissioners should be eligible for the doyenship of the diplomatic corps received wide support but, in the light of Britain's unhappiness about it, was not pressed. The committee thought some form of credentials for high commissioners should be considered, but came out firmly against the idea that they should be accredited by the King.[80] (Interestingly, the issue of diplomatic immunity for high commissioners appears not to have been raised.)

Thus although the office of high commissioner was still not assuredly safe, the deeply nagging problem of status and precedence had been largely resolved. For the moment enough had been done to avert what had seemed an imminent threat to the very existence of the office. It had been a close-run thing. Ireland's absence was probably the crucial

[80] P.M.M.(48) 14th Meeting, minute 1, 21 October 1948, TNA, PREM8/1333, referring to Report of the Committee of High Commissioners and Officials, 'Status of High Commissioners', 19 October 1948, TNA, P.M.M.(48)14, CAB133/48.

factor in the achievement of a harmonious outcome. Other contributory factors were the spirit of optimism and goodwill induced by the presence of the new dominions, especially India; and a wish not to raise unnecessary difficulties at a time when Ireland was quitting the Commonwealth and India was moving in a republican direction. And Britain congratulated herself on her 'careful handling and timing' of the discussions.[81]

E. Implementing the Prime Ministers' Decisions

The agreement to treat high commissioners and ambassadors as equal in status required the revision of national tables of precedence.[82] This led to teething troubles in a number of capitals. In Ottawa and New Delhi there were complaints that, because the precedence of high commissioners was backdated to the date of their arrival, some long-serving heads of Commonwealth missions suddenly leapt up in the relevant section of the lists. The *doyen* in Wellington protested. There, and in Colombo, ministers plenipotentiary tried for some years to insist that, as the representatives of heads of state, they had seniority over high commissioners, and in Canberra the departing Italian ambassador complained in 1952 that high commissioners 'do not exist internationally'.[83] In South Africa there was a heavy storm in the diplomatic tea cup. The necessary changes were announced as taking effect from January 1949. But high commissioners continued to receive lesser treatment as the heads of foreign missions in Pretoria refused to accept high commissioners as full members of the diplomatic corps, and the incoming French *doyen*, Armand Gazel, who had made mischief in New Zealand, proceeded in the same vein in South Africa. Ignoring a ruling by the governor-general, and without consulting high commissioners, Gazel refused to accord the traditional courtesies to the Australian high commissioner's designated consort (his sister). When the high commissioner, Alfred Stirling, learned that she was going to be seated after the wives of ministers, he boycotted a lunch for the outgoing American *doyen*.

[81] Liesching (PUS)-Clutterbuck, telegram 82, 3 February 1951, TNA, DO127/93.

[82] One authority says that in making the change 'consultation had to be undertaken with foreign states and their agreement obtained': Wheare (1960) 138. This is perhaps putting it too strongly, as it was up to each state to arrange its own table of precedence and the prime ministers had merely urged the 'maximum degree of uniformity'.

[83] C.F. Elliott (Canadian HC), 16 February 1952, NAC, RG25, 3997, 10062–40.

Stirling attributed this treatment to jealousy amongst the wives of heads of legations, but it was in keeping with Gazel's practice in New Zealand of drawing a clear distinction between Commonwealth and foreign heads of mission, and excluding the former from any official correspondence in matters involving the diplomatic corps.

In London 'many hackles'[84] were raised. Here, as had earlier been envisaged, ambassadors were demoted in the table of precedence to come (along with high commissioners) after rather than before the high officers of state. The diplomatic corps was not convinced by Britain's explanation that the change only amounted to giving 'formal recognition to what has long been the rightful place of High Commissioners as representatives of ambassadorial status'.[85] In accordance with the views of most prime ministers, however, and contrary to what had earlier been envisaged, ambassadors and high commissioners were to be treated as a single group and rank 'in a common order of seniority based on their respective dates of arrival'[86] (the FO and the CRO thus being enabled to supply their own interpretations of the last phrase).

In two other respects British practice did not, perhaps, obviously conform with the prime ministers' approach. It had been agreed that the 'practice of treating High Commissioners and Ambassadors as separate groups should be abandoned unless there are decisive technical objections to doing so'.[87] But Britain continued to distinguish in a number of ways between them. She kept them apart in her Diplomatic List (and continued doing so until the mid-1970s);[88] on certain state occasions they were seated separately; she did not regard them as part of the diplomatic corps, and therefore deemed them ineligible to become the corps' *doyen* (a view which was accepted, until the end of the 1960s, not just by local ambassadors but also by the high commissioners);[89] she

---

[84] Cockram (a senior official) minute, 14 December 1949, TNA, DO35/3212.

[85] Escott Reid (acting under-secretary) memorandum, 'Precedence and Titles of High Commissioners', 29 November 1948, *DCER* 14, 1475.

[86] *London Gazette*, 24 December 1948.

[87] Report of the Committee of High Commissioners and Officials, 'Status of High Commissioners'.

[88] The 1975 Diplomatic Service List separately listed British missions to foreign states and to Commonwealth countries. In 1976 the Diplomatic Service List placed them in one alphabetical list, using asterisks to identify high commissions. The change in precedence did not, of course, extend to the Southern Rhodesian high commissioner because of that territory's non-sovereign status.

[89] It is a curious aspect of the office of *doyen*—or leader—of the body of diplomats in a capital that, while on the face of it, the appointment lies with those diplomats,

still regarded them as supplementary, rather than normal, channels for her communications with their states; there was no rush to give them legal immunity; and she maintained a separate Whitehall department to handle relations with Commonwealth states. She was of course making the point that high commissioners were different from 'ordinary' diplomats resident in London, in that relations between members of the Commonwealth were not like those between other states. None of this appeared to arouse much unhappiness.

The prime ministers had also agreed that high commissioners should no longer be ranked among themselves on the basis of the seniority of their countries. *A fortiori*, it might be thought, this would also apply higher up in the Commonwealth. Nevertheless, the prime ministers themselves were seated (and spoke) on the seniority basis at their 1949 Meeting in London. It occasioned no walk-outs—but did not happen again. At certain British ceremonies, however, where the high commissioners but no foreign diplomats were present, they continued for a while to be ranked according to what was known as the 'order of Dominions'. But its use at the state opening of Parliament attracted comment. The limited seating at floor level meant that one or two high commissioners' wives had to sit in the gallery, and it was invariably the wives of high commissioners from the same countries. Possibly on account of this the Pakistani high commissioner suggested in 1951 that there should be one order of precedence for all occasions based (as was now usual) on personal seniority. (Alerted, a CRO official could 'only suppose' the 1948 agreement had been 'overlooked'.)[90] Subject to two qualifications, this was agreed. The first was that at the suggestion the Indian high commissioner, Krishna Menon,[91] an exception was made (and continues to be made) for the laying of wreaths on London's cenotaph during the Remembrance Day ceremony, which commemorates people from the Commonwealth who have fallen in the two world wars, and subsequently. And second, it was ruled that the Irish ambassador (neither a family member nor a foreigner), who joined the high commissioners on

in practice the receiving state often has a determining influence on it. See further, Chapter 5, Section E and Chapter 7, Section G. The exclusion of high commissioners from London's diplomatic corps was not much of an inconvenience to them: they had excellent individual access to the receiving state and, as necessary, their most senior member acted as group spokesman.

[90] R.R. Sedgwick (AUS) minute, 6 June 1951, TNA, DO35/3327.

[91] F.A.K. Harrison (a senior official) minute, 18 December 1951, TNA, DO35/3327.

these occasions, should in future follow them. This would prevent the possibility of him or her 'taking the lead over everybody [on account of personal seniority] on occasions such as receptions to meet foreign royalty when Commonwealth High Commissioners and the Ambassador for the Irish Republic are received separately in advance of the Diplomatic Corps'.[92]

There was also, for a while, a continuing differential practice regarding another matter which was discussed at the 1948 Prime Ministers' Meeting, but which had been left to individual states to decide: whether high commissioners should be accorded the style of 'excellency'. Three old Commonwealth members had not wanted this. Two of them—New Zealand and South Africa—quickly swallowed their objections. However, not only did Canada want to stop high commissioners in Ottawa being called 'excellency'; she also wanted the style to be denied to her own high commissioners. She was persuaded not to try to tell other states how they should address Canadian heads of mission in their capitals. But she refused to accord the style 'excellency' to high commissioners in Ottawa, continuing her practice (since 1942) of designating them as 'honourable'. When, a couple of years later, the Pakistani high commissioner expressed surprise about the position in Ottawa, a weighty Canadian memorandum said that not calling high commissioners 'excellencies' was 'awkward'.[93] A little more than a year later Canada quietly came into line with the rest of the Commonwealth.[94]

F. Conclusion

It was remarkable that the office of high commissioner should have survived. It had become so unpopular that it looked very much as if there was going to be no alternative to translating high commissioners into fully-fledged ambassadors. But at least a breathing space was secured, and as it happened the decision to give high commissioners the same

[92] Sedgwick minute, 6 June 1951.

[93] Norman Robertson (clerk of the Privy Council and cabinet secretary) memorandum, 17 November 1949, NAC, RG2 18, 107, U-10-11, vol. 2.

[94] In response to a request from Clutterbuck that the change should be regarded as one of form only and as not impairing intra-Commonwealth relations, the Canadians were 'splendid'. Instead of announcing it, the change was unobtrusively slipped into a new edition of the Diplomatic List, in this way making 'it clear to everybody that no political significance was involved': H.F. Feaver (Protocol Division) memorandum, 2 February 1951, NAC, RG25, 6371, 3011-A-40 part 3.

status and precedence as ambassadors took much of the steam out of the debate. It also proved to be the thin end of a wedge, as outside London the 1948 changes initiated a process whereby the distinction between Commonwealth and foreign heads of mission became increasingly blurred. But first another, and on the face of it irresistible, threat to the office of high commissioner had to be averted.

CHAPTER FIVE

SUBSTANTIVE EQUALITY, LATE 1940s–EARLY 1950s

The 1948 Prime Ministers' Meeting was probably the key event in the survival of the office of high commissioner. However, that was far from clear at the time. The Meeting's agreement that high commissioners should have equal status with ambassadors was unquestionably important. But in respect of the ever-looming issue of whether high commissioners should be turned into ambassadors, it seemed that only a temporary breathing space had been gained. And the breather was very short-lived, newly-independent India soon confirming her intention to become a republic. On the face of it that meant she would have to leave the Commonwealth, as she would no longer share the same head of state as the rest of the 'family'. In itself this would not pose a threat to the office of high commissioner; it would just mean that the pairs of states exchanging such heads of mission were reduced. But the rest of the Commonwealth was keen to keep republican India within the fold, and India was well disposed towards the idea. Somehow, therefore, the Commonwealth had to undergo the constitutional contortion which would secure this result. Given Britain's pragmatic approach to such matters (which was to a considerable extent inherited by the 'old' dominions), it was unlikely that this challenge would be insurmountable, and so it proved. But accommodating a republic within the Commonwealth seemed inevitably to involve saying good-bye to an office which appeared inextricably bound up with a shared monarchy. High commissioners were the representatives of the sovereign's several governments in their relations with each other. On becoming a republic India would place herself outside the King's realms, and appoint her own, individual, head of state. In theory, she could perhaps exchange ambassadors with her fellow Commonwealth members while they went on exchanging high commissioners with each other. But as a practical matter that was hardly 'on', especially given that there was considerable Commonwealth pressure to adopt diplomatic styles. Yet, in the event, the Commonwealth's willingness not to insist on tidying up all loose ends had the consequence that when India became a republic on 26 January 1950, she went on sending and receiving high commissioners to and from her fellow Commonwealth members (albeit with a new form of accreditation, appropriate to her republican status), enabling them to continue doing likewise. Another triumph for pragmatism.

Moreover, at this period three other steps were taken to place high commissioners in the same (or an equivalent) position as ambassadors, none of which had been discussed at the Prime Ministers' 1948 Meeting. In the first place, arrangements were made for them always to bear letters of accreditation of one kind or another. Formal accreditation was central to diplomatic ceremony, so that authorizing high commissioners in this way helped to remove the suggestion that they did not belong to the body of diplomats. Second, each Commonwealth member took (or made ready to take) the action which was necessary for high commissioners to enjoy diplomatic immunity within her jurisdiction. Their earlier lack of immunity had not much rankled, but could easily do so given its clear implication that they were less than full diplomatic agents. Third, most Commonwealth states decided that in their several capitals high commissioners should be put in the same position as ambassadors as regards their eligibility for the *décanat*—that is, for the doyenship, or deanship, of the diplomatic corps. (London was an—acceptable—exception for a further two decades.) By definition this meant that high commissioners were part of the relevant diplomatic corps, as the *doyen* of a corps could not be other than one of its members. This last change removed what hitherto had often (as has been demonstrated in this book) been a substantial grievance. Added to the 1948 agreement regarding equal status, these developments resulted in high commissioners gaining substantive equality with ambassadors, which dissolved much of the antagonism which had been felt in some quarters towards their title. Thus, in the 'new' Commonwealth which had been importantly symbolised by republican India's continued membership, the grave post-War threat to the office of high commissioner had, at least for the time being, been diverted.

While the discussions about India were going on, there was another republican issue on the Commonwealth's agenda. Ireland was known to be moving in a republican direction, and a firm statement of intent was announced (very unexpectedly) by her *taoiseach* in September 1948, during a visit to Canada. He also made it clear (as then seemed obvious) that this entailed quitting the Commonwealth, and it did. But her departure created some troublesome fallout for Britain on the high commissioner front. As a republic Ireland would, in relation to Commonwealth states, be expected to exchange and receive ambassadors or ministers rather than high commissioners; and given her vigorous hostility to the latter office, there was little expectation that there would be any delay in her doing so. Britain, however, was very much interested in delay. In part this had to do with the rather strange arrangement whereby Ireland retained a special relationship with Commonwealth members after she had formally left the association. But additionally Britain feared that the use of diplomatic titles would complicate her position regarding India. Almost to the very day of becoming a republic, India was insisting that the heads of mission exchanged with Commonwealth states had to become ambassadors. At the time of Ireland's going, Britain was still hoping that this, and with it the seemingly certain loss of the office of high commissioner, could be avoided. It would be no help at all if at this stage the high commissioners and representatives sent to and from Dublin were given traditional diplomatic titles. As it happened, Ireland did hold back, and Canada was persuaded to delay turning her high commissioner in Dublin into an ambassador. This was sufficient for republican India first to be ushered into the Commonwealth—and, most surprisingly, without thereby jeopardising the office of high commissioner. Subsequently, when existing envoys between Ireland and Commonwealth states were reaccredited and new ones accredited as ambassadors, there was sometimes much bickering about the titles of their heads of state, in one case so much so that the proposed exchange was put on one side for more than a decade. But as between members of the Commonwealth it was high commissioners who continued to be exchanged. The office had survived.

A. Keeping India in the Commonwealth

India's intention (announced even before independence) to become a republic caused much perturbation, as that form of government was deemed to strike at the heart of the Commonwealth relationship. According to constitutional orthodoxy, allegiance to the Crown was the Commonwealth's key distinguishing feature—an 'absolute condition of membership'.[1] Hence Burma had to depart when, on her independence day in January 1948, she became a republic; and so did Ireland when she became a republic in 1949. India, on the other hand, was

[1] CRO draft brief for Viscount Addison (dominions secretary), May 1947, TNA, DO35/2186.

too important to lose. Hence the assiduity with which the last viceroy, Earl Mountbatten of Burma, had wooed the incoming prime minister, Jawaharlal Nehru, into overcoming his doubts about staying in the Commonwealth. Hence, too, Britain's attempts to make the Commonwealth appealing to India by, for example, dropping the term 'dominion' and ceasing to refer to the Commonwealth as British.[2] And, having become convinced of the value of the Commonwealth, Nehru made it clear that India wanted to remain after becoming a republic. Most 'old' Commonwealth prime ministers found it hard to swallow the idea that the members of their association would not all share a common allegiance; but they recognised the need to make concessions and take risks for the sake of keeping India on board. The rather watery idea emerged that India might recognise the King as Head of the Commonwealth, and lengthy discussions revealed the dearth of acceptable alternatives to this proposition. The outcome was that, at a special Prime Ministers' Meeting in April 1949 (only days after Ireland's departure), it was amicably agreed that India would accept the King as the 'symbol of the free association' of independent Commonwealth countries 'and as such the Head of the Commonwealth'.[3] The other Commonwealth countries in turn recognised India's continuing membership. At Pakistan's insistence India was not regarded as an exceptional case, so it could be 'logically assumed' that any other members going down the republican path would be accorded the same treatment.[4]

Legally-speaking, the ingenious 'London Declaration' was said to be 'pragmatic nonsense'.[5] It was justified on the grounds that 'it would be

[2] See Clement Attlee (prime minister) cabinet memoranda, 26 October and 30 December 1948, *BDEE 1945–51* IV, 160–1, 178–9.

[3] PMM-1949 communiqué quoted in Mansergh (1958a) 251. Queen Elizabeth's headship derives from the proclamation of her accession to the throne, in which India, although a republic, participated. This was because India's high commissioner, Krishna Menon, had indicated in 1951 (when there was grave concern about the King's health) that he would like to show respect for King George VI's successor and join the other high commissioners in attending the Accession Council and signing the proclamation of the new sovereign. He also suggested modifying the wording to include the expression 'Head of the Commonwealth', whose authorship he claimed. Although the wording had not been changed for 'three or four centuries', Menon's wishes were met. In February 1952 his successor signed the proclamation, along with the other high commissioners: Dixon (1969) 64–5. Nehru also sent a message welcoming the Queen as head of the Commonwealth. In keeping with the proclamation, the Queen's royal style and titles refer to her being 'Head of the Commonwealth'.

[4] Attlee in cabinet meeting, 27 April 1949, *BDEE 1945–51* IV, 206.

[5] G. Marshall quoted in 'Introduction', *BDEE 1945–51* I, lxx.

a disservice to the Crown if Commonwealth Ministers allowed a position to develop in which the Crown was made to appear a stumbling-block' to the association's continued cohesion.[6] It was also acclaimed as a political triumph, the 'last great formal step in defining the nature of the Commonwealth'.[7] But another way of looking at it was as the first formal step in an altered direction, marking the birth of a 'new', looser, and less homogenous Commonwealth.

B. High Commissioners to and from India, Pakistan, and Ceylon[8]

India had had representation in Britain and South Africa long before the transfer of power in August 1947. Her first high commissioner had been appointed to London in 1920 to perform 'functions in connexion with the business of the [Indian] Federation, and, in particular, in relation to the making of contracts'.[9] He had no political role since his country was under the overall control of Britain's India Office, through which 'India' dealt with intra-imperial or international bodies such as the League of Nations. A few years later, in 1927, when India effectively took full responsibility for all aspects of Indian-South African relations, she sent an agent to the Union. In 1935 her representation there was raised to agent-general, and from 1941 to 1946 (when India withdrew him) he was a high commissioner. As regards the rest of the Commonwealth, India made appointments to Australia (1944), Canada and Pakistan (1947), and Ireland (1949).

At the beginning of the 1940s, Leo Amery, the secretary of state for India, tried to persuade South Africa's wartime prime minister, Jan Smuts, to send a high commissioner to India in the hope that this move might have a helpful effect on her attitude to the Commonwealth. (There was ever-growing nationalist opposition in India to Britain's continued rule.) Smuts declined: there were too few South Africans in India and not enough trade. Canada was on the face of it more co-operative. As early as 1940 she agreed in principle to have a high commissioner in India, but he only arrived in April 1947, four years after the opening

[6] Cabinet conclusions, 3 March 1949, *BDEE 1945–51* IV, 202.
[7] Miller (1966) 145.
[8] India and Pakistan became independent in August 1947, and Ceylon in February 1948.
[9] The Government of India Act, 1935.

of an Australian high commission and about as many months after Britain and Ceylon had opened missions.[10] Neither the Australian nor the Canadian high commissioner had much to do. But that was not the point. Their presence was intended to encourage the composition of Anglo-Indian differences, show solidarity with both sides and, it was hoped, demonstrate the value of the Commonwealth relationship. By contrast, Britain's high commissioner, Terence Shone, was very busy. He was in the unusual position of representing Britain in a country which was still formally under the immediate control of the British governor-general, also called the viceroy (although by then Britain had begun treating Nehru's interim government as '*de facto* . . . independent').[11] An attempt was made to square this circle by placing Shone not under the India Office but under the Cabinet Office, which was directly responsible to the prime minister. Correspondingly, his Directive gave him diplomatic tasks, instructing him to rely on 'persuasion, representation and negotiation' in his dealings with the Indian government.[12]

When India became independent under that name in August 1947, she did so as a state which encompassed only part of the former Raj. The rest went to another state, Pakistan, as Britain had been unable to arrange a single constitutional structure acceptable to the Hindu majority and the Muslim minority. India and Pakistan immediately exchanged high commissioners, and Britain sent one to Karachi (Pakistan's capital until 1959). But none of the 'old' dominions followed suit, which left Pakistan feeling somewhat cold-shouldered and discouraged. Britain found this a bit embarrassing and urged Australia and Canada (who were represented in India) to help Pakistan 'feel part of the family'.[13] She also hoped that sending high commissioners would assist in keeping Pakistan on side (or at least not hostile) in the developing Cold War. Although Australia, like Canada, faced considerable staffing problems, she managed to open an office in Karachi in March 1948 as a preliminary step towards sending a high commissioner in 1949. By then, however, Pakistan could barely house existing missions and so was not keen to receive new ones. She therefore suggested to Canada

---

[10] As Ceylon was not independent, she initially had a 'representative' in India.

[11] E.E. Bridges (Treasury)-P.J. Dixon (FO), 21 October 1946, TNA, DO133/46.

[12] Directive to Shone enclosed in cabinet secretary's circular letter, 13 November 1946, TNA, DO133/46.

[13] Sir John Stephenson (DUS) quoted in John Holmes (Canadian AHC, London), telegram 1570, 10 October 1947, NAC, RG25, 6292, 11493-A-40.

that instead of pursuing her plan to appoint a high commissioner, she should for the time being rely on her existing trade commissioner. Canada was not deflected, and opened a high commission in 1949. Ceylon followed in 1950. As far as Pakistan herself was concerned, a lack of trained officials and funds prevented her from immediately sending high commissioners to capitals other than London. But by 1952 she was also represented in Canada, Australia, New Zealand (resident in Canberra), and Ceylon. For her part, Ceylon had by 1952 established four high commissions—in Australia, Britain, India, and Pakistan. Commonwealth membership was an important factor behind the opening of high commissions in Ceylon, and their heads formed a significant proportion of the early representatives in Colombo.[14]

In the early years, there was little substance in relations between the old and the new Commonwealth. None of the former dominions had had any previous knowledge or experience of South Asia, and they were not very interested in their exotic, newly-independent brethren. The official who was asked to open Canada's high commission in Pakistan in 1949 received apologies for being so assigned (although in the event he found it a rewarding task). Another Canadian foreign service officer was thought odd in the 1950s for asking to go to India; and when the Canadian prime minister, John Diefenbaker, was planning his visit to these two states in 1958, 'the atmosphere of the prime minister's office was like that of a family preparing for a tourist excursion'.[15] Much the same was true of the rest of the old Commonwealth. When Sir Edmund Hillary went as New Zealand's high commissioner to India in 1985, he was told that he would not have to abandon his commitments elsewhere; he just had to spend most of his time in India.

However, the value of high commissions went beyond demonstrating (as a Canadian official put it) 'the importance of our connection with this "unique [Commonwealth] association", as well as our friendly relations'.[16] Everyone benefited from this early bridge-building between North and South. Newly-independent states gained easier

[14] In 1953 Colombo had an American embassy, four high commissions (Britain, Pakistan, Australia, and India) and six legations, three of which were 'more or less permanently' headed by *chargés d'affaires*: J.C. Satterthwaite (American ambassador, Colombo), no. 591, 1 April 1953, NAC, RG25, 6371, 3011-A-40.

[15] Robinson (1989) 55.

[16] D.M. Cornett (Commonwealth Division) memorandum, 'Appointment of a High Commissioner for Ceylon in Canada', 4 May 1955, NAC, RG25, 7223, 9965-A-40, part 1.

access to sources of assistance, a gentle broadening of perspectives, and additional means of trying to exert influence (especially important to Pakistan and India because of their dispute over Kashmir). The old Commonwealth gained expanded diplomatic and foreign policy horizons, and a valuable education in third world issues and perspectives through the opening of 'doors and windows in [a] hitherto blank wall of ignorance and prejudice'.[17] And the latter group also benefited from educating and socialising new states in the ways of (if not into) the Western camp. It is striking that by 1951 Canberra was sending more communications to Delhi than anywhere else except London, and that close Indian-Canadian relations in the early 1950s were of some significance at the United Nations, especially in the winding up of the Korean War. Hence general agreement emerged that the 'new' Commonwealth had 'considerable diplomatic value' and that members should make the most of it.[18]

1. *India and the question of translating high commissioners into ambassadors*

In India it was assumed by the relevant high commissioners that on becoming a republic in January 1950, she would want to exchange ambassadors rather than high commissioners. Accordingly, Britain's high commissioner charged his deputy with working out what this would involve, and his Canadian colleague caused bemusement by arranging to have his diplomatic uniform flown out. (He was the only Canadian head of mission in possession of 'the expensive uniform authorized by United Kingdom regulations for United Kingdom ambassadors'—Canada not then having its own such uniform.)[19] India certainly attached importance to this change. As Sir Girja Bajpai, the senior External Affairs official, explained, although he 'personally liked the title High Commissioner'[20] he had three objections to it. First, it

[17] Doxey (1982) 16.

[18] Holmes (1962) 292.

[19] Howard Measures (Chief of Protocol) memorandum, 27 December 1949, NAC, RG25, 4045, 10566–40, vol. 1. The other Commonwealth representatives in New Delhi had no intention of appearing in uniform on any occasion, and Britain's DHC thought 'uniforms would be an unnecessary expense, and out of place in a country celebrating its liberation from all traces of past imperialism': Frank Roberts telegram 1236, 20 October 1949, TNA, DO127/92.

[20] Ben Cockram (a senior official) minute, 10 November 1949, TNA, DO35/3212.

was 'a relic of the past relationship' and its holders were without full ambassadorial rights and immunities.[21] Second, when Indian heads of mission represented a president and carried credentials, they would have to become ambassadors. And, third, while there were no longer precedence problems in foreign capitals, there was one in India. This was because India gave her own ambassadors 'a special and high precedence' but it was 'difficult to fit Indian High Commissioners into the table' of precedence.[22] Neither the carrot of diplomatic immunity nor the contention that high commissioners 'had a much better position than any Ambassador' could dissuade Sir Girja.[23] India wanted her high commissioners to become ambassadors, and would be satisfied with nothing less.

Britain's representatives in India were firmly against obstructionism. Any such attempt would harm Anglo-Indian relations, as Britain would look as if she were trying to ignore a fundamental constitutional development and India would be justified in rebuffing her. Britain should abandon her regrettable 'tendency to die in the last ditch'.[24] Patrick Gordon Walker, the junior CRO minister, agreed: 'We don't want to be pushed reluctantly into something we must do anyway', he said.[25] Senior officials in the CRO and elsewhere also agreed that exchanging ambassadors with India would doom the office of high commissioner everywhere, and that ideally Britain would be done with the problem once and for all. It would, the cabinet secretary advised the prime minister, look better if all Commonwealth members made the switch simultaneously, as a group, rather than 'give the appearance of a progressive disintegration'. But he also pointed out the awkwardness of Britain herself suggesting this, given her stout defence of the office of high commissioner in 1948.[26] And there were other arguments against doing so. A change would bring no practical advantages; the CRO thought the existing title was distinguished and distinguishing;

[21] Frank Roberts (British acting HC, New Delhi) telegram X1257, 13 July 1949, TNA, DO35/ 3212.

[22] Cockram-Sir Girja Bajpai conversation, 10 November 1949, TNA, DO35/ 3212.

[23] Bajpai-Patrick Gordon Walker (parliamentary under-secretary, CRO) conversation, 11 December 1949, TNA, DO35/32112.

[24] Roberts minute, 19 October 1949, TNA, DO133/13.

[25] Gordon Walker minute, 1 November 1949, TNA, DO35/3212.

[26] Norman Brook (cabinet secretary) minute for Attlee, 4 November 1949, TNA, PREM8/1333.

and there was the 'minor technical argument' (as it had now become!) about the King not being able to accredit an ambassador to himself.[27] More specifically, the Board of Trade was strongly opposed because it was worried about the consequences for preferential Commonwealth trading tariffs. The title of high commissioner was indicative of the special, non-foreign Commonwealth relationship and hence, it was thought, could help Britain refute claims for similarly advantageous tariff rates from states entitled to most-favoured-nation treatment. Lastly, an all-round exchange of ambassadors would 'mean that once again the Commonwealth steam-roller would have to be run over New Zealand',[28] which would be especially regrettable as the loyal New Zealanders were 'the strongest supporters of Commonwealth integrity'.[29] It was noted in the CRO that if the exchange of ambassadors were limited to India this would have the merit of not affecting New Zealand, there being no exchange of envoys between the two.

Evidently these contrary arguments carried weight. For when, on 7 November, the Cabinet considered the suggestion that Britain should begin consultations on converting high commissioners into ambassadors, it came out against any change at all. Recollecting that in 1948 Nehru himself had 'deprecated' the title 'ambassador', ministers thought 'it would be unfortunate if this change of nomenclature had now to be adopted by all Commonwealth countries as a result of precipitate action by the Government of India'.[30] The prime minister, Clement Attlee, agreed to take up the question with Nehru (who was in London). When they spoke the next day, Nehru gave Attlee the impression that he did not feel strongly either way. He 'agreed it would be unfortunate if different titles were adopted in different Commonwealth countries. Didn't seem at all eager to press for the title of ambassador'.[31] However, Nehru 'seem[ed] to have been unbriefed' ('these formalities are not his strong point'), and after talking to Bajpai accepted that a change in titles was

---

[27] Addison (lord privy seal) cabinet memorandum, 'Title and Status of Commonwealth High Commissioners', 3 November 1949, TNA, CP(49)226, CAB129/37.

[28] Percivale Liesching (PUS, CRO) in inter-departmental meeting, 20 September 1949, TNA, DO35/3212.

[29] Addison memorandum, 'Title and Status of Commonwealth High Commissioners', 3 November 1949, TNA, CP(49)226, CAB129/37.

[30] Cabinet meeting, 7 November 1949, CM64(49), TNA, CAB128/16.

[31] Attlee-Nehru conversation, 8 November 1949, TNA, DO35/3212. The Canadian High Commission in New Delhi confirmed that Nehru was 'not greatly concerned about this matter': Paul A. Bridle, no. 493, 9 December 1949, NAC, RG25, 4045, 10566–40, vol. 1.

necessary and inevitable, though as India would regard it as 'purely formal' it 'would in no way affect the intimacy of [her] relations with her partners in the Commonwealth'.[32]

Nonetheless, there were still some favourable omens for Britain. Nehru's Commonwealth-minded high commissioner in London, Krishna Menon, was keen to retain that title. High commissioners in India seemed happy with it, too. India would be somewhat disadvantaged by a change, as her commissioners in the colonial empire would have to become consuls and so lose their current privileged status and find themselves with a somewhat restricted remit. Most importantly, Nehru was not in a hurry, and indeed disinclined 'to go into the question thoroughly'.[33] He decided to postpone reaching a decision until after the January 1950 Commonwealth conference on foreign affairs in Colombo (immediately prior to the date on which India would become a republic), when he could discuss the subject informally and explain India's views in a personal and friendly way. Also very encouraging was the fact that every Commonwealth country except Canada now wanted to retain the title. New Zealand's new prime minister, Sydney Holland, personally drafted a telegram making it clear he wanted to keep this distinguishing Commonwealth mark, and his Australian colleague, Robert Menzies, shared Holland's perturbation that a change of title 'would serve no useful purpose and might be misunderstood'.[34] Ceylon, too, preferred high commissioner, though she was willing to compromise for the sake of uniformity, and South Africa wanted to give the 1948 arrangements a longer trial.

And so, as the Colombo conference approached the CRO began feeling optimistic about the office. Perhaps Britain could persuade Nehru to continue with the status quo for the time being, or not to raise the subject on the grounds that the case for change had neither been proven nor received sufficient support. And in fact it was not openly discussed at Colombo. The reason for this non-development, however, arose out of South Africa's determination not to receive Asian ambassadors, not least for fear of one day finding herself with an Asian *doyen* of the diplomatic corps. She did not say this outright. Initially she said she wanted to continue with existing arrangements

---

[32] Sir Archibald Nye (British HC) telegram, 21 November 1949, TNA, DO127/93.

[33] Nye telegram 53, 5 January 1950, TNA, PREM8/1333.

[34] E.J. Williams (British HC, Canberra), telegram 11, 5 January 1950, TNA, PREM8/1333.

for the time being because the 1948 changes had 'brought about a considerable improvement in the position of High Commissioners and have overcome many of the difficulties and anomalies which previously existed'.[35] But then her prime minister instructed his delegation to press strongly for the title 'ambassador' and, in so doing, make it clear that the Union would insist that certain states could only be represented in South Africa at the non-diplomatic, consular, level. Any such statement would have hugely offended India, Pakistan, and Ceylon who would rightly have recognised that it was aimed at them. The only way to avoid a damaging row was not to have any formal discussion of the matter. Britain's commonwealth secretary, Philip Noel-Baker, had a quiet word with Nehru who, with other, more pressing, preoccupations agreed 'The title can wait'.[36] An important reason for this was that Krishna Menon, India's high commissioner to Britain, and Noel-Baker had agreed at Colombo that the continued exchange of high commissioners need not stand in the way of their being formally accredited (in the manner of ambassadors). And when Britain suggested the issue be left over for the time being, neither South Africa nor anyone else dissented. In this way the office of high commissioner gained another, most unexpected, lease of life.[37]

2. *Accreditation and* agréation

Diplomatic-style accreditation was politically and psychologically important for India, being seen as symbolic of an unquestionably sovereign republic. Enabling high commissioners to be so introduced between India and Britain turned out to be unexpectedly easy. After his private discussions with Noel-Baker in Colombo, Menon, had put forward as

---

[35] D.F. Malan (South African PM) 1949 telegram to Attlee, quoted in Forsyth (SDEA) memorandum, 'Status and Character of Commonwealth Representation in London and other Commonwealth Capitals', 30 September 1955, SAA, BTS 43/4, vol. II.

[36] Nehru quoted in Noel-Baker—John Dulanty (Irish HC, London) conversation, 27 January 1950, TNA, PREM8/1333.

[37] By then there was an additional argument in favour of the office, in that Indonesia and the Netherlands had recently agreed to exchange high commissioners. Noel-Baker told both Nehru and Pakistan's Liaquat Ali Khan about Dutch-Indonesian arrangements. Nehru 'was evidently impressed with the fact that the Dutch and Indonesians have almost certainly consciously copied our title of High Commissioner and took the point that it might put them both in a difficulty if we made a change': Noel-Baker minute, 27 January 1950, TNA, DO130/107. See also Dulanty secret report 5, 31 January 1950, INA, DFA, London Embassy, unnumbered files, Box 1–14, file 4.

his own an idea that had been floating around the CRO:[38] that the credentials which high commissioners should carry to and from their respective heads of state should be called 'letters of commission'. This would at one and the same time meet India's needs while differentiating Commonwealth from normal diplomatic practice and provide a link with the title 'high commissioner'. This was privately agreed, and on re-accreditation a few months later (in consequence of India having become a republic) Menon was received by the King in the manner of an ambassador (though the CRO made all the arrangements), presenting letters that did not much differ from the traditional letters of credence.[39] Meanwhile, at Menon's request, the British high commissioner's re-accreditation letters were written in 'Olde English' and contained 'plenty of flourishes'.[40] However, Britain and India had failed to consult other Commonwealth states about their idea, and as Nehru had continued to be neglectful of the matter, the rest of the Commonwealth had less than two weeks' notice of its introduction. This gave huge offence. Pakistan was particularly incensed. Believing that India had 'scored yet another point',[41] she belatedly tried to rally support for the view that all that was needed was a letter of introduction from one prime minister to another (which was her own practice). She was fighting a lost cause. In sympathy for her hurt feelings, Australia and Canada did delay their introduction of letters of commission—and Pakistan herself continued, until 1962, to use and demand prime ministerial letters of introduction for all intra-Commonwealth heads of mission.[42] But letters

[38] Francis Cumming-Bruce (Counsellor, New Delhi) did 'not suppose that Mr. Krishna Menon would have clearly developed views on this kind of problem', and attributed it to India's Ministry of External Affairs. However, S. Dutt, a senior Indian official, said Menon 'had in fact his own views on all this': Cumming-Bruce and Frank Roberts minutes, 17 January 1950, TNA, DO133/13.

[39] In 1957 Malaya became independent with her own monarch, the *Yang di-Petuan Agong*. In exchanging high commissioners with Malaya, the Queen addressed the Malayan head of state by his title. The ceremony of presenting letters of commission carried by the two states' high commissioners was the same as for all non-realm high commissioners.

[40] H.R. Horne (Canadian HCO, London), no. 2160, 14 September 1950, NAC, RG25, 6194, 3011-A-40, part 2.3.

[41] CRO memorandum, 'Accreditation of Commonwealth Representatives', November 1950, TNA, DO127/93.

[42] This was despite, first, having become a republic in 1956 and, second, having no prime minister after 1958 following General Ayub Khan's abrogation of the constitution, dismissal of legislative assemblies, and dissolution of political parties. Wanting to play down this breach in democracy, Commonwealth members displayed their usual ingenuity in accommodating one another: they avoided formal accreditation or skirted

of commission for high commissioners going to or coming from states who did not share the same head of state became the norm, as did letters of recall.

Pakistan's stand had a useful consequence in respect of another aspect of the Commonwealth's accreditation arrangements. It spurred Attlee to suggest, in February 1951, that high commissioners exchanged between the King's realms should routinely carry prime ministerial letters of introduction addressed to the receiving states' prime ministers. Hitherto there had been no uniformity of either practice or style. Some high commissioners bore no letters, others had letters from their ministries of external affairs, and those from South Africa and Pakistan had letters from their prime ministers. Attlee's proposal was readily adopted, and inter-realm high commissioners began carrying such letters[43] which were informally presented to the addressee at the first opportunity after arrival.

As regards *agréation*—the seeking of *agrément*, i.e. the receiving state's confirmation that a proposed nomination for the sending state's head of mission would be acceptable—it became the norm in inter-realm appointments for what in effect amounted to *agrément* to be sought from the receiving state's prime minister. But diplomatic-type letters of recall were never deemed necessary for high commissioners of the realms. With regard to appointments involving a republic or another Commonwealth monarchy Britain, at least, came to observe the usual diplomatic procedures, except that the term '*agrément*' was not used.

---

around the President's title in their letters of introduction. But this anomaly could not continue. In 1960 Ceylon did not consult Pakistan before accrediting her high commissioner with letters of commission; in 1961 Britain did likewise; and also in that year Canada decided off her own bat to provide the President with two letters—a formal one using titles, and a more personal one from prime minister Diefenbaker. A few months later Pakistan caved in and announced that in future she wanted to send and receive letters of commission.

[43] However, in 1952 when Norman Robertson returned to London for a second term as Canadian high commissioner, he did not carry a letter to prime minister Churchill 'mainly because he was already so well known in London': H.F. Feaver (Protocol Division) memorandum, 10 March 1953, NAC, RG25, 6371, 3011-A-40, part 3. When Robertson brought the matter to the attention of the CRO, it agreed that he 'needs no introduction': R.R. Sedgewick (head of Constitutional Department) minute, 1 August 1952, TNA, DO35/3214. Meanwhile, 'Mr. Robertson and the Queen appear[ed] to have introduced themselves, as she asked him to lunch the other day': C.H. Ronning (Commonwealth Division) memorandum, 'Letters of Introduction for High Commissioners: Your Memorandum to the Minister', 20 June 1952, NAC, RG25, 4045, 10566–40, vol. 1.

C. The Diplomatic Consequences of Ireland's Departure from the Commonwealth

It was mentioned in the previous chapter that although Ireland's *taoiseach*, Eamon de Valera, regarded the 1936 External Relations Act (ERA) as turning Ireland into a republic, he studiously avoided saying so in public. In 1945, in response to taunts in the *Dáil*, de Valera used the word 'republic' for the first time,[44] and drew attention to the fact that under the ERA the (British) King acted for Ireland in certain external matters—signing treaties and issuing and receiving letters of credence. Critics complained that this suggested Ireland was not completely sovereign—and indeed de Valera might have already worried about this, as he had sometimes left missions in the hands of *chargés d'affaires* rather than appoint new heads of mission armed with credentials from the King, and on at least one occasion had tried to make an appointment with credentials which lacked the King's signature.[45] The 1948 general election resulted in Seán MacBride taking charge of Ireland's Department of External Affairs (DEA). A former chief of staff of the Irish Republican Army (IRA)[46] with impeccable nationalist credentials, MacBride's first request of the DEA's official head, Freddie Boland (SDEA) (so Boland later claimed), was for a list of all the British agents working in the Department.[47] During the election campaign, MacBride's *Clann na Poblachta* (Party of the Republic) had called for the repeal of the ERA, a step that would unambiguously establish Ireland as a republic.

---

[44] Vincent Massey (Canadian HC, London), no. A.305, 27 July 1945, NAC, 4480, 50021-40, part 1.

[45] According to undenied reports, the de Valera government had tried to send a minister plenipotentiary to the Vatican City State bearing such a letter of credence. The Vatican refused to receive the envoy as a minister, granting him the status only of a *chargé d'affaires*. He was soon replaced by a properly-accredited representative—that is, one who bore credentials signed by the King: Turgeon (Canadian HC, Dublin), no. 121, 14 August 1948, NAC, 4480, 50021-40, part 1.

[46] The IRA fought first against the British in the years leading to the Anglo-Irish 'Treaty' of 1921, and then in the civil war of 1922–23 against the establishment under the 'Treaty' of the Irish Free State—to which objection was taken because it was both a dominion and ruled over only 26 of Ireland's 32 counties. The IRA continued to engage in acts of violence against the Irish authorities and, later, against the British authorities both on the British mainland and in Northern Ireland.

'Treaty' is in quotation marks because although in international law the agreement in question was hardly a treaty (Ireland still being part of the British Empire), the Irish regarded it as such.

[47] Patterson (2006) 100.

The new *taoiseach*, John A. Costello, was also 'a trenchant critic'[48] of the ERA, and soon diplomats were reporting that Ireland was likely to repeal the Act. Nonetheless, everyone was taken by surprise at the timing of Costello's announcement in Ottawa in September, not least ministers and officials in Dublin (including MacBride).[49]

There was much less surprise that, unlike India, Ireland showed no disposition to stay in the Commonwealth after becoming a republic. Nor, in contrast to her attitude to India, did Britain feel inclined to put herself out for Ireland. However, Australia, Canada, and New Zealand wanted to retain a connection. Britain agreed to go along with them for, given the intimacy of Anglo-Irish relations and the considerable movement between the two states, she would face enormous practical and administrative difficulties if she had to treat Irish shipping and aircraft as foreign, and Irish citizens as aliens. Hence the proposal that Ireland might, while outside the Commonwealth, be regarded as within it for such purposes of citizenship and trade. This would solve Britain's problems, and it fitted in with Ireland's wish for 'an intermediate position' in which she was 'neither a British nation nor a foreign State' and so retain 'many of the advantages of membership through a factual association based, not only on her historic relations with Commonwealth countries, but on a reciprocal exchange of trade preferences and citizenship rights'.[50] Britain's lawyers, however, saw all sorts of problems about continuing to grant Commonwealth trade preferences. They were far from convinced that it would be internationally accepted that a state which was not in the Commonwealth was anything other

[48] McMahon (2000) 181.

[49] Noel-Baker minute, 27 May 1949, TNA, DO130/104. The announcement was made on the morrow of a dinner at which, it has been suggested, Costello took offence at the dining-table centrepiece being a replica of 'Roaring Meg', a gun which was symbolic of the exclusion from Ireland of six northern Irish counties—Ulster as they are often, but not wholly correctly, called: see Garner (1978) n. 320. Others said he was influenced by the governor-general, who hailed from Ulster, toasting not 'Ireland' but 'The King': *Irish Times*, 10 July 1962. Yet others claimed it was a several-faceted and not fully thought out domestic political manoeuvre: see Lee (1990) 301, Patterson (2006) 96. A colleague thought he must have drunk too much: see McMahon (2000) 185. It has also been said—and denied—that the announcement was a deliberate government decision, which was precipitately made public because of fears of a leak: see O'Brien (1988) 179. Commonwealth prime ministers had 'thought it most unlikely that Eire would in fact take this step': Lester Pearson (secretary of state for external affairs) memorandum, 2 October 1948, NAC, RG2 18, 107, U-10-11 1948 (September–December).

[50] Cabinet conclusions, 12 November 1948, *BDEE 1945–51* IV, 166.

than foreign, and so feared that non-Commonwealth states with whom Britain had most-favoured-nation treaties (in relation to which intra-Commonwealth preferences of a more favourable kind were allowed) would claim the same rights as (foreign) Ireland. Ireland pooh-poohed these legalist worries. She said that as no new rights were being created there was unlikely to be a challenge on most-favoured-nation grounds, and few countries paid attention to the constitutional niceties of the Commonwealth. Anyway, she was prepared to take (what was for her also) a risk. Britain had another worry: that keeping Ireland within the Commonwealth trading system might encourage other groups of states with historic or cultural links to set up similar preferential schemes, and so discriminate against British trade. Britain's doubts were far from completely overcome, but were sufficiently suppressed to enable her to go ahead. Thus at informal Commonwealth talks in Paris in November 1948 (culminating in a sumptuous dinner) it was agreed that when Ireland became a republic on 18 April 1949 (Easter Monday—in tribute to the iconic anti-British rising on that day in 1916) Commonwealth states would neither treat her as a foreign state nor treat her citizens as foreigners. It was 'a very Irish solution!'[51]

There was, for Britain, still a considerable fly in the ointment. As a republic, Ireland would expect traditional diplomatic titles to be used for heads of mission accredited to and by Ireland. This was politically important for her, as well as being the final expression of her long campaign against the Commonwealth title of high commissioner. She was willing not to press for the reaccreditation (with normal diplomatic titles) of the high commissioners already in post (especially as the majority was likely soon to be replaced), but she wanted there to be no new high commissioners to or from Dublin after 18 April. For her part, Britain wanted to do nothing which would prejudice her opposition (hopeless though it increasingly seemed) to India's insistence on exchanging ambassadors after she became a republic in January 1950. The appearance at this time of ambassadors from Commonwealth states in republican Dublin, and of Irish ambassadors in their capitals, would weaken Britain's case. Nor would such a development sit easily alongside Britain's emphasis, in respect of trading arrangements, that

---

[51] Garner (1978) 320. He adds, and another former CRO official confirmed: 'The main discussion took place at a small dinner at the Ritz whose gastronomic excellence contributed to the resolution of difference and of which the astronomic cost could not be questioned in the light of the political results': 320 n. and private information.

Ireland's departure from the Commonwealth did not thereby put her in the usual sort of foreign relationship *vis-à-vis* its members—and that, indeed, they were hardly foreign to each other at all! Until, therefore, the Indian issue was resolved Britain wanted to avoid any change in the relevant diplomatic titles.

She tried to persuade Ireland 'to go slow',[52] and in an informal way sought support from the rest of the Commonwealth. South Africa and India thought it should be up to Ireland to decide, and Australia was uncooperative. On the other hand, New Zealand and Ceylon could almost certainly be relied upon; Pakistan, too, if she thought India would benefit from any Irish action; and Canada was believed to be sympathetic. But especially as there could be no question of organising a pressure group, the states who really mattered were the ones who were already represented in Dublin—Canada and Australia—and the one who intended to make an early such appointment: India. It was India who posed an immediate and serious problem, it being apprehended she would 'sell the pass' by appointing a minister plenipotentiary, and do so even before Ireland had quit the Commonwealth.[53] '[S]pecial representations' were made in New Delhi,[54] but to no avail. At the beginning of 1949 Ireland made an exception to her usual practice of refusing to accept non-resident heads of mission who were based in Britain (she feared that Dublin could easily become 'a sort of diplomatic suburb of London'), agreeing that India's high commissioner in London, Krishna Menon, could also to be accredited to her as a minister.[55] Menon claimed he had told Attlee informally about it. However, Whitehall knew nothing until the CRO was asked to transmit a telegram from Nehru to the King asking—as was usual for diplomatic appointments, but previously unheard of in respect of intra-Commonwealth ones—for his approval. The CRO assumed Nehru had not realised the 'awkward implications' of his telegram.[56] But Nehru was unmoved by Britain's appeals not to give Menon a diplomatic title, although in

---

[52] CRO circular telegram Y44, 7 February 1949, TNA, DO35/4229; 'Titles of Representatives Exchanged between Eire and Commonwealth Countries', enclosure in Sir Cecil Syers (DUS) circular letter, 22 March 1949, TNA, DO35/4229.

[53] Syers minute, 13 January 1949, TNA, DO35/4229.

[54] 'Titles of Representatives Exchanged between Eire and Commonwealth Countries'.

[55] Boland (Irish ambassador, London)-Seán Nunan (SDEA), 23 June 1952, INA, DFA, Secretary's Office, P.236).

[56] Liesching minute, 22 January 1949, TNA, DO121/74.

deference to Attlee, and despite Menon's huge eagerness to proceed to Dublin, the appointment was delayed until after Ireland had left the Commonwealth. Then, however, to Britain's consternation and Ireland's delight, Nehru made Menon an ambassador, the first Dublin had ever received. When he presented his credentials at the end of July, he was given appropriately 'gushing'[57] treatment and granted precedence over all other envoys except the *doyen* (who, as was usual in Catholic countries, was the Papal nuncio). This was entirely in order since Ireland had not been a party to the 1948 decision about high commissioners having equal status with ambassadors. But it was galling for Britain's representative, still in the second class with high commissioners and ministers plenipotentiary, to be outranked by an Indian. Ireland's part in this development was interpreted as an expression of displeasure at Britain's delay in exchanging ambassadors. When the American legation became an embassy in the spring of 1950, the position of Britain's man in Dublin became more difficult.

In October 1949 Ireland moved on Canada. Pointing out that as far as Ireland was concerned, high commissioners were 'in a "twilight zone" ',[58] Boland said that Dublin wanted to replace Hearne (who had been in Ottawa for a decade) but would not move him until she was sure that his successor would be an ambassador. Canada had no objections on grounds of protocol or policy, and thought it was up to Dublin whether she wanted to risk her tariff preferences being challenged in consequence of this action. Britain asked Lester Pearson, (the secretary of state for external affairs, 1948–57) to stay his hand while ministers considered the parallel question of exchanging ambassadors with India, and also so that Britain could set consultation in motion. Pearson 'readily agreed'[59] to a ten-day delay but said he could not hold back much longer. London then went silent and remained so; after eight increasingly embarrassed weeks her high commissioner, Sir Alexander Clutterbuck, said he could no longer justifiably try to stop the Canadians granting *agrément* for Seán Murphy, who had already been nominated as ambassador. Even then, Britain tried to get Canada to wait until

[57] Measures memorandum, 'Exchange of Ambassadors with Ireland', August 1949, NAC, RG25, 4045, 10566–40, vol. 1.

[58] D.M. Johnson (Canadian AHC, Dublin), no. 190, 3 October 1949, NAC, RG25, 4045, 10566–40, vol. 1.

[59] Sir Alexander Clutterbuck (British HC, Ottawa) telegram 1251, 24 October 1949, TNA, DO35/3212, DO127/92.

the 'major question [of India] is settled'.[60] Canada refused. The Irish case was 'clear' and distinct from that of India and, having already held back for a long while, Canada would no longer delay Hearne's departure.[61] On 31 December Hearne was told that the Cabinet had agreed to accept Murphy as ambassador. A few days later the King (as Canada's head of state) gave his approval.

At Canada's request, no publicity was given to the appointment until Ottawa and Dublin had agreed (informally and off the record) on the wording of Murphy's letters of credence. This was a potential minefield, as Ireland would not provide credentials referring to herself as the 'Republic of Ireland' (the name used in Britain's 1949 Republic of Ireland Act), and deemed 'Éire' unacceptable when the English language was being used. She insisted on 'Ireland' which, according to Article 4 of Ireland's Constitution, was the name of the state in the English language. Agreement was reached without difficulty. Canada had been using 'Ireland' since 1937, and thought it appropriate to use the form Ireland considered correct. But there was also the question of how Canada's head of state was to be addressed. At that time the King's title still described him as sovereign of Great Britain 'and Ireland'. But the DEA's under-secretary agreed it would be absurd for the President of Ireland to accredit an ambassador to the King of Ireland. 'You can strike out the reference to Ireland [in the King's title] if you desire', he declared. 'I don't know what the lawyers will say, but that's my view.'[62] Thus it was that Murphy arrived bearing a letter of credence from the President of Ireland to, simply, 'King George the Sixth'. Buckingham Palace was not amused, nor by the fact that the credentials, written in Irish, were forwarded to the King without a translation.

Canada's high commissioner to Ireland, Justice Turgeon, could not immediately be translated into an ambassador because he was not in Dublin for the first half of 1950 (being in Canada chairing a royal commission). His absence, combined with comments from Murphy about Canada being 'pathetically pro-British on anything to do with Ireland',[63] made the Irish suspect that, like Australia, Canada intended

---

[60] CRO circular telegram, 23 December 1949, TNA, PREM8/1333, DO127/92.

[61] Clutterbuck telegrams 1504 & 1505, 24 December 1949, TNA, DO127/93.

[62] Arnold Heeney in Hearne-Boland, personal & confidential, 12 January 1950, INA, DFA, London Embassy, unnumbered files, Box 1–14, file 4.

[63] Murphy-Boland, 19 May 1950, INA, DFA, Secretary's Office, P.12/5(a), Ottawa Embassy 1950–1963. Like Kiernan in Australia, Murphy paid careful attention to religion and background. In one of his first reports, he commented on the number

to keep her representation 'on a low level' until the Commonwealth had reached agreement on simultaneously turning high commissioners into ambassadors.[64] (The news that Canada's popular acting high commissioner was to be transferred heightened Irish suspicion that a hostile conspiracy was afoot.) In fact, Turgeon was 'very anxious' to return as an ambassador once he was free to do so[65] and in mid-1950, after consulting London and Canberra, the decision to that effect was taken and *agrément* swiftly granted. Whereupon Canada ran into difficulty over the wording of Turgeon's credentials. London took a very close interest in this, fussing in particular about the implications for Northern Ireland of the receiving state being referred to simply as Ireland (rather than the Republic of Ireland, which Britain deemed to be the correct name). There was also the question of the terminology to be used for the head of the sending state. Canada, recalling the Irish precedent (which had been followed by India), proposed that the King should choose between signing as 'King of Canada' (which she preferred) or 'King George the Sixth'. The Palace strongly objected. The King had only one legal title said his secretary. No other could be used. In this matter the King, as the head of the sending state, was in a stronger position than he had been with regard to Ireland's despatch of an ambassador to Canada. This was because it was customary to set out in full the title of the sending head of state, whereas that was not necessarily so with regard to the title of the head of the receiving state. With Turgeon about to set sail for Dublin, Canada explained apologetically that she had run up against insurmountable statutory difficulties. She had to use the full royal title. Rather than have Turgeon return as a high commissioner, Ireland capitulated and Turgeon was

of people of Irish origin who were 'very highly placed' in federal and provincial governments. In the DEA alone, Pearson was 'the son of a North of Ireland Methodist Preacher, Mr. Heeney the son of a Church of Ireland Parson, and Mr. Escott Reid half Scoth[*sic*] half Irish but of Presbyterian stock. All very nice fellows but I doubt if they will be much use to you. I dont[*sic*] think that your predecessor found them very sympathetic': Murphy-Boland, 27 May 1950, INA, DFA, Secretary's Office, P. 12/5(a), Ottawa Embassy 1950–1963.

[64] Boland-Murphy, 24 May 1950, INA, Secretary's Office, P.12/5A. However, a few years later Boland thought that 'of all the Commonwealth countries other than Britain, Canada is the one most interested in Anglo-Irish relations and most likely to play a useful and sympathetic role in connection with the Partition problem if the opportunity should ever arise': Boland-Nunan, 2 January 1953, INA, DFA, Secretary's Office, P.12/14a/1.

[65] Arnold Heeney (under-secretary, DEA) memorandum, 25 May 1950, NAC, RG25, 4045, 10566–40, vol. 1.

accredited by the King of Ireland to the President of Ireland.[66] He returned to so splendid a welcome—including a 19-gun salute as his boat passed Dun Laoghaire—that the President protested that the forthcoming credentials ceremony would look as if it was of 'subsidiary importance'.[67]

By this time Britain was agreeable to an exchange of ambassadors with Ireland. In 1949 MacBride had reluctantly agreed not to make a change in London until Ireland's long-serving high commissioner, John Dulanty, had departed. For her part, Britain had hastened to replace her representative, Lord Rugby, just before Ireland became a republic, though she did so with a show of goodwill by pandering to Ireland's strong desire to receive the new representative, Sir Gilbert Laithwaite, in the manner of an ambassador—complete with credentials. Whenever the subject of re-accrediting Ireland's high commissioner and Laithwaite as ambassadors was raised thereafter, Britain took the line that while she was not opposed to it, the time was not yet ripe. By May 1950 this argument was wearing very thin. First, exchanging ambassadors with Ireland had no obvious implications for intra-Commonwealth exchanges. Second, so far there had been no challenges to Ireland's preferential trading status, and it was not for others to tell Ireland not to take risks on her own behalf; moreover, a recent Irish-American commercial treaty had accepted the continuation of Ireland's Commonwealth preferences. Third, India and Canada had already broken ranks. Fourth, Laithwaite was discomforted by his lack of ambassadorial status. It caused him embarrassment, limited his effectiveness, and was a source of friction. He urged London to recognise that the question was essentially political rather than technical and that it was very important to Ireland. But fifth, and most importantly, Dulanty wanted to retire as an ambassador and he was well-liked. As Noel-Baker put it, he had been an 'admirable' Irish High Commissioner and 'at the same time a very good friend indeed to the United Kingdom'. If Britain could help him, she should.[68] When, at the end of June, the CRO learned that

[66] This was after 'an exhaustive weekend's study of *titres de pretention* satisfied them that sovereigns whose titles laid claim to territories actually held by other could still have diplomatic relations with those monarchs': Laithwaite (British representative)-Liesching telegram 26, 27 June 1950, TNA, DO130/107.

[67] McDunphy (secretary, *Taoiseach*'s Department)-Nunan, 18 July 1950, INA, Department of Taoiseach, General (S) files, S.11797B.

[68] Noel-Baker—Dulanty conversation, 27 January 1950, TNA, DO121/121.

Dulanty was going to retire earlier than expected—at the end of the following month—it was necessary to move swiftly. This was perhaps fortunate since Britain and Ireland might otherwise have got bogged down in a disagreement over the wording of credentials.

Ireland, of course, wanted Laithwaite's new ambassadorial credentials to be addressed to the President of Ireland and to refer to 'Ireland' in the body of the text. Britain refused. 'Ireland' was deemed to include the whole of the island, and Attlee had decreed in May 1949 that Britain should stand firm on the wording of her 1949 Ireland Act and whenever possible use the term 'Irish Republic' (or at least 'Republic of Ireland'). Britain also initially thought she needed to use full title of the King and the 'correct' (as she saw it) title for the President (i.e. 'President of the Republic of Ireland'). However, in order to avoid a quarrel the junior CRO minister, Patrick Gordon Walker and MacBride agreed that each would use what they considered to be the correct title for their own head of state and country, and Britain would, like Canada, accept Irish credentials addressed to 'His Majesty King George the Sixth' *tout court*. By mid-July the King had given his approval and on 26 July, less than a week before Dulanty retired, he and Laithwaite presented their credentials. Interestingly, Dulanty's credentials did not bear the usual reference to the existence of 'friendly relations' between the two states. That was deemed inappropriate in the Anglo-Irish context. They spoke, instead, of 'strengthening relations'.[69] In her next ambassador's letters of credence, Britain 'retaliated' by referring simply to the existence of diplomatic relations between the two states rather than, as was usual, to such relations 'happily' existing![70]

Later problems

Although Ireland was now outside the Commonwealth, the kind of intra-Commonwealth problems which had arisen earlier over the exchange of heads of mission continued to reverberate for a decade or so. They arose in Ireland's relations with Britain, Canada, and Australia, constituting a kind of grumbling appendix to the Irish side of the high commissioner story.

---

[69] W.P. Fay (assistant secretary, DEA) minute, 18 April 1952, INA, DFA, London Embassy, F100/2/29. The same wording was used in Boland's September 1950 credentials.

[70] Nunan-Murphy, 22 May 1952, 317/51, INA, DFA Canberra, Box 16–30, B.1.2 I.

In 1951 Sir Walter Hankinson was nominated to replace Laithwaite as Britain's ambassador at Dublin, and the CRO drafted letters of credence similar to those carried by Laithwaite in 1950. But de Valera was now back in office and taking a strict line on credentials. Any whose wording did not entirely conform to Irish requirements had to be redone. Accordingly, and despite a warning that the CRO was also going to dig in its heels, Frank Aiken (minister for external affairs, 1951–54) demanded that Hankinson's draft credentials be amended. An impasse was reached. The CRO refused to agree to the wording Aiken wanted and Aiken refused to budge. The date for Hankinson's departure came and went. Eventually, after a month, Liesching (the senior CRO official) affably suggested to Ireland's ambassador, Freddie Boland, that he might be asked to go on leave. ('There is no reason why he should be here if we cannot have an Ambassador ourselves in Dublin.')[71] Boland personally pleaded with de Valera to recognise that Ireland would be in a very uncomfortable position if they found themselves with a Conservative commonwealth secretary advised by officials whom they had alienated. (Britain was on the eve of a general election which the Labour government was likely to lose.) De Valera took the point and speedily agreed to Liesching's suggestion that they both use the names of their heads of state without any elaboration (i.e. Ireland would address her letters to 'His Majesty King George the Sixth' and Britain would address her letters, in Irish, to 'President Seán T. O'Ceallaigh'). At the customary dinner following Hankinson's presentation of his credentials, toasts were given by Aiken to 'His Majesty King George the Sixth' and by Hankinson to 'The President'.[72]

Ireland said that she had 'exceptionally'[73] agreed to the wording of Hankinson's credentials because, as close neighbours, Britain and Ireland were 'compelled... to remain in constant contact',[74] and having 'diplomatic relations at the highest level' would 'help remove partition'.[75] The exceptional, however, became the rule between the two, not least

[71] Liesching minute 28/51 for Attlee, 29 September 1951, TNA, DO35/3986.

[72] In 1950 Laithwaite and the *tainaiste* (deputy prime minister) made the same toasts.

[73] British Embassy, Dublin-Norman Costar (a senior CRO official), 15 October 1951, TNA, DO35/3986.

[74] Michael Rynne (legal adviser, DEA)-W.T. Doig (Australian CDA, Dublin) conversation, 29 October 1953, DFA, London Embassy, Box 16–30, 1953.

[75] Australian Associated Press Report, c. March 1954, INA, DFA, Canberra Embassy, Box 16–30, 1954.

because the royal title that was adopted for Britain's new Queen in 1953 was if anything even more offensive to Irish susceptibilities than the old one: it referred directly to partition by declaring Queen Elizabeth to be Queen of 'Northern Ireland'—the six counties which Britain ruled and to which Ireland laid claim. This led to Ireland refusing to send the customary special mission to the coronation. (She was represented by her ambassador, who did not go beyond the 'ordinary courtesies',[76] and made a 'contemptible effort' to wreck joint Commonwealth celebrations in Dublin by 'drawing off' heads of mission to another important event.)[77] But so far as future Anglo-Irish diplomatic exchanges were concerned, the 1951 formula was used, and succeeded in avoiding another impasse.[78]

Canada and Australia, however, ran into difficulties over the name of the Irish state. It is customary on the advent of a new monarch to reaccredit all existing envoys. Canada agreed to reaccredit Turgeon to 'Seán T. Ó'Ceallaigh, President of Ireland', but the Queen queried it, saying 'Am I not sovereign of part of that territory?'[79] Canada decided not to press the Palace, and arranged with Ireland that there should be no re-accreditation. But this was only a stop-gap. In 1952 Turgeon had already reached the retiring age of 75 and three years' later, when he was becoming frail and wanted to live in Portugal (to which he was also accredited), Pearson decided it was time to make a stand. He told the House of Commons that 'the correct form of address for the head of the Irish state is the President of Ireland'.[80] Having thus

---

[76] Aiken in the *Dáil*, 29 April 1953, INA, DFA, P238.

[77] She issued late invitations to a ceremony conferring the freedom of Dublin on President O'Kelly and Cardinal D'Alton, the Primate of All Ireland. When the Papal nuncio insisted on sticking to his original acceptance of the Commonwealth invitation, the civic ceremony was brought forward and curtailed, and a motor cycle escort rushed the diplomatic corps to the Commonwealth garden party.

[78] When, in 1996, Ireland's head of state, for the first time, paid an official visit to London, the problem of title was avoided by referring to her as 'Her Excellency President Mary Robinson'; and Britain's sovereignty over Ulster was symbolised when she arrived at Buckingham Palace by the guard of honour being formed from the Irish Guards—a British Army regiment: Goldstein (1977) 16. The 1998 British-Irish (Good Friday) agreement led in 2000 to Britain using 'Ireland' in most routine and formal documents, including her Diplomatic List. Ireland reciprocated in 2001 by switching from 'Great Britain' to 'United Kingdom' in the Dublin Diplomatic List. However, in certain legal contexts, including credentials, the two countries continue the practice hammered out half a century ago of agreeing to differ.

[79] Eoin MacWhite-Seán Ronan (DEA), 23 January 1963, INA, DFA, Secretary's Office, P276.

[80] House of Commons, 10 March 1955, 1890.

made Canada's position clear, he assured the Irish that the credentials of the next ambassador, Alfred Rive, would be in the desired form. The Australians 'gratuitously'[81] objected, and the British raised various difficulties, referring to the adverse effect this would have on Northern Irish feelings, its discourtesy to the Queen, and the legal contradiction which would be involved. For although the Queen's Canadian title did not mention Northern Ireland, by signing credentials addressed to the President of Ireland she would be recognising Dublin's claim to an area which, in her capacity as Britain's Queen, was part of her realms.[82] Nevertheless, Pearson insisted it was for the Canadian government alone to determine what its policy was. If the wording of the credentials would gravely embarrass the Queen, Canada would reluctantly ask her governor-general to sign (which Britain's lord chancellor, commonwealth secretary, and a home office parliamentary under-secretary all thought might be preferable). The Palace suggested a ministerial exchange of letters. Canada refused and again threatened to have credentials issued by the governor-general. The Queen capitulated, and signed Rive's letter—which was in Irish. It opened with Her Majesty's full Canadian title, was addressed 'To His Excellency T. Ó'Ceallaigh *Uachtarán na hEireann*', and called the state 'Ireland'.[83] At Ottawa's request, the credentials were given no publicity, but the British were put out to learn that they could be seen in Ireland's Parliamentary Library.

Meanwhile Ireland and Australia were 'feuding like Kilkenny cats'.[84] When Labor lost office in December 1949 and Robert Menzies became prime minister, the Irish representative in Canberra, T.J. Kiernan, predicted a complete change in Australia's approach to Ireland, saying the attitude of the parties in the coalition government was 'not so much the English Conservative attitude of 1950 as the English Conservative attitude of the 1890's'.[85] There would be 'no independent policy in any

[81] Irish CDA, Canberra-W.A. Irwin (Canadian HC, Canberra) conversation, 20 September 1955, A/2/2/ INA, DFA, Embassy Canberra, Box 16–30, 1955.

[82] Although a reservation could be made when accepting credentials, the writer of credentials could not effectively attach one: Annex to CRO memorandum, 'Letters of Credence of United Kingdom and Canadian Ambassadors in Dublin', November 1955, TNA, DO127/92.

[83] CRO memorandum, 'Letters of credence of United Kingdom and Canadian ambassadors in Dublin'.

[84] *Truth* (Sydney) referring to Irish-Australian differences over the style and title of ambassadors, 14 September 1958.

[85] 1949 Annual Report, INA, DFA, Embassy Canberra, Box 16–30, A/18/12.

matter of external affairs'.[86] He seemed to be right, as the new minister for external affairs, Percy Spender, displayed a wounding indifference towards Ireland, failing to replace Dignam (the Australian high commissioner) when his term of office expired in April 1950,[87] and continuing officially to address Kiernan as 'High Commissioner' after he had been reaccredited as an ambassador. Kiernan's new status had been grudgingly agreed by Spender following Britain's exchange of ambassadors with Ireland. But his presentation of ambassadorial credentials was unconvincingly postponed;[88] and when he returned from vacation to take up his new office in November 1950 he received a cold reception: he was not met at the airport, and neither Menzies nor Spender attended the credentials ceremony, which was 'cut to the bare bone of necessary formality' and not reported in the press.[89] Moreover, he was put at the bottom of the table of precedence.[90]

---

[86] 1948 Annual Report, INA, DFA, Embassy Canberra, Box 16–30, A/18/1.

[87] As the Australian *chargé d'affaires* was used as a kind of roving ambassador for work in Europe, the Irish felt most insulted. It seemed to show 'contempt for Ireland' to use Dublin as a 'home base for Australia's diplomacy-on-the-cheap to elsewhere': undated and unsigned memorandum, 2/302/1, INA, DFA, Canberra Embassy, Box 16–30, 1954; O'Farrell (1980) 16. Spender's excuses ranged from the lack of suitable appointee, the need for economy, a *chargé d'affaires* was sufficient, and the impossibility of deciding hurriedly on such an important appointment: Kiernan minute, 29 January 1952, INA, DFA Canberra, Box 16–30, B.1.2 I; Rynne-Doig conversation with Doig, 29 October 1953, INA, DFA, Canberra Embassy, Box 16–30, 1953; O'Farrell (1980) 15.

[88] The reason, according to a 'very ill at ease and shifty' Spender, was that many Australians with Irish blood would 'be annoyed at any change of status in Australia that suggested being foreign'. Moreover, according to the SDEA, John Burton, there would have to be legislation before ambassadors were exchanged since the relevant Australian law (which the DEA could not trace!) stated that Australia should be represented by a high commissioner in the then Irish Free State: Kiernan-memorandum, 27 April 1950, INA, DFA, Secretary's Office, Confidential Reports from Canberra Legation, P.12/10.

[89] The governor-general, who was 'friendly as usual' wore morning dress like Kiernan but the 'stand-in' government ministers wore lounge suits, and there was no press coverage whatsoever: Kiernan-Nunan, 13 November 1950, INA, DFA, Canberra, Box 16–30, B.1.2 I.

[90] The French and American ambassadors had complained to the Taiwanese *doyen* (Kan Nai Kuang) when Kiernan was placed third in order of precedence during the Remembrance Day ceremony in November 1950 (after Kan and the British high commissioner, and before the ambassadors). The DEA also asked Kan if Kiernan should now replace him as *doyen*. Kan said Kiernan was covered by the 1948 understanding about Commonwealth countries not becoming deans and that Kiernan's recent presentation of letters of credence eliminated any claim to precedence based on his time in Canberra as Ireland's 'representative'. Kiernan 'should accept his place as the junior Ambassador'. This dashed the hopes of ambassadors whose governments had recognised the People's Republic of China. They had hoped Kiernan might relieve

Further salt was rubbed into this wound by Australia's lack of enthusiasm for being represented in Dublin. Spender, and his successor, Richard Casey (1951–60), were uninterested in Ireland and did not think Australia needed an ambassador there[91] (the High Commission having been translated into an Embassy in step with Kiernan becoming an ambassador in Canberra). However, in late 1952 Casey decided to appoint one. Such a step might win Irish Catholic votes, and it would be useful to have a Dublin-based head of mission to undertake roving ambassadorial work.[92] Being loathe to waste a good career officer in what he considered to be a marginal post, in mid-1953 Casey chose Dominic Paul McGuire, a Catholic author and lecturer, and a friend of Menzies. But McGuire never got to Dublin. Ireland was willing to accept that his credentials should bear the Queen's Australian royal title, since governments 'should agree to accept the title legalised under the law of the other'.[93] But by the same token the credentials should be addressed in the manner regarded as proper by Ireland. Thus they should be sent to the 'President of Ireland'. Casey refused. He would neither take sides against Britain nor embarrass the Queen by asking her to sign credentials implying recognition of Dublin's claim to Ireland's six northern counties. He pointed out that recently he had, on behalf of the receiving state, 'passively' accepted Kiernan's reaccreditation by the 'President of Ireland' because the Australian government 'were not sticklers for nice formalities'.[94] Surely, he thought, Australia as the sending state could be allowed to address Ireland's head of state in the same manner as Britain had been allowed to do in 1951: 'President Seán T. O'Ceallaigh'. But de Valera was adamant. Ireland's wording

---

them of the embarrassment of having to deal with a Taiwanese *doyen*: Croft (Canadian AHC) minute, 15 November 1950, NAC, RG25, 3997, 10062–40.

[91] The DEA was short-staffed and the Australian *chargé d'affaires* in Dublin had told Casey that there was 'practically nothing to do'. Australia could, like India, service the post from London: Hudson (1986) 280.

[92] 20 to 25 per cent of Australians were Irish or of Irish descent. The Irish-born, octogenarian Catholic Archbishop of Brisbane was said to have promised to support the government in return for the appointment of an Australian ambassador at Dublin: O'Farrell (1980) 15–16.

[93] Kiernan-Rynne, 18 August 1953, INA, DFA, Canberra Embassy, Box 16–30, 1953. The Queen's Australian title was 'Elizabeth the Second, by the Grace of God of the United Kingdom, Australia . . .', and Australian law explicitly stated that this reference to the United Kingdom included Northern Ireland. In 1973 Australia dropped the reference to the United Kingdom (and also to the Queen as 'Defender of the Faith').

[94] 'Summary Account of Exchange which took place between the Irish and Australian governments in regard to the Accreditation of Mr. Dominic Paul McGuire as Australian ambassador at Dublin', INA, DFA, Embassy Canberra, Box 16–30, B.1.2.

had to be used. She was willing to assist Australia by accepting the Irish rendering of the President's title, *Uachtarán na hÉireann* (in the Roman or Gaelic script), but Australia rejected this subterfuge. The suggestion that the credentials be couched informally as a *lettre de cabinet* also fell by the wayside, as Ireland insisted that it be addressed to the 'President of Ireland'. Other proposals put forward by one side were found wanting by the other. A last-ditch Irish suggestion of a ministerial letter of appointment was initially welcomed by Menzies and the Palace, because it would be possible to avoid using the title of the President (as well as the also-vexatious issue of the name of the state). But then there was some tiresome tussling. Ireland accepted that it was for the Queen to appoint McGuire to the rank of ambassador, but wanted it to be clear that it was not the Queen but the Australian government which was sending him to Dublin; and for that to be satisfactorily clear Ireland demanded an 'official assurance'[95] that McGuire's personal commission of appointment from the Queen contained no mention of Ireland or Dublin. Casey refused, saying that a commission of appointment was a private document. By now he had had enough, and in January 1954 terminated the negotiations, McGuire went instead to Rome, and Australia and Ireland engaged in mutual recriminations. A few months later Kiernan went on leave and did not return. He was not replaced, the Irish Embassy in Canberra being left in the hands of a *chargé d'affaires* (the Australian Embassy in Dublin having been in a like state since 1950). As Ireland saw it, Australia was interested in her only as a means of serving some internal political purpose.

It was another decade before Australia and Ireland overcame their principled stands. Early in 1964 Ireland made an approach, Australia had a minister for external affairs who wanted a solution, and there ensued secret, serious, swift, and successful negotiations: each would address their ambassador's credentials as the other required—and at the same time disclaim acceptance of the significance the other attached to the title used! When, in mid-May, Ireland's Dr. Eoin MacWhite presented his credentials and Kiernan's letter of recall, Menzies was 'extremely affable', saying '"thank God I have lived to see this day" with such warmth and feeling that I might almost have believed him'.[96]

[95] Kiernan-Alan Watt (SDEA), 18 January 1954, INA, DFA, Embassy Canberra, Box 16–30, 1954, 2/302/1.

[96] MacWhite minute, 19 May 1964, INA, DFA, B.1.2, 1964. MacWhite was soon protesting about the pressure of work, and asked the DEA to 'abandon its habit of treating this mission as its lowest priority simply because it is the furthest away':

Australia's appointment came some six months or so later, when Menzies demonstrated the importance he attached to relations with Ireland by sending a cabinet minister to head the Embassy, occasioning an outpouring of 'genuine goodwill'.[97]

D. Diplomatic Immunity

In the late 1940s one substantive difference in the position of high commissioners and traditionally-titled diplomats was that the former (and their staff) lacked diplomatic immunity. As has been seen in the last chapter, this had not given rise to any real difficulties. But a court case involving the South African trade commissioner had led the CRO and FO to decide that Britain's former objections to granting immunity were no longer valid, and that it would be desirable to rectify this sooner rather than later.

However, an inter-departmental committee of officials that had been considering the status of high commissioners advised, in 1948, to the contrary. First, it said, the grant of immunity would be constitutionally inappropriate. Diplomatic immunity implied foreign allegiance, being derived from the fact that sovereigns did not sit in judgment over each other (nor, therefore, over their representatives); but high commissioners, and their staffs, were all (at that time) British subjects, and hence owed allegiance to the same sovereign. Second, to grant immunity to this group of subjects would undesirably discriminate against all the others. Third, this group was not small, so privileging it would be noticed. There had already been a sharp rise in the number of those entitled to immunity in Britain (from just over 1,000 in 1938 to getting on for 3,000), and giving it to high commission staff would increase the figure by about half—including 'large numbers of relatively subordinate staff, especially in the case of the High Commissioners for India and Pakistan'.[98] Fourth, diplomatic immunity was unpopular and its need

MacWhite-Gallagher, personal, 1 July 1964, INA, DFA Canberra, Box 1–15, Diplomatic Staff, General, 1964–5, A.3.2.

[97] Hugh S. Robertson-MacWhite, 21 January 1965, INA, DFA, B.13: 'Australian Diplomatic Representatives in Ireland, 1959–1965'. In the Australian context this was 'an element of great prestige', political appointees usually going only to London, Washington, and Wellington: MacWhite-SDEA, 15 October 1964, INA, DFA, Embassy Canberra, Box 16–30, B.1.3.

[98] Cabinet Official Committee on Commonwealth Relations, Status of Commonwealth High Commissioners and of Governors-General, Chairman's note of conclusions of meeting on 24 May 1948, C.R.(O)(48)9, TNA, CAB134/118.

was not widely understood. Obtaining parliamentary approval for the necessary legislation would be bound to arouse controversy.[99] Finally, states could be expected to waive their diplomats' immunity in serious criminal offences; and in minor cases public authorities did not bring criminal proceedings. It was therefore 'open to doubt' whether the grant of immunity was necessary.[100] The matter was put on one side.

But only a year later the government found it could no longer easily ignore the issue. If, as expected, ambassadors were exchanged with India and Ireland, they and their staff would automatically receive immunity, and high commissioners would have a powerful grievance if they were not similarly treated. Moreover, there could be serious problems if the CRO was unable to prevent a civil action against a Commonwealth diplomat. Difficulties had already arisen. The Pakistani high commissioner had been cross about several cases involving members of his High Commission and raised the subject with the prime minister, and India had protested strongly about the affront to her national prestige and international standing when Mr. Thivy, her representative in Malaya, was denied immunity.[101] Worryingly for Britain, India's perturbation over Thivy was strengthening her apparent determination to turn high commissioners into ambassadors, who would then enjoy what she regarded as their proper status and position. Meanwhile, Britain was also obliged to recognise that there was a definite danger in Asia

> that if bad relations developed, vexatious legal actions might be brought in the local courts, proceedings before which are frequently prolonged, and can be deliberately drawn out by executive interference, or prevented [*sic.*] by false witnesses. The High Commissioner for India has expressed strongly the opinion that diplomatic immunity should be secured for the representatives of the United Kingdom in India and the case is certainly as strong in Pakistan.[102]

---

[99] The lord chancellor in the 1945–51 government later said that this subject had caused him 'a great deal of trouble'. He 'used to receive protests from all quarters of the House about the vast extension which was taking place in diplomatic immunity': House of Lords *debs.*, 11 March 1952, 586.

[100] Cabinet Official Committee on Commonwealth Relations, 24 May 1948, C.R. (O)(48)9.

[101] India had a number of representatives in British colonial territories: commissioners in Nairobi, Suva, Singapore, Port Louis, and Port of Spain; and an agent in Kuala Lumpur.

[102] CRO memorandum, 'Diplomatic Immunity for Commonwealth Representatives', 14 October 1949, TNA, DO35/2225. See also Addison memorandum, 'Title and Status of High Commissioners'.

On Attlee's instructions, the Thivy case was referred to the government's law officers. They pointed out that even if the members of high commissions had had diplomatic immunity, Thivy would not have been entitled to it as he was based outside the seat of the metropolitan government; at best, therefore, he could have claimed consular immunity, which would not have protected him from being sued. However, they went on to recommend that Britain should seriously consider giving diplomatic immunity to all Commonwealth representatives. Traditionally, diplomatic immunity was only appropriate for the representatives of foreign states. But

> in practice the several countries of the Commonwealth although not regarding each other as foreign are independent and sovereign, *par inter pares*, and incapable of ordering their relations with each other save by negotiation [which is] normally carried out by the High Commissioners who are . . . in effect diplomatic representatives. It is true that they are not accredited and received in the same way as Ambassadors, but this is a matter of procedure. They are . . . received . . . as the representatives of their States and for the purpose of conducting relations with those States. . . . [They] do now perform *inter se* what is in principle essentially a diplomatic function to which immunities could—we think should—quite properly be attached.[103]

The government accepted the law officers' advice and so did the rest of the Commonwealth. The legislative process was therefore started. However, despite the best efforts of the commonwealth secretary, Patrick Gordon Walker, it went slowly. Both intra-governmental consultation and the drafting process took a measured course. Parliamentary time for the bill was hard to find. Two general elections intervened. The new, Conservative, government which emerged from the second of them ran into trouble with its predecessor's draft, and the commonwealth secretary had difficulty persuading his colleagues to agree to the legislation.[104] Further delay resulted from a financial crisis and the death of the King in February 1952. But by the end of March of that year the Diplomatic

---

[103] Hartley Shawcross and Frank Soskice (law officers of the Crown) report, 28 July 1949, annex B to CP(49)226, TNA, CAB129/37.

[104] Ministers were not happy about introducing controversial legislation and they objected to extending immunity to members of the Commonwealth family. Their objections were echoed in Parliament, where there were complaints about the legislation detracting from the Commonwealth 'family relationship' and about the inclusion in the bill of the Irish ambassador (whom Britain neither regarded nor treated as foreign): Wilson (1957) 615.

Immunities (Commonwealth and Republic of Ireland) Act had entered into force. Most Commonwealth countries passed equivalent legislation: South Africa had already done it, Australia and New Zealand did so in 1952, Canada in 1954, and Pakistan in 1957. India initially forgot to give special attention to high commissioners in legislation relating to the position of the hundreds of rulers of former princely states which were now a part of India, but made amends in 1956. Ceylon continued to rely on administrative action. Where legislation was absent it did 'not appear to have created any practical difficulties'.[105]

Interestingly, Britain's legislation had the effect of advantaging some high commission staff over their counterparts at embassies. Immunity was granted to those who were accepted by the receiving state as enjoying diplomatic status, and the CRO (for at least the rest of the decade) took a more liberal view on this than the FO, almost invariably granting requests for it. Thus while the FO would not let tourist attachés and trade agents have diplomatic status, the CRO happily gave it to a New Zealand 'Tourist Adviser' and 'a host of other officers from all parts of the Commonwealth whose exotic designations suggest[ed] the performance of duties having but a tenuous connexion with diplomacy as ordinarily understood'.[106] As regards the diplomatic sanction of declaring a miscreant *persona non grata* (which had the effect of expulsion), the CRO considered that inconceivable. It was, said a CRO official, 'contrary to the ethos of the Commonwealth' to suggest that a member of a high commission could behave in such a way as to make his presence unacceptable![107]

---

[105] CRO brief for PMM-1956, 'Title of High Commissioners', 21 June 1956, TNA, PREM11/1221.

Ireland did not introduce legislation, on the grounds that embassy staff already enjoyed immunity by virtue of their diplomatic status. This derived from Article 29(3) of the Constitution which stated that 'Ireland accepts the generally recognized principles of international law as its rule of conduct in its relations with other states': Rynne-P. Gautrey (British Embassy, Dublin) 1 December 1951, TNA, DO35/2226.

[106] T.H. Glasse (head of Protocol Department) minute, 14 July 1961, TNA, TP30015/80, FO372/7577. Some high commission staff were also differently advantaged. Britain's usual practice was to refuse diplomatic immunity to any members of London embassies who, in addition to the nationality of the sending state, also held (the recently-created status of) UK citizenship. In the case of the 'old' Commonwealth high commissions, this practice would probably have resulted in such staff being refused immunity, as anyone whose father was born in Britain enjoyed UK citizenship. The legislation therefore exempted such people from the operation of this dual nationality rule.

[107] L.J.D. Wakely (AUS) minute, 18 June 1962, TNA, DO161/143.

It is also noteworthy that the 1952 Act also gave full diplomatic immunity to the envoy of a non-sovereign territory: the high commissioner for Southern Rhodesia, Sir Kenneth Goodenough. Goodenough had long felt aggrieved about being lumped together with the agents of Australian states and Canadian provinces; but Britain's move was prompted at least as much by the fact that she was, for the first time, about to appoint a high commissioner to Southern Rhodesia, and wanted him to have the same immunities as her other high commissioners.

E. High Commissioners and the *Décanat*

In any particular capital the whole body of diplomats—the 'diplomatic corps'—is represented *vis-à-vis* the receiving state by its *doyen* or dean (who, put differently, holds the *décanat*). Correspondingly, it is through the *doyen* that the receiving state deals with the corps. Thus the *doyen* is the channel of communication between the two, and may also act on behalf of the whole corps on certain ceremonial occasions. In theory there are two stages to the appointment of a *doyen*. First it is necessary to identify which representative missions are 'diplomatic', since only their members belong to the 'diplomatic' corps and, accordingly, only their heads are eligible to become *doyen*. This is a matter for states rather than diplomats, and one on which each individual receiving state plays a key role, through the arrangement and contents of its Diplomatic List (which identifies those who enjoy diplomatic status within that state), its statements to courts of law about whether a particular person is entitled to diplomatic immunity, and the shape of its table of precedence.

Second, the *doyen* has to be selected from those eligible. In theory this is a matter for the corps, but in practice the office usually passes automatically from a departing *doyen* to the next longest serving head of mission of the highest available diplomatic class (ambassadors forming the highest class, and ministers the next highest). (One long-established exception to this arrangement is that in states where the Roman Catholic faith is the official religion, the office falls to the Papal nuncio—a resident diplomatic representative of the Holy See who has the same rank as an ambassador.) However, occasionally there are considerations which may result in this usual procedure being by-passed. It is, for example, important for the corps, and for the receiving state, that the *doyen* should be acceptable to that state, and ideally someone whose representations will not be impatiently received. If the presumptive *doyen*, for political or personal reasons, is out of favour with the receiving state, both that state and the corps may wish the office to pass to someone else. It is also important that the choice of *doyen* should not lead to difficulties or dissension within the corps, as could well happen should his or her state be one which is not in diplomatic relations with a number of the states represented in the corps, or if the individual in question has an abrasive personality. In these circumstances both the corps and the receiving state may be keen that the office of *doyen* should pass to another head of mission. Additionally, there could be factors associated with the mission of the presumptive *doyen* which suggest an alternative choice: if, for example, the mission is very small and poorly funded, which may make it hard for its head to secure the extra office-type support which the *doyen* might need, or if the head or indeed the whole mission is non-resident. An absent *doyen* is unlikely to be an effective one.

In any of these circumstances the receiving state could well become involved in the process of choosing the next *doyen*. Its participation might be passive (through account being taken of its views), but very possibly it may play an active role, by facilitating or organising a smooth and generally acceptable changeover. The likelihood of the latter is all the greater if the corps in question has as a whole not been very busy, or if a number of its members prefer to avoid the embarrassment and perhaps trouble which may ensue if the corps took the initiative in passing over the presumptive *doyen*, or if the receiving state is anyway anxious to have a significant hand in the process. On such occasions the receiving state is not uncommonly spoken of as 'recognising' a new *doyen*, from which it is but a short step to speak of that state as 'appointing' the *doyen*. Formally speaking, this is not so: in principle it is up to the corps to appoint its *doyen*. But these terms express what now and then is a key aspect of the situation. In practice, and out of necessity, the corps and the receiving state almost always come to a fairly easy understanding about who is to hold the *décanat*. But—as will be seen in the next section but one—not always.

1. *Further equality*

Before the 1948 Prime Ministers' Meeting high commissioners had been regarded as ineligible for the *décanat* because, in the context of the British Empire and Commonwealth, they were 'non-foreign'—and hence were judged to be 'non-diplomatic'. At the Meeting the question was raised as to whether there should be any change in this approach.

The Committee of High Commissioners and Officials who had been asked by the prime ministers to consider this and other related matters saw 'no good reason' why a high commissioner should not enjoy the office of *doyen*, but also thought it 'unnecessary to press the point'.[108] It was not pressed. Those who were against the idea, such as Britain, argued that the corps might object to a member of 'the family' (i.e. a Commonwealth *doyen*) speaking to another 'family' member (i.e. a Commonwealth receiving state) on behalf of '*foreign* representatives on matters touching their privileges and possible grievances'.[109] This, it was suggested, might be especially awkward in London, where high commissioners enjoyed special privileges that were denied to ambassadors. More specifically, Britain was anxious to maintain as many marks as possible of the Commonwealth's distinctive character. And so, for the time being, no high commissioner became *doyen*. In terms of general status and dates of precedence they might now rank with ambassadors. But not wholly so.[110]

Three years later, however, the situation began to change, Canada declaring that the exclusion of high commissioners from the *décanat* was out of keeping with the Commonwealth's constitutional evolution. A more urgent consideration also pointed in this direction: her wish to avoid being in the 'impossible position'[111] of the next *doyen* being from Nationalist China (Taiwan, or Formosa), an island territory which was not recognised by many of the states represented in Ottawa. (They had, instead, chosen to recognise the mainland, communist, People's Republic of China.)[112] The diplomats of these states could, of course, have distinguished between the Taiwanese in his capacity as dean (with whom they could properly have had dealings on *décanal* matters) and as ambassador (with whom they should have had no dealings). But this would have been embarrassing. Canada therefore checked that

---

[108] Report, 19 October 1948, TNA, CAB133/88.

[109] J.P. Erichsen-Brown memorandum, 18 November 1949, NAC, RG25, 4045, 10566–40 vol. 1.

[110] Thus although Hearne had served longer in Ottawa than anyone else, he was denied the *décanat*. However, as the *doyen* was a widower, Mrs. Hearne was given precedence over all the other diplomatic wives at a tea party given by the governor-general's wife.

[111] Minute, signature illegible, 30 December 1952, TNA, DO127/116.

[112] This became a not uncommon situation, as Taiwan often left ambassadors in place indefinitely, for fear of the receiving state seizing the opportunity of a change of ambassador to withdraw its recognition of Taiwan and recognize the mainland government.

the Chilean ambassador, who was next in line for the office, had no objections to the change. (He did not, being anyway due to depart.) She also checked that Britain, whose high commissioner was the next most senior head of mission, was agreeable[113] and she let the rest of the Commonwealth know what was in the offing. She then informed the Ottawa diplomatic corps that she had decided that high commissioners were entitled to hold the *décanat*, and that British high commissioner, Sir Alexander Clutterbuck, would 'consequently' become dean.[114] Because Clutterbuck was popular and highly regarded, Canada's action was generally well received, and no inconvenience arose.[115] A few months later he was succeeded by another high commissioner, the Australian F.M. Forde.[116] There were no formal protests, but there was some diplomatic grumbling.[117] Moreover, the Irish ambassador to Canada, Seán Murphy, deduced not only that the 1948 non-decision on the *décanat* had been aimed at preventing his predecessor, Hearne, becoming *doyen*, but that it had now been lifted for Clutterbuck's sake!

[113] The CRO understood that in Ottawa high commissioners 'are regarded as part of the Diplomatic Corps and that being so we are advised by the Foreign Office that the question whether they should be eligible for the position of Dean in the same way as foreign Ambassadors is one for the local Diplomatic Corps, with whom the choice lies': R.R. Sedgwick (AUS)-Clutterbuck, 28 November 1951, TNA, DO127/116.

[114] DEA note to diplomatic corps, 14 December 1951, NAC, RG25, 3997, 10062–40.

[115] A few years later, however, another British high commissioner doubted the wisdom of becoming *doyen* in a capital like Ottawa, where relations 'were so close and informal' that 'some of the foreign sticklers for diplomatic niceties' might doubt whether a British dean would fight sufficiently vigorously for their diplomatic rights: CRO note, 'Deanship of Diplomatic Corps in Commonwealth Countries', 8 January 1962, enclosed in G.W. St.J. Chadwick (AUS) circular telegram, 9 February 1962, TNA, FCO57/88.

[116] Forde was *doyen* from May 1952 to April 1953. When he left, the Taiwanese was again next in line. However, the Chinese agreed to Canada's suggestion that he should not become dean due to responsibilities necessitating his absence from Ottawa. This continued for some years: DEA memoranda, 4 and 26 December 1952, 5 February 1953, 7 and 12 June 1957, NAC, RG 25, 3997, 10062–40.

[117] The Italian ambassador, di Stefano, called on the *chef de protocol* to complain very strongly that, as far as the diplomatic corps was concerned, high commissioners 'do not exist internationally', and used the 1815 Congress of Vienna to support his case. Jules Léger (assistant under-secretary) later took the opportunity of a meeting with di Stefano, to say that 'taking the accords of the Congress of Vienna as a landmark in world history he could go a step further and make a good case against Canada ever having become an independent country'. T.J. Endemann (South African HC, Ottawa) minute, 2 February 1952, SAA, BTS, 180/3; Léger memorandum, 27 December 1951, *DCER 1951*, http://www.dfait-aeci.gc.ca/department/history/dcer/details-en.asp?intRefid'5416

In Australia, meanwhile, political and personal factors had already resulted in high commissioners informally serving as *doyen*,[118] and in 1952 she, together with Pakistan, Ceylon, and India, decided to allow them to hold the *décanat*. New Zealand soon followed suit. Only Britain and South Africa resisted the trend—and in Ceylon the American ambassador observed that the British high commissioner had 'not only not encouraged this development', but 'done [his] best to discourage it' on the grounds that high commissioners could not, properly, be members of the diplomatic corps.[119] But change was clearly in the air, and as the 1950s progressed high commissioners were generally seen as, and felt themselves to be, fully integrated into their respective diplomatic corps. Even South Africa, whose *apartheid* régime did not want to be confronted with 'the menace of doing business with a coloured *doyen*',[120] recognised a high commissioner as acting doyen in 1956. That event, however, provoked quite a contretemps.

2. *South Africa and the* décanat, *1956*

Until 1956 South Africa, like Britain, did not regard high commissioners as members of the diplomatic corps—hence their car licence plates bore the letters 'HC' rather than 'CD'. Some members of the Pretoria diplomatic corps shared that view rather firmly, including the Dutch *doyen*, Jan van den Berg (who in this was continuing the

---

[118] The Taiwanese *doyen* took care to keep out of the picture on the odd occasion when the diplomatic corps met (e.g. to arrange a farewell for a parting colleague) because the Soviet ambassador 'refused to attend any meetings called by him, holding that he does not represent any head of State'. In consequence, the British high commissioner informally took over the functions of *doyen*: Kiernan-Nunan, 13 November 1950. Then the Soviet ambassador became *doyen* but he was 'a sick man' and 'not very articulate in English'. Once again a high commissioner, from Ceylon, effectively took over, and was often called 'sub-Dean or Acting Dean'. The British HC (Sir Stephen Holmes) predicted that the corps would want the Ceylonese to succeed the Soviet, and evidently the Australian government did too, announcing at the end of November 1952 that, in keeping with what had happened elsewhere and in the light of an imminent review of her order of precedence, high commissioners in Canberra would be allowed to hold the *décanat*. 'This', said the British high commissioner, 'removes almost the last differentiation [here] other than the name' between high commissioners and ambassadors: Holmes telegrams 196 and 209, 28 November and 15 December 1952, TNA, DO127/116. 'If I had been regarded as dating from my first appointment here, I should be first in the list', instead of seventh said Kiernan glumly: minute, 8 December 1952, INA, DFA, Canberra Embassy, Box 16–30, 2/302/1, B.1.2 I.

[119] Satterthwaite (Colombo), 1 April 1953.

[120] Forsyth (SDEA) reported in Chadwick (HCO Ottawa) minute, 6 December 1949, TNA, DO127/93.

line taken by his French predecessor, Armand Gazel). However, the minister for external affairs, Eric Louw, had 'an affectionate regard'[121] for the second most senior head of mission, the Australian Colonel W.R. Hodgson (1952–57), and when van den Berg went on leave in 1956 he decided that Hodgson should be acting *doyen*. Louw claimed this was 'in fulfilment' of the decision of the 1948 Prime Ministers' Meeting, and that it 'did not accord with the constitutional evolution of the Commonwealth' for high commissioners not to be regarded as 'in all respects assimilated with the Corps'.[122] Van den Berg nonetheless made representations against Hodgson acting in his place, but Louw replied that it would be a derogation from sovereignty to suggest that high commissioners did not have the same status as ambassadors.

Heads of mission were furious. It was most improper of Louw to tell the diplomatic corps who should represent them—although they would almost certainly have accepted anyone but Hodgson. For although Hodgson went down well with the South Africans, he was the corps' *enfant terrible*: an outspoken, bottom-pinching,[123] 'rugged, raucous, hard-drinking Australian'.[124] A 'very hectic', 'very heated' meeting of the corps at one stage 'got quite out of hand'.[125] Van den Berg then told Louw that high commissioners were not regarded as members of the diplomatic corps, that they would not be so regarded until the diplomatic corps unanimously agreed otherwise, and that some of his colleagues were consulting their governments. Now it was Louw's turn to lose his temper. His government could not agree 'that the question as to whom it will recognise as the Doyen . . . is one for decision by any other Government'. High commissioners and ambassadors had not been regarded as separate groups since 1949, and he was only revising the position in one respect. It was 'fully in accordance with recognised diplomatic practice' for the senior head of mission to be appointed acting *doyen*.[126] Louw went on to make an announcement to this effect; the corps accepted it as settling the matter; and Hodgson apparently obtained 'considerable satisfaction from his new role'.[127] In

121 E.W.I. Gill (Canadian HC), no. 126, 28 May 1956, NAC, RG25, 3997, 10062-40.

122 Louw-van den Berg, 12 June 1956, NAC, RG25, 6371, 3011-A-40, part 3.

123 See Tothill (1995), citing Dr. Joan Rydon.

124 Woodard (2000) 80.

125 Gill-Herman Schoch (Netherlands Embassy) conversation, Cape Town, 18 July 1956, NAC, RG25, 6371, 3011-A-40, part 3.

126 Louw-van den Berg, 8 August 1956, NAC, RG25, 6371, 3011-A-40, part 3.

127 Gill, no. 207, 17 August 1956, NAC, RG25, 6371, 3011-A-40.

this way high commissioners in South Africa—as almost everywhere else in the Commonwealth—came to be recognised as unquestionably members of the diplomatic corps and, as such, entitled to the *décanat*. Now only Britain continued to regard high commissioners as outside the diplomatic fold and hence ineligible to become *doyen*. In London's special circumstances—where high commissioners were particularly well looked after—this caused no problem.

This South African affair had an interesting appendix, which testified to the increased appeal of the office of high commissioner. The diplomatic corps' hostile response to Louw's decision about Hodgson had led Louw to talk of raising the question of the title of 'high commissioner' when he went to London for the Prime Ministers' Meeting at the end of June 1956. Louw had no personal liking for the office (which he had held briefly in 1929), and wanted to do away with it. Hence he appointed a 'minister' rather than a 'deputy high commissioner' to London; he gave instructions that *agrément* should be sought for South Africa's new high commissioner to London;[128] and said he intended to remove 'HC' from cars belonging to Commonwealth missions. Putting the subject on the prime ministers' agenda might also reap political rewards in republican quarters, and he was thought to 'be influenced by special motives touching the Gold Coast' which would become independent, as Ghana, early in 1957.[129] For although Afro-Asia was moving towards boycotting the *apartheid* state rather than exchanging missions with her, now that high commissioners had been assimilated into Pretoria's diplomatic corps the remote prospect of a black or brown *doyen* could only definitively be avoided by doing away with the office of high commissioner. That would enable South Africa to restrict, say, Ghanaian representation to the level of minister rather than ambassador, which (assuming there was at least one ambassador in Pretoria, which to all intents and purposes was certain) would exclude the Ghanaian from the *décanat*.

As it turned out, Louw decided not to raise the subject. If he had, only India and Ceylon were likely to have supported him, and neither of them was pressing for a change. Canada had no strong views, believing the pros and cons were fairly evenly balanced—though it was notewor-

[128] His instruction was not carried out either because it was overlooked or not understood by South Africa House.

[129] CRO brief for PMM-1956, 'Title of High Commissioners', 21 June 1956, TNA, PREM11/1221.

thy that, in contrast to her attitude half a dozen years earlier, she now valued the high commissioner 'badge': it was one of the few distinctive and distinguishing marks of Commonwealth membership and created 'a bond of fellowship', marking out its bearers as 'a distinct group' enjoying a 'specially close and confidential relationship'.[130] Australia, New Zealand, and Pakistan wanted no change, and Britain would have strongly opposed Louw, contending that intra-Commonwealth relations were 'different in kind' from those with foreign states and 'at all costs' should not be 'whittled away by changes in nomenclature'.[131] It seemed clear that the balance of opinion had shifted in favour of the office. However, had there been a discussion which looked like going the 'wrong' way, Britain planned to prevaricate by suggesting 'that the matter required careful thought and should be left over for further consideration on some future occasion'.[132]

F. Conclusion

The challenges facing the office of high commissioner at the end of the 1940s were formidable. Developments regarding India seemed very clearly to point in the direction of its holders soon becoming ambassadors. That this did not happen is attributable to several factors. On the positive side, Britain skilfully postponed the day of reckoning; two key individuals were greatly in favour of the existing title (India's Krishna Menon who liked being a high commissioner, and Britain's Philip Noel-Baker who probably believed it when he said that high commissioners had become 'more important' than ambassadors now that 'every "tuppeny hapenny"[*sic.*] country had an Ambassador');[133] and, most importantly, a third key individual, Nehru, responded to India's smooth translation to a republic within the Commonwealth by agreeing not

[130] DEA memorandum, 'Proposed Change of Designation of High Commissioners', 18 June 1956, NAC, RG25, 2370, s/228/1.

[131] Percivale Liesching (British HC)-Gilbert Laithwaite (PUS), personal and confidential, 25 August 1956, TNA, DO35/5015.

[132] CRO brief for Cabinet, Commonwealth Prime Minister's Meeting 1956, 'Title of High Commissioners', 21 June 1956, TNA, PREM11/1221.

[133] Dulanty Secret Report 5, 31 January 1950. Cf. Laithwaite 'thought Noel Baker[*sic*] had a bee in his bonnet about the title High Commissioner, and he [Laithwaite] was afraid that he might influence other Commonwealth Ministers against the idea of adopting the title Ambassador': Dulanty-Boland, 5 January 1950, INA, DFA, London Embassy, unnumbered files, Box 1–14, file 4.

to raise the issue at the Colombo conference in 1950. Negatively, the campaign against the office was, at two crucial moments, undone. The first was in 1948, when the Irish *taoiseach*'s precipitate announcement that Ireland would become a republic and leave the Commonwealth meant that he was not present at the Prime Ministers' Meeting. This probably tipped the balance in favour of the agreement that the office should be allowed to survive *ad interim*. The second occasion was in 1950, when the Commonwealth's Colombo meeting agreed to let the titular sleeping dog lie. That particular dog would not slumber indefinitely. But the office of high commissioner had survived, and its future was improved by the removal of most remaining differences between the position of its holders and that of ambassadors: they were to be (distinctively) accredited, enjoy diplomatic immunity, and almost everywhere be eligible for the *décanat*, and hence members of the relevant diplomatic corps. At the same time the office continued to benefit from the intimacy of the Commonwealth connection. Seemingly its holders were now advantaged rather than disadvantaged. They had become, it appeared, ambassadors plus.

CHAPTER SIX

'AMBASSADORS PLUS',[1] EARLY 1950s–MID-1960s

In the 1950s all was by no means always well with the Commonwealth. One member, South Africa, was moving towards pariah status because of her policy of racial discrimination. Two others, India and Pakistan, had fought in 1947–48 over the princely state of Kashmir—whose Hindu ruler had opted to join India but whose Muslim majority favoured Pakistan. The unsettled issue rumbled on, with the state's territory split between the claimants. During the Cold War, most Commonwealth members became part of or favourable to the Western alliance system, but India took a stance which was called 'neutralist' (later, 'non-aligned'). When Pakistan fell under military rule in 1958, the rest of the Commonwealth fidgeted uneasily. In Britain senior members of the government worried (privately) about the diluting impact on the Commonwealth of Asian-African decolonisation. Some bilateral Commonwealth relationships lacked much substance. Most strikingly, the British (and French) assault on Egypt in 1956 following the nationalisation of the Suez Canal brought the Commonwealth to 'the verge of dissolution'.[2]

Paradoxically, however, the Commonwealth emerged from the Suez crisis in a seemingly strengthened condition. Shortly thereafter two British possessions became independent within the Commonwealth—Ghana (formerly the Gold Coast) and Malaya. They were the first new members for almost ten years. This measured rate of expansion posed no threat to the association's cosy intimacy, its leaders, officials, and military men seeing one another at regular Commonwealth meetings and often being in touch at other times. Nor was it expected that there

---

[1] 'High commissioners as *doyen* argument', note attached to B.G. Smallman (Commonwealth Co-ordination Department) minute, 11 June 1969, TNA, FCO68/34.

[2] Pearson (secretary of state for external affairs, Canada) quoted in Doxey (1982) 5. Only Australia and New Zealand supported Britain. The Commonwealth's Asian members talked openly of leaving it; South Africa sat on the sidelines; and Canada was openly critical. It was like 'finding a beloved uncle arrested for rape': *The Economist*, quoted in Holmes (1982) 357.

would be any upsetting acceleration in the winding up of colonialism. So the outlook for the Commonwealth could certainly be judged as favourable. As one close observer put it, the late 1950s 'perhaps marks the apogee of the Commonwealth idea'.[3] There was even a tendency, especially in Britain, to extol the Commonwealth as a unique and 'great experiment in co-operation', 'a bridge' between states, continents and peoples, and 'a model of what the whole world might one day become'.[4] These sentiments were not the preserve of the idealist left; influential figures on Britain's right, too, were similarly optimistic, seeing the Commonwealth not just as something of an international asset but also exemplifying the sort of civilised political values which elsewhere seemed in increasingly short supply. Thus the commonwealth relations secretary in the Conservative government, the Earl of Home, said (privately) in 1958 that the Commonwealth was such an 'exciting prospect that the written word can scarcely capture [its] spirit or its unity of purpose'.[5]

The Commonwealth's singular diplomatic practices and differential dealings with high commissioners symbolised, emphasised, and (it was hoped) strengthened this unusual association. Its distinctiveness was underlined. Probably because of this, the 1950s and early 1960s were good years for high commissioners, when the advantages of their office were obvious and appealing. They had become, like ambassadors, the normal channel of communication between governments, and apart from being denied the *décanat* in London, they had all the rights and benefits of ambassadors plus some special treatment which went well beyond what most outsiders might have guessed. These developments contributed in 1956 to a potential challenge to the office not being pursued (as indicated in the previous chapter), and to the Commonwealth's ability, during the negotiation of the 1961 Vienna Convention on Diplomatic Relations, to put on a united (and successful) front to retain and protect the now long-established office of high commissioner.

A few of the advantages of the office discussed in this chapter predate the period on which it is focused, so that high commissioners were already in some small measure 'ambassadors plus' at the start of the 1950s. Other advantages survived for much longer than the chapter's

---

3 Garner (1978) 339.
4 Mansergh (1969) 410–1.
5 In a confidential Conservative Party paper, 2 May 1958, quoted in Miller (1974) 411.

period. As late as 1972, for example, no one responded to an intra-Foreign and Commonwealth Office (FCO) 'invitation to identify any [Commonwealth] conventions to which only token respect is paid';[6] and although at about this time the importance of the Commonwealth in foreign policy was fading and high commissioners were ceasing to be able to take special treatment for granted, important distinctions remained and they could still often count on benefiting from the Commonwealth factor, especially in Britain. For these reasons not all the references in this chapter date from the years with which it mainly deals, and the present tense is sometimes used. But it was during the 1950s and first half of the 1960s that the benefits of being a high commissioner were most strongly marked; and at this time they were enjoyed in a very supportive political context.

A. Pageantry and Protocol

1. *Royal occasions*

One instance of the special treatment of high commissioners concerns their relations with Britain's head of state. All of them have claims on Buckingham Palace: those from the sovereign's realms (the 'realm high commissioners') because she (and before her, the King) is their sovereign; the others because she is Head of the Commonwealth. Hence the greater intimacy of her relationship with high commissioners than with ambassadors, and her wish that 'every opportunity be taken to stress the family relationship between Commonwealth countries at events at which She is present'.[7] The number of republics and indigenous monarchies[8] in the Commonwealth grew hugely during her reign, but

---

[6] R.E. Allen (Commonwealth Co-ordination Department) minute, 13 July 1972, TNA, FCO68/411.

[7] Lt.-Col. J.M. Hugo (ceremonial secretary, CRO) minute, 29 April 1968, TNA, FCO49/138.

[8] States with their own monarchs at the end of the period covered in this book are Brunei, Lesotho, Malaysia, Samoa, Swaziland, and Tonga. Unusually, CRO Lists described Britain's mission in Brunei as 'H.M. High Commission'. The others were 'British High Commissions'. For a short while after the creation of the Foreign and Commonwealth Office in 1968 its annual Diplomatic Service List continued this nomenclature in respect of Brunei, but early in the 1970s the mission there, like all other missions to Commonwealth states, became 'British High Commission'.

This is an appropriate point at which to note that British high commissioners are never called 'Her Majesty's' high commissioners. This is because even if they are posted

this only minimally affected the formal aspects of high commissioners' relations with the Queen.

Thus on ceremonial and state occasions in Britain high commissioners are privileged. At the funeral of King George VI in 1952, they walked in a body immediately behind heads of state and royalty, and before the heads of foreign delegations. (The ambassador of Ireland, which had left the Commonwealth but was not regarded as foreign, was placed immediately after the high commissioners.) At the Queen's coronation in the following year they were seated separately from the diplomatic corps. They have separate and preferential seating arrangements for the opening of Parliament and royal weddings and funerals. Moreover, unlike ambassadors—and to the chagrin of some of the latter—high commissioners (and the Irish ambassador) are seated in the British prime minister's stand for Trooping the Colour (the military ceremony marking the Sovereign's official birthday) and treated to refreshments afterwards. They also received a disproportionate number of invitations to official functions such as the Royal Ascot horse race meeting, and special invitations to royal garden parties; have 'special privileges for seats in Royal boxes e.g. Wimbledon' (Britain's leading tennis tournament);[9] and tickets for cricket matches at Lords (Britain's premier cricket ground).

It was a matter of policy that 'the importance of the Commonwealth should be emphasised every time The Queen entertains foreigners'.[10]

---

to a non-realm they do not hold a commission or warrant of appointment from the Queen. It is thought that this practice stems from the origins of the office, when all high commissioners operated in an imperial context and hence did not need to be furnished with the sort of commission which authorised ambassadors to act (formally speaking) as the sovereign's personal representative in a foreign state. Rather, high commissioners represented the government of one part of the sovereign's domain *vis-à-vis* the government of another part. The practice has effectively been continued, in that Britain's letters of commission, although signed by the sovereign, are still couched in a quasi-governmental way, the high commissioner being spoken of as the representative of the United Kingdom and not of the head of state. Inter-realm letters of introduction, of course, are unambiguously government to government.

[9] Undated G. Duggan note, 'Similarities and Differences between Ambassadors and High Commissioners', April 1969, TNA, FCO68/66. See also annex to Paul Gore-Booth circular memorandum, 'Relations with the Commonwealth', 5 November 1968, TNA, FCO49/138.

[10] Earl of Home (commonwealth secretary) minute, 28 June 1960, TNA, DO35/7879. In 1961, when there were 11 high commissioners in London, it was proposed that on state visits the City of London entertainment should consist of an evening banquet rather than a luncheon, which would mean that the usual opera or theatrical performance would disappear. The prime minister did not approve: 'No. I think this is a pity.

In consequence high commissioners and their wives used always to be invited to state banquets; ambassadors only went if they had 'a special interest in the guest'.[11] Eventually, however, there were more high commissioners than could be conveniently accommodated. But in 1969 the Queen still invited about a third of them to the banquets. Also, at Buckingham Palace receptions to meet foreign royalty or distinguished visitors, high commissioners are received separately and in advance of ambassadors.

Palace protocol on ceremonial occasions also delicately underlines the Irish ambassador's special status. When the Queen ascended to the throne, she received his credentials before those of foreign ambassadors, and he was 'shepherded' by the commonwealth secretary rather than the foreign secretary. Until the creation of the Foreign and Commonwealth Office (FCO) in 1968, newly-arrived Irish ambassadors travelled to the Palace in the ambassadorial coach but in the company of the CRO's ceremonial and protocol secretary, and the commonwealth secretary was present when they presented their credentials. And at any receptions for the diplomatic corps during state visits, the Irish ambassador is presented after high commissioners but before ambassadors, and the same order applies at the state opening of Parliament.

State visits by the Queen[12] have provided another opportunity for her to demonstrate her relationship to Commonwealth heads of mission, who used to figure prominently in her programme. Thus in Stockholm in 1956, 'The Commonwealth note was struck from the moment of Her Majesty's arrival, escorted by a Canadian vessel and welcomed by the five Commonwealth Heads of Mission, and was strikingly brought home by the sight of the Royal Standard being hoisted successively at each Commonwealth Mission' as she visited it.[13] And in Paris in 1957, the 'Commonwealth *doyen*' was 'in the forefront as much as possible'.[14] The growth of the Commonwealth made it impractical to continue

Nothing should ever be changed in the way of ceremony and ritual': Harold Macmillan minute, 15 December 1961, TNA, PREM11/4795.

[11] Master of the household, Buckingham Palace, memorandum for Sir Michael Adeane (private secretary to the Queen), 9 June 1960, TNA, DO35/7879.

[12] Her visits to Commonwealth countries were not normally so designated until 1979.

[13] British ambassador, Stockholm, 23 June 1956, CAP, BTS, PM12/12, vol. 2. All Commonwealth missions participated on an equal footing. They co-hosted a reception and their heads of mission attended all state functions and were present during private parts of the visit.

[14] British ambassador, Paris, no. 96, 25 April 1957, CAP, BTS, PM12/12, vol. 2.

in this vein, but the Queen receives high commissioners first at diplomatic receptions, and invites them to stand with her when she receives ambassadors. The latter sometimes complained, but the Queen resisted all attempts to introduce Commonwealth envoys and ambassadors to her in one body.[15] In 1962, on a visit to Sierra Leone, one ambassador was so disgruntled about foreign heads of mission being treated 'like poor relations' that he walked out of one of the functions.[16] However, on these occasions intra-Commonwealth sensitivities about status and precedence also came to the fore, in particular the concern of other Commonwealth countries that the British high commissioner should not automatically assume the senior role. Thus any joint Commonwealth functions called for 'great tact and care'.[17] In 1957 in Lisbon, where there had been problems over the South African and Canadian ambassadors being given 'proper recognition', it was suggested that the joint Commonwealth reception be held 'in a "neutral" place' or at the South African Embassy (as its ambassador was 'the senior Commonwealth representative').[18] And later that year in Washington, 'things got to such a pitch that they nearly had to hold a Commonwealth reception in a hotel' rather than an embassy.[19] However, all passed off well. Commonwealth heads of mission and their wives jointly welcomed the Queen in her capacity as Head of the Commonwealth and attended her dinner for President Eisenhower; and the ten Commonwealth flags were frequently flown together—in alphabetical order.

On royal visits to Commonwealth states the role played by the British high commissioner to that state depends on whether or not it is one of the Queen's realms. When the Queen visits one of her realms, the high commissioner neither escorts her nor accommodates her. He or she fades

---

[15] Adeane memorandum for Lord Chamberlain, 14 July 1969, TNA, FCO57/88.

[16] Jack Johnston (British HC)-G.W. St.J. Chadwick (AUS), 18 January 1962, TNA, DO161/186.

[17] Sir Gilbert Laithwaite (PUS) minute, 31 October 1957, TNA, DO35/7804. The position of the spouse may also need to be considered. Canada's DEA was put out when, in Havana in 1954, the wife of the Canadian head of mission was asked to act as official hostess at a British Embassy reception to celebrate the Queen's official birthday. Shared celebrations were not a bad thing, but sharing in this way might be seen as implying the Canadian Embassy was subordinate to Britain's. Nor was it appropriate to 'use' 'another fellow's wife' who, not being 'male & equal', would have found it very difficult to refuse: Undated E.A. Côté (head of American Division) minute, June 1954, NAC, RG25, 8196, 7753-A-40, part 2.1.

[18] R. Jones (acting SDEA)-Stephanus du Toit (South African ambassador, Lisbon) 19 December 1956, CAP, BTS, PM12/12, 2.

[19] Lord Selkirk (Admiralty)-Home, 17 October 1957, TNA, DO35/7804.

into the background, being the representative in the realm not of the Queen but of the British government. The Queen's representative in a realm is the governor-general who, in her absence, acts for her in her capacity as the realm's head of state. But when the Queen visits one of the non-realm states, her representative there is the British high commissioner. Accordingly, as with her ambassadors in non-Commonwealth states, he or she plays a leading role in making arrangements for the visit, and accompanies the Queen during her time there.

2. *Presentation of credentials*

A new high commissioner to Britain from a state which is not one of the Queen's realms goes to the Palace to present his or her letters of commission in a semi-state landau (i.e. coach) pulled by four horses, the two nearside ones being ridden by postillions. (The ambassadorial landau is pulled by a pair of horses driven by a coachman.) The presentation ceremony itself is identical to that for ambassadors. It is a formal occasion at which everyone stands. First the Queen receives the high commissioner and the accompanying permanent under-secretary (PUS) of the Commonwealth Relations Office (CRO) (or another senior official) (after 1968, when the CRO was merged with the Foreign Office, it was the PUS or a senior official of the Foreign and Commonwealth Office who was in attendance); then the high commissioner may present up to eight members of his or her mission (the number that fits into the coaches which complete the procession to the Palace); after which the high commissioner's spouse is conducted informally into the room for a short audience with the Queen.[20] In the realms, the presentation of credentials to the governor-general (representing the Queen) by high commissioners not of the realms seems to be conducted in varying ways—sometimes with the same formality as the presentation of ambassadorial letters of credence; sometimes with a little less.[21]

---

[20] The reason for the private audience for the spouse was that when George VI was King, all ambassadors were male and the Queen used to entertain their wives to tea. When the Queen came to the throne and was faced with the two tasks that had been carried out by her parents, they were combined into one, multi-part, audience.

[21] It appears, for example, that in New Zealand and Australia the former is the case; in Canada, at least in 1965, the latter. This perhaps disappointed the Tanzanian high commissioner who had expected to make a few formal remarks. But the chief of protocol was told that the governor-general felt this was 'a family occasion', and did 'not wish there to be an exchange of speeches when he receives new High Commissioners': Esmond Butler (governor-general's secretary)-C. Eberts, 13 July 1965, NAC, RG25,

On the other hand, high commissioners to Britain from one of the Queen's realms (who present their letters of introduction to the prime minister) customarily have an informal audience with the Queen soon after their arrival. Being representatives of a government (not of a head of state) and subjects of the Queen, they cannot travel to the Palace in the ambassadorial state landau. They go by car. (This is sometimes a matter of regret.) But once there the high commissioner, together with her or his spouse, receives a private, informal audience of about twenty minutes at which the group sits and no-one else is present. It has been described as a 'pleasurable', 'relaxed', 'family-like occasion'.[22] In addition, high commissioners of the realms are at some point invited to Windsor Castle for an overnight stay—a privilege shared by few ambassadors. This may not make much difference to diplomacy, but it is flattering and enjoyable. Sometimes high commissioners of the realms also have the privilege of a farewell meeting with the Queen. In the realms high commissioners from another realm present their letters of introduction to the prime minister in an informal way. The governor-general may also host a relatively informal reception for them.

So far as precedence in a particular capital is concerned, throughout the 1950s high commissioners of the realms generally had an advantage over other high commissioners. The precedence of the latter was determined by the date (and, if need be, time) of the presentation of their letters of commission. But except in South Africa (where, from 1948, the presentation of the letter of introduction was the crucial date), high commissioners of the realms, not being formally accredited to the receiving state, and hence having no credentials to present to its head, had their precedence dated from their arrival either in the capital (Australia) or on the territory of the receiving state (Britain, Canada, and New Zealand). This meant, for example, that in 1951 the Chinese ambassador to Pakistan received lower precedence than the British high commissioner because he had not presented his credentials when the latter arrived. It also meant that such high commissioners had a head start in being able fully to get down to work at once rather than wait until they had presented credentials. These practices mostly changed in the 1960s, however, in consequence of the Vienna Convention on Diplomatic Relations.

11016, 22-7-1, part 1.1. Conceivably, the practice may vary with the disposition of individual governors-general.

[22] Scott (1981) 138, and private information.

B. The Activity of High Commissioners

1. *Relations with the receiving state*

One potential advantage enjoyed by high commissioners of the Queen's realms is having a prime ministerial letter of introduction, as it probably ensures an earlier meeting with the host prime minister than would otherwise be the case. This is an opportunity for the incoming head of mission not just to have a perhaps useful discussion but, right away, to seek a favourable relationship with the head of government. It has been said that this meeting may 'be among the most useful and significant of a head of mission's tour of duty'.[23]

An advantage which all high commissioners have is the right of direct access to the receiving state's head of government and its governmental ministers and departments. This ability to go to the top sometimes valuably facilitated the conduct of business—especially useful in countries like Ghana in 1969, where, it was said, 'If ever we found ourselves obliged to channel our relations with the Ghana Government through the Minister of External Affairs, the wheels would come to a grinding halt'.[24] Although there had, by the early 1970s, been 'some slippage of this convention in certain Commonwealth countries notably in Africa',[25] many high commissioners continued to deal directly with heads of government and went on doing so for many more years. (It was useful in this connection to be able to point out that the right of access was reciprocal.) The CRO regarded this as the principal difference between high commissioners and ambassadors who—at least in theory—dealt only with the foreign ministry.

High commissioners' contacts with governmental figures were sometimes close, and brought helpful benefits. In Australia, an external affairs minister provided 'a good deal of... information that would not have reached us for some time, including information his senior officials might not have known and, if they had, might have felt unable to share'.[26] A Canadian wrote of his service in Pakistan in the early 1950s that many of the ministers and officials, influenced by their pre-independence

[23] Personal communication.

[24] H.K. Matthews (British HC)-R.J.M. Wilson (West Africa Department), 18 September 1969, TNA, FCO65/115

[25] FCO note on Commonwealth traditions, August 1972, TNA, FCO68/411.

[26] Major-General L.R. La Flèche (Canadian HC), no. 174, 28 May 1950, NAC, RG25, 4480, 50019-A-40, part 1.

experiences, were 'frightfully British'; and that through meeting the British military adviser on board ship en route to his posting, he got 'quite close' to some key figures in the Pakistan Defence Department.[27] In newer Commonwealth states, personal associations sometimes provided an acceptable 'cover' for cooperation between armed forces which might otherwise easily have been seen as neo-imperialism. These links sometimes resulted in extremely relaxed personal relationships with individual ministers and officials throughout the machinery of government. Thus when Canada's high commissioner, Norman Robertson (1946–49, 1952–57), left London in 1949, the foreign secretary was in tears. The friendship between Britain's high commissioner to India, Sir Archibald Nye (1948–52), and the Indian prime minister, Jawaharlal Nehru, was said to be 'equalled by no other diplomatic representative at any time'.[28]

The establishment of warm personal relations was often assisted by the smallness of some capitals and their diplomatic corps, as well as by a sense of Commonwealth kinship. Lord Carrington, British high commissioner (1956–59), found the Australian prime minister, Robert Menzies, 'warm, friendly and hospitable, often inviting us to his house (which was near ours) and dining with us, alone or with others'.[29] The South African high commissioner, A.M. Hamilton (1957–61), also enjoyed a close friendship with Menzies—who in March 1960 on his walk home from Parliament (which took him past South Africa House) stopped by on Hamilton to give him 'moral support'[30] after a parliamentary debate over the shooting of African protesters at Sharpeville, which had aroused outrage worldwide and marked a turning point in attitudes to the Union. When the British deputy high commissioner in Kenya visited the Foreign Ministry in the early 1970s, its permanent secretary 'would call out down the corridor..."Now then Len you

[27] Personal communication. These advantages 'wore away in time, especially after the Commonwealth expanded rapidly, the UK Government grew less enthusiastic, some of the "new" members found more interest in other international affiliations and much less in the Commonwealth, even after it developed its own Secretariat in London': *ibid.*

[28] Garner (1978) 310.

[29] Carrington (1988) 126. When Carrington presented his letter of introduction (at 3 p.m.), 'Menzies led me into the ante-room, took from a cupboard an enormous jug and poured what looked to me like a whole bottle of gin into it, to which he added a thimbleful of French vermouth and started mixing the martini. He handed a large tumbler to me, soon insisted on topping it up. I wandered unsteadily out of the Parliament House': *ibid.* 127.

[30] Tothill (1996).

imperialist rogue, what are you coming to tell me today?"'[31] And in 1973 the permanent under-secretary of the FCO, who had spent most of the overseas part of his career in the uptight East European milieu, was 'astonished at the informality' of the British high commissioner's relations with the official in charge of New Zealand's Department of External Affairs (DEA).[32] This kind of evidence for the advantages of being a high commissioner is often found in archival material, interviews, and memoirs.

Another difference between ambassadors and high commissioners, at least in the third quarter of the twentieth century, was the latter's wider relations with the receiving state. Some high commissioners continued to spend an appreciable amount of time on commercial matters, which brought a number of contacts of a 'non-diplomatic' type. They and their staff also engaged in a 'new style'[33] of diplomacy, which focused on public relations and regarded the primary duty of a high commissioner as 'making contacts with the people of the country'.[34] In this their work was subtly different from that of embassies, 'less formal... more widely pervasive, and often goes deeper down'.[35] Connectedly, the title 'high commissioner' had advantages in the broader community: a certain cachet, sounding important but not foreign, which led to invitations that would not come the way of an ambassador and meant that 'ex officio many doors are open to him to which a foreign Ambassador may only later and sometimes hardly ever gain access'.[36] In addition, high commissioners 'normally' lived as integrated members of local communities and were sometimes automatically admitted to important clubs not open to ambassadors; they also tended to find themselves 'involved in a range of activities more reminiscent of minor royalty than of diplomacy'.[37]

---

[31] Jane Barder interview with Sir Leonard Allinson, 5 March 1996, CAC, DOHP 6.

[32] Scott (2003) 181.

[33] Garner (1978) 307.

[34] Norman Brook (cabinet secretary) memorandum, 'Foreign Office and Commonwealth Relations Office', 8 May 1956, TNA, PREM11/1233.

[35] Viscount Amory (British HC, Ottawa 1961–63), House of Lords *debs.*, 7 April 1964, 55. In 2006 a member of Trinidad and Tobago's London High Commission visited an undistinguished and provincial British football club (Port Vale), as one of its players (who had never himself lived in Trinidad and Tobago) was a member of the state's World Cup squad.

[36] A.W. Snelling (DUS) draft note, 'Similarities and Differences between Ambassadors and High Commissioners', 31 March 1969, TNA, FCO68/66.

[37] Garner (1978) 378.

In London high commissioners and their staff were favourably placed in a number of respects. High commissioners were regularly briefed by the prime minister. Britain's 1952 immunities legislation had had the effect of advantaging some high commission members over their opposite numbers in embassies, and all high commission staff already had marginally superior privileges. High commissioners could ask Britain for technical assistance of certain kinds: for the vetting of local applicants for positions at their high commissions; for security inspections of their premises; and for help with communications, including telegram facilities and courier services. And, as will be discussed below, they benefited considerably from the fact that there was a separate government department—the CRO—which handled all relations with Commonwealth states.

Caution should be exercised, however, both in estimating the difference which high commissioners' perquisites and practices made to the substance of relations, and in supposing that ambassadors were always at a disadvantage in these respects. The establishment by a high commissioner of a good relationship with senior governmental figures is indeed likely to pay some diplomatic dividends. But such a relationship is most unlikely to prevail against a major interest of the receiving state, nor against adverse personal attitudes to the sending state or its leader. Public diplomacy (as it has come to be called) is more about public relations than the achievement of foreign policy goals. And when a high commissioner does seem to deliver the political goods, there is always the question of the extent to which other factors in the relationship of the two states influenced the outcome. As for ambassadors, they too will build up some beneficial personal contacts; and it is always open to them to ask to see the head of government when delivering a message from their own head of government. To take an admittedly extreme example, it is hard to conceive of American ambassadors losing out because they do not belong to the high commissioner club. It is also doubtful whether the prohibition on foreign missions dealing with home government departments was ever rigorously applied. Nonetheless, during the 1950s and early 1960s high commissioners undoubtedly felt well treated, and were favourably placed to advance their states' interests to the maximum possible degree.

2. *The influence of British high commissioners*

While all high commissions tended to have good access to the receiving state's government, the access enjoyed by members of the quite generously staffed British missions was generally outstanding. This contributed not just to some warm personal relationships but also, so it was often thought, to a high level of political influence. It started at the top, as dealings between high commissioners and prime ministers were 'in most cases close and frequent',[38] and in Australia only the British High Commission retained right of access to the Prime Minister's Department. More generally, contact with the Australian authorities was so frequent that it was 'as if one were dealing with another Whitehall department'.[39] In Ottawa Britain's High Commission enjoyed 'an influence far greater than that of any other Commonwealth mission'.[40] Elsewhere, her missions used to good advantage their occasional need to approach heads of government with personal prime ministerial messages and government communications—'something which no foreign ambassador (and few if any other Commonwealth high commissioners) would do'.[41]

In the newly-decolonised third world, British high commissions had additional advantages. First, in the run-up to independence the CRO established an intimate relationship with the prospective government, a CRO officer (informally called a 'John the Baptist') being attached to the governor's staff to help set up a Department of External Affairs (DEA) and make preparations for post-independence representation including, to the extent requested, the conduct of international relations. This could lead to close friendships. Second, acting as *doyen* of the diplomatic corps (discussed in Chapter Seven) put Britain's representative in 'double harness' *vis-à-vis* the host state.[42] Third, pre-independence attachments to British diplomatic missions and British training courses for new diplomats, as well as, in a large number of cases, a British university education made for good personal relations and common ways of going about things. Fourth, members of high commissions

---

[38] Snelling draft note, 'Similarities and Differences'.

[39] T.D. O'Leary (first secretary and defence secretary, HCO)-R. Walker (head of Commonwealth Planning and Policy Department), 30 November 1966, *BDEE 1964–1971* II, 351.

[40] 'The Commonwealth as a British Interest: Canada and the Commonwealth', Annex to E.J. Emery (counsellor HCO)-Walker, 1 December 1966, *BDEE 1964–1971* II, 357.

[41] G.P. de T. Glazebrook (Commonwealth Division) memorandum, 'Status of Commonwealth High Commissioners', 30 September 1959, NAC, RG25, 6371, 3011-A-40, part 3.

[42] J.E.A. Miles (governor's secretary's office, Jamaica)-M.B. Chitty (Constitutional Department), 16 March 1962, TNA, DO200/50.

in Africa sometimes had the chance to build up contacts with African 'freedom fighters' who were in exile from their own territories. This went down well on most sides. And, fifth, there tended to be much goodwill towards the British including, on the whole, those who had been directly involved in colonial rule.

However, this last resource was not much exploited, as the CRO was reluctant to take on former Colonial Office (CO) officials or Colonial Service officers, and initially took a principled decision not to appoint the latter to territories in which they had held significant responsibility. It was feared that such men might have the 'wrong' tenor or give an unfortunate impression to the outside world. Occasional evidence suggested this apprehension was sometimes justified: Britain's first high commissioner to Zambia, whose career had been in colonial affairs, was openly shunned. On the other hand, Malay[si]a's prime minister, Tunku Abdul Rahman (1957–70, and generally referred to as 'the Tunku'), asked why none of his country's 'friends'—from colonial days—had been sent to Kuala Lumpur.[43] And when the former head of the CO's Far Eastern Department, Jack Johnston, became high commissioner in 1971, he was most warmly welcomed, both in the press and by the Tunku's successor. In Nigeria there was evident respect and affection for two former district officers who became deputy high commissioners; the High Commission was often turned to for advice or expertise; and it was thought to have 'greater influence than most'.[44] The same was said of the High Commission in Uganda. Newly-independent Sierra Leone was 'a wonderful posting', where the British high commissioner 'could do no wrong'. He had access to all the top people, and was invited to everything including school speech days and choir concerts. He was as 'busy as a beaver'—'a fairly languid beaver'.[45] In Asia, the British had a 'special position' in Singapore;[46] while in the Caribbean the British High Commission in Jamaica had 'the edge over all other Diplomatic Missions in Kingston' in terms of its standing with ministers and senior officials.[47]

One thing, however, which Britain was loathe to do for her former possessions was to represent their interests in other Commonwealth

[43] Greenhill (1992) 94.

[44] E.N. Larmour (minister, HCO)-Walker, 26 January 1967, *BDEE 1964–1971* II, 391.

[45] Personal communication.

[46] P.C.H. Holmer (DHC)-Walker, 12 December 1966, *BDEE 1964–1971* II, 373.

[47] R.G. Britten (DHC)-Walker, 12 December 1966, *BDEE 1964–1971* II, 377.

states. She was perfectly willing to do this in foreign states where they were not represented. But within the Commonwealth she would only speak on their behalf if there were overwhelming reasons for it, or if the circumstances made it notably churlish or unfriendly not to do so. The reason for this was that the Commonwealth was different. If states did not have high commissions, the 'proper course'[48] was to correspond direct. This was 'a feature of the unique and intimate atmosphere of intra-Commonwealth relations and emphasizes the special relationship between the Members'. She did not want 'to blur the special [Commonwealth] relationship' by moving in the direction of foreign diplomatic procedures.[49] Nor did she want to give the erroneous impression that one Commonwealth member was protecting another *vis-à-vis* a third, or for her high commissioner to be asked to take action which, in the Commonwealth context, could be embarrassing. She also wanted to encourage Commonwealth countries to appoint high commissioners.

3. *Collegial relations*

It was said in the early 1960s that 'one of the great benefits of the Commonwealth association [was] that the political leaders and the officials of Commonwealth countries are almost invariably able to establish close, friendly and useful relationships with their Commonwealth colleagues wherever and whenever they meet'.[50] This special quality, that made Commonwealth contacts more than ordinarily valuable, does not preclude other special relationships; but Commonwealth countries had things in common that they did not share with others in quite the same way. This was sometimes summed up as a sense of being British; Australia's prime minister, Robert Menzies (1949–66) used sometimes to say, 'I'm British to my bootstraps'.[51] Culture and sentiment does not guide foreign policy, but 'instinctive links' at a personal level not only played a welcome and 'highly important part in the lives of

[48] C.W. Dixon (constitutional adviser) minute, 11 July 1957, DO35/5223.
[49] A.R. Adair (Constitutional Department)-M.Z. Terry (CO), 12 November 1956, DO35/6211. See also Alan Lennox-Boyd (colonial secretary)-officer administering the Gold Coast government, no. 1711, 14 December 1956, TNA, DO35/6211.
[50] J.G. Hadwen, 'The Commonwealth in 1960', NAC, DEA, RG25, 9593, 10-1960/1.
[51] Carrington (1998) 118.

Member countries'; they were '[i]n many ways the life-blood of the Commonwealth association':[52]

> We speak the same language and understand each other—all the more so because we have largely common systems in administration, the law, the armed forces, education, British merchanting and banking traditions and interests. Oxbridge, Sandhurst, Shakespeare, the authorised version of the Bible are all genuine links. Even if the Commonwealth were a "farce" it is not "phoney".[53]

Such links and the weight they carried were by no means limited to the 'old' Commonwealth.

Thus high commissioners and their staffs generally found it easy to work with their Commonwealth counterparts. A new head of mission would make a special point of calling on other high commissioners, and the already-resident colleagues could generally be relied upon to be helpfully welcoming, not least in the sharing of information. (There was likely to be a similar camaraderie among Commonwealth ambassadors in non-Commonwealth states.) In the mid-1960s a deputy high commissioner said, 'One need only sit in on a Drafting Sub-Committee... to realise the degree of cohesion which exists among professionals who have been reared in the same public service tradition. That alone offers great opportunity for consultation and solid understanding. It even cuts across trivialities and play-acting which the politicians inflict on us.'[54] In London, good relations were facilitated by meetings of bodies like the Commonwealth War Graves Commission, Commonwealth occasions such as the multi-faith Commonwealth Day service, and (from 1965) dealings with the Commonwealth Secretariat. Such relations frequently survived even quite sharp political differences. At the start of the 1950s the Indian and South African high commissioners in London were firm friends, and at least at one time those states' representatives in Canberra were also close. Although Canadian-Indian relations deteriorated in the mid-1960s, a closely-involved Canadian said there was never 'any friction or unpleasantness in professional relations with

[52] CRO confidential print, 'The British Legacy: The "Intangible" Links of the Commonwealth Association', 9 August 1960, *BDEE 1957–64*, II, 645. In 1956 Macmillan (soon to be prime minister) regarded Britishness as 'the strongest cohesive force in the Commonwealth': Macmillan-Patrick Maitland MP, 19 March 1956, TNA, DO35/5012.

[53] H. Bowden (commonwealth secretary) cabinet memorandum, 'The Value of the Commonwealth', 24 April 1967, TNA, C(67)59, CAB 129/129.

[54] Private information.

Indian reps. [*sic*] whether in Karachi, the UN, Ottawa or London. I attribute this to our shared "cultural" background in the British modus operandi.'[55] Of course, friendships between high commissioners were not just attributable to the Commonwealth link—and there were plenty of similar developments in non-Commonwealth contexts. But especially at this period the fact remained that being in the Commonwealth meant something special which, while it was impossible to weigh with any accuracy, could not for that reason be discounted. High commissioners were different not just in name.

From time to time and in various places high commissioners (and also other Commonwealth heads of mission) gathered to discuss whatever was on their minds. It happened that such meetings in London were not very successful (as will be explained in the next chapter). But there were plenty of helpful Commonwealth meetings elsewhere, including ones between the resident group of high commissioners and senior political visitors. In non-Commonwealth capitals, too, useful meetings were held. In Moscow, the ambassadors of (at least some) Commonwealth states gathered on Saturday mornings to share information and exchange grievances, and in Washington, Paris, Beijing, and other capitals they held weekly or fortnightly meetings at which discussion ranged widely. Behind the Iron Curtain these meetings would sometimes be held in 'safe speech rooms'.

A noteworthy forum for regular and frequent Commonwealth consultation was the United Nations. Although the participants were not 'high commissioners' or from 'high commissions', but came from the offices of 'permanent representatives' (to which the title of ambassador was added), their activities call for brief mention as they provide an excellent example of the collegiality of Commonwealth representatives. At the UN's inception the existence of a Commonwealth group was taken for granted, reflecting its contribution to the war and the fact that its members did not fit into specifically regional groups. This worked to the benefit of Commonwealth members, most notably in having a non-permanent seat on the Security Council reserved for one of them. More generally, their delegates liaised closely, and thought it appropriate and useful to do so. This was facilitated by the attachment of one or two CRO officials to the British delegation with the job of keeping in touch with the other Commonwealth delegations. Commonwealth heads

[55] Personal communication.

of mission at the UN also met regularly at British-convened meetings. They were generally friendly and constructive, and as such a welcome relief from the often-chilly atmosphere of other meetings in the Cold-War dominated UN. Despite some difficult personalities like H.V. Evatt (Australian minister for external affairs, 1941–49) and Krishna Menon (Indian delegate 1946–47, 1952–62), and much candour, tension arising from divergent policies did not trespass on personal relations. At the end of the 1946 Assembly, for example, Vijaya Lakshmi Pandit of India (a non independent UN member), who had clashed bitterly with the South Africans, sought out the Union's prime minister, General Smuts, to ask his pardon lest anything she had said had failed to match up to the high standard of conduct set by Mahatma Gandhi (who had formed an indestructible friendship with Smuts before the First World War).

All Commonwealth members got something out of these UN meetings. Newer, weaker states were said to find them 'essential'.[56] They might not have changed votes, but they helped create 'understanding and respect even amid disagreement',[57] encouraged friendships, and reinforced the Commonwealth's 'strong old-boy network'.[58] The willingness of Britain—at the start of the UN's life one of the 'Big Three'—to take the time and trouble to explain her views and listen to theirs was appreciated. The result was 'a consulting team' that had 'more coherence in perspective than most of the regional groups',[59] although in the early years the frequency of meetings and closeness of consultation was not advertised lest it be construed as 'a ganging up' of the Commonwealth.[60] A couple of decades later this type of liaison was still continuing, and still judged useful and influential, although by then it was also recognised as a 'wasting asset'.[61]

---

[56] Holmes (1982) 169.

[57] Millar (1962) 745.

[58] Holmes (1982) 295. The network was further strengthened by attaching to 'old' Commonwealth delegations trainee diplomats of about-to-become independent territories.

[59] Holmes (1979) 267.

[60] Bevin (foreign secretary) at PMM-1948, 21 October 1948, NAC, RG2 18, 107, U-10-11 (vol. 1). See also 'Commentary on proposals for Commonwealth consultation', secret, 4 November 1948, NAC, RG2 18, 107, U-10-11 (vol. 1).

[61] P.J.S. Moon (first secretary, British Mission New York)-Walker, 5 December 1966, *BDEE 1964–1971* II, 362.

C. The Commonwealth Relations Office

1. *CRO Diplomacy*

Britain was the only Commonwealth country with a government department dedicated to dealings with independent Commonwealth states. It symbolised the importance Britain attached to the Commonwealth, and by its nature thought not just in terms of British interests but also approached particular issues from the perspective of the Commonwealth as a whole. It also meant that the Commonwealth had, in the commonwealth secretary, a spokesman at the heart of government, and high commissioners (and the Irish ambassador) did not have to jostle with others for ministerial attention. On the contrary, they were made to feel special. With the exception of Duncan Sandys (1960–64), the commonwealth secretary held small luncheon parties for them and their wives at the start of their posting in London, and at its end. These occasions, at which the guest list was 'purely social', played 'an important part in the special relationship between Commonwealth countries'.[62] So, too, did the CRO's Ceremonial Section, which liaised closely with high commissioners (and all the other Commonwealth visitors who passed through London). In the fifties it was still 'a Foreign Office with a family feeling':[63] small enough for there to be easy contact between officials; kindlier and warmer than the FO; and dedicated to treating its clients well, though not necessarily with kid gloves.

But the CRO was not a strong department, and although it grew in size and responsibilities it had difficulty shaking off jibes about being paternalistic, inefficient and slow-moving, insufficiently vigorous in pressing its case, and sanitising material to avoid upsetting anyone. Churchill said it was 'the Department which translates *oratio recta* into *oratio obliqua* and sends it out to the Dominions'.[64] Nor were many CRO officials a match for the FO's 'Rolls Royce' types, who tended to look down on the CRO people as 'a bunch of wets'.[65] Accordingly, if high commissions wanted 'hard information' and a broader perspective, they tended to go to the FO. In addition, during the early 1950s none

[62] Hugo minute, 8 August 1968, TNA, FCO49/138.
[63] Walter Runciman in the House of Commons, July 1925, quoted in Cross (1967) 72.
[64] Sir Richard Best interview with Sir Harold Smedley, 22 May 1997, CAC, DOHP 23.
[65] Interviews.

of the Conservative government's first three commonwealth relations secretaries carried much political weight. The CRO then fared better under the Earl of Home (1955–60), an intelligent and popular man who was regarded in several quarters as the best of all commonwealth secretaries.[66] His successor, Duncan Sandys, had the merit of fighting hard in cabinet, and also succeeded in shaking out and sharpening up the Office. But he was a bully with peculiarly frustrating working habits and a penchant for over-lengthy meetings; and after the colonies were added to his responsibilities in 1961 he devoted much more time to them than to the Commonwealth. In the mid-1960s the CRO was accused of clinging to the 'fiction' that the Commonwealth remained 'a close-knit family in which the members really did maintain "English" standards and really did, literally and metaphorically, play cricket'. It was alleged that CRO diplomacy 'has never been diplomacy as the Foreign Office knows it. It has been rather the practice of a maternal relationship, the proud and tolerant kindness of the mother country towards her adolescent brood'. And it was said that whereas FO posts appraised events 'objectively and expertly', CRO posts 'too often' consisted of 'dedicated idealists' emitting 'a vague effusion of good will'.[67]

This is perhaps unfair. The CRO by no means wallowed in sentimentalism, and when interests clashed 'frankness and, at times, toughness were all the greater because of the family relationship'.[68] Even if (for understandable reasons) the CRO attached overmuch value to the Commonwealth, the policy of 'being nice to the rest of the Commonwealth', was not a CRO invention. It 'originate[d] to a very large extent outside this Office, in a cloud of emotion, as well as in cooler-headed reasoning'.[69] For until at least the early- to mid-1960s the British government regarded the Commonwealth as very important, and intra-Commonwealth relations as different from foreign relations. They were seen as more intimate and informal; having a different 'feel'; based on friendship, frankness, and partnership; and having often-distinctive procedures. Thus it was said that whereas almost all British missions in foreign states tended 'to report on basis of observation of what is going

[66] Thorpe (1996) 160.

[67] Kirkman (1966) 187. In the mid-1960s it took a three-month stint in the CRO's Intelligence Department to 'shatter' one CRO official's 'illusions of the cosy commonwealth [sic] relationship': Sir Colin Imray memoir, CAC, DOHP 54.

[68] Garner (1978) 44.

[69] Walsh Atkins minute, 5 March 1963, TNA, DO193/62.

on, [high commissions did] so on the basis of fairly frank discussions with Commonwealth Government Departments concerned'.[70] High commissions were judged to reach more widely into the host community than embassies, and their staff were thought to be much readier to contact opposition parties than their counterparts from the FO.

The difference between CRO and FO attitudes were highlighted by the former's response to a 1963 memorandum written by a retired Foreign Office PUS, Lord Strang. He had suggested that perhaps Britain was 'too apt, by the tradition and bias of our service, to do the giving and leave the taking to others'.[71] She might take a leaf from the French book and give her diplomacy 'a new look': instead of altruistically 'casting [her] bread upon the waters', she should practise 'tough diplomacy' and be 'rather more self-regarding' and unsentimental.[72] It is unlikely that the drift of Strang's remarks upset many people in the FO, and in the CRO, too, there were those who felt that British foreign policy had 'become blunted since the war by over-much deference to the views of other Commonwealth Governments, particularly Mr. Nehru and Dr. Nkrumah' (of Ghana).[73] However, others were 'surprised—and appalled' by Strang's words, including Joe Garner, the CRO's PUS: 'I cannot believe that a reversion to eighteenth century diplomacy, to emphasis on selfish national interests and, in effect, to the rule of the jungle, is in the best interests of this country', he said.

> It would strike at the root of our partnership in the Commonwealth; it would delay any possibility of our getting into Europe, and it would immensely prejudice our relationship with the United States. We should also, no doubt, have even more trouble with the United Nations.
>
> More broadly, I feel this line is quite out of keeping with the conditions in the second half of the twentieth century, and with what we should be aiming at. The Prime Minister has consistently laid emphasis on the need for 'interdependence'; surely that is right, with all that that involves. One de Gaulle is quite enough at a time![74]

---

[70] E.N. Larmour (counsellor, HCO Canberra)-D.L. Cole (head of Personnel Department), 11 September 1962, TNA, DO197/3. Washington and New York were the two exceptions.

[71] Sir Harold Caccia (PUS, FO), circular letter to heads of mission referring to the question posed by Strang, 1 March 1963, TNA, DO193/62.

[72] Strang quoted in Caccia circular letter, 1 February 1963 TNA, DO193/62, Beck (2004).

[73] Shannon minute, 25 February 1963, TNA, DO193/62.

[74] Garner minute, 14 February 1963, TNA, DO193/62.

No one in the CRO questioned Britain's right to stand up for herself. Britain could, and should, be tough with the Commonwealth. But she should also recognise that Commonwealth members 'still expect negotiations with Britain to be different in kind from negotiations with other countries',[75] and should try to retain that different atmosphere. In addition to there being objections in principle to 'tough diplomacy', it would 'be the surest road to failure with the new Commonwealth States in Africa'.[76] When dealing with 'new shorn lambs'[77] Britain should adopt 'a policy of "contained appeasement"'[78]—not out of altruism but self-interest. This was, first, because of the importance of building up a post-colonial relationship during an 'initial period of hypersensitive nationalism'.[79] Second, it was in Britain's long-term interest to promote 'tolerable relationships between whites, browns and blacks' and the Commonwealth was 'a useful instrument' for this purpose.[80] Third, if newly-independent states were 'economically and financially shaky it [wa]s because of the conditions in which we handed them over at independence'. Taking advantage of their inexperience and trying to extract every last penny out of them would frustrate Britain's 'necessary objective of securing their stability and peaceful progress'.[81] Fourth, in most cases Britain did not hold the whip hand:

> It is the weaker countries, with everything to gain and little to lose, who have the bargaining power. Of course, if we withheld military support, capital investment, technical aid, from new Commonwealth countries, we could gravely harm them. But they could do far more damage to us, (for example, by expropriating business interests, or in supporting the Soviet bloc in the United Nations); and they would not hesitate to do so if they felt so inclined. And even if we ignore moral considerations (i.e. the pledges reiterated by successive Governments to continue to assist in the development of countries for whose administration we have been responsible in the past), we cannot afford to neglect the British interests which are at stake in Commonwealth countries overseas.... With newer,

[75] Viscount Amory (British HC, Ottawa)-Garner, 9 April 1963, TNA, DO193/62.

[76] Note attached to Garner comments on Lord Strang's 'New Look Diplomacy', 'The Issue as it Affects our Relations with the Commonwealth in Africa', 5 April 1963, TNA, DO193/62.

[77] Pritchard (British HC, Dar es Salaam)-Garner, secret & personal, 29 March 1963, TNA, DO193/62.

[78] Note attached Garner comments on Strang's 'New Look Diplomacy'.

[79] *Ibid.*

[80] Walsh Atkins minute, 5 March 1963, TNA, DO193/62.

[81] Pritchard-Garner, 29 March 1963.

less resilient countries, experience has already shown that a more subtle and flexible approach eventually brings larger dividends.[82]

2. *Information sharing*

At the start of the 1950s, the Commonwealth's members were still heavily dependent on Britain for information about the wider world, which was channelled to them by the CRO through high commissioners. Indeed, the CRO regarded it as the duty of a British high commissioner 'to keep the Commonwealth Government informed of all current developments especially in the sphere of international affairs, particularly in those foreign countries where that Government maintains no diplomatic representation'.[83] The one notable limitation was of information about other Commonwealth members.

However, distinctions were drawn between the old and new Commonwealth when distributing certain documents and deciding how far to consult and share information. This was justified on the grounds of security, efficiency, and the unwillingness of the new Commonwealth to share in certain commitments. Precautions were in order. In the late 1940s and early 1950s, the Indian high commissioner in London, Krishna Menon, was thought to have a personality disorder, take drugs, have a communist amongst his mistresses, and himself have a strong pro-Soviet bias. His mission was allegedly 'honeycombed with Communist sympathisers'.[84] In 1957 the commonwealth secretary said that such was the 'divergency of view' between Britain and India, 'We simply would not dare' exchange information as freely with India as with Canada.[85] Meanwhile, Kwame Nkrumah, a former member of the Communist Party and nationalist leader in the Gold Coast (Ghana), had long been thought 'dangerous' by the FO.[86]

On the other hand, most old Commonwealth members (Canada, Australia, and New Zealand) and their high commissioners received much fuller, and immensely useful, information as well as (on a personal and confidential basis) certain secret telegrams. The 'rule of thumb' was 'to tell them freely and frankly everything except the little which it was

---

[82] Garner comments on Strang's 'New look diplomacy'.
[83] Commonwealth secretary memorandum, in House of Commons (1959) 57.
[84] F.H. Boland (Irish ambassador), 1 Aug. 1952, INA, DFA, P.12/14(a)/1.
[85] Home-Malcolm MacDonald (British HC, New Delhi), 10 December 1957, *BDEE 1957–64* II, 627.
[86] FO Research Department memorandum, June 1950, *BDEE Ghana* I, 273.

necessary to keep back'.[87] This meant that they expected, and enjoyed, free and frank exchanges of views, and Britain, in turn, benefited from receiving a certain amount of information from them. Their London high commissioners felt splendidly placed for knowing what went on in the world.[88] In connection with the United Nations General Assembly some briefs were exchanged, and at least one preparatory meeting was held. Additionally, there was important intelligence and defence collaboration between them. So far as the other old Commonwealth member—South Africa—was concerned, things were not quite the same following the Nationalist victory in 1948. However, at some levels cooperation remained good. When at the end of the 1950s the Canadian DEA was 'encountering serious obstacles' in setting up a new section dealing with Africa (which was 'almost virgin' to her officers),[89] they approached the South Africans who gave the Canadian High Commission in Pretoria 'all the information they wished to have'.[90]

Of course Britain's behaviour was self-serving inasmuch as information was not only a sign of Commonwealth membership but also a means of trying to keep others on side. As Britain's cabinet secretary pointed out,

> In practice, the only means of ensuring that... on attaining independence, [states] will turn to us for help and advice in the conduct of their external relations is to make available to them from the outset information and guidance on such international questions as are of direct concern to them. Their first steps in the conduct of external relations will be of crucial importance. It will therefore be most desirable that they should from the outset exchange representatives with other Commonwealth countries and that through this medium they should be provided with a flow of information and guidance, selective at first but progressively enlarged, on international matters of direct concern to them and of common concern to the Commonwealth as a whole.... It is only by this means that we can hope to develop, in new Commonwealth members, that similarity of approach to the main problems of international relations which enables the Commonwealth to exercise its influence in world affairs. But these procedures, viz., the exchange of high commissioners, the interchange of information and views on foreign policy, and attendance at periodical

[87] T.J. Duggin memorandum, 'Relations with the Commonwealth High Commissions after the FO/CO merger' (first draft), 24 July 1968, TNA, FCO49/138.

[88] Interview.

[89] C.B.H. Fincham (first secretary, South African HCO, Ottawa), 'Exchange of Information on Africa', 22 July 1959, SAA, BTS, 1/28/3, vol. 1.

[90] W.C. Naudé (DEA)-Fincham, 12 January 1960, SAA, BTS, 1/28/3, vol. 1.

> meetings of Commonwealth Ministers, are in fact the outward marks of full Commonwealth membership.[91]

Similarly, the main purpose of consultation was to try to win support for, or at least avoid opposition to, British policies. The price Britain had to pay was giving greater attention to others' views than she would normally do, though it could be presented as a positive characteristic of intra-Commonwealth relations and an exemplification of Britain's 'wisdom & good faith'.[92]

3. *Ireland and the CRO*

Seán MacBride, the Irish minister for external affairs (1948–51), had assumed that once Ireland had left the Commonwealth she would deal with the FO, and had spoken of breaking off all relations with the CRO. However, thanks to some 'complex manoeuvring'[93] in Whitehall, the British prime minister decided that transferring responsibility for Ireland to the Foreign Office 'would be inconsistent with the Government's policy that Eire should not be regarded as a foreign country'.[94] This satisfied everyone. It accorded with the wishes of the Palace. The foreign secretary was glad to avoid involvement in problems likely to arouse Irish-American feelings. The CRO was happy since it had feared for its future if Irish dealings were moved to the FO and, as discussed below, did what it could to retain its Irish responsibilities. It also turned out to please the Irish, although MacBride's decision not to press for a change is remarkable given Irish attitudes only a few years earlier. In 1945 Joe Walshe (the secretary of external affairs—the senior official) had spoken of the DO's barely-concealed 'anti-Irish animus' and its Colonial Office mentality,[95] and in 1946 his successor, Freddie Boland, said Ireland would be much better off if the DO were wound up.

It is true that the CRO had sympathy for Northern Ireland, and was sometimes frustrated and irritated with 'the South': one official who was 'noticeably soured'[96] while working on the CRO's Irish desk, told

---

[91] Brook report, 'The Future of Commonwealth Membership', January 1955, TNA, PREM11/1726F.
[92] See Walsh Atkins minute, 2 January 1957, TNA, DO35/5012.
[93] Dean (1992) 410.
[94] Liesching (PUS) minute, 10 November 1950, TNA, DO35/3984A.
[95] Walshe conversations in London enclosed in report to de Valera, 21 September 1945, INA, P 12/14(2).
[96] O'Brien (1988) 181.

the cabinet secretary that the 'underlying difficulty is that while views in Whitehall are formed on a basis of reason and common-sense... this approach may be inapplicable to Eire'.[97] However, the election of a Labour Government in 1945 was before long seen by Ireland as having produced a British 'change of heart'.[98] The influx of new blood in 1947 when the India Office was merged with the Dominions Office to form the CRO (plus the transfer of staff from the Burma Office when it was abolished in 1948) was also from Ireland's point of view a change for the better.

And so, when Britain and Ireland exchanged ambassadors in 1950, MacBride said 'he had no intention' at that time of raising the question of moving over to the FO.[99] For its part, the CRO thought there were several 'powerful' and 'very cogent' arguments against such a step.[100] The CRO link was all that remained of Ireland's former Commonwealth association. If Anglo-Irish relations were transferred to the FO and the Irish ambassador was deemed 'foreign', Britain's argument that Ireland was non-foreign would be much weakened. This would make it all the more difficult to reach an arrangement with Ireland to secure her return 'to the Commonwealth and the use of her ports';[101] it would encourage Northern Ireland extremists to argue that there was no chance of a political accommodation with 'the South'; and would pose a threat to Ireland's preferential trading arrangements with the Commonwealth. On the wider international front, putting Ireland under the FO would set a bad example to the new Commonwealth members 'who were already inclined to vie with each other in eliminating any marks of Commonwealth relations'.[102] It would also hearten men like Australia's minister for external affairs, H.V. Evatt, who wanted to deal with the FO. And on the domestic bureaucratic front, it would encourage the FO to resume 'their intrigues for absorbing into their empire the whole field of Commonwealth relations'.[103]

---

[97] Norman Archer (AUS, principal secretary to British representative 1941, 1944–48)-Brook, 23 December 1948, quoted in *ibid.*, 181.

[98] Boland (SDEA)-Kiernan (Irish representative, Canberra), 31 December, 1946, INA, DFA, Ottawa Embassy, D/30/1.

[99] Ben Cockram (AUS) minute, 15 August 1950, TNA, DO35/3984A.

[100] Liesching minute, 10 November 1950, TNA, DO35/3984A.

[101] CRO memorandum, 'Responsibility for Relations with the Irish Republic', c. 10 November 1950, TNA, DO35/3984A.

[102] *Ibid.*

[103] *Ibid.*

By giving the new Irish ambassador, Freddie Boland (1950–56), first-class treatment and helping the embassy in its dealings with other departments, the CRO did no harm to its cause. At the same time it 'shrewdly put no obstacles' in the way of Ireland's pre-1950 'ambition' to escape to the FO.[104] Boland, who was said to wield a good deal of influence, recognised he was well off and also the advantages of the CRO's wide knowledge of Ireland and its leaders. He was

> dealing a good deal more with the Commonwealth Relations Office than his predecessor ever did and had no complaint to make about the consideration that Irish questions were getting in London. . . . they were probably better served with a substantial share of Gordon Walker's attention than they would be by the infinitesimal [*sic.*] fraction of Bevin's which would be all they could expect to get from the Foreign Office in these times.[105]

Thus it was that not only did Ireland not suggest a transfer, she resisted it. She was proved right, for after the merger of the Foreign and Commonwealth Relations Offices, Anglo-Irish relations did not loom large on the new department's horizon. Meanwhile, keeping Ireland in the CRO meant that to the FO she remained 'mysterious and unknown . . . geographically, politically and diplomatically'.[106]

D. Safeguarding the Office: The 1961 Vienna Convention on Diplomatic Relations

1. *Preparation*

During the negotiation of the Vienna Convention on Diplomatic Relations (VCDR) the members of the Commonwealth collaborated closely to protect the office of high commissioner, so underlining the value they attached to it. The Convention was the first comprehensive treaty setting out the rules of diplomatic intercourse, these rules having evolved over centuries on the basis of the customary practices of

[104] Robertson (Canadian HC)-Boland (Irish ambassador) conversation, 4 January 1951, NAC, RG25, 4481, 50021–40, part 3; *The Irish Times*, 31 August 1959.

[105] Robertson-Boland conversation, 4 January 1951.

[106] Peck (1978) 16. Peck also found striking ignorance and prejudice: 'We had not been long in Ireland when the wife of a very distinguished British ex-soldier, retired from public life, said to Mariska, "Tell me, my dear, what is it like now, living in Government House?" I'm afraid I wouldn't know," Mariska answered very gently. "The President moved in before we came here"': *ibid.*, 18.

states. The project was an ambitious and 'hazardous task',[107] involving detailed, 'complicated and difficult' negotiations.[108] Their immediate starting point was a draft convention that the UN's International Law Commission had spent several years preparing. The Commission's members sat in their individual capacities, but took full account of governmental views.

However, one matter which neither the Commission nor the relevant government departments took into account at all was the existence of the office of high commissioner. When, late in the day, a shocked CRO discovered this, it was hardly in a position to complain as it had paid no attention to the paperwork (which it had received) about the emerging convention. Only at the end of 1960, when the FO asked whether it wanted high commissioners to be specifically mentioned, did it wake up. Minds were now concentrated, to find not only that there was no mention in the draft of high commissioners (or of acting high commissioners), but that some of the wording was unsuitable and in some respects 'entirely wrong in relation to the Commonwealth'.[109]

The first problem had to do with the functions of a diplomatic mission (Article 3 in the final Convention—this discussion uses the final numbering of the Convention's Articles). The draft stated that a mission represented a state and protected the interests of its nationals. High commissioners of the Queen's realms, however, represented governments, and strictly speaking they did not protect nationals, as in theory each Commonwealth member protected all Commonwealth nationals within its jurisdiction. Nor did the CRO think the Commonwealth 'would like formally to commit itself' to another provision in the draft Article 3, which said that diplomatic missions engaged in 'internal political reporting'.[110]

Second, the draft's reference to the making diplomatic appointments was unsatisfactory, as its insistence on *agrément* (Article 4) failed to take account of the fact that this was not formally sought between

[107] Sir Francis Vallat (legal adviser, FO), 'Report on the International Conference on Diplomatic Intercourse and Immunities held at Vienna, March 2 to April 18, 1961', TNA, TP30015/85, FO372/7578 (Vallat report).
[108] F.R. Hoyer-Millar (PUS, FO) minute, 5 June 1961, TNA, TP30015/85, FO 372/7578.
[109] D.L. Cole (head of Personnel Department), minute 2 January 1961, TNA, DO161/137.
[110] *Ibid.*

the Queen's realms.[111] Third, requiring the receiving states' express consent to the appointment of their nationals to the staff of a sending state's mission (Article 8) was not 'the sort of thing'[112] the CRO wanted. Commonwealth states neither sought nor received permission for such appointments, which were thought (erroneously, it later emerged) to be common. (This problem arose out of all Commonwealth citizens being treated in British law as British subjects or British citizens.)

Fourth, requiring a uniform procedure for receiving heads of mission (Article 18) could lead to the Queen or her governors-general having to start ceremonially receiving high commissioners of the realms in formal audience. Fifth, Article 41 (which related to the duties of a mission towards the receiving state) said that they were to conduct all their official business with or through foreign ministries. This ignored both the role of the CRO in London and the high commission practice of sometimes dealing with departments other than DEAs. Finally, the provision that the International Court of Justice would have jurisdiction in disputes arising out of the interpretation of the Convention (Article 45 in the draft—it did not appear in the Convention) was objectionable to the CRO, which regarded it as a 'a point of principle...that Commonwealth countries should not take each other to the International Court'.[113] (Of those Commonwealth states which had accepted the Court's compulsory jurisdiction, all but Pakistan had excluded Commonwealth disputes from their acceptances.)

Altogether this was a sorry prospect, the more so because there was little Britain could do. There was no question of trying to exclude the Commonwealth from the convention: it was too late in the day; foreign states would object; India was unlikely to agree (she was thought to be anxious that high commissioners and ambassadors should be treated the same); and others would be 'reluctant to see the Commonwealth exhibited as a peculiar entity in this way'.[114] Nor was there any mileage in suggesting a Commonwealth understanding or reservation to restrict the application of the convention, since the new Commonwealth (and

---

[111] Initially realm governments simply notified each other of the name of an appointee but it became the norm to seek informal approval. In January 1961 the CRO said there had never been any objection to an inter-realm appointment.

[112] Cole minute, 2 January 1961.

[113] Undated G. Cunningham (CRO adviser attached to British delegation to Vienna Conference) minute, c. 18 February 1961, TNA, DO161/137.

[114] L.J.D. Wakely (head of Constitutional Department) minute, 3 January 1961, TNA, DO161/137.

even some of the old) might interpret it as an attempt 'to deny them the full trappings of independence'.[115] Old and new alike wanted the Convention to apply to intra-Commonwealth relations. Nor would any references to protecting the specialness of intra-Commonwealth relations or high commissioners get far. It would have little resonance for, say, Pakistan *vis-à-vis* India, or in capitals where high commissioners were already becoming less 'special', and so might do more harm than good. In any case, in some states it might be better to have 'the protection of an agreed text, rather than relying on local goodwill and legislation which can be altered'.[116]

For these sorts of reasons Britain decided only to try for amendments that were deemed essential. Accordingly, after consulting the rest of the Commonwealth through her high commissioners, the British delegation went to the conference seeking, first, to make *agréation* and the consent of the receiving state to the employment of its nationals in a sending state's mission permissive rather than compulsory; second, to insert references to the titles 'high commissioner' and 'acting high commissioner'; third, to allow missions to deal with departments other than foreign ministries; and fourth, to obtain an 'all-important'[117] phrase permitting, 'more favourable treatment' where this was already extended 'by custom or agreement'. Such a form of words would be sufficiently 'inconspicuous' as to be 'unlikely to awaken objection';[118] make it unnecessary to seek a number of other amendments; and permit Commonwealth governments to continue exercising 'less formality and control in their relations *inter se* than in relations with foreign countries'.[119]

2. *The Conference, 2 March–18 April 1961*

The Vienna Convention was negotiated in an unusually constructive, good-natured, and amicable way by 320 delegates from 81 states. This included only ten Commonwealth delegations as the eleventh member,

---

[115] CRO circular telegram W36, 23 January 1961, TNA, TP20015/18, FO372/7573, DO161/137.

[116] C.D. Lush (assistant legal adviser, FO) minute, 16 January 1961, TNA, TP30015/18, FO372/7573.

[117] 'Report of the Canadian delegation to the UN Conference on Diplomatic Intercourse and Immunities', NAC, RG25, 3477, 9–1961/1 (Canadian delegation report).

[118] Legal Division memorandum, 9 February 1961, NAC, RG25, 6371, 3011-A-40, part 3.

[119] CRO circular telegram W36.

New Zealand, decided that the benefit of attendance would be outweighed by its cost.

Despite the Cold War being at its height, there was a 'remarkable'[120] absence of East-West acrimony. Such divisions as there were tended, on the more important issues, to be 'between the major and the minor Powers, and the minor Powers being in the majority tended to be able to impose their will'.[121] This, however, was significantly counterbalanced by the leadership that was given by Britain and the Soviet Union. (The Americans were 'very weak' and 'strangely out of touch'.)[122] Britain took the initiative in, and put much effort into, meetings of the West European and Commonwealth groups, which the FO legal adviser, Sir Francis Vallat, usually chaired. They helped simplify issues, threw light on the wide field covered by the draft articles, and produced an agreed line on particular points. This paid off since Commonwealth members found these consultations useful for exchanging views, planning approaches, and expressing reservations, especially when Britain planned to introduce a controversial amendment to the Article dealing with the employment in a mission of people with the nationality of the receiving state. In addition, a member of the CRO was on hand to liaise with the Commonwealth states for the first part of the Conference, and they consulted the British a good deal. The Commonwealth delegations also made an 'outstanding' contribution to the proceedings[123] by providing three committee chairmen (one of whom chaired the Committee of the Whole, which did the main work), and playing a valuable role in overcoming the most difficult controversy of the conference—the privileges and immunities of administrative and technical staff. There was also an 'unusually happy relationship between the Commonwealth and Afro-Asian group', thanks largely to the Ceylonese ambassador at Washington who chaired the Afro-Asian meetings and 'acted as a sympathetic liaison officer between them and the Commonwealth group'.[124] All this meant that it was possible 'to achieve agreement

[120] Vallat report.
[121] *Ibid.*
[122] D.P. Waldron (assistant legal adviser), 'Report of Irish Delegation to the Conference on Diplomatic Intercourse and Immunities, Vienna, March 2 to April 18, 1961', INA, DFA, 417/224 (Waldron report).
[123] Vallat report.
[124] *Ibid.*

on many points before they came before the Main Committee',[125] to decide whether amendments protecting Commonwealth practices should be in the name of the Commonwealth or Britain, and to have Commonwealth practices accommodated (notably in Articles 14 and 47). (On other matters, Commonwealth delegates went their own ways, making no attempt to vote as a group, and they were sometimes seriously divided—as over the use of wireless transmitters.)

There were five ways in which the draft Convention was amended in a manner which suited the Commonwealth. First, insertions into Articles 10, 13, 19, and 41 recognised the role of the CRO as the channel of communication with the receiving state, though '[i]t required both persistence and persuasion to convince the Conference to accept this modification'.[126] Second, with the support of every Commonwealth delegation (except that of the about-to-depart South Africa), Article 47 was amended to allow more favourable treatment in accordance with 'custom or agreement'. This amendment was passed effortlessly, thanks to 'certain delicate manoeuvres'; Soviet support (which provoked 'extreme and unavoidable' American annoyance);[127] and the fact that the conference was running out of time so that the amendment's implications were not fully examined. Third, after Article 8 (employment of nationals of the receiving state in a sending state's mission) had been 'given a very rough treatment' by delegates who thought the practice 'was, and ought to be obsolescent',[128] the British delegation succeeded in ensuring that, while consent for this was required, it did not need to be express. Fourth, the draft article about the settlement of disputes was relegated to an optional protocol. And fifth, Article 14 was amended to recognise 'other heads of mission of equivalent rank' to ambassadors.

This last achievement was hard won, taking 'no less than forty interventions and a four-day adjournment' before an acceptable wording was agreed.[129] During the discussion of the presentation of credentials (Article 13), Britain's remarks about wanting to cover the 'well-established practice' of high commissioners dealing with the CRO, had

[125] Undated Cunningham report on Vienna Conference, TNA, DO161/138.
[126] Vallat report.
[127] Lush-Cunningham, 7 April 1961, TNA, DO161/138.
[128] Cunningham-Wakely, 10 March 1961, TNA, DO161/137; undated Cunningham report.
[129] Canadian delegation report.

'prematurely set off the debate'[130] about the office. Then the British explanation about why high commissioners should be mentioned in Article 14 drew undesirable attention to differences between high commissioners and ambassadors. Nor was the Commonwealth cause helped when it was pointed out that the former FO legal adviser, Sir Gerald Fitzmaurice, had 'unaccountably slipped up' by telling the International Law Commission 'that High Commissioners were not "ambassadorial" but "domestic" and therefore did not need special mention here'.[131] Then, as they had warned, the French demanded that mention should also be made of their *haut-représentants de la Communauté* (French envoys to former colonies who had adhered to the French Community). Other delegations, especially the Latin Americans and Soviets, strongly opposed a specific reference to special titles in a general convention. However, there were sympathetic suggestions that the position be covered with a general formula, so Ghana proposed adding a reference to 'other heads of mission of equivalent rank'. This, however, outraged France and Tunisia: they had not been warned beforehand; they considered a specific mention of *hauts-représentants* was particularly appropriate (since they were accredited to heads of state); and they wrongly thought that the new amendment was intended to replace, rather than be in addition to, a reference to *hauts-représentants*.

The debate grew acrimonious and there were calls for a return to the original wording. However, after further Commonwealth consultations, and in view of the fact that no one had suggested high commissioners were *not* equal to ambassadors, Ghana proposed that Article 14 should just refer to 'other heads of mission of equivalent rank', and make no explicit reference to high commissioners and *hauts-représentants*. This was appreciated as a reasonable move but the vote was delayed to allow for further consultation and, reportedly, so that the leader of the Soviet delegation, G.I. Tunkin, could consult Moscow. During this period, it increasingly seemed that the fate of the amendment lay in Tunkin's hands, and much behind-the-scenes effort went into trying to influence him. Four days later, when the vote was taken, the formula was approved by 71-0-5. It meant that, when the Convention came into force, high commissioners and their equality with ambassadors would be recognised in diplomatic law.

---

130 *Ibid.*
131 Waldron report.

3. *Impact*

As the Convention did not lead to any large immediate changes, high commissioners and ambassadors were still sufficiently distinct to allow the CRO to argue that the moves towards 'normal' diplomacy 'should not be over-rated'.[132] Nonetheless, the office of high commissioner had been weakened by the Convention.

In the first place, the CRO had had to swallow its objections to a number of articles so as not to 'draw attention to our abnormal practices'.[133] The articles in question included ones relating to the functions of a mission, *agrément*, and the reception of heads of mission. Maintenance of these Commonwealth practices might therefore need to be justified by reference to Article 47.2 (b), which permitted flexibility stemming from custom or agreement. But that would mean their undesired exposure.

Second, the disparities between representation in foreign and Commonwealth countries had been reduced, or were likely to be reduced. It was now open to receiving Commonwealth states to place limits on the size of high commissions (Article 11) and to declare a member of a high commission *persona non grata* (Article 9). High commissions' service staff and servants lost certain jurisdictional immunities. In high commissions there was a growing trend towards the use of diplomatic nomenclature, their acting high commissioners increasingly being called *chargés d'affaires*, and their senior personnel soon being termed ministers or counsellors. By the early 1970s the Australian High Commission in London was the only one still using the old, Commonwealth, designations—and within a couple of years it, too, had adopted the usual diplomatic terminology. It was now necessary for the receiving state to consent to the appointment of its nationals to the diplomatic staff of a high commission, even if they also had the citizenship of the sending state (Article 8). And except in Australia and New Zealand (who continued—and still continue—their old practices),[134] high commissioners exchanged between the Queen's realms ceased being considered as hav-

---

[132] CRO memorandum for Committee on Representational Services Overseas, 'History of the CRO', 20 September 1962, TNA, DO197/2.

[133] Cunningham minute, 17 February 1961, TNA, DO161/137.

[134] At least in Australia this does not appear to have become an issue with other heads of mission, perhaps because only a handful of high commissioners are involved (in 2006, those from Britain, Canada, New Zealand, Papua New Guinea, and Solomon Islands).

ing taken up their functions, and taking precedence, from the moment their feet touched the soil of the host state or its capital. Instead, they were only fully in business (and therefore took precedence) as of the date on which they presented their equivalent of credentials—i.e., letters of introduction (Articles 13 and 16).

The CRO was gloomy about this last change. It envisaged an ex-cabinet minister, charged with urgent business, being unable to execute it because he had not presented his letter to an absent prime minister; or a 'temporarily ill-disposed' Commonwealth country keeping the British high commissioner designate 'in a state of vacuum for weeks'.[135] However, it was a theoretical rather than a real problem. Delays in presenting letters tended to be brief where the diplomatic corps was small; when the prime minister was away the letter might be presented to the acting prime minister; or in some cases the high commissioner might 'pursue'[136] the prime minister if the latter was visiting another part of the country. In any event, among friends there were always ways around problems.

Third, the Convention assisted those Commonwealth states who wished to adapt their practices to 'normal' international use, as they could cite the requirement of the first paragraph of Article 47 that, except in the circumstances mentioned in its second paragraph, the receiving state should not discriminate between states. Even in the CRO there was some feeling that changes in the character of the Commonwealth now made it appropriate to treat Commonwealth diplomats much like foreign ones. This was signified by a less sweeping grant of diplomatic status, so that tourist advisers, trade agents, and the like from Commonwealth states could no longer rely on easy access to diplomatic immunities.[137]

Thus the CRO had not got all it wanted for the Commonwealth out of the negotiation of the Convention, but it had not done badly.

---

[135] P.A. Grier minute, 18 November 1963, TNA, DO161/139.

[136] C.H. Imray minute, September 1962, TNA, DO161/39.

[137] However, in 1966 it did not appear that members of Commonwealth missions in London were being harshly treated: the Ghanaian and Nigerian High Commissions had a remarkably large number of 'diplomatic agents' compared with their 'administrative and technical staff'; and there were noticeably high numbers of the latter in the Canadian (184), Australian (334), and Indian (618) High Commissions. Under the Vienna Convention diplomatic agents enjoyed its full range of privileges and immunities, while administrative and technical staff had them all except immunity from the civil and administrative jurisdiction of the receiving state in respect of their non-official acts.

However, Britain's chancellor of the exchequer was implacably opposed to provisions that went further, in the matter of excise privileges, than his country's existing practice. These provisions apparently required the abandonment of hitherto sacrosanct rules which prevented high commissioners (and ambassadors) and their staffs from obtaining British goods which were normally subject to excise duty without payment of that duty—notably, Scotch whisky and British-manufactured cigarettes. So fierce was the argument, so implacable the chancellor, and so strong the doubts raised in the foreign secretary's mind that the latter wondered whether the Convention was worth ratifying. Eventually the FO legal adviser came up with an ingenious interpretation that enabled Britain to maintain that her existing practice did not conflict with the Convention. She ratified it in September 1964, a few months after it had come into force.

E. Conclusion

The satisfaction that was so often expressed with the office of high commissioner from the early 1950s onwards contrasts sharply with the previous attitude. One reason was the prevailing optimism about the Commonwealth and decolonisation. Another was the fact that high commissioners felt more confident about their office. They had been put on a par with ambassadors in the very important areas of status and immunities; they enjoyed certain advantages over them in respect of protocol, form, and ceremony (especially on royal occasions); and in London they benefited from dealing with the CRO. Moreover, they were no longer a tiny—and beleaguered—band. By the beginning of 1962 there were thirteen high commissioners in London, and members of high commissions comprised about a quarter of the diplomatic community. In all Commonwealth capitals they put themselves out for each other. They were 'on to a good thing'. Hence it was not surprising that the Commonwealth 'came through' during the negotiation of the Vienna Convention on Diplomatic Relations. Here Britain championed the office determinedly and well, and had a fund of goodwill to call on in the other Commonwealth delegations. This reflected both the emphasis she placed on the Commonwealth in her foreign policy, and the importance to the Commonwealth of Britain's central position. The title of high commissioner and the benefits associated with the office signified the existence of a particular historical and contemporary relationship, which all members valued. The Commonwealth was still very much a going concern. So much so that in the mid-1950s there was even talk of it being extended to include France, Norway, and other European countries.

However, by the early 1960s the Commonwealth was perceptibly becoming a looser and more diverse organisation, and its members were showing signs of a disinclination, except on ceremonial occasions, to bother distinguishing between themselves and foreign states. There was no clear indication that dramatic developments lay at hand, either in relation to the Commonwealth itself or to the office of high commissioner. But there was a discernable hint in the air that for high commissioners the way ahead lay downhill.

CHAPTER SEVEN

NORMALISATION, EARLY 1960s–MID-1970s

The Commonwealth's occasional tribulations during the 1950s had not tarnished its general reputation as 'a good thing'.[1] But then the pace of change accelerated, the Commonwealth was assailed by unpredictable crises, problems arose in all quarters, and within a few years the association was being viewed in a different, more critical, light. The old members suspected the newer ones of taking a coldly instrumental approach towards it. Lament for the loss of earlier, and allegedly sounder, values was in the air. It was most keenly expressed in Britain.

Britain lay at the heart of the Commonwealth. She had created it and without her it would not have survived. She also benefited from it, as the Commonwealth greatly facilitated her honourable extrication from colonial responsibilities, and cushioned her adjustment to the decline of imperial might. In 1956, when she joined France and Israel in invading Egypt, she was dismayed to find that her prized Commonwealth housed some 'critical & uneasy lodgers'.[2] These scars soon healed. But a decade later things had perceptibly gone downhill, even in relation to the older members. When in 1967 Charles Ritchie became Canada's high commissioner in London, he discovered that while '[w]e and the British were excellent friends...we were no longer members of the same family.'[3] Australia was going through the same process of adjustment and by 1972 was said to be at last ready 'to emerge finally from the [colonial] chrysalis'.[4] Meanwhile, in March 1961 another founder member, South Africa, had in effect been expelled (she left formally at the end of May); and in 1972 Pakistan made an abrupt departure. The South African question was the first important occasion on which Britain had failed to prevail within the Commonwealth, and an 'utterly miserable and distressed'[5] Harold Macmillan (Conservative prime

---

[1] Miller (1966) 180.

[2] L.B. Walsh Atkins (West Indies Department, CRO) minute, 2 January 1957, TNA, DO35/5012.

[3] Ritchie (1983) 90.

[4] Laking quoted in Templeton (1991) 8.

[5] Lord Kilmuir quoted in Horne (1989) 393.

minister, 1957–63) said it was also his 'first real defeat'.[6] The event has been linked to Britain's subsequent decision to seek entry into the European Economic Community (EEC), but minds had been turning in that direction for some time, and Macmillan was already personally committed to making an application. When that was done in August 1961 it could hardly fail to suggest, despite Britain's protestations to the contrary, that she was starting to put Europe above the Commonwealth in her list of priorities. As it happened she was not admitted until 1973, but the writing was on the wall. The Commonwealth had started to look like a normal international arrangement.

Nowhere was this process more sharply evident than at the Commonwealth Prime Ministers' Meetings. During the 1950s they had been gentlemanly 'occasions where problems [we]re discussed informally, as among friends, not as at the United Nations where words are weighted, and contacts soured with suspicion or preserved in a deep-freeze of protocol'.[7] They had been 'agreeable as well as valuable. There was... the charm of the Royal presence, and all on a scale that was like a small and pleasant house party'.[8] By 1962 they were 'becoming a sort of miniature United Nations', and Macmillan shrank from these 'troublesome' occasions.[9] The two 1966 Meetings were, for Harold Wilson (Labour prime minister, 1966–69, 1974–76), 'purgatory' and 'hell on earth';[10] and Wilson's commonwealth secretary spoke of Britain 'clutching vipers to her bosom—and paying for it'.[11]

Other leaders in the old Commonwealth were also distressed. Australia's prime minister, Robert Menzies (1949–66) found having Archbishop Makarios of Cyprus as a colleague 'almost as bitter a pill to swallow' as the South African affair,[12] and objected to associating with states 'like Ghana', who were 'more spiritually akin to Moscow than to London'.[13] Nor did the disruptive influence of racism go away with the departure of South Africa, for then the Commonwealth focused

[6] Harold Evans quoted in *ibid.*
[7] Carrington (1955) 145.
[8] Macmillan-Robert Menzies (Australian PM) personal telegram, 8 February 1962, *BDEE 1957–64* II, 664.
[9] *Ibid.*
[10] Ziegler (1995) 238.
[11] H. Bowden (commonwealth secretary) cabinet memorandum, 'The value of the Commonwealth', 24 April 1967, TNA, C(67)59, CAB 129/129.
[12] Woodard (2000) 89.
[13] Menzies-Macmillan, personal, 15 January 1962, *BDEE 1957–64* II, 659.

on ('Southern' until 1964) Rhodesia's determination to maintain white minority rule, which led her unilateral declaration of independence in November 1965. When Britain rejected African demands that she end the rebellion by force, two African members (Tanzania and Ghana) broke off diplomatic relations with Britain; some of the Commonwealth's African delegations walked out of the United Nations (UN) General Assembly when the British prime minister addressed it; and they contributed to the buckets of abuse which were poured on Britain's head. By any yardstick, her Commonwealth critics were behaving much like unfriendly foreign states. Britain could now hardly claim that political relations between its members were inherently different from those between other states. There were a number of areas in which this move towards normalisation was evident.

A. Consular Relations

Consular work focuses on the protection of a state's nationals who are abroad, and on their being conveniently provided with a number of technical services; it also seeks to promote a state's commercial and economic interests. It therefore tends (unlike diplomatic work) to be done on the political periphery. Moreover (unlike diplomatic agents) consular officers in any particular state are often, with its permission, quite widely spread: some in the capital, but others in such cities and towns as suit the requirements of the sending state. For these reasons it is, in principle, not difficult for two states to agree that their consular officers should receive special privileges and immunities. Furthermore, the very character of Commonwealth relations made it easily possible for consular services to be provided not by the 'parent' state but by the host state. In consequence, consular arrangements within the Commonwealth differed in many important ways from those found elsewhere, which complicated things for its members during the negotiation of the Vienna Convention on Consular Relations (1963) (VCCR).

1. *The Commonwealth's consular arrangements*

The roots of consular relations lie in commerce, and the territories that later became dominions began to protect their interests in this sphere at an early date. Being dissatisfied with the British diplomatic and consular officials who had hitherto looked after her trade interests, Canada began in 1884 to appoint 'commercial agents' within and beyond the Empire.

But as people assumed that the job of agents was to purchase goods, such full-time (but not the part-time) officers were in 1907 re-named 'trade commissioners', the title being chosen because the presence of high commissioners in London had given the word 'commissioner' 'the established connotation of a government representative'.[14] The other dominions and Britain followed suit. These and later quasi-consular posts outside Commonwealth capitals became known as 'outposts'.

Britain's trade commissioners in the Commonwealth, who often had bailiwicks 'larger than the British isles', were 'frequently obliged by circumstances to play a representative role quite outside their commercial functions'.[15] But formally-speaking they, like information officers, had no general representative character and no official access to governments (although sometimes they were given favourable privileges, usually of the kind enjoyed by consuls in foreign states and territories but occasionally of the diplomatic sort). They were a different species to members of high commissions: their work was specialised and non-political; in each state they operated under a senior trade commissioner (based in the capital); and (until 1965) were creatures of a service run by the Board of Trade. Senior trade commissioners and high commissioners were said to work closely together, but their relations were not always free of friction and there was sometimes duplication of effort.

One activity for which neither service was equipped was that which is often regarded as of a purely consular kind: helping visitors and residents from home when they were in trouble, looking after their formal needs by (for example) drawing up or certifying contracts or deeds and solemnizing marriages, and undertaking certain functions in relation to national shipping. This was because in the Commonwealth special arrangements for such work were considered unnecessary. A convenient, economical, and tacitly-accepted 'convention' had grown up that each Commonwealth country accepted responsibility for looking after the consular-type needs of visitors or residents from other Commonwealth countries—even to the extent of issuing them with passports. This arose from the Commonwealth's history, which resulted in its people all being British subjects and (at least until the middle of the twentieth century) most of its members sharing common standards and similar legal systems. In short, Commonwealth relations were not foreign. Hence

[14] Wilgress (1967) 15.
[15] *The Manchester Guardian*, 'The Dominions', 28 December 1946.

Britain avoided using the word 'consular' in a Commonwealth context, and regarded high commissions, other than in emergencies or where there were agreements to the contrary, as having no consular functions. The Commonwealth 'convention' also resulted in Britain being willing to perform consular services for Commonwealth countries in foreign states where they were not represented, and Britain went on doing so for Ireland after she left the Commonwealth and, in a much more limited way, for South Africa after she was (in practice) expelled.

However, on the independence of India and Pakistan in 1947 Britain took a major step in the consular direction by opening in each of the new dominions three high commission outposts (the equivalence being more for the sake of parity than need), each with a deputy high commissioner in charge.[16] India had the largest British community outside the British Isles, and it was important that it should not be worse off than in foreign states. But India was not expected to be able either to maintain 'standards' or to fulfil her responsibility towards British citizens 'to the same extent as... in a "white" Dominion where there is the bond of sympathy for a fellow "white" in distress'.[17] Furthermore, each of the new states was vast (and Pakistan, the smaller of the two, was at this time made up of separate parts, East and West, divided by about 1,000 miles of Indian territory), and Britain's citizens were widely scattered. It was important, Britain felt, that such people should not be discouragingly far from home officials and consular-type facilities—although these, like other outposts, did little work of a purely consular kind, all of which, under existing Commonwealth arrangements, continued to be handled by the host state. What they did offer people from Britain was a form of comfort and protection.

These outposts were treated as detached but integral parts of the high commissions in the capitals; and their staff were high commission personnel, acting as Britain's political representatives in the receiving states' most important provinces. In Pakistan they received diplomatic privileges, and in India extended consular privileges. In India the outposts' heads received precedence immediately after provincial prime ministers, which was much valued for the good treatment and excellent

[16] In India these were in Calcutta, Madras, and Bombay; in Pakistan in Dacca, Lahore, and Peshawar. Pakistan and India also opened two outposts in each other's territory.

[17] Minute, no note of name (?Shone, British HC), April/May 1948, TNA, DO133/48.

access it brought. Formally speaking, they were not consular posts (so their heads did not need *exequaturs* enabling them to perform consular acts). *De facto*, however, Britain was moving, inside the Commonwealth, towards the provision of consular services, and as decolonisation proceeded her practice elsewhere resembled that in India and Pakistan. Similar outposts headed by deputy high commissioners were set up in Malaya and Nigeria, and by 1961 there was 'an understanding in all the newer Commonwealth countries that the British representative should have access to any U.K. citizen in distress, and it [was] customary for the British representative to be informed of cases such as imprisonment'.[18] The tide was perhaps turning in the direction of something like normal consular relations, an issue which had to be faced head-on at the imminent negotiation of a multilateral convention on the subject.

2. *The 1963 Vienna Convention on Consular Relations*

i. *Preparation*

Like the 1961 Convention on Diplomatic Relations (VCDR), that on Consular Relations was based on a draft prepared by the UN's International Law Commission (ILC). It was negotiated in Vienna between 4 March and 24 April 1963. Britain was apprehensive of the project, not least because it might 'prejudice, or even destroy'[19] arrangements outside capital cities in the Commonwealth. Her 'wide variety of representation' did not fit into the 'uniformed and formalized limits of a Consular Convention', and while the draft would benefit trade commissioners it would 'strike a serious blow at the status and functions' of deputy high commissioners,[20] who had 'something more than Consular, but something less than Diplomatic status'.[21] If their offices (which were becoming known as deputy high commissions) became consulates, they would no longer automatically be free to engage in political work and political reporting, and if they had to take on the full range of consular functions, they would need additional staff. The last point would be even truer of the

[18] C.H. Imray (Constitutional Department, CRO)-W.V.J. Evans (deputy legal adviser, FO), 27 February 1963, TNA, FO369/5659.
[19] Undated draft brief for United Kingdom delegation to the 17th session of the UN General Assembly, TNA, DO161/141.
[20] HCO Colombo telegram 44, 30 May 1962, TNA, DO161/145.
[21] HCO New Delhi telegram 800, 4 June 1962, TNA, DO161/145.

missions sent by the states of the old Commonwealth (and Ireland) to each other, as so many of their nationals moved between them.

The Foreign Office (FO) suggested Britain should try arguing that intra-Commonwealth consular practices did not fall within the scope of the draft convention. The Commonwealth Relations Office (CRO) disagreed. Given that the object of the convention was 'to secure uniformity', it would be difficult to suggest that the Commonwealth should not be covered.[22] Nor would it be wise to try for the exclusion of specific Commonwealth practices, or to attach reservations regarding them: the CRO did not 'want to provoke an inquisition into Commonwealth arrangements';[23] new Commonwealth states were probably not much interested in or attached to them, so it might not be possible to get a united Commonwealth front; and Britain was opposed to making reservations to international conventions unless vital interests were at stake. Consideration was given to trying to obtain an amendment to what became Article 72 of the Convention which would permit (on the lines of Article 47 of the Diplomatic Relations Convention) more favourable arrangements sanctioned by 'custom or agreement'. But Canada thought that would be hard, and there were doubts whether it would meet Commonwealth needs: the difference was not so much that Commonwealth countries gave better treatment to one another, but that consular relations were narrower and less formal. Instead, there was strong support in the CRO for trying to get Commonwealth practices covered by the draft article (it became Article 73) which said that the Convention would not affect other international agreements. This found favour in Canberra, Wellington, and several other capitals. However, the lawyers said the draft's intention was to cover only 'formal written conventions and other international agreements' and could not embrace 'informal Commonwealth arrangements'.[24] And any attempt to make it do so would be unlikely to receive general acceptance. Britain therefore reverted to the idea that a 'special arrangements' amendment to Article 72 'may be the best thing to go for'.[25]

After asking her high commissioners to sound out the views of their receiving states, and thrashing out her position, Britain explained it to

---

[22] H.L.M. Oxley (assistant legal adviser, CRO) minute, 11 July 1962, TNA, DO161/141.
[23] CRO circular telegram 451, 4 September 1962, TNA, DO161/145.
[24] William Dale (legal adviser, CRO) minute, 28 June 1962, TNA, DO161/141.
[25] CRO circular telegram 451.

representatives from Commonwealth high commissions at a meeting in February 1963. It was well received. The three who expressed firm views (Australia, New Zealand, and India) wanted to keep the existing, informal arrangements, and the meeting agreed about 'the necessity of ensuring that the Convention was drafted with sufficient flexibility'[26] to meet Commonwealth requirements *inter se*. This accorded with such governmental views as had been reported,[27] and seemed to be confirmed when the Commonwealth delegations first met in Vienna.

ii. *The Conference*

The Consular Convention was unanimously adopted by the delegates of 92 states on 24 April 1963, and the Commonwealth made a valuable contribution to the proceedings. The British were the best prepared, 'the most active and well-briefed Western delegation', and their leader, Vincent Evans (the FO's deputy legal adviser), played a key role. The heads of the other ten Commonwealth delegations were almost all good, and 'contributed conscientiously and sensibly to the work of the Conference'.[28] Britain did not achieve all she sought by way of protecting current arrangements with the Commonwealth and Ireland. But she secured her principal object of amending Article 72 to ensure flexibility in the application of the Convention. Further, Article 73 was amended with the addition of a new paragraph expressly affirming the right to conclude 'international agreements confirming or supplementing or extending or amplifying the provisions', so guaranteeing 'elbow room'[29] for drawing up Commonwealth agreements which departed from the Convention's terms. To the extent that the Commonwealth wished to protect Commonwealth practices, it could.

However, the Conference revealed that that might not be the Commonwealth's wish. The British put much effort into relations with

[26] Meeting of representatives from high commissions and representatives of British government departments, 19 February 1963; A.A. Russell (Consular Department, FO) minute, 20 February 1963, TNA, FO369/5658.

[27] Undated CRO brief for 19 February meeting, 'ILC's Draft Articles on Consular Convention', c. 18 February 1963, TNA, DO161/145.

[28] Report of the Canadian Delegation to the United Nations Conference on Consular Relations, Vienna, 4 March to 24 April 1963, NAC, RG25, 3477, 9–1968/2 (report of the Canadian delegation).

[29] CRO memorandum, 'The Question of Exclusion of Commonwealth Quasi-Consular Arrangements from the Draft Convention on Consular Relations', 8 February 1963, TNA, FO369/5657.

their Commonwealth brethren at the Conference. They hosted an early party, liaised effectively, were available to talk to Commonwealth representatives at any time, and at least once a week held informal and 'extremely useful'[30] Commonwealth meetings under Evans' chairmanship. (He suggested sharing it with other delegations on a rotating basis, 'but the general feeling was that it would be more convenient if the United Kingdom continued to take the Chair').[31] Probably as a result of this activity, delegates were 'in many cases'[32] persuaded to abstain rather than vote against Britain. But there was also a noticeable lack of Commonwealth cohesion.

In the first place, it seemed that some individuals gratuitously failed to keep in step. India's Krishna Rao, who chaired the Drafting Committee and was 'the most prominent' Commonwealth representative, did not always exercise his often decisive influence in debates to Britain's advantage. Ceylon's R.S.S. Gunewardene chaired the Afro-Asian group in a way that was 'very much against the British delegation's interests', played into the hands of the Soviets, and at one stage caused 'considerable embarrassment' to the Nigerians.[33] E.K. Dadzie of Ghana was effective, experienced, and personally affable but not much influenced by the British. And the Australians 'did not show up too well'.[34] Their leader was 'too laconic in his utterances to be really effective',[35] 'their position was often unpredictable', and they not uncommonly voted 'against the stand taken by other members of the "old" Commonwealth group'.[36]

Second, Commonwealth members were on opposing sides in respect of the major issue over which there was a fundamental difference of approach—between those who, like Britain, adopted a restrictive approach to the granting of privileges and immunities to consuls, and those who sought in this regard to assimilate consuls with diplomats. In drafting the Convention, the ILC had tended in the latter direction, and this was the line taken by the Soviet bloc and by the many delegations which had been instructed that, when in doubt, they should support

---

30 Undated CRO report, 'Negotiation of Vienna Convention on Consular Relations', TNA, KK2/114, FO369/5661. See also CRO circular telegram 106, 9 February 1963, TNA, DO161/145.

31 *Ibid.*

32 *Ibid.*

33 *Ibid.*

34 Report of the Canadian delegation.

35 Undated CRO report.

36 Report of the Canadian delegation.

the ILC draft. Ghana, Ceylon, India and, to a lesser extent, Pakistan and Sierra Leone belonged to this group, which was aligned with a few West Europeans. Britain, the old Commonwealth, Nigeria, and Malaya took a more restrictive approach, as did a number of others, including, to a lesser extent, the USA.

But, third, and most disturbingly, the Commonwealth's achievement in securing the amendment of Article 72 began to look futile. For towards the end of the Conference it emerged that some Commonwealth states were abandoning the consensus that had been reached in London in February. As the CRO had anticipated, some Commonwealth delegations favoured 'formalizing the existing quasi-consular relations'[37] and applying the Convention *inter se*, and as the Conference progressed, their views grew stronger. It was therefore agreed that after the Conference the CRO 'should circulate a memorandum for consideration by other Commonwealth Governments setting out the advantages and disadvantages of applying the Convention and what modifications would be either necessary or desirable if it were so applied'.[38] Moreover, Commonwealth arrangements were already being challenged in practice. Cyprus had applied to appoint 'honorary commissioners' performing specifically consular functions in Britain, Tanganyika, and Australia, and did so in at least the first two; New Zealand, Pakistan, and Jamaica also intended to appoint 'honorary' officers of a consular type; and many thought it would be better straightforwardly to use the designation 'honorary consul'. Britain was not among them, and continued to maintain that 'consular relations, as such, do not exist within the Commonwealth'.[39]

iii. *From the Vienna Conference to consular relations*

Reflecting the comparative lack of general enthusiasm for the VCCR as compared with the VCDR, it took slightly longer to enter into force (just over four years as opposed to just under three) and secured fewer signatories.[40] In Britain's view, many of the rules laid down in the

---

[37] Abdul Rahim (2005) 290.

[38] W.V.J. Evans, 'Report on the International Conference on Consular Relations held at Vienna from March 4 to April 24, 1963', 3 July 1963, TNA, KK2/109, FO369/5661.

[39] C.J.B. Larby (legal assistant, CRO)-R.G.H. Watts (head of Consular Department, FO), 28 August 1963, TNA, FO369/5662.

[40] At the end of 2006 all but ten Commonwealth members were bound by the Convention.

Convention were 'salutary and useful', but there was too much that was 'obnoxious and contrary to British interests, policy and practice'.[41] Nonetheless she had signed within a year, passed the necessary legislation by the end of 1967, and ratified it in 1972. At that time only five other Commonwealth countries were bound by the Convention, though one—Ghana—had deposited the first ratification.

By 1965 Britain had come to see that there would be advantages in adopting consular titles and practices. Her various outposts did 'a great deal' of work of the consular sort; they were 'bound to develop' an 'essentially "consular" relationship to the "expatriate" (non-emigrant) British community';[42] and her high commissions in the old Commonwealth supported the 1964 Plowden Report's recommendation that consular titles should be used at British outposts—without, however, taking on additional consular functions. But 'after prolonged consideration' Britain decided that it would 'probably in practice be difficult to reconcile' using consular titles at outposts 'with the kind of informal relationship we should like to see maintained'.[43] She hoped, therefore, that her fellow Commonwealth members would agree it would be disadvantageous to apply VCCR *inter se.* This would avoid translating her deputy high commissions into consulates, and so losing the benefits they got from being part of diplomatic missions.

In mid-1966 'a very large majority'[44] of Commonwealth states appeared to agree about not applying the Convention. But Australia had joined some of the new Commonwealth in wanting to adopt normal international practice, and New Zealand, too, was edging in the same direction. In 1970 the latter reopened discussions on the issue, and by then there was a noticeable feeling that it was time for a change. Commonwealth membership rose in that year to 32; intra-Commonwealth relations were substantively the same as foreign relations; there was a divergence of laws and administrative practices; and the huge rise in intra-Commonwealth trade and personal travel was accompanied by an increasing expectation of a full range of consular services. Thus at a 1972 conference there was a fair amount of support for the view that that the traditional Commonwealth convention

---

[41] Russell minute, 30 October 1963, TNA, KK2/112, FO369/5661.

[42] W.A.B. Hamilton (AUS)-DHCs Ottawa, Canberra, Wellington, 3 May 1965, TNA, DO161/316.

[43] Hamilton (CRO)-G. Kimber (DHC, Canberra), 3 May 1965, TNA, DO127/27.

[44] Sir Neil Pritchard (DUS)-J.C. Morgan (DHC, Canberra), 17 August 1966, TNA, DO126/27.

(whereby the host provided consular services) was 'less than satisfactory'[45] and that outposts should be turned into consulates. What was needed were clearly-understood and accessible consular arrangements, and accurate and easily-recognised titles (there were 24 different ones for officers in charge of outposts) instead of the existing 'rather haphazard practices'.[46] It was time to standardise practices and procedures in line with the 1963 Convention.

Britain was unhappy. There were, she said, public relations advantages in having 'special titles', which were 'one of the distinguishing marks'[47] of Commonwealth membership. She did not think uniformity mattered much, and saw no practical advantage in going further with the adoption of the VCCR's practices; nor was she keen on the loss of privileges and precedence that would be involved; and like the small states who preferred the *status quo*, she was concerned about the cost and staffing implications. Privately, though, she admitted that the Commonwealth convention only operated satisfactorily in the old Commonwealth, and (as will be discussed below) she knew Australia was champing at the bit to adopt the usual consular (and diplomatic) titles.

In traditional Commonwealth style, neither side tried to force its views on the other. Britain did not want to be obstructive, and New Zealand did not want others to abandon the Commonwealth convention unwillingly (also emphasising that any change need not have an impact on the 'tradition of informal access' which 'rests on the closeness of the Commonwealth relationship').[48] A live-and-let-live compromise was reached. Consular exchanges (including honorary consuls) were acceptable, but not obligatory. Members could adopt as much of the VCCR as they wished. And an unrepresented Commonwealth country could make whatever arrangements were most satisfactory for her and the receiving state, including reliance on the Commonwealth convention

[45] New Zealand government memorandum, 'Consular Relations within the Commonwealth', January 1971 (New Zealand government memorandum), Appendix B to 'Consular Relations Within the Commonwealth. Report and Record of Meeting of Commonwealth Officials, 16–18 May 1972', NAC, RG25, 3132, 1-1972/2 (Commonwealth Officials' Meeting, May 1972).

[46] 'Views of the Governments of Trinidad and Tobago, Fiji and Canada', conveyed in circular letter, 18 August 1971, Appendix E to Commonwealth Officials' Meeting, May 1972.

[47] UK government memorandum, 'Consular Representation within the Commonwealth', April 1972, appendix G to Commonwealth Officials' Meeting, May 1972.

[48] New Zealand government memorandum.

or on a third Commonwealth country. The outcome was submitted to the Heads of Government (until 1971, Prime Ministers') Meeting (CHOGM) which met in Ottawa the following year and adopted in the shape of what became the (never published) '1973 understandings'.[49]

In the 'old' Commonwealth some rather significant developments followed, which for a long while had been under periodic discussion. In the mid-1960s Britain's trade and information outposts there had been re-designated and given a wider remit. In Australia and New Zealand they became 'offices' of the high commissions (and in Australia were headed by deputy high commissioners, who enjoyed diplomatic status and privileges), and in Canada, British 'government offices'. It was now agreed that they should all be transformed into consulates-general. (There was no change of nomenclature in India and Nigeria.) The Commonwealth's hitherto distinctive representative arrangements had moved further towards the norm.

B. Comings—and Goings

At the start of 1961 the Commonwealth had eleven members, almost exactly balanced between the old and the new. At the end of 1973 it had exactly three times that number. In fact 24 newly-independent states had joined, all bar two (Cyprus and Malta) from outside Europe, most with fewer than a million people, and virtually all of them poor.[50] But—something which had never been thought of as part of Commonwealth practice (Ireland's departure being widely seen as the exception which proved the rule)—two earlier members (including one of the old guard) had left: South Africa and Pakistan. These happenings had more than a whiff of normal international behaviour. They also meant (among other things) that the diplomatic missions South Africa and Pakistan exchanged with Commonwealth states had to change their names from high commissions to embassies; and they each had to embark on a lot of additional consular work.

[49] See Abdul Rahim (2005) 326.

[50] At about the time Kenya became independent (December 1963) its leader, Jomo Kenyatta, was asked whether he had expected his country to be free of colonial rule during his lifetime. 'He laughed uproariously and replied, "Certainly not; I never even expected to see India independent in my lifetime. In Africa we assumed it would take much longer"': Malcolm MacDonald (commonwealth secretary's Special Representative in Africa), 21 September 1968, TNA, FCO68/32.

1. *South Africa*

South Africa was never an entirely comfortable Commonwealth member. Like the Irish, the Afrikaners (who comprised about three-fifths of the European population) had bitter memories of British imperial rule, and specifically of her anti-Boer discrimination and the Boer War, in which about twenty-six thousand women and children died in concentration camps. Like the Irish, too, Afrikaners were natural republicans. And many Afrikaners thought South Africa should have joined Ireland in staying neutral in the Second World War. But whereas the British tended to appreciate the affable Irish, they were uncomfortable with the 'alien' Afrikaners, with their 'strange language', 'fundamentalist religion', 'rigid morality' and 'obstinate refusal to be assimilated in the British way of life'.[51] The National Party (Nationalist) victory in South Africa's 1948 election, and the determined application of *apartheid* at a time when the rest of the world was (at least officially) moving in the opposite direction, led to a cooling in official relations and South Africa's increasing ostracization. This did not discomfort the Union one whit. Afrikaners were an inward-looking people who were significantly cut off from many currents of the contemporary world, and their prime ministers were not keen on travel. Thus when international criticism reached a new pitch in 1961, Dr. Hendrik Verwoerd (prime minister 1958–66) declared that South Africa would 'stand like walls of granite because the survival of a nation is at stake'.[52]

Meanwhile, a referendum had been held in October 1960 on whether South Africa should become a republic, and Verwoerd's 'prayers [we]re answered' with an affirmative vote.[53] He then set about fulfilling his promise to English-speakers to try to keep South Africa in the Commonwealth. In 1949 it had been assumed that other countries who followed India down the republican path would be accorded the same treatment, and when Pakistan (1955), Ceylon (1956), and Ghana (1960) became republics no difficulties had been raised about them remaining. However, in 1960 South Africa had become 'the polecat of the western world',[54] when the killing of two protesters at Langa and 67

[51] Garner (1978) 57.
[52] Quoted in Geldenhuys (1984) 23.
[53] Beyers (ed.) (1987a) 738. The majority was quite small: 52 per cent or 74,580 votes out of the 1,632,583 votes cast. Natal voted overwhelmingly against becoming a republic.
[54] *Die Burger* quoted in Brown (2000) 50.

demonstrators at Sharpeville was denounced world-wide. Cocooned in his 'cloud-cuckoo-land of self-righteousness',[55] Verwoerd did not recognise that the situation had fundamentally changed. As he saw it, the rest of the world was 'wrong' and the Commonwealth was 'tiresome and impertinent'.[56] Britain lobbied hard on South Africa's behalf, and no Commonwealth member was publicly committed to opposing her continued presence in the Commonwealth. But at the Prime Ministers' Meeting of March 1961 there was a bitter confrontation between Tunku Abdul Rahman of Malaysia and Verwoerd. The Meeting went on to discuss a declaration of Commonwealth principles (including racial equality), to which South Africa would have to subscribe if she were to stay in the Commonwealth. In response to a suggestion that it would make things easier if she would agree to exchange diplomatic representatives with Afro-Asian Commonwealth members, Verwoerd said this was 'not immediately practicable'.[57] During the Second World War there had been an Indian high commissioner in the South African province of Natal; in the late 1950s Egypt (then in union with Syria under the name of the United Arab Republic) had a legation in Pretoria; and in March 1961 South Africa and Japan had agreed to exchange embassies. But, Verwoerd said, the presence of diplomatic missions from black Africa would cause 'confusion' and 'incidents',[58] not least as Ghana had said that her purpose in having representation in South Africa 'would be to incite the Bantu against the Government'.[59]

This, in Macmillan's view, was the key moment. If Verwoerd had been willing to make a 'small gesture' and say he would receive a black high commissioner 'we could have won through'.[60] That he did not was 'the final straw'[61] that released an 'all out', 'unbridled' and 'often

---

[55] Sir John Maud (British HC) telegram 897, 31 October 1960, TNA, DO161/106.

[56] *Ibid.*

[57] Colin Legum, 'The story behind the walk-out. Suggestion changed atmosphere', *The Observer*, 19 March 1961.

[58] Verwoerd quoted in Geldenhuys (1984) 13.

[59] Miller (1961) 65.

[60] Macmillan-Menzies personal telegram, 8 February 1962, *BDEE 1957–64* II, 660. However, he went on to say that he sometimes thought 'that the whole thing was plotted against us from the start': *ibid.* In retrospect, trying to keep South Africa in the Commonwealth looks like a lost cause.

[61] Walter Farr, 'S. Africa forced out by Britain. Loss of influence may mean U.N. expulsion', *Sunday Telegraph*, 19 March 1961; Miller (1961) 65. The commonwealth secretary told the Commons: 'The close special relationship of the Commonwealth can be maintained in one way only. That is by continuous and intimate consultation

insulting'[62] attack on the Union. The Meeting came unstuck over what was to be said about racial equality, Verwoerd withdrew his request to stay in the Commonwealth, and South African membership duly lapsed. This was not what Verwoerd had ostensibly intended, but he was delighted with the guidance he felt God had given him. Jet aircraft escorted his plane from South Africa's border to the airport, where he received 'a hero's welcome'.[63] It was the highpoint of his life. Black South Africans burned his effigy.

South Africa's departure from the Commonwealth on 31 May 1961 made little difference to her overall bilateral relations with its individual members. But it had a huge symbolic impact, which was underlined in November of that year at the UN General Assembly where, for the first time, the Commonwealth united in voting for a resolution condemning her racial policies. There were also a number of practical consequences, not least on the diplomatic front. The word 'Foreign' was substituted for 'External' in the names of her Department and minister of external affairs. High commissioners to and from South Africa were reaccredited as ambassadors (without losing their precedence), although Britain's ambassador remained also high commissioner for the High Commission Territories. High commission staff with Commonwealth titles exchanged them for diplomatic ones. In Britain's case this meant that her deputy high commissioner became minister/counsellor, her senior trade commissioner became minister (commercial), and her chief information officer a counsellor (information). Her service advisers became *attachés*, but the collective designation 'Service Liaison Mission' was retained in the hope of forfeiting as little as possible of the former 'special' defence relationship with South Africa. The high commissioners exchanged between South Africa and the Federation of Rhodesia and Nyasaland became accredited representatives (although South Africa's representative added the word 'diplomatic' to his title). On 1 December South Africa was 'transferred' from the CRO to the FO.

---

between the Governments. Yet, while applying for continued membership, the South African Government—and this is something which bit very deep—still firmly refused to receive diplomatic representatives from non-European members of the Commonwealth. This makes a mockery of consultation, and in any case we cannot accept that because of the colour of their skins certain members of the Commonwealth are to be treated as lepers': *Keesing's Archives*, April 1961 (online version).

[62] Verwoerd broadcast, 17 March 1961, SAA, BVV, 48/1, vol. 1.

[63] Redcliffe-Maud (1981) 91.

The consular impact of South Africa's departure promised to be large for both her and Britain. The British community in South Africa was considerable—about 300,000 people. Hitherto, in line with the traditional Commonwealth practice, the usual sort of consular work had been unnecessary. That had now changed so, as well as her trade commissioners and information officers at outposts in South Africa becoming consuls, extra dispositions would need to be made. Britain was also responsible for about 185,000 Africans from the High Commission Territories who were working in South Africa, and perhaps tens of thousands from other British dependencies. The nature of South African law (especially the pass laws) made it difficult to perform consular services for them, but it would now be politically embarrassing to give the impression that this was being avoided.

South Africa, which had given little prior consideration to the practical consequences of leaving the Commonwealth, was also faced with having to take on additional consular work. Initially, she hoped Britain would continue undertaking consular functions for her in the states and territories in which she was not represented. There were quite a number of those as, apart from her trade commissioner in Singapore (who became a consul), she had no diplomatic, consular, or quasi-consular representation in Asia or the communist bloc, and little in Africa and Latin America. Britain, however, would do nothing for her in the Commonwealth or Ireland, where such activity would be highly embarrassing; in foreign African states (other than the Congo, which was covered by an earlier agreement) she would not, for the same reason, go beyond occasional *ad hoc* and urgent consular acts on behalf of South African citizens; and as to elsewhere, the commonwealth secretary reluctantly agreed that British officials could oblige only on a strictly temporary basis. (Over a decade later, however, and despite the waning of their relationship, Britain was still 'at least theoretically taking care of consular affairs for South Africa in certain countries',[64] though this amounted to very little in practice.) The situation led to the establishment of a consular division in South Africa's Foreign Ministry, but it took a while to get properly under way.

Other noticeable losses for South Africa were the Commonwealth's information-sharing arrangements; automatic access to reports from

[64] Grace Thornton (head of Consular Department) minute, 15 March 1972, TNA, FCO47/580.

British missions; and Britain's considerable assistance with cyphers, codes, courier services for diplomatic mail, and security matters. Her growing isolation was compounded by the fact that her overseas representation remained small, and by instructions (given to missions in the 1970s) saying they should discontinue 'general political reporting and...focus only on the way South African issues were "playing" in individual countries'. She was not much interested in 'what made other countries tick'.[65]

2. *Pakistan*

When the British left India, both the sub-continent and Pakistan were divided, East and West Pakistan being separated by about a thousand miles (and having little in common beyond religion). Moreover, although West Pakistan had the smaller population, it was politically and economically dominant. This created tensions that eventually erupted into violent conflict, and (assisted by India's armed intervention) East Pakistan seceded at the end of 1971 under the name of Bangladesh. After a number of Commonwealth states, including Britain, had recognised her (or made known their intention of doing so), the Pakistani President, Zulfikar Ali Bhutto, announced at the end of January 1972 that his country was quitting the Commonwealth (to which Bangladesh was soon admitted). The Commonwealth meant little to the average Pakistani and their governments had long had a jaundiced attitude to it. Bhutto himself regarded it as an arrangement which had 'passed the point of mutual benefit'.[66] He flew to Beijing where he toasted Afro-Asian solidarity.

In this way Pakistan became the third state to withdraw from the Commonwealth, and she went much more abruptly than the earlier two. Britain was well-prepared. In addition to having dealt with the consequences of South Africa becoming a foreign state, she had drawn up a 'blueprint' of action in 1966 because it looked as if President Kenneth Kaunda of Zambia might march out of the Commonwealth over Britain's failure to use force to end the Rhodesian rebellion and, in so doing, take more than half its members with him. The blueprint had been updated in 1968, and again in 1970 when the Commonwealth was in crisis over a proposed sale of arms by Britain to South Africa.

---

[65] Tothill (2000).
[66] Quoted in Smith (1981) 144.

Had the sale gone ahead, the Commonwealth Secretariat (set up in 1965, as indicated below) thought up to 20 states might leave.

The consequences of Pakistan's departure fell into five categories. First, she excluded herself from a variety of official and semi-official bodies and meetings where participation depended on Commonwealth membership, and also lost the benefits of certain legislation which applied to Commonwealth states. Second, at the diplomatic level all high commissions to and from Pakistan became embassies and the ex-high commissioners, now ambassadors, received new credentials. However their formal presentation in Islamabad (and in at least some other states) was not deemed necessary, the chief of protocol in Islamabad saying that he saw 'no necessity' for it and was 'ready to let sleeping dogs lie'.[67] Hence these new ambassadors retained their existing precedence. In London the Pakistani ambassador could still see the foreign and commonwealth secretary, but lost his right of access to any other minister (including the prime minister) and high officials in their ministries. (However, on any particular occasion he could always seek access, as other ambassadors were beginning to do, often with success.) There was a similar loss in other Commonwealth states for Pakistan, and in Pakistan for Britain, but in some of them it was only theoretical, as not all members now accorded the privileged access which was still the norm in Britain and some other capitals. The Pakistani ambassador in London no longer enjoyed special treatment on certain state occasions and the more favourable scale of official hospitality enjoyed by high commissioners. In the old Commonwealth, New Zealand's contacts with Pakistan were minimal, so there was little to change; Australia wanted to 'retain as much as possible of the special connection with and treatment of Pakistan';[68] and Canada decided there was no point in going out of her way to be awkward with Pakistan because of her departure.

Third, Pakistan now had to enter into consular relations with those Commonwealth states where she wanted such amenities, and Britain had to do so with Pakistan. Correspondingly, Britain had to turn her high commission outposts in Pakistan into consulates, and Pakistan had to do likewise in respect of her outposts in Britain and her trade missions in Hong Kong and Brunei. In so doing Britain's ex-outposts

---

[67] HCO Islamabad telegram 968, 15 March 1972, TNA, FCO37/1177.

[68] Interdepartmental meeting, Canberra, 4 February 1972, TNA, FCO37/1144.

lost their diplomatic status, but—on a reciprocal basis—suffered no significant diminution in their privileges and immunities. (In 1969, on pain of having them reduced, Britain had reluctantly granted similar privileges and immunities to Pakistan's outposts.) These outposts had undertaken the protection side of consular work, 'dealing with relief and repatriation, emergency evacuation planning, reporting of arrests, deaths and accidents, etc.'[69] However, as consulates they now had also to take on such matters as notarial work, registering births, marriages, and deaths, and dealing with visas, migration, and shipping (the last of which would, at Karachi, be very demanding for Britain).

Britain was willing, at least for a while, to provide Pakistan with consular assistance in countries where it was needed. But she did so unenthusiastically, the head of the Foreign and Commonwealth Office's (FCO) Consular Department saying Britain did 'not want this burden and the sooner we can get rid of it the better'[70]—thinking of possibly embarrassing clashes of interest between the two states over, for example, immigration.[71] As it happened, Britain was not much called upon: six months after Pakistan's departure, Lesotho was the only Commonwealth country in which she had formally undertaken consular responsibility for Pakistan; and beyond the Commonwealth she was equally unburdened, other than providing assistance with the evacuation of Pakistanis from Vietnam.

Fourth, in the economic sphere there was the issue of whether Pakistan should lose the valuable aid and technical assistance she received from Britain on account of her Commonwealth membership. Britain did not take a hard line on these matters. As to trade, the preferential Commonwealth arrangements enjoyed by Britain and Pakistan (which were detailed in a bilateral agreement) were in any event on the verge of being phased out, in consequence of Britain joining the EEC. So in this area there was not much change which was attributable to Pakistan's withdrawal. Finally, there was the question of the status of the large Pakistani community in Britain. Pakistani citizens would now become aliens. Many of them, being British subjects, had been eligible, through their length of residence, to register as British citizens (a different process from naturalisation). Here too Britain wanted to avoid

[69] W.R. Loveridge (Consular Department) minute, 13 June 1972, TNA, FCO37/1177.
[70] Thornton minute, 30 June 1972, FCO47/580.
[71] *Ibid.*

unnecessary hardship, having a particular eye to community relations and the possibly inflammatory charge that 'we are taking punitive actions against coloured Pakistanis that we did not take against white South Africans when they left the Commonwealth'.[72] A transitional period was therefore instituted, during which resident Pakistanis could take advantage of their soon-to-disappear right.

While, therefore, in principle Britain wanted to maintain the line taken in 1961, 'that a country which leaves the Commonwealth should not enjoy the privileges which go with Commonwealth status',[73] she also wanted to refrain from imposing needless discomfort on Pakistan or unnecessarily damaging relations. Thus the adverse consequences of this departure did not seem great. A number of African states were disturbed by the apparent 'lack of retribution',[74] and in danger of concluding that there were no material costs in quitting the Commonwealth. The head of the FCO's Commonwealth Co-ordination Department, Leonore Storar, was accordingly asked 'to produce a list designed to be as intimidating as possible, of the penalties of leaving the Commonwealth'.[75] Storar found it hard to produce a convincing case.

Nonetheless, it was not long before Pakistan had second thoughts about her decision. She made conciliatory moves in 1973, but abandoned them when there was a leak to the press. In 1978 further soundings were taken, but scuppered by India's opposition. Eventually, in October 1989, Ali Bhutto's daughter, Benazir (now prime minister), took Pakistan back into the Commonwealth, with 'a brief and characteristically dramatic appearance' at the Commonwealth Heads of Government Meeting (CHOGM—the renamed Prime Ministers' Meeting) in Kuala Lumpur'.[76] Although the Commonwealth did not

[72] J.A.N. Graham (private secretary to foreign secretary)-G.L. Angel (private secretary to home secretary), undated, c. March 1972, TNA, FCO68/206; FCO memorandum, 'The Withdrawal of Pakistan from the Commonwealth', 13 July 1972, TNA, FCO37/1143.

[73] Quoted in P.D. McEntee (Commonwealth Co-ordination Department) brief for Martin Le Quesne (DUS), 11 May 1972.

[74] Denis Greenhill (PUS) minute, 13 March 1972, TNA, FCO68/206.

[75] Leonore Storar (head of Commonwealth Co-ordination Department) minute, 7 April 1972, TNA, FCO68/206.

[76] *The Round Table* (2000) 158. But her visit placed her hosts in 'an embarrassing linguistic dilemma. It had escaped them until the moment of her arrival that "Bhutto" in Malaysian is the term used to describe a very private part of the male anatomy. When the Malaysian prime minister greeted Ms. Bhutto, he found himself rambling on in a rather confusing and nonsensical manner for several minutes, while he was franticly trying to avoid addressing Ms. Bhutto by her last name. The Malaysian press,

matter hugely to Pakistan, she was evidently of the view that it was better to be in than out.[77]

C. The Commonwealth Secretariat

Among the Commonwealth's peculiarities was the fact that it had no secretarial support of its own. At its prime ministers' regular meetings (always, until the mid-1960s, in London), the CRO organised things and Britain's cabinet secretary traditionally acted as secretary-general. The idea of a Commonwealth secretariat had occasionally been floated, but resisted as superfluous or too much like a step backwards, towards centralisation. As late as 1963 it was still '[b]arely conceivable'. But times changed so quickly that two years later it was considered 'not merely desirable but...essential'.[78] The newer members, Britain observed, were sometimes 'disregarding the old rules', while she felt 'inhibited' by her dual role from 'making full use of [her] position'.[79] Although she wondered what a permanent secretariat would find to do, and 'feared it might develop into an African pressure group',[80] it should on balance be useful. In any event opinion was moving in that direction, and at the 1964 Prime Ministers' Meeting the go-ahead was given. The Commonwealth Secretariat, headquartered at Marlborough House in London, began life in the following year with a Canadian diplomat, Arnold Smith, as its secretary-general. He was given the status of a high commissioner.

In the words of one authority, this was 'the most important landmark in the evolution of the modern Commonwealth'. It represented the 'decolonising' of its management, and Smith, 'by his personal impact and low-key rhetoric', ensured the Commonwealth's ongoing 'de-Britannicization'.[81] His dynamic interpretation of his office earned

however, simply referred to the visitor from Pakistan as "Miss Benazir"': Mousavizadeh, Lee and Lu (1990) 28. This last usage is the Malaysian style of address.

[77] This was also true of Fiji, who left in 1987 and rejoined in 1997. Then, after being suspended in 2000, she was restored to full membership a year later. She was suspended once more in December 2006. South Africa rejoined in 1994 following the end of the *apartheid* regime.

[78] Chadwick (1982) 55.

[79] P. Rogers (Cabinet Office) minute on new concept of Commonwealth, 1 July 1965, *BDEE 1964–1971* II, 342.

[80] Quoted in McIntyre (2000) 144.

[81] McIntyre (1991) 46 and 56. Smith's successor, Sonny Ramphal was also active. On

him Afro-Caribbean goodwill, but he was 'rather too active and earnest' for the old Commonwealth and India.[82] They were also irritated by his 'efforts at self-inflation'[83] which included much pressure to be accorded the title 'excellency' (which was granted in 1968). He was, however, thought to have saved the Commonwealth from an angry African exodus over Rhodesia.[84] More generally, the Secretariat resulted in a broader role for high commissioners to Britain, as they secured a link to the whole, complex Commonwealth network. It has been said that most of them have taken good advantage of it. In reverse, the Commonwealth's secretaries-general have enjoyed easy access to the London high commissioners. More generally still, however, the Secretariat gave the Commonwealth a little of the look of a normal international organisation.

D. Meetings of High Commissioners and of Commonwealth Heads of Mission

During the Second World War the daily meetings of high commissioners in London provided a useful forum for discussion and passing on information, and high commissioners were, in overall purpose, united. With the War's end, attempts were made to continue this pattern. First the high commissioners met weekly, and then fortnightly, often accompanied by an adviser or two, and with CRO and FO officials present. The meetings were an opportunity for consultation and information gathering. But they were not necessary for the former, and potentially useful for the latter only on the rare occasions when the foreign secretary attended. They soon '"peter[ed] out" from inanition'.[85] With

the anti-*apartheid* front, he sided with the rest of the Commonwealth against Britain in wanting sanctions against South Africa. He was prepared to lobby the British government and openly criticised its policy; he orchestrated the Commonwealth's approach to *apartheid* at the 1986 London mini-summit; and he 'did not make a strenuous effort to prevent the boycott of the Edinburgh Commonwealth Games in 1986': Parks (1997) 171.

[82] Introduction, *BDEE 1964–1971* I, lxxxii.

[83] Background note to Commonwealth Office brief for Mr. Bowden's visit to Australia, January 1967, *BDEE 1964–1971* II, 381. Smith annoyed his former Canadian colleagues by describing himself as 'the senior Canadian ambassador', which led to 'a big exchange' with one of them: personal communication.

[84] See Doxey (1989) 119.

[85] Norman Robertson (Canadian HC, London) quoted in F.H. Soward, 'Canadian External Policy 1946–1952', NAC, RG25, 3843, 36–1946/1.

the arrival in 1947 of a new and idealistic commonwealth secretary, Philip Noel-Baker, an attempt was made to inject new life into such meetings, and to 'make our little mob into a corps'.[86] He failed. Noel-Baker's successor tried holding informal gatherings of just the high commissioners, which worked better. Nonetheless, by the early 1950s their meetings 'had ceased to be of any significance'.[87] There were both political and personal reasons for this. The arrival of the Asian dominions changed the tenor of the meetings. There was less intimacy, and a growing number of subjects which could not conveniently be discussed with everyone present.[88] Sometimes there were furious arguments: the Australian high commissioner, J.A. Beasley, 'struck a new note of aggressiveness';[89] India's Krishna Menon was a 'strange, contorted figure...who indulged in bitter tirades of personal abuse';[90] and on one occasion Sir Oliver Goonetilleke of Ceylon was 'obstructive, argumentative...ill-mannered and at times almost insolent'.[91] The war-time focus and cohesion had been lost.

However, London meetings did not vanish altogether. In the 1950s there were very occasional ones with foreign secretaries or prime ministers. And in the 1960s there were meetings on specific issues, such as Britain's 1961 application to join the EEC, which were a supplementary means of keeping high commissioners informed. Later in the 1960s the commonwealth secretary sometimes called informal meetings (probably in an attempt to prevent the new Commonwealth Secretariat from monopolising this aspect of things). And high commissioners still came together by virtue of being trustees of the Imperial War Museum and the Commonwealth War Graves Commission, and members of the Governing Board of the Commonwealth Foundation.[92] But the focus of high commissioners' collective attention in London was now the Secretariat, where meetings were convened on subjects remitted to them by the Prime Ministers'/Heads of Government Meetings. Some

---

[86] Robertson-Pearson (under-secretary for external affairs), 13 November 1947, NAC, RG25, 4480, 50020–40, part 1.

[87] Holmes (1982) 166.

[88] See note of ministers' meeting, 'Arrangements for Consultation with Commonwealth Countries', 28 July 1948, TNA, DO121/22.

[89] Garner (1978) 299.

[90] *Ibid.*

[91] Patrick Gordon Walker (commonwealth secretary) telegram-British HCs, New Delhi and Colombo, secret, personal, 3 May 1950, TNA, DO35/9014.

[92] Established in 1966, the Commonwealth Foundation promotes co-operation at professional and non-governmental levels.

discussed routine matters, but others, like the Sanctions Committee (set up in 1966 to monitor the progress of sanctions against Rhodesia) were highly-charged and uncomfortable for Britain.[93] African impatience became well-nigh uncontrollable. As a deputy high commissioner put it, he once spent three hours

> listening to African neophytes expressing suspicion and disbelief, based largely on press reporting, of categorical assertions by British Government spokesmen.... The experience is not unlike that which I suffered through long hours of fruitless United Nations oratory.[94]

Such friction and mud-slinging 'poisoned'[95] Anglo-African relations and had a negative impact on British prime ministerial attitudes towards the Commonwealth. Edward Heath (prime minister, 1970–74) felt 'undisguised disrespect'[96] towards it and African leaders, and Margaret Thatcher (prime minister, 1979–90) saw it as a nuisance.

Outside London occasional meetings were held. There were standing instructions to all British posts to encourage contact with Commonwealth colleagues, and in a number of places there were close social relations, a comparing of notes on political problems, and a pooling of information. But gatherings of Commonwealth heads of mission were patchy in terms of both frequency and value. Moreover, in some Commonwealth states there was a danger that get-togethers of high commissioners might lead governments to suspect they were being 'ganged up against'.[97] In Nkrumah's Ghana the British high commissioner thought that even attempting to organise such meetings would be 'dangerous, and lay us open immediately to the charge of neo-colonialism and other embarrassments'.[98] Other reasons for not holding meetings were the paucity of high commissioners; the belief that the local Commonwealth representation had the wrong complexion ('in Freetown the Ghana high commissioner is the joker of the Commonwealth pack; the Pakistani high commissioner fills the same

---

93 See Alexander (2003) 201. Alexander says that with the acrimonious 1966 Prime Ministers' Meeting, Wilson underwent 'a revulsion from his Commonwealth responsibilities' and became convinced of the need to apply for EEC membership.

94 Private information.

95 The word 'poison' often crops up in this context. On this occasion it was used by Garner (1978) 423.

96 Pimlott (1996) 399.

97 N.E. Costar (British HC, Port of Spain)-Garner (PUS), 6 May 1963, TNA, DO161/188.

98 T.W. Keeble (DHC, Accra)-Garner, 25 May 1963, TNA, DO161/188.

function here' in New Delhi);[99] or simply the view that they would be a waste of time. Nor, generally, did there seem to be any disposition on the part of receiving states to call Commonwealth meetings. Bilateral contacts, both between high commissions and with the receiving state, were of course a different matter.

At the UN in New York there were still more or less monthly meetings. But after the 1956 Suez crisis Commonwealth unity there 'was never quite the same';[100] and as decolonisation speeded up delegates from the new Commonwealth became absorbed in their regional groups and began campaigning as regional representatives. One consequence was the loss in 1965 of the 'Commonwealth seat' on the Security Council. Another was that less importance was attached to sometimes 'appallingly dull'[101] Commonwealth meetings. A third was that in these meetings, as in other fora, Britain came in for some very rough treatment over her handling of the Rhodesian problem and her insufficiently critical attitude towards South Africa. Until 1963 she chaired Commonwealth meetings, and so was able to contain discussion 'within reasonable limits'.[102] But then the chair began rotating monthly (in alphabetical order), and by the second half of the 1960s Commonwealth meetings more or less ground to a halt.[103] The Commonwealth Secretariat's 1969 suggestion that they be revived met with no enthusiasm, and it was even difficult to get representatives together for a short meeting with the 'commonwealth' secretary-general (as Arnold Smith called himself—a title which became accepted).

Altogether, the frequency and quality of high commissioners' meetings were like those of any international association which lacked a central purpose.

---

[99] Paul Gore-Booth (British HC, New Delhi)-Garner, 1 June 1963, TNA, DO161/188.

[100] Doxey (1982) 6.

[101] Personal communication.

[102] Sir Patrick Dean (British permanent representative, New York) reported in Ross Campbell memorandum, 'Commonwealth meetings in New York—Rotation of Chairmanship', 9 October 1962, NAC, RG25, 4482, 50024–40, part 4.

[103] There continued, however, to be 'a constant exchange of views and ideas at all levels' between Commonwealth delegations: P.J.S. Moon (first secretary, New York)-R. Walker, 5 December 1966, *BDEE 1964–1971* II, 361.

E. The Position of High Commissioners

In terms of access, the distinction between high commissioners and ambassadors was already being whittled away by the start of the 1960s. On the one hand, foreign missions in some states dealt on an informal and fact-finding basis with departments other than the foreign ministry. On the other, high commissioners could no longer count on seeing all government ministers and officials. As the decade progressed, some new Commonwealth states (most notably Nigeria) sought to abolish or curtail high commissioners' wide ranging right of access. Direct government-to-government communication, too, was ceasing to be distinctive to Commonwealth diplomacy. Non-Commonwealth foreign ministers, especially in the EEC, increasingly exchanged personal messages without going through their accredited diplomatic representatives. At the political level, something in the nature of a two-tier Commonwealth system was emerging. Even Britain no longer tried 'to deal in the same way and on the same footing with all countries of the Commonwealth'.[104] Her relations with the newer members were becoming 'more like' those which she had with 'foreign countries', or like those between 'other Western countries and the developing countries in which they have substantial economic interests'.[105]

There was still plenty of consultation, which was proclaimed in the 1965 *Agreed Memorandum* establishing the Commonwealth Secretariat as 'the life blood of the Commonwealth'.[106] It was also to be found in the numerous meetings of ministers and officials, and the various co-operative institutions and advisory boards dealing with matters such as agriculture, forestry, shipping, economics, and telecommunications. But to assert, as Britain's commonwealth secretary did in 1962, that informal consultation on and the sharing of information about current events was 'constant'[107] was, in the view of his man in Jamaica, 'at best a pious aspiration and at worst plain humbug'.[108] Some in the CRO thought this was going too far. But undoubtedly there was, at least in respect of the new Commonwealth, a considerable imbalance.

---

104 Bowden cabinet memorandum, 'The value of the Commonwealth'.

105 *Ibid.*

106 Commonwealth Secretariat (1971) 170. See also McIntyre (2000) 147.

107 Duncan Sandys (commonwealth secretary) quoted in J.S. Bennett (AUS seconded from the CO) minute, 5 March 1963, TNA, DO161/188.

108 Alexander Morley (British HC, Kingston)-Garner, 22 April 1963, TNA, DO161/188.

A number of factors contributed to this: suspicion or colonial hang-ups; officials who were not always sure what their states' policy was, or lacked experience in international matters; insufficient confidence to discuss policy with Britain's representatives; and not having much worthwhile information to divulge. Few new Commonwealth states had much interest in, or knowledge of, more than limited aspects of international relations; sometimes they did not have an organised system of reporting to the foreign ministry, and in any event they tended to have few overseas missions; the quality of such reports as were received was said to be sometimes rather poor; and their foreign ministries did not always display great efficiency or zeal. Thus, in 1963 Pakistan's DEA was dismissed by Britain's high commissioner, as 'limp, dilatory, sometimes unhelpful and at all times lacking in drive and interest'.[109] And it was observed from New Delhi that the return Britain got for the information she gave was 'disappointingly small'.[110] In the old Commonwealth consultation and information sharing was appreciably better, but even here there could be exceptions. Australia's DEA, perhaps chiefly for internal bureaucratic reasons, was in the early 1960s reluctant to take the British High Commission into its confidence, and its head was said to have instructed officials not to disclose information without his specific authorisation.

So far as traditional diplomatic practices were concerned, a minister of state at the CRO took pride, in 1960, in the Commonwealth having evolved 'a set of procedures which avoided the formalities and stiffness of normal protocol. We do not despatch formal notes of protest to each other, shrouded in the blinding light of the latest publicity technique'.[111] 'Goodwill was taken for granted even in cases of violent disagreements, which were much easier to resolve because of the informality of such diplomacy'.[112] However, the informal Commonwealth approach functioned well only as long as there were no serious tensions: as a former CRO official recollected, 'when relations between [Commonwealth] countries became less than cordial (as they were most of the time between India and Pakistan), the arrangements moved into the normal

[109] Morrice James (British HC, Karachi)-Garner, personal and confidential, 29 May 1963, TNA, DO161/188.

[110] Gore-Booth—Garner, 1 June 1963.

[111] Lord Alport quoted in Miller (1974) 388.

[112] Miller (1974) 388.

intergovernmental mechanism'.[113] Even Britain no longer considered informality adequate in the enlarged Commonwealth. One reason the CRO and FO had wanted immunity legislation was to protect British officials; and there was no inclination to think that the privileges and immunities provisions of the 1961 Convention on Diplomatic Relations were inappropriate in the Commonwealth. Which was just as well. For the 1960s saw the development in the Commonwealth not just of relations of a 'normal' kind, but also of some hitherto inconceivable behaviour.

For example, President Nkrumah of Ghana chose, at a 1961 diplomatic gathering in Hungary, to describe Britain's record in Africa as that of a 'colonial oppressor'—whereupon Britain's representative 'slammed down his drinking glass and strode from the room'.[114] There was a difficult passage of events in 1963 over Trinidad and Tobago's high commissioner in London, Sir Learie Constantine (formerly a famous cricketer). He complained (mistakenly) to a *Daily Mirror* reporter that a decision of the commonwealth secretary discriminated against West Indians, and was reprimanded by his prime minister, Dr. Eric Williams. Constantine, who regarded himself as 'something unique among the species of High Commissioner'[115] and at home was thought to have a 'swollen head',[116] flew to Trinidad to protest. But to no avail. Within a few weeks a bitter and dispirited Constantine had tendered his resignation (but he did not leave office immediately). Early in 1964 Britain's high commissioner to Zanzibar, Timothy Crosthwait, was ordered to leave, following Britain's reluctance to recognise the new revolutionary regime. Allowed back a month later he was again expelled—on the day he presented his credentials—for having, on instructions, criticised the new leader's recent description of the British as 'devils'.[117] In 1970 Zambia's President Kaunda announced on arrival in London that he had come to appeal to the British people about British policy towards South Africa over the head of their prime minister. Later, at dinner, when the latter 'quietly and logically' explained why Britain had to do business with South Africa, Kaunda suddenly 'sprang up' and 'rushed

[113] Private information.

[114] Sir Nicholas Cheetham obituary, *The Times* 13 February 2002.

[115] Costar-Arthur Snelling (DUS), 19 June 1963, TNA, DO200/80.

[116] J.A. Davidson (first secretary, HCO)-C.W.F. Footman (West Indies Department) 16 December 1963, DO200/80.

[117] Timothy Crosthwait obituary, *The Times* 29 November 2006.

from the room', crying 'My God, my God, I never expected a British Minister to speak to me like that!'[118]

But the most extraordinary event of this kind concerned another Zambian, Mr. Ali Simbule. Soon after the 1967 announcement of his appointment as high commissioner in London, he told a press conference that Britain was 'a "humbled, toothless bulldog, wagging its tail in front of Rhodesian Premier Ian Smith and fearing him like hell"'. This provoked headlines and angry demands that Britain's acceptance of Simbule's nomination to London ('*agrément*' in non-Commonwealth contexts) should be withdrawn. Ineffective efforts were made to persuade President Kaunda not to proceed with the appointment. Simbule arrived in May professing friendship with Britain, but was not allowed to present his letters of commission until Britain and Zambia had agreed on the wording of a formal expression of regret for his remarks. Then, in August, as he departed for a trip to Zambia, he reiterated his 'toothless bulldog' gibe to the *Sunday Telegraph* and pointed out that far from withdrawing it, he was repeating it.[119] He made similar statements during a stop-over in Nairobi.

Now the fat was in the fire. The Zambian Ministry of Foreign Affairs was reportedly 'having heart failure';[120] Kaunda was 'very annoyed' and had decided 'Simbule was unfit to hold the London post';[121] but did not want to appear to be sacrificing him in response to British pressure. Accordingly, he appointed him as a UN delegate, and a spokesman announced he 'would return to his base as soon as his other assignments were over'.[122] In New York, Simbule proceeded to make a speech describing Britain as 'the worst offender' against sanctions;[123] asserting she was 'racialist', applied 'double standards', and 'showed a total disregard for human suffering...in Rhodesia'; and insisting Zambia 'would not be intimidated' from exposing Britain's '"wickedness and treachery" and would not be misled [into] bogus and deceitful statements'.[124] Simbule saw nothing wrong in what he had said: 'they

[118] Greenhill (1992) 149.

[119] Defensive brief for the commonwealth secretary's visit to Africa October/November 1967: Mr. Simbule, 17 October 1967, TNA, FCO29/33.

[120] British HCO telegram 3211, 3 October 1967, TNA, FCO29/33.

[121] Defensive brief for commonwealth secretary's visit to Africa.

[122] British HCO telegram 3210, 3 October 1967, TNA, FCO29/33.

[123] 'Call to bomb bridges and blockade ports', *Scotsman*, 17 October 1967.

[124] British delegation to UN, telegram 2722, 16 October 1967, TNA, FCO29/33.

were only words which did not necessarily mean very much'.[125] But there was uproar in the British press. Kaunda felt obliged publicly to support Simbule. But privately he promised to withdraw him, and this was gracefully achieved in December. Simbule returned to London to wind up his affairs and sought a farewell call on the Queen. The request was 'not pressed' by the CRO,[126] but the Queen agreed to it. Simbule also said goodbye to the commonwealth secretary (whom he was meeting for the first time). Courtesies continued to be observed by Britain, her high commissioner greeting Simbule at the airport when he and his family returned to Lusaka. Zambia, however, swiftly posted him to Ivory Coast.

More dramatically, and dangerously, British Commonwealth missions and representatives were beginning to be subjected to violence. During the 1956 Suez crisis the British Information Service office in Dacca (East Pakistan) was burnt down. The British trade commissioner in Montreal was kidnapped in 1970. In Ireland, Britain's Embassy was burnt in 1972 after the 'Bloody Sunday' shooting by paratroopers of thirteen demonstrators in Northern Ireland. This sort of thing continued into the next decade. Britain's ambassador to Ireland was assassinated in 1976, and her deputy high commissioner in Bombay in 1984. In 1980, when Britain's high commissioner to Zambia said that Britain would not take responsibility for an attack on that state by the illegal Rhodesian regime, he was condemned by the press as an 'arrogant, irrelevant and insolent' 'fascist hyena' and there was a huge demonstration, which included many students, outside the High Commission. When the high commissioner's wife commented on this to the local university's vice-chancellor, he disclaimed the demonstrators, saying 'my lot are coming tomorrow'. They were worse:

> loudspeaker vans were going round telling students to report for voluntary demonstrations.... Windows were smashed and they started trying to break down the outside wall.... we started burning our secret documents.... [President Kaunda] was raving and shouting, a sort of continual speech at the State House being broadcast.... It really was quite unsettling.... I was called to the ministry and I was not allowed to say anything. I was given the crime sheet of all the dreadful things I'd done by the foreign minister... who really hated the British. I wasn't terribly unhappy to find

[125] Evan Luard (Labour MP, British delegation to UN)-G.A. Crossley (DHC Lusaka) 23 November 1967, TNA, FCO29/33.

[126] CRO-British HC, telegram 3398, 19 December 1967, TNA, FCO29/33.

> that he [later fell from grace]....The atmosphere really was awful....the government (or Lord Carrington) said, 'You better come home.'...I left that night....[Lord Carrington was supportive and] appointed me as Assistant Under Secretary for Africa. It was a moment of great pleasure when Richard Luce, the Minister of State, who dealt with Africa said then, 'Come and join me, the Zambian High Commissioner is coming in'....he said to her, 'You know Len, don't you? He's going to look after Africa for us.'
>
> Her hair practically stood on end.[127]

In the 1960s British high commissioners were withdrawn on a dozen occasions, mostly from African states. Sometimes there were personal reasons; sometimes they were the unlucky casualties of poor inter-state relations; and on more than one occasion it was not easy to disentangle these factors. It was said that high commissioners to Kenya had been removed from office because the Kenyans got upset with them.[128] And it was said of one high commissioner who was expelled that this was after his 'secretary mixed up two letters he had written, putting each in the other's envelope: one letter thanked the President for his gracious hospitality at dinner the previous evening, the other reported to London in vivid language the latest corrupt deals and sexual excesses of the same President'. (According to a colleague, hardly anyone believed that it was a mistake.)[129] In 1961 the British high commissioner to Ghana fell foul of President Nkrumah's unfounded belief that he had been stirring up people in London against the country, and that critical opinions in the press had been taken from one of his despatches. It meant, he wrote, that any 'usefulness I may have had in this post has thus come to an end'.[130] In 1965 Ghana and Tanzania broke off diplomatic relations with Britain over the Rhodesian affair. (The day after giving the high commissioner a week to leave the country, Ghana's President Nkrumah, not untypically, invited him over for a chat.) In 1976 the leader of a failed coup and two heavily-armed guards turned up at Britain's High Commission in Nigeria, and insisted on seeing the high commissioner, Sir Martin Le Quesne. When he informed the Nigerian authorities, they 'asked him to hush the incident up', but Reuters, which

---

[127] Jane Barder interview with Sir Leonard Allinson, 5 March 1996, Cambridge: Churchill College, Churchill Archives Centre (CAC), DOHP, 6.

[128] Private information.

[129] Private information.

[130] Snelling (British HC)-Sandys, valedictory despatch, 5 December 1961, *BDEE* 1957–64 II, 260.

the government believed was 'the voice of the British government',[131] reported the incident. Le Quesne had done nothing wrong, but Nigeria demanded his withdrawal. There was then a breach in diplomatic relations. In 1972 President Idi Amin of Uganda 'spectacularly' televised his announcement of the expulsion of the British high commissioner, Dick Slater, along with 20,000 Ugandan Asians. Once Slater had enjoyed unrestricted access; he was Amin's 'best friend' ('along with the Queen and Moshe Dayan'). Now he sat 'silently on a sofa twirling his spectacles while the Ugandan dictator wagged his finger at him like an admonishing schoolmaster'.[132] Four years later Britain broke off relations with Uganda, on the grounds that the tyrannical Amin 'had rendered impossible the proper functioning of the United Kingdom High Commission in Kampala'.[133] Amin declared he had beaten the British and 'conferred on himself the decoration of CBE which, he said, stood for "Conqueror of the British Empire"'.[134]

The refusal of a nomination for the headship of a high commission (the Commonwealth's equivalent of *agrément*) is much less likely to attract attention than the head's expulsion or a breach of diplomatic relations. But this previously unheard of event in Commonwealth relations certainly occurred in 1964, when Cyprus' President, the bearded Archbishop Makarios, turned down Cyril Pickard, who had been Britain's very effective acting high commissioner. His blackballing was thought to be connected with a rumour that he had called His Beatitude the Archbishop a 'barefaced liar'. In denying it in public, Pickard added fuel to the fire by saying that 'the adjective was obviously mistaken'.[135]

It almost seemed during these years as if it was not a matter of the normalisation of Commonwealth relations, but of their straying beyond the bounds of normality.

F. Titular Flexibility—and Orthodoxy

The title 'high commissioner' had started life in relation to territories which were self-governing but not sovereign. By the second half of the

---

[131] Obituary, *The Times*, 28 April 2004.
[132] Richard Slater obituary, *The Times*, 10 October 2001.
[133] Gore-Booth (1979) 190.
[134] Patrick Keatley, Idi Amin obituary, *The Guardian*, 18 August 2003. He also awarded himself a 'Victorious Cross': Tom Boyden, *The Times*, 26 August 2003.
[135] Canadian HCO Nicosia telegram, 24 March 1964, NAC, RG25, 21498, 2146.1.6.

twentieth century it was being used within the Commonwealth by the heads of diplomatic missions sent by one of its sovereign members to another—but not exclusively so, as Britain thrice bestowed the title on her representatives to Commonwealth entities which were less than sovereign. The first such case arose (as was mentioned in the previous chapter) in 1951, when she appointed a high commissioner to Southern Rhodesia, a self-governing territory. Like other such officers, he was responsible to the CRO.[136]

Britain had found it 'a great inconvenience' to be without a diplomatic-type mission in Salisbury, as although the governor was expected to keep Britain informed of what was going on 'it came low in his priorities and...it was difficult to expect him to comment on internal affairs in the way that a British diplomat could'.[137] There was much to be said for the appointment of a political representative, especially in view of plans to create a federation of the two Rhodesias (Southern and Northern) and Nyasaland. This is what happened, and he was titled a high commissioner. (When in 1953 the anticipated Central African Federation was established, he was accredited to it.) His tasks were those of a normal British high commissioner, with modifications taking into account the territory's constitutional position and relationship with neighbouring colonies. For example, although he and his South African colleague had full diplomatic status, like his counterpart in London he was not styled 'excellency' and the governor remained responsible for native affairs. The Southern Rhodesian (and then the Federal) prime minister was not happy that foreign envoys in Salisbury could not have diplomatic status or titles, and as the Gold Coast (Ghana) and Malaya approached independence insisted 'it was essential that the Federation should not be left behind in the race'.[138] His 'people would not contemplate with equanimity' the Federal high commissioner 'having to walk behind the High Commissioner for the Gold Coast'.[139] They felt

---

[136] South Africa had already sent a high commissioner to Salisbury, in April 1950 (and Southern Rhodesia reciprocated). After South Africa left the Commonwealth in 1961 the South African mission was re-named the 'South African Diplomatic Mission' and headed by an 'Accredited Diplomatic Representative'. As has been mentioned earlier, Southern Rhodesia had been represented in London by a high commissioner since she became self-governing in 1923.

[137] Sir Richard Best interview of Sir Harold Smedley, 22 May 1997, CAC, DOHP 23.

[138] Home—Lennox-Boyd—Malvern (Southern Rhodesian PM) meeting, 15 June 1956, TNA, DO35/4672.

[139] Malvern-Home, 21 June 1956, appendix B to *ibid.*

they were 'being held back and wish[ed] to find some opportunity for enhancing their status in the eyes of the world'.[140] Partly to ease this pressure for independence, in 1957 Britain gave the Federation the right to conduct such relations as it had or might have with other Commonwealth countries and with foreign countries, subject to Britain's ultimate responsibility for the Federation in international law. In this way the Federation obtained the right 'to exchange "diplomatic agents"' and appoint consular or trade representatives.[141] But no such exchanges took place before Rhodesia's illegal, unilateral declaration of independence (UDI) in 1965, and the level of overseas representation in the Federation never rose above that of consul-general or commissioner (although from 1957 American consuls-general had the personal rank of minister).

In January 1964, following the break-up of the Federation, Southern Rhodesia reverted to her original identity and as such sent a high commissioner to, and received one from, Britain. In October 1964 she became 'Rhodesia'. As, then, the likelihood of UDI grew, the British high commission was emptied of confidential documents. But the high commissioner made no departure preparations lest the Rhodesians should think Britain was resigned to accepting UDI. When UDI was declared on 11 November 1965, Britain broke off diplomatic relations. She withdrew her high commissioner from Salisbury and gave the Rhodesian high commissioner in London two days to leave the country. However, until 1969 each High Commission retained a rump staff to undertake consular work.

Meanwhile, in 1963 Britain had also appointed a high commissioner to another dependent federation: that of South Arabia, which brought together the colony of Aden and the British protectorates in its hinterland (the high commissioner also serving as the colony's governor). The Federation was initially under the CO, and then transferred to the FO—so that, most unusually, that last Office had an administrative-diplomatic high commissioner on its books. This novelty did not last long, as in four years, and as many high commissioners, the Federation's internal situation deteriorated sharply, culminating in an ignominious

[140] CRO brief for Home, 'Status of Foreign Representatives in Salisbury', 15 November 1955, TNA, DO 35/5225.

[141] Undated G.E.B. Shannon (AUS) minute, May 1961, TNA, DO161/185.

British departure. The successor state of South Yemen did not join the Commonwealth.

The third such case also arose in 1963, when Britain appointed a high commissioner to the protected state of Brunei (previously she had had a 'resident' there). Brunei had become self-governing in 1959 and, although small, was wealthy on account of her oil and natural gas resources. Possibly this might have had something to do with the titular upgrading of Britain's representative, although it was said in 1967 that the high commissioner acted more as an old-style colonial resident than as head of a diplomatic mission. Be that as it may, the high commissioner at that time endeared himself to the Sultan (the ruler) so much that the latter tried to prevent the official's departure to a higher-graded post. He offered to reimburse Britain for the cost she would incur if she kept him there on an improved salary, and when the offer was declined threatened to resign from his throne. Britain was unmoved, and the Sultan resigned. High commissioners continued to be appointed to Brunei up to her becoming independent in 1984—and afterwards, as she became a member of the Commonwealth.

While, however, these cases demonstrated the flexibility of the title of high commissioner, two other cases indicated that at the level of diplomatic relations, it could only be used between those who were full Commonwealth members. A sovereign state's possible or potential Commonwealth membership was insufficient to justify the bestowal of the title on the head of the mission to that state. This was the new orthodoxy. The first instance signifying this was Cyprus, which had become independent in 1960. Britain had nursed the hope, for a variety of dubious reasons, that it might be possible to shunt Cyprus into a 'Special Association' with, rather than full membership of, the Commonwealth. Was the Commonwealth, the prime minister later asked, 'to be the R.A.C. or Boodles'?[142] (two Gentlemen's Clubs in London, the latter being much the more exclusive of the two). This scheme was very soon seen to be a lost cause, so the question which remained was whether Cyprus was to be admitted to the Commonwealth. While discussions on this matter proceeded—as languidly as Britain could arrange them—her representative to Cyprus was so termed (but although Cyprus was at this time a 'foreign state' he came under the CRO). Only after Cyprus was admitted to the Commonwealth in March 1961 did he become a high commissioner.

---

[142] Quoted in James (2002) 27.

The second such case led to the appointment of a 'British Government representative *ad interim*' in Singapore. From 1946 to 1963 Singapore had been a British colony. She then joined with two other dependent territories and the sovereign state of Malaya to form the Federation of Malaysia. Insofar as Singapore was concerned it was a short union, as in August 1965 she was 'expelled by the Tunku'.[143] The above title was then hurriedly devised, the 'interim' part reflecting the expectation that Singapore would be quickly admitted to the Commonwealth. However, it took much longer to obtain the necessary indications of willingness from all the other members, as Singapore had deeply upset Pakistan. After a month, Britain's representative, J.V. Rob (who came under the CRO), told London that although his 'unusual title' did not harm his position or his relations with the government, it 'has inevitably been a source of some misunderstanding and has provided the basis for a number of amiable witticisms...but it is now beginning to wear a little thin'.[144] Malaysia had exchanged high commissioners with Singapore, and Australia and India had translated their representatives into acting high commissioners. As Rob was without a recognised diplomatic title, he was for purposes of precedence placed in the lowest possible category—even below consuls. He was not much cheered by the fact that he was joined there by the New Zealand envoy, who had no title at all! He was concerned, with Armistice Day coming up, about how the British community would feel at seeing him in this 'artificially humble position'.[145] He wanted to be made an acting high commissioner, and a CRO official thought 'it would be reasonable to consider whether protocol could not be stretched [that] little bit further'.[146] But it was ruled that Rob could not bear that title until the Commonwealth membership question was resolved, which did not happen (positively, for Singapore) until mid-October.

G. CRO Diplomacy and the Demise of the CRO

One of the distinguishing characteristics of Britain's relationship with the Commonwealth was that she had a separate department (and minister) of state to handle all issues relating to its other members—first

[143] Introduction, *BDEE 1964–1971* I, liv.
[144] J.V. Rob-J.C. Morgan (AUS), 14 September 1965, TNA, DO169/544.
[145] *Ibid.*
[146] Morgan minute, 22 September 1965, TNA, DO169/544.

the Dominions Office, and then, from 1947, the CRO. Her high commissioners received their instructions from it and reported to it, and many—but by no means all—of them came from its ranks. In London it was the resident high commissioners' immediate, and day-to-day, port of call. Its very existence marked Britain's close and benevolent interest in her imperial offspring, and in the institution which was indicative both of their history and their continuing association. In 1968 it came to an end.

As early as 1944, Britain's first high commissioner, Sir William Clark, had called for a merger of the FO and CRO so that Britain and the Dominions could be put 'on a more comfortable parity'.[147] Four years later, the FO suggested the CRO had 'outlived its purpose',[148] and that it would be 'in the interests of efficiency and co-ordination'[149] if it took over the CRO's functions in regard to foreign affairs or, indeed, the whole CRO. The technique of dealing with Commonwealth states was, it thought, little different from what was needed for foreign states. Regular contact with foreign policy experts was what was required, and without it Britain's high commissioners were 'less competent to discuss foreign affairs as frankly and fully'[150] as they would be if they represented the foreign secretary and spoke on his behalf.

The CRO responded vigorously to what were possibly 'the first rumblings of a landslide which would in the end destroy the C.R.O.'[151] In so doing, it had had an ally in the cabinet secretary, Sir Norman Brook. He thought the FO's proposal would 'give rise to grave difficulties'. First, it assumed the foreign secretary would deal directly with ministers for external affairs (MEAs). But four prime ministers were their own MEAs, and this was one reason why the prime ministerial channel was used for consultations on major foreign policy issues. Nor did Britain's prime minister, Attlee, want to do anything that might upset the arrangement whereby high commissioners in London were responsible to their prime ministers rather than their MEAs. Second, the CRO's standing would be seriously affected if it lost its responsibility for foreign policy, which

[147] Cross (1967) 754

[148] S.Y. Dawbarn minute, 16 February 1953, TNA, ZP1/5, FO371/125029.

[149] Orme Sargent (PUS FO)-Percivale Liesching (PUS CRO designate), 6 December 1948, TNA, DO121/22.

[150] Joint FO/CRO memorandum, 'Relations with Other Commonwealth Governments on Foreign Affairs', 25 February 1949, TNA, DO121/22.

[151] Liesching-Philip Noel-Baker (commonwealth secretary), 11 December 1948, TNA, DO121/22.

in turn could set a train of events in motion which would remove any justification for the CRO's existence as a major department of state. Third, public opinion was 'insistent that the Cabinet should include a senior Minister who can voice the interests of the Commonwealth'.[152] Finally, Britain had always regarded special arrangements for handling relations as necessary in view of the distinctive nature of the Commonwealth relationship. Attlee sympathised with Brook's arguments (perhaps because he was a former dominions secretary), and a meeting of senior ministers endorsed the cabinet secretary's conclusions. A few months' later there was another FO foray, leading to a short and sharp inter-departmental battle which ended with the foreign secretary agreeing to leave the matter in abeyance.

A 'period of calm' in FO-CRO relations then set in as the two departments developed 'more realistic and cooperative' relations.[153] The CRO promised to overcome its shortcomings, and set up a Foreign Division; British high commissioners were told to give greater emphasis to foreign affairs; and there were some cross-postings to overseas missions. But the CRO was not out of the wood. For a number of reasons it lacked many high-calibre senior officials, and men of 'no more than average ability'[154] were over-promoted to become high commissioners. In 1956 the foreign secretary gave the prime minister an FO memorandum complaining acidly about this, and in particular about the neglect of Australia's demand for a change of high commissioner. The immediate problem was solved by a first-class political appointment (Lord Carrington), and other political appointments followed. In fact, 'outsiders' had commonly headed a minority of high commissions (and in 1951 the FO had provided its first high commissioner). But reliance on them looked bad, and in 1959 a House of Commons committee said there was 'clearly something wrong with a Service when so many of its top posts are offered to men who have made their careers elsewhere'.[155]

Meanwhile the idea of an FO-CRO merger had never gone away. During a 1954 parliamentary debate, a minister found it necessary to insist that it was essential to have 'a special department' on the grounds

---

[152] Norman Brook minute for Attlee, 17 July 1948, Annex 1 to note of meeting of ministers, 'Arrangements for Consultation with Commonwealth Countries', 28 July 1948, TNA, DO121/22.
[153] Garner (1978) 302.
[154] *Ibid.* 376.
[155] House of Commons (1959) vii; Sir Gilbert Laithwaite (PUS CRO) in *ibid.*, 138.

that intra-Commonwealth relations were 'quite different from our relations with foreign countries'.[156] And in 1956 Sir Norman Brook again rallied to the flag by dissuading a (now different) prime minister from doing anything about a merger. He advanced bureaucratic and domestic political reasons for leaving things as they were, and also international ones: high commissions should not be thought of in the same breath as embassies, as our 'relations with Commonwealth countries *are* different from our relations with foreign countries'. High commissions should certainly

> contain one or more people with special knowledge and experience of international affairs who can speak on level terms, as experts, with officials of the local Department of External Affairs. But they have another function viz., to provide a link between the United Kingdom and the people of the country where they serve.[157]

If closer departmental links were in the air, Brook concluded, it was not those between the CRO and the FO which should be strengthened during the next, crucial decade in the evolution of the Commonwealth, but those between the CRO and the Colonial Office (CO).

However, neither the CRO nor CO saw much virtue in the idea. The CRO, which saw itself as 'a progressive Department with an exciting future',[158] tended to look down on the CO as an administrative-type department and did not want to be 'tarred with the Colonial brush':[159] 'When the CRO referred to what it called the C.O. people, it was using the tone of an anthropologist discussing a backward tribe with somewhat backward rituals'.[160] Thus in 1959 the CRO shunned

---

[156] Quoted in Cross (1967) 75.

[157] *Ibid.*

[158] Garner (1978) 408.

[159] *Ibid.*, 303.

[160] George Thomson (a front-bench Labour spokesman) in 1960, quoted in *ibid.* 408. For its part, the CO despised the CRO only a little less than did the FO: 'Both the FO and the CO had genuine jobs and functions to perform: the only function of the CRO was to try to keep the Commonwealth sweet, which was a pretty thankless task...the Colonial Office was more concerned to fulfil its responsibilities to the colonial territories and to bring them to independence in the best possible conditions than to worry about whether on independence the CRO would have a lovely, placid, trouble-free relationship with them....I remember very well the persistent whining from the CRO ("please try not to upset them!") when we in the CO were busting a gut to get safeguards for the ethnic minorities into the Nigerian independence constitution....negotiating...post-independence arrangements...required a degree of diplomatic finesse and determination that the anti-colonial movement in the wings and our critics at the UN never dreamed of': personal communication.

as 'retrograde'[161] the suggestion that the two Offices combine. It made much of the fact that the Commonwealth's members had no wish to deal with a department which exercised colonial responsibilities. Nonetheless, in 1960 a House of Commons committee endorsed the idea. It advanced no further because the prime minister thought it would be premature. But two years later he was better disposed towards it, not least because the two Offices now shared a single Cabinet minister. They were amalgamated in 1966.

On the FO side, plans for an arranged marriage with the CRO were gathering steam. In 1962 the Plowden Committee was set up to examine the organisation of Britain's three overseas Services—Foreign, Commonwealth, and Trade Commissioner—and its deliberations included an intense examination of the question of a CRO-FO merger. The CRO put up a stout defence, speaking of the 'profound importance' of the Commonwealth for Britain and 'the free world generally', the administrative disadvantages of a merger, and the usefulness of the CRO's expertise and contacts.[162] It also insisted that the significance of moves towards 'normal' diplomacy 'should not be over-rated'. Changes were 'by no means general' and they 'had little effect on the real substance of the Commonwealth relationship'.[163] The Committee, however, tentatively concluded that the 'right amalgamation' was 'between the two "diplomatic" departments'.[164] This elicited a prime ministerial explosion. '**NO**. I think the Plowden Ctee [*sic.*] are on the wrong track—*altogether*,' said Macmillan. 'I should **oppose** strongly merging Commonwealth with F.O. *Politically*, it wd. be worse for us than the Common Market.'[165]

When the Committee's Report appeared in 1964, there was a different prime minister, Sir Alec Douglas-Home, the former Earl of Home (and the later Baron). He was undisturbed by its conclusion that the division of the world for representational purposes into Commonwealth and non-Commonwealth countries 'impedes the development and execution

---

161 Introduction, *BDEE* 1957–1964 I, xxxii.

162 CRO memorandum for Committee on Representational Services Overseas, 'The Role and Work of the Commonwealth Relations Office', 24 September 1962, TNA, DO197/2.

163 CRO memorandum for Committee on Representational Services Overseas, 'History of the CRO', 20 September 1962, TNA, DO197/2.

164 Philip de Zulueta (private secretary to prime minister) minute for Macmillan, 5 December 1962, *BDEE* 1957–1964 I, 336.

165 Macmillan minute, 6 December 1962, *BDEE* 1957–1964 I, 336.

of a coherent foreign policy' and 'that the logic of events' pointed towards the creation of a 'a single Ministry of External Affairs'.[166] But he also agreed with the Committee that the time for it was not yet opportune, since such a step 'might be misinterpreted as implying loss of interest in the Commonwealth partnership',[167] and this view was endorsed during a parliamentary debate. However, the Committee's recommendation that the CRO and the FO, while remaining separate, should draw their staff from a single service found widespread acceptance, and the three overseas Services were amalgamated into a single Diplomatic Service, in 1965. Announcing this decision, the new Labour prime minister, Harold Wilson, was careful to emphasise that Britain continued to value the special nature of the Commonwealth relationship. But it was another, and significant, nail in the CRO's coffin.

The change, however, was not without benefit to the CRO. The single service brought economic and commercial work in the Commonwealth into a closer and more efficient relationship with political work. It provided a buffer that enabled the CRO to avoid the shock of sudden amalgamation; to develop 'a sense of unity' with the FO and a 'new sense of identity'; and to work out the 'techniques of a Single Service before facing the major surgical operation involved in a full merger'.[168] (It also brought material advantages in conditions of service.) The following year, the Commonwealth Office was created by merging the CRO and CO, and a junior FO minister was elevated to the Cabinet with the job of being 'particularly nice to the Commonwealth countries'.[169] By then, the creation of the Commonwealth Secretariat had provided an alternative focus for Commonwealth members; domestic opposition to a merger was evaporating; and even CRO officials who had been 'resolutely opposed'[170] to it came to accept its inevitability, and worked towards it. It was becoming obvious that the expansion of the Commonwealth called for greater regional specialisation, which could best be developed in conjunction with the FO, which would also offer useful general experience as well as wider and more varied career

---

[166] Plowden Report (Cmd. 2276) paragraph 44.

[167] R. Butler (foreign secretary) cabinet memorandum, 'Plowden Committee's Report on the Representational Services Overseas', 3 February 1964, TNA, CP(64)34, CAB129/116.

[168] Garner (1978) 414, 416.

[169] Malcolm MacBain interview with Denis Doble, 29 March 2004, CAC, DOHP 58.

[170] Dixon (1969) 67.

prospects. It was odd that the FO lacked specialist knowledge about Britain's relations with a significant portion of the world (in October 1968 only one of its senior officers had any substantial African experience), and that the (former) CRO was in the same position about most of the world, running high commissions whose staff had only a limited practical experience of foreign affairs.

Thus there was thus little protest when, in 1968, the two departments were combined into the carefully-named Foreign and Commonwealth Office. In taking this step, Britain went out of her way in both word and deed to emphasise there had been 'no change in our attitude or approach to the Commonwealth connection',[171] and to reassure high commissioners in London that their position would not be eroded. The prime minister claimed that Commonwealth prime ministers 'put the view "very strongly"' that the merger 'was in the better interests of the Commonwealth; "they liked to have one Department to deal with"'.[172] But they would, anyway, have had few grounds for complaint, given their increasing tendency to organise their own foreign ministries on a purely geographical basis, without drawing distinctions between Commonwealth and non-Commonwealth states.

Still, the merger reflected Britain's turning away from the Commonwealth, and was seen as such. This was particularly so in New Zealand, where there was 'much unfavourable comment' about Britain wanting 'to be rid of the Commonwealth in order to become more European'.[173] Inevitably it further diminished the intimacy of Commonwealth relationships, and was a loss for Britain's Commonwealth partners. They no longer had their own spokesman in the Cabinet; and their high commissioners had to accustom themselves to dealing generally with heads of departments rather than ministers or a permanent under-secretary. An attempt was made to sweeten the pill by the relevant 'geographical Minister of State' giving new high commissioners a welcoming luncheon to introduce them to people who would be useful; and, when possible, the foreign and commonwealth secretary hosted luncheons for departing high commissioners, which put them in the same league as ambassadors from important states or those who had been in London for a long time or had otherwise distinguished

[171] Wilson to House of Commons, 28 March 1968, 333.
[172] Wilson to House of Commons, 11 February 1969, 1118–9.
[173] Introduction, *BDEE 1964–1971* I, lxx

themselves. Nonetheless, it was a pill. Despite 'a crash programme of cross postings'[174] Commonwealth states remained, for a while, unknown to many FCO staff; and officers posted in the Commonwealth often found themselves writing home to people whom they had not met. High commissions, which had been relatively well staffed compared to embassies, were scaled down.

Nor did CRO people remain long in top positions, and thirty who were considered not up to FCO work were given early retirement. For the rest, they had to adopt the practices of the larger and more impersonal FO, whose identity was stronger, discipline stricter, and conduct of business more formal. For their part, FO people, rather than cherishing the Commonwealth, were said often to find it 'very irritating and troublesome'.[175] They thought it did nothing for Britain's standing and were critical of the 'indulgent favouritism' afforded to ex-colonies.[176] One official admonished an ex-CO colleague to 'remember that Britain can't be bothered with these potty little places any more'.[177] Neither of two further reports on Britain's representation overseas (the 1969 Duncan Report and the 1977 Berrill Report) respected the once sacrosanct distinction between Commonwealth members and 'foreign states'. Britain's procedures regarding high commissioners resident in London were becoming ever more 'normal'; but in this respect they were also catching up with what was already the norm elsewhere in the Commonwealth.

H. Britain and the *Décanat*

1. *British high commissioners and the* décanat *in newly-independent states*

In former colonies it was usual for the representative of the ex-imperial power to provide the first *doyen* of the diplomatic corps. This could be formally agreed in advance between colonisers and colonised, or achieved by ensuring that he or she was the first to present credentials, or (in the interests of safety) both routes could be followed. However, as mentioned above, in the 1950s Britain was strongly of the view that high commissioners could not be seen as part of the 'foreign' diplomatic

[174] Sir Colin Imray memoir, CAC, DOHP, 54.
[175] Jane Barder interview with Sir Leonard Allinson.
[176] Imray memoir, CAC, DOHP, 54.
[177] Quoted in Alexander (2006) 317.

corps. Presumably for this reason, when the question of the *décanat* arose in regard to Ghana in 1957, the CRO earnestly hoped the new state would follow London's example in excluding high commissioners from the diplomatic corps, and thereby avoid saddling the British high commissioner, Sir Ian Maclennan (1957–59), with the *décanat.* Since, however, he was for several months the only substantive head of mission in Accra, he could not escape the office. Then the CRO did an about-turn, deciding as 'a matter of direct policy',[178] to seek the *décanat* for British high commissioners, who therefore (there being no formal agreement to this effect with the states concerned) had to make sure that they presented their credentials ahead of anyone else, so ensuring they weren't 'jumped'. This could necessitate an early start on independence day: in Nigeria (1960) the appointment was at 8.30 a.m.; in Tanganyika (1961) 8.15 a.m. (an 'excessively rushed' occasion, just 15 minutes before the independence ceremony);[179] and in Sierra Leone (1961) 7 a.m. The British high commissioner also became the first *doyen* in Malaya (1957) but in Cyprus (1960) it was the Greek ambassador who secured the post.

However, in 1961 the Nigerian press began complaining that Viscount Head (1960–64) was too bossy, and his role as *doyen* was cited as 'yet another example of the way in which he exerted a malign influence over the Nigerian Government'.[180] When, therefore, the Duke of Devonshire (the junior CRO minister) learned that Britain intended 'to follow the usual practice'[181] in Tanganyika, he wondered whether Britain should, in this way, gratuitously give 'the "anti-imperialists" yet another stick to beat us with, without any compensating advantage'.[182] In consequence, the CRO canvassed everyone who had acted in this capacity in newly-independent states. There was no consensus, the advantages and disadvantages of being *doyen* appearing fairly evenly balanced.

On the negative side, Head (who had not been keen on becoming *doyen*) believed it gave ill-wishers, especially ill-informed ones, an excuse

---

[178] A.L. Mayall (vice-marshal of the diplomatic corps)—Rear-Admiral the Earl Cairns (marshal of the diplomatic corps), 1 August 1969, TNA, FCO57/88.

[179] Neil Pritchard (British HC)-G.W. St. J. Chadwick (AUS), 24 February 1962, TNA, DO161/186.

[180] A.E. Furness (secretary to Duke of Devonshire, parliamentary under-secretary) minute, 1 December 1961, TNA, DO161/186.

[181] *Ibid.*

[182] Devonshire-Head, personal and confidential, 15 January 1962, TNA, DO161/186.

to rail against Britain's alleged 'desire to maintain a "neo-imperial" status'.[183] He thought it 'best for the representative of the "ex-boss country" not to be boss of anything'.[184] (The CRO agreed that it might be disadvantageous to have a British *doyen* 'in suspicious countries like Kenya and British Guiana').[185] Maclennan observed that there was 'a considerable risk' in some states 'of kicks, and very few ha'pennies or bouquets'. Hence when he had been high commissioner in Accra he had been reluctant, as there

> were so many difficulties between us and the Ghanaians to complicate life further by functioning actively as Dean of the Corps, something which might involve me in squabbles with the Government over alleged indignities and lack of privilege involving some of my colleagues, especially those who had nothing to do but think of such things...I modelled my performance on King Log rather than King Stork.[186]

It was observed that being a *doyen* sometimes complicated the job of 'promoting the outwards signs of Commonwealth kinship', as it could look to a critical eye as if the British high commissioner was getting special treatment.[187] It was also usually time-consuming and could involve 'a good deal of tiresome and unnecessary work'.[188] Even where the diplomatic corps was small

> The British high commissioner in newly-independent country could expect to be busy with arrangements consequent upon independence, paying attention to British-owned companies working locally; strings of visitors, and because of the historic connection being invited to everything that was happening locally....When, after a while, one British high commissioner called a meeting of the diplomatic corps, which he regarded as his duty as doyen, the other diplomats started having ideas about having a diplomatic ball and other social activities, and it was quite clear that the doyen was expected to organise such events. He solved the problem by doing nothing about them and never calling another meeting.[189]

---

[183] CRO note, 'Deanship of Diplomatic Corps', April 1961, TNA, FCO57/88.

[184] CRO note, 'Deanship of Diplomatic Corps in Commonwealth Countries', 8 January 1962, enclosure in Chadwick circular telegram, 9 February 1962, TNA, FCO57/88.

[185] Chadwick minute, 2 February 1962, TNA, DO161/186.

[186] I. Maclennan (former British HC Accra)-Chadwick, 8 January 1962, TNA, DO161/186.

[187] CRO note, 'Deanship of Diplomatic Corps', 8 January 1962.

[188] Dixon minute, 1 February 1962, TNA, DO161/186.

[189] Personal communication.

On the positive side, there was a strong view that it was 'right and proper when power is transferred in friendly circumstances'[190] that Britain should assume the diplomatic helm. It could be easier for the receiving state to turn for advice on protocol and related matters to a representative of the former metropolitan power than to a 'Dean whom they do not know'.[191] In the course helping the authorities or inexperienced diplomatic colleagues in the role of *doyen*, it was possible to exercise a sensible influence, and this could be particularly advantageous 'in an immature place like Uganda',[192] or where the alternative was someone who would be incompetent, 'inefficient or unwilling to press the local authorities',[193] or where the diplomatic corps was small. In Malaya, being *doyen* afforded 'frequent and regular social opportunities of talking informally with key Ministers', and the high commissioner's prominence on state occasions pleased the British community.[194] And if there were no other heads of mission on the ground on independence day, the office would seem unavoidable. Furthermore, the work of a *doyen* did not seem markedly to absorb the 'goodwill which might be needed for our own United Kingdom purposes'.[195] On the contrary, British doyens usually earned genuine gratitude and goodwill for being helpful and lending their diplomatic experience to states taking their first diplomatic steps.

The CRO concluded that instead of being 'inclined to go for the Deanship as a matter of principle',[196] Britain should weigh each case on its merits, and neither 'engage in an ugly rush' to be first in the queue, nor 'deliberately loiter round the corner in order to join it further down'.[197] In practice, however, Britain continued actively seeking the *décanat*. In Zimbabwe (1980) she was unsuccessful, the staunchly

---

[190] Garner (PUS, CRO) minute, note for the record, 5 February 1962, TNA, DO161/186.

[191] Jack Johnston (British HC, Freetown)-Chadwick, 18 January 1962, TNA, DO161/186.

[192] Chadwick minute, 2 February 1962.

[193] Sir A. Morley (British HC-designate, Kingston) in L.B. Walsh Atkins (AUS) minute, 18 April 1962, TNA, DO200/50.

[194] Geofroy Tory (British HC)-Chadwick, 12 January 1962, TNA, DO161/186.

[195] CRO note, 'Deanship of Diplomatic Corps', April 1961.

[196] Chadwick circular telegram, 9 February 1962.

[197] Maclennan (British ambassador, Dublin 1959–64, British HC Accra 1957–59)-Chadwick, 8 January 1962, TNA, DO161/186 and CRO note, 'Deanship of Diplomatic Corps'.

pro-China President Mugabe arranging for that state's ambassador to be the first to present his credentials (ahead not just of Britain but also the Soviet Union), and so to become *doyen*. But she obtained it for her high commissioners in Jamaica (1962) and Trinidad and Tobago (1962) (being actively encouraged to do so by both these states), and also in Kenya (1963), Guyana (1966), Lesotho (1966), and Mauritius (1968). In so far, therefore, as the nationality of the *doyen* in newly-independent countries was concerned, Britain was following the usual practice.

2. *The* doyen *in London*

By the mid-1950s high commissioners were entitled to enjoy the *décanat*—that is, the doyenship or deanship of the diplomatic corps—in all capitals except London. This was because Britain (who, as the receiving state, had an important practical say in the matter)[198] did not regard high commissioners 'as part of the Diplomatic Body'.[199] Instead, what London seems to have done since at least the early 1950s was to give informal recognition to a Commonwealth *doyen*, in the person of the senior high commissioner. Thus the South African high commissioner was referred to as having, 'in his capacity as Dean', spoken to the commonwealth secretary about a Ceylonese complaint.[200] Elsewhere, too, there were occasional references to a 'Commonwealth Corps', and its '*doyen*'.[201]

One reason why London was able for so long to evade the issue of high commissioners and the *décanat* was that some ambassadors there were 'good stayers'[202]—so much so that some high commissioners might not have known that they were regarded as ineligible for it. In 1969, however, Britain was confronted with the prospect that within a few years a high commissioner—either Sir Laurence Lindo of Jamaica or Dr. J.N. Karanja of Kenya—was likely to become the longest-serving head of mission. If one or other of them were denied a highly-prized position that was available elsewhere, they would personally 'be most upset',[203]

---

[198] See chapter 5, section E.

[199] J.A. Gutteridge (FO)-Sir Cecil Syers (DUS-CRO), 18 September 1950, TNA, TP10017/44, DO35/2225.

[200] Minute, signature illegible, September 1952, TNA, DO35/3327.

[201] See John Freeman (British HC, New Delhi)-Snelling (DUS), 17 January 1966, TNA, FO372/8041.

[202] A.L. Mayall (head of protocol/vice-marshal of the diplomatic corps) minute, 1 August 1969, TNA, FCO57/88.

[203] Mayall minute, 7 August 1969, TNA, FCO57/88.

and the decision could easily be seen 'as discrimination against the new Commonwealth'.[204] Since the newly-merged FCO was, anyway, tending to treat ambassadors and high commissioners alike, it proposed removing the prohibition on the *décanat*.

The Palace objected, as did Earl Cairns (the marshal of the diplomatic corps), the FCO's protocol person, and Lord Cobbold (the lord chamberlain). Their objections hardly withstood scrutiny. One, that it might be constitutionally improper for one of the Queen's representatives to act on behalf of other heads of mission in relation to Her Majesty, had already been breached by Britain herself: at the end of 1951 she had told Canada that she had no objection to her high commissioner becoming *doyen* of Ottawa's diplomatic corps; and she had subsequently 'taken great pains'[205] to try to ensure that she provided the first *doyen* in her newly-decolonised states. In any case, a 'monarchical', Jamaican, *doyen* in London would be approaching the Queen's government in his capacity, *inter alia*, as the representative of the Queen of Jamaica; and Kenya was a republic, with her own head of state. (Cairns allowed that a non-realm *doyen* would be less objectionable, but thought it unacceptable to distinguish between them and realm high commissioners.)

Another objection was that it might 'cut across or derogate from the special "family" position which High Commissioners enjoy'.[206] However, British high commissioners had demonstrated that *décanal* duties could be differentiated from those carried out 'as a member of the family'.[207] Moreover Britain's acceptance of high commissioners as eligible for the *décanat* would not stop her from continuing to treat 'high commissioners as "more equal" than the others in their family relationship to the Head of the Commonwealth with all the special distinctions that go with that'.[208] She would certainly, however, find herself in difficulties if she tried to persuade high commissioners that the doyenship was 'something below their dignity'.[209]

---

[204] Barry Smallman (head of Commonwealth Co-ordination Department) minute, 22 August 1969, TNA, FCO57/88.
[205] Mayall minute, 1 August 1969.
[206] *Ibid.*
[207] *Ibid.*
[208] Smallman minute, 22 August 1969.
[209] *Ibid.*

Cairns yielded, but the Palace did not. It felt strongly 'that a High Commissioner should always be something more than an ambassador',[210] and the Queen's secretary did not think logic should be 'carried too far'. What went on elsewhere was not 'a sound guide'. While the Queen was only intermittently in her other capitals,

> In London Her Majesty is generally there in person and this is what is important to the Heads of Missions accredited to the Court of St. James's.... the Doyen of the Diplomatic Corps in London should be the senior Ambassador present and the Doyen of the Commonwealth High Commissions [*sic.*] (so far as The Queen is concerned a different and more closely related body both to herself and to each other than the Ambassadors) should be the senior High Commissioner. To make the senior High Commissioner the doyen of the Diplomatic Corps is to lump High Commissioners and Ambassadors together as Heads of Missions and this would not be in accordance with what I understand to be the contemporary doctrine about the Commonwealth.
>
> I do not know what The Queen's opinion about the appointment of a Doyen is because I have not asked her but... she has more than once successfully resisted attempts in other Commonwealth Countries to introduce Ambassadors and High Commissioners to her in one body; she has always insisted that the High Commissioners should be separate and should be received apart from the diplomats.[211]

Here was a dilemma. It was Cairns who came up with a solution: to allow high commissioners to become *doyen*, but with the distinctive Commonwealth title of 'Senior High Commissioner and *Doyen* of the Diplomatic Corps'. This would mark 'the special "family" position' of high commissioners and ensure that they were given 'no grounds for feeling slighted'.[212] It was judged an 'excellent' idea—it would make a Commonwealth *doyen* a 'Doyen plus';[213] there was back-slapping all round; and no indication of royal displeasure. The way was prepared for its implementation by the inclusion in the December 1969 Diplomatic List of a new position, that of senior high commissioner. As Lindo pointed out, it had 'no real substance'.[214] However, it meant that in 1972 there were no problems at all about him becoming *doyen.* High commissioners had taken another step along the ambassadorial road.

---

[210] Mayall minute, 29 October 1969, TNA, FCO57/88.

[211] Michael Adeane (secretary to the Queen) memorandum for lord chamberlain, 14 August 1969, TNA, FCO57/88.

[212] Smallman minute, 31 October 1969, TNA, FCO57/88.

[213] Mayall minute, 29 October 1969.

[214] Mayall-Rear Admiral the Earl Cairns (marshal of the diplomatic corps), 5 November 1969, TNA, FCO57/88.

I. Australian Sniping

At the end of the 1960s the anti-high commissioner campaign was re-opened by Australia. Developments in Britain might have had something to do with this. The Labour government that won power in 1964 had a quite different general philosophy from the Menzies government in Australia, and there were no old friendships between Australian and British ministers. British immigration controls, her moves to join the EEC, and policy differences over Vietnam (where for the first time Australia fought alongside the USA without Britain), and Rhodesia (where many Australians felt 'an instinctive affinity with the white settlers')[215] indicated that Britain and Australia were drifting apart. Relations were then badly damaged by Britain's decision (after earlier prevarication) to withdraw her forces from South East Asia, and especially by her reference to 'white faces' doing 'more harm than good' on the Asian mainland. For Australia the defence of that area was 'a matter of national survival', and her prime minister, Harold Holt (1966–67), 'simply exploded'. As the British high commissioner explained,

> For us to tell them that we were withdrawing our forces, and to offer them instead a piece of trendy left-wing theology [about 'white faces']....accentuated the flibbertigibbet impression which...our country all too often gave....We...appeared as a giddy butterfly flitting unsteadily round the fringe of world politics. It was a heart-breaking period for British representatives on this side of the globe.[216]

Australia was changing, too, and her relationship with Britain became 'sounder', 'healthier', and more mature.[217] John Gorton (prime minister 1968–71) had a low opinion both of Wilson's Britain and of her continued espousal of the expanded Commonwealth. The latter was now 'an alien, artificial, contraption',[218] whose prime ministerial meetings no longer had much value. This attitude easily spilled over to the office of high commissioner, and Australia's External Affairs people had an additional and specific gripe about it, in that (exceptionally) until 1972 both the British high commissioner and the Australian high commissioner

---

215 'Australian Attitudes towards the Monarchy', enclosure in Sir Charles Johnston-Garner, 26 January 1967, *BDEE 1964–1971* II, 397.
216 Johnston valedictory despatch, 2 April 1971, TNA, FCO24/1072.
217 *Ibid.*
218 Geoffrey Tebbutt, 'New Phase in Crown Relations', *The Guardian*, 9 March 1970.

in London dealt in Canberra with the Prime Minister's Department rather than with them. It was their Minister, William McMahon (MEA 1969–71), who made a move against the office, floating the idea of its abolition at a private lunch party for high commissioners. He found an ally in Britain's envoy, Sir Charles Johnston (1965–71), who thought the title was not understood by the general public, and that getting rid of it would appear to modernise Commonwealth relations by liberating them from 'musty mystiques and dreary mumbo-jumbo'.[219]

In consequence, the FCO made an exhaustive examination of the office of high commissioner, obtaining comments from all its British holders. These revealed that the Commonwealth did not have a uniform practice towards it, and that the political access afforded to high commissioners varied considerably. The extensive benefits they enjoyed in London were often not fully reciprocated. It was thought that such advantages as high commissioners did enjoy had little to do with Commonwealth nomenclature, or even to the existence of the Commonwealth. Rather they derived from the former colonial association, a common language, and cultural and business links—all of which, as one top official put it, added up 'in an indefinable way to a relationship which is to our advantage'.[220] But above all, whether and the extent to which a high commissioner enjoyed wider and closer contacts than an ambassador depended—as it did with ambassadors—on the bilateral relationship between Britain and the receiving state.

As to the value of the office in these circumstances, there were divided opinions, a small majority of incumbents being mildly in favour of change. In more detail, four felt uneasy with 'an old imperial title' and wanted 'to bring our practice robustly up to date'; four others preferred to make haste slowly; half a dozen counselled caution on the grounds that 'to define might be to destroy'; and five believed 'there is a lot in a name' and that 'things might be eroded' if they became ambassadors.[221] (These views did not correlate with the way in which their holders had, as high commissioners, been treated.) More particularly, the argument that the title should be changed because it was misunderstood by the

---

[219] Commonwealth Co-ordination Department brief, 20 April 1971, TNA, FCO68/328.

[220] Greenhill (PUS)-Johnston, 26 November 1969, TNA, FCO68/328.

[221] 'Change of Title from High Commissioner to Ambassador: Summary of High Commissioners' Opinions', enclosure in Smallman-Sir L. Monson (DUS), 12 February 1971, TNA, FCO68/328.

public and had imperial overtones was dismissed: it was understood in the circles that mattered, and any remaining imperial flavour would fade. There was no argument for change on the basis of high commissioners having a lower status than ambassadors: that day had long gone.

With regard to whether Commonwealth members would welcome a change (on which more than one view was sometimes expressed, explaining the occasional duplication in what follows), only five were expected to favour an immediate move in an ambassadorial direction (Australia, The Gambia, Ghana, Lesotho, and Uganda); two would probably be opposed (India and Trinidad and Tobago); eight would probably fall in with whatever was the prevailing view (Barbados, Ceylon, Cyprus, The Gambia, Malaysia, Nigeria, Sierra Leone, and Singapore); and it was thought that at least seven would be governed by their desire for their envoys to retain their special position in London (Barbados, Ghana, Jamaica, Kenya, India, Mauritius, and Trinidad and Tobago).

In response, Britain decided in November 1969 that she would probably lose more than she gained if high commissioners became ambassadors. There were still marginal advantages in retaining the title: the importance many people attached to names; the value Commonwealth members put on their London privileges; the desire for distinctive Commonwealth titles to reflect (and justify) distinctive treatment (as well as the difficulty of finding an adequate alternative); and the political disadvantage to Britain of being seen to be associated with any initiatives for change. But if there were such an initiative and it found general support, 'we should not wish to be seen as standing in the way, and would probably come to no great harm by it'.[222]

As it happened, McMahon did not raise the subject bilaterally until he spoke to the British prime minister, Edward Heath, at the Singapore CHOGM in January 1971. His interest in renaming high commissioners had been revived in November 1970 when he became Minister for 'Foreign' Affairs, as he seemed to regard a change 'as a sort of pendant' to his own new title.[223] But he also held an unquenchable belief that Australia's High Commission in London would be better off as an embassy, and seemed unaware that high commissioners there received superior treatment, with 'fringe benefits, particularly in their

[222] Greenhill-Johnston, 26 November 1969.

[223] Johnston-Sir Stanley Tomlinson (DUS) 15 December 1970, TNA, FCO68/328. The DEA had changed its name to DFA in November 1970.

relationships with the Palace'.[224] Gorton had ignored McMahon's request to put the office of high commissioner on the 1971 CHOGM agenda, possibly because relations between the two were 'notoriously bad',[225] and the latter's keenness for a change might have curbed his own enthusiasm. Partly, too, Gorton might have been influenced by the success of the five-week royal tour of Australia in 1970. Undaunted, McMahon privately told Heath that Australia wanted to abandon the title 'high commissioner'. That step, he said, would receive widespread support because 'a number of other Commonwealth Governments took the same view'[226] and in many capitals high commissioners were regarded, and treated, as less important than ambassadors.

There was 'obviously some feeling about this'[227] and McMahon wanted to discuss the issue further when he visited London in February 1971, so Heath asked the FCO to consider whether anything should be done. However, nothing had happened in the previous eighteen months to make the FCO change its view that while Britain would not gain from a change, she might lose out. For although high commissioners and ambassadors did much the same work, and the title as such did not matter very much, it was

> an outward and visible sign of the special relationships between Commonwealth countries.... [making] it easier for those Commonwealth Governments who wish to do so (not all do) to continue to accord High Commissioners more favourable treatment.[228]

Further, it was now even less politically advisable for Britain actively to promote a change, as to do so when she was seeking to enter the EEC would suggest she was losing interest in the Commonwealth. But if Australia wanted to make the running and there was general support for a change of title, Britain (as before) would 'not wish to be seen as standing in the way, and would probably come to no great harm by it'.[229]

---

[224] Smallman-McEntee (Commonwealth Co-ordination Department) and Duggan (first secretary), 4 January 1971, TNA, FCO68/328.

[225] FCO brief for January 1971 CHOGM, 'Australia', TNA, FCO68/256.

[226] Robert Armstrong (cabinet secretary)-Graham, 30 January 1971, TNA, FCO68/328.

[227] *Ibid.*

[228] Smallman memorandum, 'Title of High Commissioner', enclosure in Smallman-Monson, 12 February 1971, TNA, FCO68/328.

[229] Greenhill-Johnston, 26 November 1969. Cf. Monson-Johnston, 26 February 1971. TNA, FCO68/328.

The Palace, however, was firmly opposed to taking such a line. It would, in the Queen's view, be a downward step, and Johnston was therefore told to remind McMahon 'that the Queen has, of course, an interest in this question' and 'would not be in favour of a change'.[230] Silence descended again, to be broken once more by McMahon (now prime minister) at the year's end. But there was 'not much real steam' behind his suggestion for a change of name,[231] and the matter lay dormant, so far as Australia was concerned, until early 1973.

It was, however, touched on at a 1972 Commonwealth conference on consular relations, when the Nigerian, J.A.O. Akadiri, suggested that the Secretariat should study the nomenclature of high commissioners and high commissions. He received no support but nonetheless he returned to the theme on the last day, whereupon the chairman called 'a welcome and strategic tea-break'.[232] The New Zealand delegate told Akadiri he would strongly oppose him, and the Nigerian director of the Commonwealth Secretariat's International Affairs Division, Emeka Anyaoku, advised him to drop the proposal. He did, and 'that dangerous corner' (as an FCO official put it) was safely rounded.[233]

But in 1973, Australia's newly-elected Labor prime minister, the talented 'urbane, polished and quick tongued barrister',[234] Gough Whitlam, made a final thrust. Whitlam had 'something of an obsession about relics of old colonial links', and the need to assert Australia's 'sovereignty',[235] and was therefore intent on ridding Australia of all vestiges of constitutional subordination. The office of high commissioner fell into this category, so he began exploring the idea of asking that year's CHOGM in Ottawa to consider turning high commissioners into ambassadors, on the ground that this would 'appropriately reflect the changing relationship between Commonwealth countries'.[236]

The FCO, which still saw no particular benefit in taking this step, thought it was 'tiresome' of Whitlam to raise the issue, but that it did

---

230 Monson-Johnston, 26 February 1971.

231 McEntee-T. O'Leary (assistant secretary, Cabinet Office), 19 November 1971, TNA, FCO68/328.

232 Thornton-Kenneth East (minister, Lagos) 2 June 1972, TNA, FCO68/449.

233 *Ibid.*

234 D.P. Aiers (AHC, Canberra), 6 September 1972, TNA, FCO68/391.

235 M. Reith (Commonwealth Co-ordination Department) minute, 20 March 1973, TNA, FCO68/516.

236 John Armstrong (Australian HC, London)-Greenhill, 7 March 1973, TNA, FCO68/516.

not much matter.[237] As one official put it, Britain should neither support nor resist Whitlam on this, especially since there was no need unnecessarily to expand the range of subjects on which her Conservative government was going to clash with him. Nor could she at that time afford to be associated in any action that could be seized on as evidence of her declining devotion to the Commonwealth. On the other hand, the Queen and the Commonwealth Secretariat did 'not like the idea of dropping any distinctive Commonwealth features such as the title of High Commissioner'.[238] Nor did the Secretariat even want Whitlam's proposal discussed in Ottawa. For while no one seemed to feel much inclined to move in an ambassadorial direction, an Australian lead might well be followed. So Arnold Smith, the head of the Commonwealth Secretariat, told Whitlam he 'felt very strongly' that it 'would be wrong'[239] to change the title. It was unnecessary and would give the impression that Commonwealth links were weakening. Moreover, not only had the title's 'connotation of subordination to Great Britain'[240] long since vanished, but most African, Asian, and Caribbean states quite liked the title and wanted to retain it and the material advantages that came with it.

Unlike his predecessors, Whitlam was showing 'considerable enthusiasm for the Secretariat',[241] so Smith's arguments might have had some effect, especially as Whitlam appeared to have given little thought to the subject. Nor did it come high in his priorities. Thus, when in April he visited and was charmed by the Queen, and found her entirely agreeable to changing her Royal Style and Titles in Australia, and to the governor-general issuing and receiving letters of credence on her behalf, he did not even raise the subject. A few days later he told Britain's foreign and commonwealth secretary that 'if this issue were likely to prove an obstruction at Ottawa he was not determined to raise it'.[242] He did not, though it was a few months before he completely

[237] J.K. Hickman (South West Pacific Department) minute, 30 March 1973, TNA, FCO68/516.

[238] Storar (head of Commonwealth Co-ordination Department) minute, 23 March 1973, TNA, FCO68/516.

[239] Duncan Watson (DUS) minute 26 March 1973, TNA, FCO68/516.

[240] Watson minute, 18 April 1973, TNA, FCO68/508.

[241] Draft Watson-James letter, March 1973, TNA, FCO68/516.

[242] Douglas-Home—Whitlam meeting, 24 April 1973, TNA, FCO68/517.

relinquished the idea.[243] The office of high commissioner lived on to fight another day.

J. Conclusion

The early 1960s to the mid 1970s marked a chastening coming down to earth for many high commissioners. They no longer met regularly (nor did Commonwealth ambassadors do so very often in foreign capitals); the meetings which were held did not always seem very worthwhile; and here and there the receiving states viewed such activity suspiciously. Meetings of Commonwealth representatives at the UN were often unpleasant. Privileged access for high commissioners to heads of government and ministers continued to be afforded by some members, but in many places could by no means be relied upon. The death knell was sounding for the Commonwealth's distinctive arrangements in the consular field; in one old Commonwealth state the part-consular office of deputy high commissioner disappeared; and the same state toyed with the idea of getting rid of high commissioners. But it was in and in respect of the oldest part of the Commonwealth—Britain—that the most symbolic developments took place. High commissioners in London lost 'their' separate department of state. They were placed alongside ambassadors so far as eligibility for the *décanat* was concerned (which doubtless delighted them, but also removed an element of their distinctiveness). British high commissioners occasionally found themselves being subjected to treatment which was the stuff of diplomatic nightmares. And the London-based Commonwealth Secretariat sometimes seemed like a venue for high commissioners to engage in anti-British activity.

Of course this was not the whole story. Some high commissioners' meetings were enjoyable and valuable; Commonwealth 'goodwill' was often evident; a few of its members were notably 'Commonwealth-minded' (Jamaica, for example, was 'a sort of tropical West Indian New Zealand');[244] there were still advantages to be had from the office,

[243] In July 1973 the Australian high commissioner was rebuffed by Sheikh Mujib (Bangladeshi PM) when, on instructions, he raised the question. Mujib said he did not want 'to rock the boat' or 'to be involved in any controversy on the matter': A.A. Golds (British HC Dacca) telegram 661, TNA, GK331/8/3, FCO47/672.

[244] Sir Alexander Morley (British HC Kingston, 1962–3) quoted in R.G. Britten (DHC Kingston)-Walker, 12 December 1966, *BDEE 1964–1971* II, 379.

especially in London; and Britain continued to receive appreciation, as well as brickbats. But there was no question that being a high commissioner was by the mid 1970s rather far removed from what it had usually been at the start of the 1960s.

This development reflected, as it was bound to, the Commonwealth's changing character. From being a small and fairly intimate club it had become a larger, noisier, and much less homogeneous association. The Asian dominions had been accommodated smoothly, but the new African states failed to adhere to 'the normal standards of Commonwealth membership'[245] and were openly hostile to Britain. Meanwhile, the admission of small, 'internationally insignificant' states 'debased'[246] the Commonwealth and many Third World leaders were not Commonwealth-minded. Even Indira Gandhi—the daughter of Jawaharlal Nehru who was 'the principal architect'[247] of the new, multiracial Commonwealth and its saviour during the 1956 Suez crisis—had 'no Commonwealth conscience or consciousness'.[248] Moreover, newer members tended to use the Commonwealth (like the UN) to try to get Britain to employ her power in pursuit of their agenda, even beyond what she thought was feasible, and meetings organised by the Commonwealth Secretariat provided a vehicle for their purpose. At the same time, however, the Secretariat provided some institutional underpinning for the association, which gave it additional stability, and not just in the political area but also in respect of its wide ranging technical and non-governmental work. Paradoxically, therefore, while the parent organisation was looking more like a going concern, its office of high commissioner was possibly becoming a historical curiosity—which, like many such, might be thought worth preserving but had diminishing contemporary relevance. The office remained dependent on its parent, in the sense that without the Commonwealth it would disappear (just as states leaving the Commonwealth had to appoint ambassadors rather than high commissioners), but the same was not true in reverse. The Commonwealth could, in both theory and practice, do without high commissioners, who were becoming not very different from 'normal' heads of mission.

[245] Garner minute, 'Commonwealth membership', 10 May 1962, *BDEE 1957–1964* II, 688.
[246] *Ibid.*
[247] Mansergh (1982) 235.
[248] D.A. Scott (DHC, New Delhi)-Walker, 14 February 1967, *BDEE 1964–1971* II, 400.

From now on, therefore, the office of high commissioner would be rather exposed. It did not seem in immediate danger. The many smaller Commonwealth members, especially, valued it; and as a distinctive Commonwealth arrangement the office could probably rely on being warmly championed by the Commonwealth's wide-ranging body of supporters. The protectiveness of the Secretariat and the Queen towards it was seen when it came under some Australian sniping. But another, and very significant, aspect of that episode was that Britain, and a majority of her high commissioners, showed no very great enthusiasm for the office. Things had indeed changed. High commissioners would now do well to tread warily if their office was not to attract a further and perhaps terminal assault.

CHAPTER EIGHT

SURVIVAL, MID-1970s–2006

In 1974 it was still possible for a leading Commonwealth scholar to say that intra-Commonwealth relations were 'different from ordinary diplomacy'.[1] He added that the Commonwealth's 'system of parallel diplomacy' reflected the assumption that intra-Commonwealth relations 'had a family quality which other sorts of international relations did not, and that this family quality justified a different structure of consultation and negotiation from that which normally obtained'.[2] But, as this book has shown, when these remarks were made they carried much less weight than they would have done a decade or two earlier. A process of evisceration had been underway.

It was noted in the late 1960s that Commonwealth arrangements had 'increased the scope for certain types of pressure' on Britain.[3] The considerable discomfort this caused her leaders had had a disillusioning effect, and encouraged her move towards Europe. When, in January 1973, Britain became a member of the European Economic Community (EEC), a significant turning point had been reached. Britain had created the Commonwealth, held it together, and was now in some measure turning away from it. On the eve of entering the EEC, a 'deliberately radical'[4] reconsideration of the Commonwealth by the Foreign and Commonwealth Office's (FCO) Planning Department concluded that in multilateral terms the Commonwealth was 'a declining force'.[5] Its main significance for Britain lay in bilateral relations with individual members, those with the 'old' Commonwealth being the most important. But they were less important than those with the USA and the EEC. As the foreign and commonwealth secretary put it,

> Australia, New Zealand and Canada are members of the family and important centres of our national interest. They are likely to remain

[1] Miller (1974) 384.
[2] *Ibid.*
[3] Sir Paul Gore-Booth—Garner, 15 February 1967, *BDEE 1964–1971* II, 407.
[4] Sir Alec Douglas-Home (foreign and commonwealth secretary) memorandum for Defence and Oversea Policy Committee, 13 October 1972, TNA, FCO68/438.
[5] J.E. Cable (planning staff) minute, 21 November 1972, TNA, FCO68/439.

> so. But...we exercise very little influence over the new members of the Commonwealth and will exercise less. It is almost impossible to reconcile the practices of African dictatorships and one-party states with our own. The Asian members have democratic roots but, with the departure of the officials directly trained under us, they are trending to return to a corrupt form of democracy. Nevertheless, having built up the multilateral image of the Commonwealth...it would be extremely difficult for us to liquidate it.... Britain's interests require us to keep up our intimate bilateral relationships with the Old Commonwealth...in the New Commonwealth we should concentrate on the handful who, for one reason or another are the most important. There is certainly residual value in the multilateral aspect of the Commonwealth. Clearly we should not throw this away but we have paid a very high price in the past in support of the multilateral Commonwealth and I doubt if we can afford to do so in future....the aces will only appear if we are rich and powerful in our own right and that means giving priority to Europe.[6]

It would hardly be surprising if, elsewhere in the Commonwealth, its worth was being assessed in a broadly similar way.

From this perspective, the distinctive Commonwealth diplomatic nomenclature and its differential treatment of high commissioners was a 'useful' 'symbolic' practice. But it was 'liable to erosion' in countries other than Britain and could 'come to seem increasingly incongruous'.[7] The fact that Commonwealth titles were not always understood did not help. High commissioners have sometimes been thought to have an administrative or police role; they have been mistaken for with trade commissioners; and it has even been known for them occasionally to be confused with commissionaires who stand outside hotels and expensive restaurants. Because of this sort of possibility, high commission staff and foreign ministries have been known to use the terms 'ambassador' and 'embassy' when referring to a high commissioner or a high commission, wishing thereby unequivocally to convey the full dignity of the post or the mission.[8] On other occasions such usage may simply be due to human error. In 1971 the Lesotho High Commission in London produced crested paper with the embossed heading, 'Embassy of the Kingdom of Lesotho'.[9] And in 1999 an official Canadian publication listed (in both French and English) its high commission in Mozambique

[6] Douglas-Home memorandum, 13 October 1972.

[7] FCO planning paper, 'The Commonwealth after Accession', appended to Douglas-Home memorandum, 13 October 1972.

[8] Personal communication.

[9] *The Times*, 16 February 1971.

as being headed by a non-resident 'Ambassador'.[10] Other instances are not hard to find. Whatever the reasons, they rather suggest that the office of high commissioner has neither a prominent nor a particularly appealing profile.

Yet despite the unquestionable dilution of the former intimacy of intra-Commonwealth relations, the office has survived. Tracing its fortunes during the period of this chapter is a somewhat impressionistic process, on account of the general unavailability of archival material. But reliable pointers can be found in diplomatic memoirs, and from interviews and correspondence with serving and retired diplomats and politicians who have had experience of high commissions. The chapter will also try to identify the factors on which the future of the office is likely to depend.

A. The Position of High Commissioners

1. *Information sharing and collective meetings*

In overseas posts during the early 1970s there was still a fair amount of Commonwealth cooperation. So far as Britain was concerned, her consultation and information sharing with the 'old' Commonwealth members was markedly more intimate and informal than with her European allies, and covered some matters, such as intelligence, for which there was no European parallel. But with other Commonwealth states it was 'at best intermittent, *ad hoc* and erratic',[11] and the trend was downwards. Meanwhile, the EEC's impact on the conduct of diplomacy began before Britain's formal admission. She was fully included in the process of political consultation from March 1972, which involved close links with EEC missions in its member states, participating elsewhere in EEC heads of mission meetings, and helping to prepare joint reports for Brussels (where the EEC had its headquarters) when this was required. Of course Britain did not have to throw discretion about Commonwealth matters and members to the wind, or abandon Commonwealth consultation. But meetings of EEC heads of mission

[10] *Canadian Representatives Abroad* (Ottawa: Department of Foreign Affairs and International Trade, January 1999) 95, 106.

[11] FCO planning paper, 'The Commonwealth after Accession'.

'considerably altered' the dynamics of high commissioners' meetings. Until then the latter were

> an innovation for most participants and held their interest. When [EEC] Heads of Mission began holding meetings, which had precise multilateral objectives, such as setting up aid projects, answering development questionnaires from Brussels etc., the Commonwealth meetings rather faded. Countries like India were keen to keep them going as information *fora* and they did continue, but didn't have the same zip as earlier.[12]

This was not necessarily a matter for regret, given the bad-temperedness of many Commonwealth gatherings between the mid-1960s and the early 1990s. Some intra-Commonwealth discussions did gain substance from the common struggle to end racism in Southern Africa. But criticisms of British policy towards Rhodesia, and of her opposition to certain policies advocated by other states in respect of South Africa (especially when Margaret Thatcher was prime minister, 1979–90), meant that Commonwealth meetings were also marked by barbed conversations and, on occasion, by nasty exchanges. Such policy differences could even spill over on to the sort of multilateral occasions which some would regard as non-political. The 1986 Edinburgh Commonwealth Games, for example, were boycotted by 32 of the 58 Commonwealth states and territories which were entitled to participate.

More generally, Commonwealth meetings in some capitals had nothing substantive to discuss, making them a waste of time or plain unedifying. It often appeared to be simply a matter of inclination whether or not high commissioners got together at all. In at least one country they continued doing so simply because no high commissioner wanted to be the one to call a halt. Nonetheless, meetings of Commonwealth heads of mission neither disappeared nor completely lost all value. Thanks to the geographical spread of Commonwealth membership and good personal relations, high commissioners continued to share confidences and glean otherwise inaccessible information. At the United Nations there were still useful discussions, and occasional collaboration. In London meetings were periodically arranged by the Commonwealth Secretariat, and high commissioners were also brought together in connection with the work of certain Commonwealth bodies such as the Commonwealth Foundation. The extent to which all such gatherings were useful depended a lot, as always but now perhaps more

[12] Personal communication.

so, on personal chemistries. Where fruitful interaction did occur, the Commonwealth nexus could still prove diplomatically valuable, adding something to the normal exchanges of diplomatic life.

It has to be noted, however, that the link between the holding of collective meetings and the titles of the participants is unclear. If high commissioners were called ambassadors, they might well continue meeting in their capacities as representatives of Commonwealth states—as, indeed, they have done in some non-Commonwealth capitals. Thus there may be no such link at all. But it cannot be completely excluded that the distinctiveness of the title of high commissioner has given a modicum of independent impetus to decisions to hold such gatherings.

2. *Relations between individual high commissioners*

Bilateral contacts between high commissioners have frequently been more than ordinarily valuable. The almost universal legacy of British rule means that Commonwealth members have things in common which they do not share with others in quite the same way: history, their manner of approaching issues, education, the English language, at least a proclaimed respect for the ethos of public service and democracy, and (not least) cricket and rugby. For all the diversity of their backgrounds, they have an easy affinity, an 'inclination to interact',[13] 'a sense of "belonging"', 'a perhaps unidentifiable commonness'.[14] In some countries there are annual cricket matches between the high commission 'corps' and foreign ministries (in one state the wives, being discontented with trailing around after their husbands, demanded their own game, which was duly arranged—and repeated). Newly-arrived high commissioners may still be warmly welcomed: in 1985 when New Zealand re-opened its mission in New Delhi after a three year break, Sir Edmund Hillary 'went straight from the flight to lunch with a group of Ambassadors and High Commissioners.... We finished off the day with a formal dinner at the residence of Sir Robert Wade-Gery, High Commissioner for the United Kingdom.'[15] Even after more than over 30 years' of being 'pretty well shunned',[16] some South African diplomats (including those who had at best been children in 1961)

[13] Interview.
[14] Millar (1967) 13 and xii.
[15] Hillary (2000) 336.
[16] Interview.

found that after their country rejoined the Commonwealth they still, as high commission members, related most easily to diplomats from other Commonwealth states. One high commissioner gave a lunch for his South African colleague to celebrate his 'elevation' to the office of high commissioner, and another gave a farewell dinner for all the Commonwealth high commissioners.

Sentiment and social occasions do not guide foreign policy, but easy personal relations can facilitate the speedy establishment of relatively close and relaxed relationships, which makes it easier to get work done and to speak frankly. In this context high commissioners have an *additional* relationship that may sometimes make a marginal difference, in much the same way as it is said to be useful for two people engaged in a discussion to wear the same school tie or be freemasons. (In the Commonwealth context having been jailed by the British might have been the equivalent qualification some years ago.) Being a high commissioner can also occasionally pay off handsomely in terms of information gathering and diplomatic assistance. In Zambia in the late 1970s, when relations with Britain were 'poisoned' by the Rhodesian problem, the African and West Indian high commissioners were 'a great help' to the British high commissioner, reflecting their shared concern about the situation.[17] And the Commonwealth link is useful in foreign states: the Swahili-speaking East Africans were very useful members of a strong 'Commonwealth mafia' in the Democratic Republic of the Congo;[18] Commonwealth ambassadors helped Britain when she was restoring diplomatic relations with Argentina; and as the representative of a leading European Union[19] state, Britain's ambassador at Paris may on occasion be able to assist his Commonwealth colleagues.

But as these last illustrations suggest, close relationships may have little, if anything, to do with the individuals concerned being called high commissioners, and a lot, or everything, with their being the representatives of Commonwealth states, or of certain Commonwealth states, or because of who they are. (Sir Edmund Hillary, for example, was invited to certain meetings in New Delhi because he was so nice.)

---

[17] Jane Barder interview with Sir Leonard Allinson, 5 March 1996, Cambridge: Churchill College, Churchill Archives Centre, DOHP, 6.

[18] Interview.

[19] In 1967 the EEC and two other European bodies merged to form the European Communities, although each of them retained its distinctive legal identity. In 1993 the European Community (as it had become known) became the European Union.

Thus the same benefits would perhaps have emerged if the people involved had been called ambassadors.

3. *High commissioners and the receiving state*

So far as the extra-diplomatic scene in Commonwealth countries is concerned, special treatment has become much less common. But in some there remains at least a residue of the old feelings of intimacy with certain Commonwealth representatives, enabling members of some high commissions to continue to have relatively close relations with their local communities. These attitudes may in part result from the use of the term 'high commissioner', in that it adds emphasis to the existence and distinctiveness of the Commonwealth connection.

At the official level, high commissioners of the Queen's realms have, in general, continued to enjoy the benefit of meeting the receiving state's prime minister at an early date to present letters of introduction. In Australia one high commissioner had 'pretty well immediate access' to present his letter—'a non-ceremonial occasion providing an opportunity for a substantive discussion and future "recognition"'.[20] One Canadian prime minister did not bother about formally receiving a British high commissioner's letter of introduction. They just got down to business. (Occasionally, too, high commissioners are invited to a farewell chat with the prime minister.) In London, however, this practice was was ended in 1997 when Tony Blair became prime minister (it sometimes, so it was said, being impossible for him to arrange even a relatively early appointment with a newly-arrived high commissioner). Nor are formal calls necessarily helpful. It must have been hugely discomforting for the Canadian high commissioner, Paul Martin (1975–79), who was a vain man, to learn during his farewell call on Mrs. Thatcher that she was ignorant of his lengthy and distinguished political career.

So far as access to governmental ministries is concerned, the Commonwealth connection can still count. High commissioners to and from the old Commonwealth have continued to gain fairly easy access to the highest levels in each other's foreign ministries, as well as deal with other departments of state, in all of which they often establish close and relaxed official relations. (However, foreign ambassadors may also now have access to government departments other than the

[20] Personal communication.

foreign ministry.) In India, because New Zealand's high commissioner, Sir Edmund Hillary, was regarded as 'one of us'[21] he had no difficulty seeing ministers or chief secretaries who were said to be inaccessible, and Paul Martin found British ministers 'generous...with their time and their prompt acceptances of an offer to see them.[22] One of his successors also recalled that British ministers would see him at 'very short notice'.[23] Pressing Commonwealth business can sometimes provide a handy way of securing a ministerial appointment. In London and some other capitals even foreign ministers may try to make time for certain high commissioners when they would not do the same for ambassadors. And generally, many high commissioners have felt they enjoyed privileged access in London, benefiting from all the advantages and privileges of an ambassador plus the sort of treatment members of a club expect from each other. These benefits may not be much more than marginal for the representatives of Commonwealth countries with substantial bilateral interests and weight; but the representatives of smaller members have felt very real benefits in terms of *entrée* and breadth of access. In other Commonwealth capitals, however, things may be very different. In one, getting access to a minister or a department was, for high commissioners and ambassadors alike, 'like trying to pull hen's teeth'.[24] And access to a head of government can by no means be relied upon. In that regard even the Commonwealth connection may be insufficient.

Just as London has proved a very good capital in which to be a high commissioner, it has sometimes been the case that British high commissioners have been implicitly regarded as 'higher' than other heads of mission, and given preferential treatment. For example, one recollected that Hastings Banda (Malawi's prime minister and President 1964–94) used to contact him freely at all hours; during one of the smoother patches in Zambian-British relations President Kaunda invited the British deputy high commissioner to join him in the front row of the Cathedral for a National Day Service; towards the end of the century the British high commissioner in Nigeria was often regarded as the senior diplomat, and accordingly given higher *placement* than ambassadors who had sometimes spent years there; and on non-government

[21] Hillary (2000) 340.
[22] Diary, 2 September 1976, 4 February 1975 in Young (ed) (1988) 12.
[23] Personal communication.
[24] Interview.

occasions in Australia British high commissioners may be singled out for special treatment by Australians (possibly because they are wrongly assumed to be the Queen's representatives). In another capital, 'my status as High Commissioner conferred the benefits of being primus inter pares in the diplomatic corps... and of access to the President at any hour and in conditions of absolute privacy and discretion (no private secretary present, for instance). This in turn gave muscle to my representations in ways that were denied to ambassadors, amounting to "substantive advantage".'[25] And, recalling the days when he had privileged access to Kenya's President, Daniel Arap Moi, a former American ambassador compared himself to his British colleague, commenting that the latter probably saw Moi as often and 'no doubt'[26] went more often to the farm where Moi spent his weekends. Moreover, there have certainly been occasions when British high commissioners have quoted 'the special rights of High Commissioners in London (and the principle of reciprocity)' in support of claims to gain access to government departments without going through the foreign ministry, which, in one instance, 'would have been (a) intensely suspicious of what I was up to, and (b) quite unable to make me an appointment with a Minister of another department, even if they had wanted to'.[27]

But the crucial factor in respect of access during the years covered by this chapter is often not the Commonwealth connection. Rather, it is the calibre of the diplomat; the perceived importance of his or her state; the quality of relations between the two states; and the nature of the announced need for an appointment. Any access and special standing enjoyed by British high commissioners is probably because they are British, not because they are high commissioners. Paul Martin's political standing would have given him the same quick and easy access whatever his title. The Commonwealth link may make access a bit easier in an otherwise thin relationship; and it may make slightly more difference where relations are reasonably substantial. But so far as access is concerned most high commissioners are for most of the time in much the same position as ambassadors. And in any event, nowhere does access straightforwardly translate into influence.

---

[25] Personal communication.
[26] Hempstone (1997) 270.
[27] Personal communication.

B. The Office and the Commonwealth

It would therefore seem that while being a high commissioner is semantically distinctive, its substantive advantages are no longer appreciable. Heads of diplomatic missions exchanged between Commonwealth states could be called 'ambassador' without any loss of status or standing. Nor would such a change make an obvious difference to their ability to do their job, in that both the task and relations between the relevant states would remain the same. The breadth of access might lessen in some capitals. Here and there (or perhaps only in London) some peripheral elements of preferential treatment would probably disappear, if only to avoid overt discrimination between identically-titled heads of mission. But in almost all matters there would be little or no noticeable difference. Especially would this be so if the adoption of the traditional diplomatic title was not accompanied by any other alteration in the Commonwealth relationship. To the extent to which the latter embodies the warm feelings which are often associated with being part of a family, the situation could continue as before.

However, unlike the situation in the 1930s and 1940s, there is at the start of the twenty-first century little apparent unhappiness with the title of high commissioner. Equality of status with ambassadors was achieved long ago, and other changes putting high commissioners on virtually the same footing as their diplomatic seniors soon followed. This seems to have taken all the steam out of the once fairly vigorous campaign against the office. It may be that this is because the maintenance of a semantic oddity is seen as to all intents and purposes an irrelevance—a quaint historical leftover, which has no intrinsic utility but neither does any harm. Why waste even minimal time and effort, it might be thought, bothering about such an essentially trivial matter. 'If it ain't broke, don't fix it.' But there is, perhaps, a little more to the situation than that.

It may be that the very title, 'high commissioner', has a resonance and significance which reaches beyond mere semantic convention. The day-to-day perquisites of the office have not been completely eroded—maybe less so than might have been expected—and they are especially valued by some of the beneficiaries. The use of a distinctive terminology may facilitate and encourage the emergence of an occasionally advantageous pattern of diplomatic behaviour, in relation both to intra-Commonwealth issues and to third parties. These associated considerations may not be hugely important in the larger scheme of things. But even marginal attractions and benefits are likely to be seen—by high commissioners, by their staffs, and by their states—as worthwhile: a state of affairs which should be appreciated rather than gratuitously endangered. Seen in isolation, therefore, there would appear to be little likelihood of the title of high commissioner being abandoned.

But the title also signifies the Commonwealth link between the sending and the receiving states. It is indicative of their both being members of a wider, and exclusive, group. It is, in fact, a function of the very existence of that group, in that—as ever—the title could not subsist without the Commonwealth, whereas the Commonwealth could dispense with the title. In practice the relationship between the two is rather less stark than these words suggest. The Commonwealth is not so strong that it can rely on being undamaged if it discarded one of its notable distinguishing features. Assuming, therefore, that the association has an interest in its own survival (as associations almost universally do), it behoves the Commonwealth's decision-makers to foster the office of high commissioner. Similarly, those outside official circles who have a regard for the Commonwealth's health (and they are fairly numerous and sometimes favourably placed) have a stake in the maintenance of what helps to make it distinctive, in that its distinctiveness is part of its strength. But at bottom the survival of the Commonwealth does not turn on the maintenance of its office of high commissioner, whereas the office only has a future if its parent body has one too. And over the past half century or so the Commonwealth has undergone a major change, resulting in a sharp decline in its political cohesion. Indeed, at the level of high politics it is almost totally without this quality. But paradoxically, at other levels it has flourished. There is, however, an uncertainty about the depth of the 'modern' Commonwealth's roots. Should they prove shallow, and fail, the Commonwealth's high commissioner offspring would fail also. To assess the prospects for the office, therefore, a brief examination of the vitality of the contemporary Commonwealth is required.

1. *Unexpected applicants—and lost sheep*

One measure of an association's well-being is whether it continues to attract members from among those who are eligible and may be expected to join. On that score the Commonwealth has, since the early 1970s, done well. Indeed, exceptionally so. All Britain's colonies and protected states who became independent during this period, and one who did so some time before, have become members of the Commonwealth, most of them being very small or tiny island states in the Caribbean, Oceania, and the Indian Ocean. Two or three who had left or been suspended (for failing to meet the Commonwealth's asserted standards in the areas of democracy and human rights) chose to rejoin. Two others were admitted although their previous constitutional connection with Britain was at best tenuous, and one new member had no such connection at all.

Of the last three, two—Namibia and Cameroon—had been German colonies which were taken from her after her defeat in the First World War and made into League of Nations mandates: dependent territories administered largely in the manner of colonies by mandatory powers under the loose supervision of the League. South Africa so administered South West Africa, and Britain and France each so administered part of Cameroon. After the Second World War South Africa refused to transfer South West Africa to the UN Trusteeship system, and became in the UN's eyes the occupying power of what was soon called (by the rest of the world) Namibia. After a long struggle, Namibia achieved independence in 1990. She applied for, and was immediately granted, Commonwealth membership. She had not been under British jurisdiction, but her history had given her a Commonwealth connection. There were a couple of precedents for this development, in that part of Papua New Guinea had been an Australian mandate and trust territory (the rest being under British control), and on becoming independent had joined the Commonwealth; and Samoa (then called Western Samoa) had been a New Zealand mandate and had formally entered the Commonwealth some years after becoming independent ('formally', because she had been treated as such since independence).

The French-administered part of Cameroon became independent in 1960, and part of British-administered Cameroon joined it in the following year, the ex-British section making up about one-fifth of the whole. There was therefore a small British link, but overwhelmingly the state was French speaking and initially there was no question of Commonwealth membership. And when in the late 1980s Cameroon showed such an interest, its historical link with Britain was so scant that, for the first time, a Commonwealth paper was produced discussing the criteria for membership. Cameroon had to wait six years and undergo scrutiny before being accepted in 1995, and that was conditional on her agreeing to observe the Commonwealth's principles and use English in all official Commonwealth communications.

At the same time another African state was admitted which had never been wholly or even partly ruled by Britain or any other Commonwealth member. This was Mozambique, which had been a Portuguese colony for about half a millennium before becoming independent in 1975. On the face of it there was no case at all for her entry. But it was argued by Africans that she bordered on no fewer than six Commonwealth states (one, Zimbabwe, has since departed), and had suffered much for the sake of 'democracy and human dignity' in Zimbabwe and South Africa.[28] More important was the fact that South Africa's President Mandela was strongly championing Mozambique's case, and was widely regarded as a hero who could do no wrong. Hence, as an 'exceptional' case which was not to be taken as a precedent, Mozambique became a Commonwealth member, but 'on condition that it improved the teaching of English'.[29] Then Rwanda (1996) and Yemen (1997) applied, but without success. There has been talk of Palestine and even Israel (both of which were once part of the British mandate of Palestine) eventually applying, and Sweden, too. And in December 2006 it was reported that Algeria had applied for membership. Clearly Commonwealth membership is an attractive proposition.

There are two other states which should also be mentioned in this connection, one who has rejoined, and one who has not but who has notably been mending her rather poor fences with Britain. They are South Africa and Ireland. Both were in the Commonwealth from its beginning, were once its most awkward and discontented members, and were leaders of the campaign against the office of high commissioner.

i. *Return of the prodigal*

As South Africa's President Mbeki put it, South Africa left the Commonwealth but in its vigorous opposition to *apartheid* 'the Commonwealth never left South Africa'.[30] To older leaders of the African National Congress (ANC—the indigenous anti-*apartheid* party), re-entry was 'the right thing to do'.[31] That was also the view of the iconic Nelson Mandela, who was released from captivity in 1990. It was not shared by all South African. Some old-school Nationalists 'did not give

---

[28] Southern African Research and Documentation Centre (1997).
[29] *The Times*, 26 November 1998.
[30] Interview.
[31] Anyaoku (1994).

a stuff' for the Commonwealth, and had no wish to rejoin a group that had attacked them for so long. The minister for foreign affairs, 'Pik' Botha, and 'Africanists' in his Department, thought South Africa should concentrate on regional affairs. Certain sections of the ANC were also opposed, such as the communists who associated the Commonwealth with Britain and Mrs. Thatcher. (It has also been suggested that the French tried to stop South Africa rejoining.)[32] But it was no contest, the arguments in favour being overwhelming. As South Africa's anglophile head of mission in London, Kent Durr (1991–95), put it, rejoining would 'symbolise the country's full return to international respectability',[33] would not harm her, and could do her a lot of good. A quarter of Commonwealth members were African, most of her neighbours belonged, and the Commonwealth link would

> open doors... create new diplomatic contacts... open up many commercial avenues and opportunities.... [provide] educational funds... improved opportunities for socio-economic development, for close-up contact with the very nexus between the developed and developing world, and certainly for ordered involvement with a regional grouping such as the South African Development Community. Contacts with countries spread across the globe and sharing in different regional economic subsystems would certainly be enhanced.[34]

Pretoria agreed Durr could explore the idea of returning, so long as he kept a low profile. It emerged that the British prime minister, the Palace, and the Commonwealth secretary-general, Emeka Anyaoku, were all much in favour.[35] The latter was especially enthusiastic, and after the Harare Heads of Government Meeting (CHOGM) in October 1991, visited South Africa to begin the process of reconciliation. This led to the despatch of a Commonwealth group of distinguished observers to the opening of the Convention for a Democratic South Africa, which marked the beginning of multi-party negotiations regarding a change in the country's governmental system. Thereafter, the Commonwealth remained deeply involved in the democratisation process: in 1993, for the first time, the Commonwealth Fund for Technical Co-operation

---

[32] An interviewee was informed of this by a friend who was high up in the French government.

[33] Durr (1993). The old régime took South Africa out of the Commonwealth; rejoining the Commonwealth was in part symbolic of there being a new government: interview.

[34] Durr (1993).

[35] Interviews.

provided technical assistance to a non-Commonwealth country to back up the work of observers, and during the 1994 elections that ushered in majority rule, it fielded a larger electoral observer mission than ever before. Within South Africa's Department of Foreign Affairs, the 'death throes of *apartheid*' produced, one insider thought, an atmosphere 'akin to the Wild West or the Chicago underworld' as its head availed himself of a last opportunity to dole out rewards to his and his ministers' 'camp followers and hangers-on'.[36]

The 1993 CHOGM agreed after the briefest discussion that it would welcome back a 'non-racial and democratic South Africa'.[37] In May 1994 Mandela was sworn in as President; just under a fortnight later South Africa applied for membership; and on 1 June resumed her place in the Commonwealth[38] (together with her former seniority on Remembrance Day and her seat in Westminster Abbey—the original plaque having been retrieved and screwed back into place). The following month, there was a stirring commemorative service at the Abbey and the Commonwealth Secretariat hosted a garden party at Marlborough House, attended by the Queen and members of the royal family. Kent Durr had an hour-long audience with the Queen (he had had ten minutes when he had arrived as an ambassador). (There was, however, no need for reaccreditation, as when states return to, or join, the Commonwealth their representatives do not present new letters on changing their title from ambassador to high commissioner.) South Africa's newly-'elevated' high commissioners were welcomed back by their diplomatic colleagues. And through the assistance it provided in human resource development and institutional capacity building, the Commonwealth then played 'an important role...in the transfer of public administration skills to the South African Government'.[39] The 'prodigal'[40] had come home.

As regards the conduct of diplomacy, the number of resident missions to and from South Africa mushroomed after April 1994, but the advent of the new government made little substantive difference

[36] Tothill (2003) 18.

[37] Ian Black, 'Commonwealth extends invitation to South Africa', *The Guardian*, 26 October 1993.

[38] She had joined the Organization of African Unity on 23 May and the Non-Aligned Movement on 30 May.

[39] Personal communication.

[40] Archbishop Tutu during Commonwealth Service of Thanksgiving, 20 July 1994: Annika Savill, 'Joy as S. Africa rejoins the Club', *The Independent*, 21 July 1994.

as there had been an ongoing diplomatic thaw since the late 1980s.[41] Nor was the lot of high commissioners in South Africa better than that of ambassadors, though there were more points of contact, both official and unofficial. Still, given the importance the Commonwealth had attached to the anti-*apartheid* crusade, and its secretary-general's belief that the organisation's chief achievement had been its role in the ending of *apartheid*,[42] South Africa's return to the Commonwealth had huge symbolic importance.

ii. *The question of Ireland*

Just as Harold Macmillan, Britain's prime minister in 1961, had hoped South Africa would return to the fold, so did his predecessor, Clement Attlee, share a similar dream of Ireland in 1949. But when Ireland burnt her boats she had also received special, non-foreign treatment, so there was no obvious inducement for her to consider rejoining. Thus, in 1951 when an Irish ambassador hinted at the possibility, the Canadian embassy at Dublin pointed out that

> there may be no percentage in it that would make it worth de Valera's while. I should not be at all surprised if Ireland was still getting almost the same benefits in the way of information and discussion at high levels that she had in pre-Costello days. And in tangible benefits, it seems to me, she is cut in on supplies by Britain, furnished with... dollars by the U.S.A.... and generally kept viable, partly for her nuisance value, partly for her useful value as a food supplier to the U.K.[43]

Yet the question did not go away. Well-informed Irish observers thought Costello had made regrettable mistake. By 1957 the hitherto 'somewhat fanatical' anglophobe minister for external affairs, Frank Aiken, was now 'very temperate and reasonable',[44] and in 1958 the idea of rejoining was brought up when he made a private visit to Britain with the *taoiseach* (Eamon de Valera). In 1961 de Valera's successor, Seán Lemass, took a conciliatory line on the matter. But there was only one context in

---

[41] Relations between heads of mission had gone a long way beyond the minimum courtesies by 1992, and many states entered into diplomatic relations with South Africa quite early in the transition period.

[42] McIntyre (2001) 133–4.

[43] H.L.E. Priestman (Canadian Embassy, Dublin)-A.J. Pick (Head of Commonwealth Division), 22 February 1951, NAC, RG25, 4481, 50021–40, part 3.

[44] Horgan (1999) 146.

which it was then conceivable—the unification of Ireland—and that was a complete non-starter during the thirty-year Northern Ireland 'Troubles' that began in 1968.

As, towards the end of the century, the North stuttered towards internal peace and the 1998 Belfast (Good Friday) Agreement was negotiated, the issue of rejoining was resurrected. In accordance with the Agreement, Ireland's Constitution was amended: instead of asserting that Ireland was a single, 'national territory', it was recognised that unity should 'be brought about only by peaceful means with the consent of a majority of the people'.[45] Later that year, the *taoiseach*, Bertie Ahern, pointed out that the Commonwealth was 'a very different thing now' to what it was in 1949, and suggested an Irish debate on rejoining.[46] At the same time President Mary Robinson said Commonwealth membership 'would act as a comfort to [Protestants in Northern Ireland] feeling threatened by the future prospect of a united Ireland'.[47] This was followed by the Commonwealth secretary-general visiting Dublin; Britain's ambassador at Dublin moving on to a job in the Commonwealth Secretariat; the Queen's acceptance of an invitation to pay a state visit;[48] President Mary McAleese breaking with precedent by attending a royal event (the Queen Mother's state funeral) and having meetings with the Queen (including one in Northern Ireland); and in April 2006 by the British ambassador breaking taboo by attending the commemoration of the 1916 Easter Rising. McAleese described relations as 'the best they have been in 800 years'.[49]

It was, however, not evident that the benefits of rejoining would outweigh the political costs. There was some strong opposition to the idea, and Commonwealth membership was probably 'a bridge too far for poplar sentiment'.[50] It is, however, not altogether inconceivable that one day there might be a sufficient spirit of reconciliation for it to become a possibility, and thus for some Irish ambassadors to become high commissioners once more.

---

[45] Constitutional amendment to Article 3, June 1998.
[46] *The Times*, 26 November 1998.
[47] *Ibid.*, 30 November 1998.
[48] As of the end of 2006 this visit has yet to take place.
[49] *Irish Independent*, 17 April 2006.
[50] Horgan (1999) 147.

2. *A Commonwealth constituency*

Be that as it may, the manner in which the Commonwealth has continued to expand suggests that it is in pretty good shape. Relevant states (and a few not so obviously relevant) clearly feel that it is beneficial to belong. It may not be the cosy club of intimates that it once was, and it does not offer the hard benefits which flow from a tight and purposeful political front. Nor does much of its work receive the recognition that it deserves. But after the United Nations and its specialised agencies it is one of the world's largest inter-governmental organisations. It is also one of the oldest and, with more than a quarter of the UN's members, about a third of the world's population, and about a fifth of its trade, is a forum which, while on the margins of international politics, appears to be quite highly valued by its widely-disparate members. They could live without it, but prefer to live with it. As Canada's prime minister, Pierre Trudeau (1968–79)—who was initially dismissive of the Commonwealth—put it, it is 'in some inexplicable way, worthwhile'.[51] It is a going concern.

At its political summit is the CHOGM, which is usually held every other year. It is a somewhat brittle phenomenon, but not thereby of little appeal to its participants and those who travel to observe and report on it. The dinners the Queen gives as head of the Commonwealth, are much appreciated, as are her audiences with Commonwealth leaders (see below). Rather less prominent, but more useful in terms of obvious output, are the meetings (some of them annual) of ministers and officials in a variety of fields, from finance and business through education to agriculture, science, and women's affairs. They swell the numbers of those who are likely to have something to say in favour of the Commonwealth. Possibly even more useful is what has come to be known as the 'people's Commonwealth', the several hundred Commonwealth non-governmental organisations which link professional people, sportspersons, and interest groups. They contribute, among other things, to the strengthening of personal skills and encourage the exchange of individual members, so giving many people the opportunity to 'experience' the Commonwealth at first hand, and reasons

[51] Opinions expressed by Commonwealth leaders over dinner during the 1969 Prime Ministers' Meeting: N.J. Barrington (assistant private secretary to foreign and commonwealth secretary) minute, 15 January 1969, *BDEE 1964–1971* II, 446. As another, more recent, observer put it, 'the Commonwealth's tangible benefits are difficult to quantify but real': interview.

for being grateful to it. The work of these organisations is facilitated and improved through the financial support of the Commonwealth Foundation (an autonomous, governmentally-funded body, founded in 1966).[52] At the bilateral Commonwealth level, getting on for a third of the aid programmes of the 'old' members is directed towards their Commonwealth fellows. All this is cocooned by the emotional adhesive which stems from the Commonwealth being a kind of old boys club. It results in a constituency which may lack independent political clout, but in its multitudinous parts amounts to a considerable whole that cannot be easily ignored. It is therefore an important fount of indirect support for the office of high commissioner.

As has been mentioned, the Commonwealth has since 1965 had the underpinning of a Secretariat, through which multilateral communication is channelled and events organised. Consultation and cooperation is promoted by the Secretariat in a variety of areas, information dispensed, and technical assistance arranged. Formally speaking the Secretariat is the servant, and the heads of government the collective master. But in practice, especially as the Commonwealth is such a loose organisation, there is scope for an appreciable degree of Secretariat initiative. As a whole, and through its several hundred personnel (drawn from about 35 of the Commonwealth's member states), the Secretariat has a keen stake in the health and distinctiveness of its parent body, and can be expected to act accordingly. Here, too, is another important source of support for the office of high commissioner.

In sum, there is a lively, fairly large, and potentially influential constituency of states, officials, and citizens which is both aware and appreciative of the Commonwealth's multifarious doings. It is reasonable to suppose that, should the Commonwealth or its arrangements—such as the office of high commissioner—come under threat, it would rally to the cause. Moreover, it is a constituency which has a form of royal patronage.

C. The Queen as Head of the Commonwealth

Queen Elizabeth II is Head of the Commonwealth, and accepted as such by each of its members as the symbol of their free association.

[52] In addition, since 1989 the Vancouver-based Commonwealth of Learning—a unique inter-governmental organisation—has been promoting distance education and learning.

She is also a very Commonwealth-minded person. In London this is reflected in the close attention she pays to all high commissioners, so demonstrating her special relationship with them. Those who represent her realms, and hence are her subjects, receive particularly privileged treatment, in the form of private, relaxed, and informal audiences when they arrive, and invitations to stay overnight at Windsor Castle at some time during their posting. But all are privileged in some meaure at, for example, the Trooping the Colour ceremony when the representatives of small Commonwealth states are better placed than the American ambassador. At royal receptions with the diplomatic corps during state visits to London, high commissioners (and the Irish ambassador) are still received before other heads of mission. When in 1968 the Commonwealth and Foreign Offices were merged, the Queen expressed the hope that it 'would not in any way diminish the special arrangements made for Commonwealth representatives'.[53] It is this sense of being marked out as a special, advantaged group on such occasions that probably accounts for the belief that there would be an outcry in London if it were proposed that high commissioners should become mere ambassadors. Abroad, too, high commissioners are sometimes singled out. The Queen has insisted that during visits to Commonwealth states they be received separately and apart from other heads of mission. In Ottawa in 1997 and Accra in 1999 she even received the high commissioners but not the ambassadors.

The increasing size of the Commonwealth has necessarily had an impact on the attention the Queen has been able to bestow on high commissioners. During her reign of more than 50 years the proportion of high commissioners who could rely on an invitation to all state banquets has fallen from 100% to, on occasion, nil. Special invitations to royal garden parties used to be available for high commissions, but nowadays all missions are treated alike, receiving tickets proportionately to their size. However, high commissions may propose some extra, non-diplomatic, guests. Further, the loosening of Commonwealth ties has contributed to the Queen no longer always playing a part in the issue of letters of commission, credence, and recall to the representatives of one of her realms. In 1977 Canada's governor-general was permitted to approve (and receive) them; and in 2005 this was taken a step

[53] J.R. Williams (private secretary to commonwealth secretary) minute, 30 April 1968, TNA, FCO49/138.

further, with such letters being issued in his or her name, and letters presented by heads of mission coming to Ottawa being addressed to the governor-general directly.[54] It would be surprising if this example was not followed.

However, the Queen does what she can to demonstrate firmly that she does not wish her Commonwealth responsibilities to be curbed. To her, CHOGMs are 'occasions of pleasure and reinforcement, offering the world a reminder of her continued global role'. On the other hand, British prime ministers have not infrequently found them dreaded and difficult events, as well as occasions on which they 'became just another Commonwealth premier'.[55] Edward Heath (prime minister 1969–74) effectively prevented the Queen from attending the 1971 Singapore Meeting (because of the likelihood of angry exchanges over Britain's proposed arms sales to South Africa), and then said he did not want another CHOGM until '1975 at the earliest'.[56] He only attended the 1973 Ottawa CHOGM, it has been suggested, because the Queen insisted 'that she at any rate would be in Canada'.[57] Six years later, the Queen's wishes prevailed over those of Mrs. Thatcher, who did not want either the Queen or herself to attend the Lusaka Meeting, being worried about their safety. In the event, the Zambians greeted the Queen with extraordinary warmth, and she brought 'a healing touch of rather special significance'.[58] It is very possible that the Queen was influential in ensuring that Mrs. Thatcher generally spoke with a degree of politeness to the Commonwealth. Her subsequent prime ministers have been better disposed towards it, and have also been fortunate in that since the early 1990s CHOGMs have become much less uncomfortable. They, and other Commonwealth events, may for the Queen be among the more pleasureable of her official activities. And as a key Whitehall figure of the 1970s and 1980s observed, '"she is entitled to feel that, whereas she just inherited the title of Queen of

[54] Privy Council Office news release, 'Canada Updates Diplomatic Practice', 29 December 2004, http://www.pco-bcp.gc.ca/default.asp?Language=E&Page=archivemartin&Sub=newscommuniques&Doc=news_release_20041229_368_e.htm.

[55] Pimlott (1996) 464.

[56] Smith (1981) 272.

[57] *Ibid.*

[58] Sonny Ramphal (commonwealth secretary-general, 1975–90) quoted in Pimlott (1996) 467.

England, her Headship of the Commonwealth is something she has striven for and earned"'.[59]

Unquestionably, the Queen is liked as a person and admired for her sense of duty, hard work, unrivalled experience, and (as early as 1955) her 'extraordinary knowledge of all that is going on'.[60] Fifty years later it was said that she can 'melt' even 'the toughest republicans...in two seconds flat'.[61] A British ambassador at (the non-Commonwealth but non-foreign) Dublin in the late 1970s found his audience with the Queen 'the most encouraging experience of my diplomatic career'. She 'had not only read but had evidently studied with care all my despatches and telegrams, all the correspondence from Northern Ireland, and all the Whitehall papers about Ireland, and she appreciated all the nuances of Ireland *as a whole*. We left Buckingham Palace enchanted and comforted'.[62] According to the former Commonwealth secretary-general, Sonny Ramphal (1975–90), the Queen understood that the Commonwealth had become a post-colonial association, 'something even senior members of the Foreign Office [*sic.*] didn't understand', and she brought to it 'a new quality of caring, a sense that it was important to her reign'.[63] She understands and relates to its leaders who, during CHOGMs, emerge from audiences with 'visible delight and satisfaction':

> 'They would tell her their troubles and worries,' says one lady-in-waiting. 'She's like a mother confessor,' says another. 'They all troop to listen to her'.... 'She used to talk to Hastings Banda as if he were a long lost friend,' says a close observer. Prince Philip was fond of describing her role as that of Commonwealth psychotherapist.
>
> 'The Queen attracts a personal loyalty in the Commonwealth context that is complex,' says a former leading Whitehall official, '—but it exists.' 'You'll see them getting up and slipping away in the middle of the meeting,' [Commonwealth secretary-general Sonny] Ramphal [said]...'for a private meeting on *Britannia* or at the Governor-General's house...It's very friendly, but it's not small talk. She always knows the political situation in the country, the key issue confronting it and where the shoe is pinching economically.' A senior minister...recalls that the Queen was

---

[59] Pimlott (1996) 464.

[60] Harold Macmillan diary, 24 April 1955 in Catterall (ed.) (2003) 416.

[61] Sir Anthony Figgis (marshal of the diplomatic corps) quoted in Rebecca English, 'Just another day at one's office', *Daily Mail*, 19th April 2006.

[62] Peck (1978) 137. When he went, earlier, to Senegal, the Queen, 'in a few minutes gave me a more perceptive commentary on Africa than I found anywhere in Whitehall': *ibid.*

[63] Quoted in Pimlott (1996) 465.

> very conscious of the sense of the Commonwealth, not just as a post-colonial institution, but as a genuinely multi-national one—and she put that impression across a the meeting. 'They all responded with deference,' he says, 'and with an affection that was returned. She liked to regard them as part of the extended family.'[64]

In sum, the Queen is held in huge respect on all Commonwealth sides.

By the time of her Golden Jubilee in 2002 she had made more than 200 visits to Commonwealth countries, including every single member bar one (Cameroon). During that year she visited Jamaica, New Zealand, Australia, and Canada (all of which she had also visited on her first such tour towards the end of 1953, Jamaica then being a colony). To celebrate her Jubilee, 2 June was appointed as a day on which there were be church services and bell-ringing throughout her realms; on 3 June a chain of beacons was lit across the Commonwealth's then 54 countries; a national festival on the Mall in London included various Commonwealth features and pageants; on 4 June there was a state procession to Saint Paul's Cathedral for a thanksgiving service, the procession being accompanied by over 1,000 musicians, including a specially formed golden jubilee steel orchestra and other Commonwealth musicians.

There is thus a real sense in which the Queen is part, and a hugely influential part, of the pro-Commonwealth constituency. Any attempt to diminish it, or its office of high commissioner, could hardly be seen as not also involving a snub to her as the Commonwealth's head. For this reason especially, it is almost impossible to imagine such an attempt while she continues to sit on the throne. Under her successor, however, things may be different. Even if the position of Head of the Commonwealth should pass to the next British monarch (and there is no guarantee of that, as the position is not hereditary), her successor is unlikely to be held in the same esteem, and feelings about the Commonwealth may not be as warm. It could lose some of its allure. It might undergo serious political rifts. There might still be keen support for it at the non-official level and amongst its smaller members, and—probably—in Britain. But other important movers and shakers might conclude that the Commonwealth had had its day. For the moment, however, the Commonwealth, and hence its office of high commissioner, seems safe.

---

64 *Ibid.*, 465–6.

APPENDIX ONE

GLOSSARY

Accreditation	Furnishing a prospective head of mission with the credentials which are necessary for him or her to take up such an appointment.
Accredited representative	Title of South African head of mission in Ottawa 1938–45, and in (Southern) Rhodesia after the illegal unilateral declaration of independence in 1965.
Acting high commissioner	Commonwealth equivalent of *chargé d'affaires ad interim.*
Adviser	Commonwealth equivalent of *attaché.*
Agent-general	Representative of a constituent province or state of a (con)federation.
Agrément/agréation	A receiving state's formal agreement to receive a person nominated by a sending state as the head of its diplomatic mission.
Ambassador	Diplomatic agent of the highest class. The full title is 'Ambassador Extraordinary and Plenipotentiary'.
Attaché	Specialist attached to a resident mission for particular duties.
Chargé d'affaires ad interim	Acting head of mission during the temporary absence of the head of mission or pending the appointment of a new head of mission (often abbreviated to *chargé d'affaires a.i.*).
Commission	Document the head of state gives to a new head of mission appointing him or her to the position in question.
Commonwealth Office	British government department created by the merger of the Colonial Office and Commonwealth Relations Office, 1 January 1966.

Commonwealth Relations Office	British government department handling relations with the Commonwealth, July 1947–January 1966. It absorbed the India Office in August 1947, and the Burma Office in 1948.
Consul	Representative of a state, who is often posted outside a metropolitan capital, who looks after her or his state's commercial interests and the interests of her or his fellow nationals. In order of seniority consuls are ranked consul-general, consul, vice-consul, and consular agent.
Consular privileges and immunities	The privileges and immunities enjoyed by consular officers, viz (chiefly): exemption from customs or excise duties on first arriving in a state, inviolability of consular premises, and immunity from jurisdiction in respect of official acts.
Consulate(-general)	A consular post.
Credentials/letters of credence	Letter from the sending head of state asking the receiving head of state to (for example) 'give entire credence to all that [the ambassador] shall have occasion to communicate to you in my name'.
Dean/*doyen*	Head of the diplomatic corps, and hence the channel of communication between the receiving state and the corps. The office is usually held by the longest-serving member of the corps in the capital in question.
Décanat	The office of the dean/*doyen* of the diplomatic corps.
Deputy high commissioner	The name sometimes given to the number two in a high commission. Also, in a few Commonwealth states, the head of a post that is located outside the capital.

Diplomatic corps	The body of diplomats, including *attachés*, accredited to a particular state. Their corporate identity is founded on a common interest in defending their privileges and immunities.
Diplomatic list	The list maintained and (usually) published periodically by the receiving state which gives the names of those who have been granted diplomatic status.
Diplomatic privileges and immunities	Special legal position accorded to diplomatic agents. Their residences, missions, and communications are inviolable; they and their families may not be subjected to civil or criminal proceedings or detention; they are exempt from certain taxes and customs duties; and they are not liable to public service or to submit to customs inspections.
Dominions Office	British government department handling relations with the dominions, 1925–July 1947.
Embassy	Diplomatic mission headed by an ambassador. Also the building housing it.
Exequatur	Document whereby receiving state authorises the head of a consular post to exercise consular functions within the post's district.
Foreign and Commonwealth Office	British government department created by the merger of the Foreign Office and Commonwealth Office, October 1968.
High Commission	Commonwealth equivalent of an embassy. Until the 1960s the term 'Office of the High Commissioner' was used.
High commissioner	Head of one Commonwealth state's diplomatic mission to another such state.
Legation	Diplomatic mission headed by a minister plenipotentiary, a head of mission of the second class. Also the building housing it.

Letter of commission	Credentials used by Commonwealth states who are not part of the Queen's realms.
Letter of introduction	Credentials provided by the head of the sending government to the head of the receiving government in Commonwealth states that are part of the Queen's realms. Their style is usually informal.
Minister of state	Second most senior government minister in a British government department.
Minister plenipotentiary	Name given to head of legation whose full title is, ordinarily, 'envoy extraordinary and minister plenipotentiary'.
Outposts	Representative missions (sometimes diplomatic but usually not) located outside capitals.
Permanent under-secretary	The senior official in certain British government departments.
Parliamentary under-secretary	Junior British minister.
Persona non grata	Term used by receiving state to indicate that a diplomatic agent or consular officer is unwelcome and must depart.
Representative	Title of British head of mission in: Australia 1931–36; Ireland 1939–50; Cyprus between independence in August 1960 and joining the Commonwealth in March 1961; Singapore between separating from Malaysia in August 1965 and joining the Commonwealth in October 1965. Also title of certain Commonwealth heads of mission to and from non-sovereign entities (for example, Britain to Kenya 1963 and Ceylon to India 1946–48). Ceylon's head of mission is India retained this title until 1949.
Secretary	Variously used: sometimes a governmental minister; sometimes the senior official

	in a ministry or department; and once the second most senior member of high commissions.
Secretary of state	The title given, in conjunction with the name of their departments, to the some British government ministers, such as secretary of state for foreign affairs.
Table of precedence	Official list setting out the order in which foreign envoys (among many others) take precedence, for example, at dinners and on formal and ceremonial occasions.
Under-secretary	The senior official in Canada's Department of External Affairs

APPENDIX TWO

COMMONWEALTH MEMBERS

State	Year of Membership	Notes*
Britain		Indigenous monarchy Realm of Queen Elizabeth II
Canada	1867†	Realm of Queen Elizabeth II
Australia	1901†	Realm of Queen Elizabeth II
New Zealand	1907†	Realm of Queen Elizabeth II
South Africa	1910†	Republic 1961 Withdrew 1961 Rejoined 1994
Pakistan	1947	Republic 1956 Withdrew 1972 Rejoined 1989 Suspended 1999–2004
India	1947⊕	Republic 1950
Ceylon/Sri Lanka	1948	Republic 1972 Changed name 1972
Ghana	1957	Former Gold Coast Republic 1960
Malaya/Malaysia	1957	Indigenous monarchy Three colonial territories joined Malaya to create Malaysia 1963
Nigeria	1960	Republic 1963 Suspended 1995–99
Cyprus	1961	Independent 1960 Republic
Sierra Leone	1961	Republic 1971
Jamaica	1962	Realm of Queen Elizabeth II
Trinidad and Tobago	1962	Republic 1976
Uganda	1962	Republic 1967
Kenya	1963	Republic 1964
Tanzania	1964	Union of Tanganyika (independent 1961) and Zanzibar (independent 1963) Republic

Table (*cont.*)

State	Year of Membership	Notes*
Malawi	1964	Former Nyasaland Republic 1966
Malta	1964	Republic 1974
Zambia	1964	Former Northern Rhodesia Republic
The Gambia	1965	Republic 1970
Singapore	1965	Republic
Guyana	1966	Former British Guiana Republic 1970
Botswana	1966	Former Bechuanaland Republic
Lesotho	1966	Former Basutoland Indigenous monarchy
Barbados	1966	Realm of Queen Elizabeth II
Nauru	1968	Former UN Trust Territory, administered jointly by Australia, Britain, and New Zealand Republic Special member§ 1968–99 Full member 1999–2005 Special member 2005
Mauritius	1968	Republic 1992
Swaziland	1968	Indigenous monarchy
Tonga	1970	Indigenous monarchy
Western Samoa/ Samoa	1970	Independent 1962 Indigenous monarchy Changed name 1997
Fiji	1970	Republic 1987 Withdrew 1987 Rejoined 1997 Suspended 2000–01 Suspended 2006
Bangladesh	1972	Republic
The Bahamas	1973	Realm of Queen Elizabeth II
Grenada	1974	Realm of Queen Elizabeth II
Papua New Guinea	1975	(in part) Former UN Trust Territory, administered by Australia Realm of Queen Elizabeth II
Seychelles	1976	Republic
Solomon Islands	1978	Realm of Queen Elizabeth II

Table (*cont.*)

State	Year of Membership	Notes*
Tuvalu	1978	Former Ellice Islands (part of Gilbert and Ellice Islands) Realm of Queen Elizabeth II Special member[§] 1978–2000 Full member 2000
Dominica	1978	Republic
St Lucia	1979	Realm of Queen Elizabeth II
Kiribati	1979	Former Gilbert Islands (part of Gilbert and Ellice Islands) Republic
St Vincent and the Grenadines	1979	Realm of Queen Elizabeth II
Vanuatu	1980	Former British-French condominium of New Hebrides Republic
Belize	1981	Former British Honduras Realm of Queen Elizabeth II
Antigua and Barbuda	1981	Realm of Queen Elizabeth II
The Maldives	1982	Independent 1965 Republic Special member[§] 1982–85 Full member 1985
St Christopher and Nevis	1983	Realm of Queen Elizabeth II
Brunei	1984	Indigenous monarchy
Namibia	1990	Former South West Africa Former League of Nations Mandate, administered by South Africa Republic
Cameroon	1995	Former UN Trust Territories, one administered by Britain, the other by France Independent 1960 Republic
Mozambique	1995	Former Portuguese colony Independent 1975 Republic

Thus, at the end of 2006, the Commonwealth had 53 members, of whom one was a special member and another was suspended

FORMER COMMONWEALTH MEMBERS

State	Year of Membership	Notes*
Newfoundland	1907[†+]	Self-government suspended 1934 Joined Canada 1949
Irish Free State/Ireland	1922[†]	Changed name 1937 Withdrew 1949
Tanganyika	1961	United with Zanzibar to create Tanzania 1964
Zanzibar	1963	United with Tanganyika to create Tanzania 1964
Zimbabwe	1980	Former Southern Rhodesia/ Rhodesia Republic Suspended 2002–03 Withdrew 2003

* Dates are only given when there has been a change since joining.

† Year in which dominion status was granted to a non-sovereign entity.

⊕ Although India only became a dominion on independence, since the First World War she had in some ways been treated as a full Commonwealth member.

§ A special member does not attend Heads of Government Meetings but may, as an observer, attend meetings of ministers and of officials.

\+ The year in which Newfoundland became a dominion is obscure, but there is evidence to suggest it was not later than 1907.

APPENDIX THREE

THE GROWTH OF INTRA-COMMONWEALTH REPRESENTATION 1880–1957[1]

From	To	Year of arrival
Britain	Canada	1928
	South Africa	1928 Imperial Secretary and Representative[2] (High Commissioner 1931)
	Australia	1931 Acting Representative (High Commissioner 1936)
	New Zealand	1939
	Ireland	1939 Representative (Ambassador 1950)
	India	1946
	Pakistan	1947
	Ceylon	1948
	Ghana	1957
	Malaya	1957
	Southern Rhodesia/ Federation of Rhodesia and Nyasaland (1953–63)	1951
Canada	Britain	1880
	Australia	1939
	Ireland	1940 (Ambassador 1950)
	South Africa	1940
	New Zealand	1940
	India	1947
	Pakistan	1949
	Sri Lanka	1953
	Ghana	1957
	Malaya	1957

[1] This table only includes representation at a senior level. Unless otherwise stated, the title of the representative is high commissioner.

[2] 'Representative' was added to the title of the then imperial secretary.

Table (*cont.*)

From	To	Year of arrival
Australia	Britain	1910
	Canada	1940
	New Zealand	1943
	India	1943
	South Africa	1946
	Ireland	1946 (*Chargé d'affaires a.i.* 1950–64, Ambassador 1964)
	Ceylon	1948
	Pakistan	1949
	Malaya	1957
New Zealand	Britain	1905
	Australia	1943
	Canada	1944
	Malaya	1957 (resident in Singapore)
South Africa	Britain	1911
	Canada	1938 Accredited Representative (High Commissioner 1945)
	Australia	1946
	Southern Rhodesia/ Federation of Rhodesia and Nyasaland (1953–63)	1950 (Accredited Diplomatic Representative 1961)
Irish Free State/Ireland	Britain	1922 (Ambassador 1950)
	Canada	1939 (Ambassador 1950)
	Australia	1946 Minister Plenipotentiary Representative of Ireland in Australia (Ambassador 1950)
India	Britain	1920
	South Africa	1927 (Agent, Agent-General 1935, High Commissioner 1941, withdrawn 1946)
	Australia	1944
	Canada	1947
	Pakistan	1947
	Ceylon	1947
	Ireland	1949 Ambassador (resident in London)

Table (*cont.*)

From	To	Year of arrival
	New Zealand	1951 (resident in Canberra)
	Ghana	1957 Acting High Commissioner
	Malaya	1957 (resident in Singapore)
Pakistan	Britain	1947
	India	1947
	Canada	1949
	Australia	1950
	New Zealand	1950 (resident in Canberra)
	Ceylon	1952
Ceylon	Britain	1948
	India	1946 Representative (High Commissioner 1949)
	Australia	1949
	Pakistan	1950
	New Zealand	1956 (resident in Canberra)
	Canada	1957 (resident in New York)
Ghana	Britain	1957
	India	1957
Malaya	Britain	1957
	Australia	1957
	India	1957
	Pakistan	1957
Southern Rhodesia/ Federation of Rhodesia and Nyasaland (1953–63)	Britain	1923
	South Africa	1950 (Accredited Representative 1961)

APPENDIX FOUR

RELEVANT ARTICLES FROM THE VIENNA CONVENTIONS

1. Vienna Convention on Diplomatic Relations, 1961

Article 3

1. The functions of a diplomatic mission consist, *inter alia*, in:

   (a) representing the sending State in the receiving State;
   (b) protecting in the receiving State the interests of the sending State and of its nationals, within the limits permitted by international law;
   (c) negotiating with the Government of the receiving State;
   (d) ascertaining by all lawful means conditions and developments in the receiving State, and reporting thereon to the Government of the sending State;
   (e) promoting friendly relations between the sending State and the receiving State, and developing their economic, cultural and scientific relations.

2. Nothing in the present Convention shall be construed as preventing the performance of consular functions by a diplomatic mission.

Article 4

1. The sending State must make certain that the *agrément* of the receiving State has been given for the person it proposes to accredit as head of the mission to that State.
2. The receiving State is not obliged to give reasons to the sending State for a refusal of *agrément.*

Article 8

1. Members of the diplomatic staff of the mission should in principle be of the nationality of the sending State.
2. Members of the diplomatic staff of the mission may not be appointed from among persons having the nationality of the receiving State, except with the consent of that State which may be withdrawn at any time.

3. The receiving State may reserve the same right with regard to nationals of a third State who are not also nationals of the sending State.

Article 9

1. The receiving State may at any time and without having to explain its decision, notify the sending State that the head of the mission or any member of the diplomatic staff of the mission is *persona non grata* or that any other member of the staff of the mission is not acceptable. In any such case, the sending State shall, as appropriate, either recall the person concerned or terminate his functions with the mission. A person may be declared *non grata* or not acceptable before arriving in the territory of the receiving State.
2. If the sending State refuses or fails within a reasonable period to carry out its obligations under paragraph 1 of this Article, the receiving State may refuse to recognize the person concerned as a member of the mission.

Article 14

1. Heads of mission are divided into three classes, namely:

   (a) that of ambassadors or nuncios accredited to Heads of State, and other heads of mission of equivalent rank;
   (b) that of envoys, ministers and internuncios accredited to Heads of State;
   (c) that of *chargés d'affaires* accredited to Ministers for Foreign Affairs.

2. Except as concerns precedence and etiquette, there shall be no differentiation between heads of mission by reason of their class.

Article 18

The procedure to be observed in each State for the reception of heads of mission shall be uniform in respect of each class.

Article 29

The person of a diplomatic agent shall be inviolable. He shall not be liable to any form of arrest or detention. The receiving State shall treat him with due respect and shall take all appropriate steps to prevent any attack on his person, freedom or dignity.

Article 30

1. The private residence of a diplomatic agent shall enjoy the same inviolability and protection as the premises of the mission.
2. His papers, correspondence and, except as provided in paragraph 3 of Article 31, his property, shall likewise enjoy inviolability.

Article 31

1. A diplomatic agent shall enjoy immunity from the criminal jurisdiction of the receiving State. He shall also enjoy immunity from its civil and administrative jurisdiction, except in the case of:

   (a) a real action relating to private immovable property situated in the territory of the receiving State, unless he holds it on behalf of the sending State for the purposes of the mission;
   (b) an action relating to succession in which the diplomatic agent is involved as executor, administrator, heir or legatee as a private person and not on behalf of the sending State;
   (c) an action relating to any professional or commercial activity exercised by the diplomatic agent in the receiving State outside his official functions.

2. A diplomatic agent is not obliged to give evidence as a witness.
3. No measures of execution may be taken in respect of a diplomatic agent except in the cases coming under sub-paragraphs (a), (b) and (c) of paragraph 1 of this Article, and provided that the measures concerned can be taken without infringing the inviolability of his person or of his residence.
4. The immunity of a diplomatic agent from the jurisdiction of the receiving State does not exempt him from the jurisdiction of the sending State.

Article 34

A diplomatic agent shall be exempt from all dues and taxes, personal or real, national, regional or municipal, except:

(a) indirect taxes of a kind which are normally incorporated in the price of goods or services;
(b) dues and taxes on private immovable property situated in the territory of the receiving State, unless he holds it on behalf of the sending State for the purposes of the mission;

(c) estate, succession or inheritance duties levied by the receiving State, subject to the provisions of paragraph 4 of Article 39;
(d) dues and taxes on private income having its source in the receiving State and capital taxes on investments made in commercial undertakings in the receiving State;
(e) charges levied for specific services rendered;
(f) registration, court or record fees, mortgage dues and stamp duty, with respect to immovable property, subject to the provisions of Article 23.

Article 35

The receiving State shall exempt diplomatic agents from all personal services, from all public service of any kind whatsoever, and from military obligations such as those connected with requisitioning, military contributions and billeting.

Article 36

1. The receiving State shall, in accordance with such laws and regulations as it may adopt, permit entry of and grant exemption from all customs duties, taxes, and related charges other than charges for storage, cartage and similar services, on:

   (a) articles for the official use of the mission;
   (b) articles for the personal use of a diplomatic agent or members of his family forming part of his household, including articles intended for his establishment.

2. The personal baggage of a diplomatic agent shall be exempt from inspection, unless there are serious grounds for presuming that it contains articles not covered by the exemptions mentioned in paragraph 1 of this Article, or articles the import or export of which is prohibited by the law or controlled by the quarantine regulations of the receiving State. Such inspection shall be conducted only in the presence of the diplomatic agent or of his authorized representative.

Article 37

1. The members of the family of a diplomatic agent forming part of his household shall, if they are not nationals of the receiving State, enjoy the privileges and immunities specified in Articles 29 to 36.

2. Members of the administrative and technical staff of the mission, together with members of their families forming part of their respective households, shall, if they are not nationals of or permanently resident in the receiving State, enjoy the privileges and immunities specified in Articles 29 to 35, except that the immunity from civil and administrative jurisdiction of the receiving State specified in paragraph 1 of Article 31 shall not extend to acts performed outside the course of their duties. They shall also enjoy the privileges specified in Article 36, paragraph 1, in respect of articles imported at the time of first installation.
3. Members of the service staff of the mission who are not nationals of or permanently resident in the receiving State shall enjoy immunity in respect of acts performed in the course of their duties, exemption from dues and taxes on the emoluments they receive by reason of their employment and the exemption contained in Article 33.
4. Private servants of members of the mission shall, if they are not nationals of or permanently resident in the receiving State, be exempt from dues and taxes on the emoluments they receive by reason of their employment. In other respects, they may enjoy privileges and immunities only to the extent admitted by the receiving State. However, the receiving State must exercise its jurisdiction over those persons in such a manner as not to interfere unduly with the performance of the functions of the mission.

Article 41

1. Without prejudice to their privileges and immunities, it is the duty of all persons enjoying such privileges and immunities to respect the laws and regulations of the receiving State. They also have a duty not to interfere in the internal affairs of that State.
2. All official business with the receiving State entrusted to the mission by the sending State shall be conducted with or through the Ministry for Foreign Affairs of the receiving State or such other ministry as may be agreed.

Article 47

1. In the application of the provisions of the present Convention, the receiving State shall not discriminate as between States.
2. However, discrimination shall not be regarded as taking place:

(a) where the receiving State applies any of the provisions of the present Convention restrictively because of a restrictive application of that provision to its mission in the sending State;
(b) where by custom or agreement States extend to each other more favourable treatment than is required by the provisions of the present Convention.

2. Vienna Convention on Consular Relations, 1963

Article 5—Consular Functions

Consular functions consist in:

(a) protecting in the receiving State the interests of the sending State and of its nationals, both individuals and bodies corporate, within the limits permitted by international law;
(b) furthering the development of commercial, economic, cultural and scientific relations between the sending State and the receiving State and otherwise promoting friendly relations between them in accordance with the provisions of the present Convention;
(c) ascertaining by all lawful means conditions and developments in the commercial, economic, cultural and scientific life of the receiving State, reporting thereon to the Government of the sending State and giving information to persons interested;
(d) issuing passports and travel documents to nationals of the sending State, and visas or appropriate documents to persons wishing to travel to the sending State;
(e) helping and assisting nationals, both individuals and bodies corporate, of the sending State;
(f) acting as notary and civil registrar and in capacities of a similar kind, and performing certain functions of an administrative nature, provided that there is nothing contrary thereto in the laws and regulations of the receiving State;
(g) safeguarding the interests of nationals, both individuals and bodies corporate, of the sending State in cases of succession *mortis causa* in the territory of the receiving State, in accordance with the laws and regulations of the receiving State;
(h) safeguarding, within the limits imposed by the laws and regulations of the receiving State, the interests of minors and other persons lacking full capacity who are nationals of the sending State,

particularly where any guardianship or trusteeship is required with respect to such persons;

(i) subject to the practices and procedures obtaining in the receiving State, representing or arranging appropriate representation for nationals of the sending State before the tribunals and other authorities of the receiving State, for the purpose of obtaining, in accordance with the laws and regulations of the receiving State, provisional measures for the preservation of the rights and interests of these nationals, where, because of absence or any other reason, such nationals are unable at the proper time to assume the defence of their rights and interests;

(j) transmitting judicial and extrajudicial documents or executing letters rogatory or commissions to take evidence for the courts of the sending State in accordance with international agreements in force or, in the absence of such international agreements, in any other manner compatible with the laws and regulations of the receiving State;

(k) exercising rights of supervision and inspection provided for in the laws and regulations of the sending State in respect of vessels having the nationality of the sending State, and of aircraft registered in that State, and in respect of their crews;

(l) extending assistance to vessels and aircraft mentioned in subparagraph (k) of this Article and to their crews, taking statements regarding the voyage of a vessel, examining and stamping the ship's papers, and, without prejudice to the powers of the authorities of the receiving State, conducting investigations into any incidents which occurred during the voyage, and settling disputes of any kind between the master, the officers and the seamen in so far as this may be authorized by the laws and regulations of the sending State;

(m) performing any other functions entrusted to a consular post by the sending State which are not prohibited by the laws and regulations of the receiving State or to which no objection is taken by the receiving State or which are referred to in the international agreements in force between the sending State and the receiving State.

Article 31—Inviolability of the consular premises

1. Consular premises shall be inviolable to the extent provided in this Article.

2. The authorities of the receiving State shall not enter that part of the consular premises which is used exclusively for the purpose of the work of the consular post except with the consent of the head of the consular post or of his designee or of the head of the diplomatic mission of the sending State. The consent of the head of the consular post may, however, be assumed in case of fire or other disaster requiring prompt protective action.
3. Subject to the provisions of paragraph 2 of this Article, the receiving State is under a special duty to take all appropriate steps to protect the consular premises against any intrusion or damage and to prevent any disturbance of the peace of the consular post or impairment of its dignity.
4. The consular premises, their furnishings, the property of the consular post and its means of transport shall be immune from any form of requisition for purposes of national defence or public utility. If expropriation is necessary for such purposes, all possible steps shall be taken to avoid impeding the performance of consular functions, and prompt, adequate and effective compensation shall be paid to the sending State.

Article 32—Exemption from taxation of consular premises

1. Consular premises and the residence of the career head of consular post of which the sending State or any person acting on its behalf is the owner or lessee shall be exempt from all national, regional or municipal dues and taxes whatsoever, other than such as represent payment for specific services rendered.
2. The exemption from taxation referred to in paragraph 1 of this Article shall not apply to such dues and taxes if, under the law of the receiving State, they are payable by the person who contracted with the sending State or with the person acting on its behalf.

Article 33—Inviolability of the consular archives and documents

The consular archives and documents shall be inviolable at all times and wherever they may be.

Article 41—Personal inviolability of consular officers

1. Consular officers shall not be liable to arrest or detention pending trial, except in the case of a grave crime and pursuant to a decision by the competent judicial authority.

2. Except in the case specified in paragraph 1 of this Article, consular officers shall not be committed to prison or liable to any other form of restriction on their personal freedom save in execution of a judicial decision of final effect.
3. If criminal proceedings are instituted against a consular officer, he must appear before the competent authorities. Nevertheless, the proceedings shall be conducted with the respect due to him by reason of his official position and, except in the case specified in paragraph 1 of this Article, in a manner which will hamper the exercise of consular functions as little as possible. When, in the circumstances mentioned in paragraph 1 of this Article, it has become necessary to detain a consular officer, the proceedings against him shall be instituted with the minimum of delay.

Article 43—Immunity from jurisdiction

1. Consular officers and consular employees shall not be amenable to the jurisdiction of the judicial or administrative authorities of the receiving State in respect of acts performed in the exercise of consular functions.
2. The provisions of paragraph 1 of this Article shall not, however, apply in respect of a civil action either:

   (a) arising out of a contract concluded by a consular officer or a consular employee in which he did not contract expressly or impliedly as an agent of the sending State; or
   (b) by a third party for damage arising from an accident in the receiving State caused by a vehicle, vessel or aircraft.

Article 49—Exemption from taxation

1. Consular officers and consular employees and members of their families forming part of their households shall be exempt from all dues and taxes, on personal or real, national, regional or municipal, except:

   (a) indirect taxes of a kind which are normally incorporated in the price of goods or services;
   (b) dues or taxes on private immovable property situated in the territory of the receiving State, subject to the provisions of Article 32;
   (c) estate, succession or inheritance duties, and duties on transfers, levied by the receiving State, subject to the provisions of paragraph (b) of Article 51;

(d) dues and taxes on private income, including capital gains, having its source in the receiving State and capital taxes relating to investments made in commercial or financial undertakings in the receiving State;
(e) charges levied for specific services rendered;
(f) registration, court or record fees, mortgage dues and stamp duties, subject to the provisions of Article 32.

2. Members of the service staff shall be exempt from dues and taxes on the wages which they receive for their services.
3. Members of the consular post who employ persons whose wages or salaries are not exempt from income tax in the receiving State shall observe the obligations which the laws and regulations of that State impose upon employers concerning the levying of income tax.

Article 52—Exemption from personal services and contributions

The receiving State shall exempt members of the consular post and members of their families forming part of their households from all personal services, from all public service of any kind whatsoever, and from military obligations such as those connected with requisitioning, military contributions and billeting.

Article 55—Respect for the laws and regulations of the receiving state

1. Without prejudice to their privileges and immunities, it is the duty of all persons enjoying such privileges and immunities to respect the laws and regulations of the receiving State. They also have a duty not to interfere in the internal affairs of that State.
2. The consular premises shall not be used in any manner incompatible with the exercise of consular functions.
3. The provisions of paragraph 2 of this Article shall not exclude the possibility of offices of other institutions or agencies being installed in part of the building in which the consular premises are situated, provided that the premises assigned to them are separate from those used by the consular post. In that event, the said offices shall not, for the purposes of the present Convention, be considered to form part of the consular premises.

Article 70—Exercise of consular functions by diplomatic missions

1. The provisions of the present Convention apply also, so far as the context permits, to the exercise of consular functions by a diplomatic mission.
2. The names of members of a diplomatic mission assigned to the consular section or otherwise charged with the exercise of the consular functions of the mission shall be notified to the Ministry for Foreign Affairs of the receiving State or to the authority designated by that Ministry.
3. In the exercise of consular functions a diplomatic mission may address:

   (a) the local authorities of the consular district;
   (b) the central authorities of the receiving State if this is allowed by the laws, regulations and usages of the receiving State or by relevant international agreements.

4. The privileges and immunities of the members of a diplomatic mission referred to in paragraph 2 of this Article shall continue to be governed by the rules of international law concerning diplomatic relations.

Article 72—Non-discrimination

1. In the application of the provisions of the present Convention the receiving State shall not discriminate as between States.
2. However, discrimination shall not be regarded as taking place:

   (a) where the receiving State applies any of the provisions of the present Convention restrictively because of a restrictive application of that provision to its consular posts in the sending State;
   (b) where by custom or agreement States extend to each other more favourable treatment than is required by the provisions of the present Convention.

Article 73—Relationship between the present Convention and other International Agreements

1. The provisions of the present Convention shall not affect other international agreements in force as between States parties to them.
2. Nothing in the present Convention shall preclude States from concluding international agreements confirming or supplementing or extending or amplifying the provisions thereof.

APPENDIX FIVE

'HIGH COMMISSIONER'—A HISTORICAL NOTE

The title 'high commissioner' suggests that that the person so designated has been charged with a commission to do something or other, and is rather senior. Its use for the heads of intra-Commonwealth diplomatic missions has been prominent and long lasting, and has acquired a significance of its own. But periodically the title has also been given to officials operating in a variety of other international or quasi-international contexts. The circumstances in which this has occurred may be loosely categorised as follows.

A. Vassal States

Vassal states (a now unfashionable term) usually have some measure of international personality, but are firmly under the political thumb of another state. A very early case of the use in this context of the title of high commissioner occurred in the fourteenth century BC, when Egypt sent officials to keep the Pharaoh informed about conditions in subordinate territories, and to control any unruly behaviour. They were called *rabisu*, which is generally translated as 'commissioner', and senior such officials were described as 'high commissioners'. More than two millennia later Egypt, formally a Turkish vassal but effectively a British one, was from 1914 to 1922 governed by high commissioners (and Britain continued to be represented there by such officials until 1936, despite the fact that Egypt had supposedly become independent outside the Commonwealth). When Cyprus fell under British control in 1878 (although remaining formally part of the Ottoman Empire) it was governed until 1925 (when it became a crown colony) by high commissioners. In 1592, before the Act of Union between England and Scotland, it was stipulated that if the King of England could not be at the Church of Scotland's annual assembly, he would be represented by a high commissioner (an office that still exists).

B. Protected States

Protected states are those with unquestioned international personality, but which have formally agreed to let another protect them and act for them internationally. Britain's representatives in some states under her protection were called high commissioners, such as those in the (now Greek) Ionian Islands in the first half of the nineteenth century, and the Malay States (later the Malayan Federation) from 1874 to 1957. France did likewise after the Second World War in relation to the states of Indo-China—Cambodia, Laos, and Vietnam.

C. Protectorates and Other Colonial-Type Situations

In British constitutional law a protectorate is a territory not formally part of the monarch's domain but treated as if it were. Effectively, therefore, it is a colony under another name. Britain's protectorates were sometimes governed by high commissioners, for example Northern Nigeria and Zanzibar in the earlier part of the twentieth century, and the 'High Commission Territories' of Basutoland (now Lesotho), Bechuanaland (now Botswana), and Swaziland until the 1960s. Also in the twentieth century the British and French representatives in their Pacific condominium of New Hebrides (now Vanuatu) were high commissioners. In the inter-War period, certain mandates (territories administered by individual states under the loose supervision of the League of Nations) were headed by a high commissioner, for example, those of Britain in respect of Palestine and Iraq, and that of France in respect of Syria. A high commissioner was appointed to the British Antarctic Territory in 1962 (an office which was later 'reduced' to that of 'commissioner').

D. Occupied Territories

After the First World War Turkey was until 1923 controlled by an inter-allied commission headed by high commissioners, and the members of the Inter-Allied Rhineland High Commission (which for a decade after the War controlled the German west bank of the Rhine) were also styled high commissioners. After the Second World War the top American, British, and French representatives in West Germany during her transition from military occupation to full independence (1949–1955) were called high commissioners. Conterminously a Soviet high commissioner fulfilled the same role in East Germany.

E. International and Quasi-International Enquiries

The British head of an 1858 enquiry into trouble in the Ionian Islands, William Gladstone, had 'high commissioner' as part of his title. Anglo-American problems after the mid-nineteenth century American civil war, many of which involved Canada, were dealt with by a joint high commission, and the Canadian Sir John A. Macdonald was one of the first high commissioners. This is the same Sir John Macdonald who, as recounted in this book, was later responsible for the introduction of the title to the imperial—and hence the Commonwealth—context.

F. International Administration

When, between the two World Wars, the Free City of Danzig (now part of Poland and called Gdansk) was under the protection of the League of Nations, its administration was headed by a high commissioner.

G. Humanitarian Activity

The title has been bestowed on international civil servants dealing with humanitarian matters. In 1920 Fridtjof Nansen of Norway, on behalf of the League of Nations, became high commissioner for the repatriation of prisoners of war, and then for refugees. At the invitation of the International Committee of the Red Cross he also acted in the early 1920s as high commissioner for aid to famine-stricken Russians. His refugee work has been continued by the United Nations high commissioner for refugees, and the UN has also appointed, in 1994, a high commissioner for human rights. In 1993 the Organization for Security and Cooperation in Europe appointed a high commissioner on national minorities.

H. Support for New Entities

States have sometimes expressed their political support for newly-emerged, but often unrecognised, entities by appointing a high commissioner to them. After the First World War Britain's first representatives to the successor states of Austria and Hungary and the defeated state of Bulgaria were briefly termed high commissioners. In the civil strife which followed the 1917 Bolshevik revolution in Russia, Britain and her allies sent high commissioners to Siberia and to the short-lived Transcaucasian entities of Georgia, Erivan, and Azerbaijan.

BIBLIOGRAPHY

Note: This bibliography includes secondary works that are cited in the text, and some others that have been particularly helpful.

Unpublished Documents

Government archives

Dublin: National Archives of Ireland.
Kew: The National Archives: Public Record Office.
London: India Office Records
Ottawa: National Archives of Canada.
Pretoria: National Archives Repository.

Collections of private papers

Birmingham, University of Birmingham Library: Sir Austen Chamberlain.
Bloemfontein, Institute of Contemporary History, University of the Orange Free State: W.C. du Plessis, Nicholas Diederichs, Brand Fourie, J.E. Holloway, G.P. Jooste, Eric Louw, Henrich Verwoerd.
Cambridge, Churchill Archives Centre: Duncan Sandys; Philip Noel-Baker, Baron Noel-Baker of Derby.
Cape Town, University of Cape Town Libraries: S.F. Waterson, Sir William Clark.
London, The British Library: Arthur James Balfour, 1st Earl of Balfour; Robert Cecil, Viscount Cecil of Chelwood.
Ottawa, National Archives of Canada: William Lyon Mackenzie King.
Oxford, Rhodes House Library: Sir Harry Batterbee.
Pretoria, National Archives Repository: Field Marshal Jan Christian Smuts, Charles Te Water.

Oral histories

Cambridge, Churchill College, Churchill Archives Centre, British Diplomatic Oral History Programme: Sir Walter Leonard Allinson, Denis Doble, Sir Colin Imray, Stephen Miles, Sir Harold Smedley, Sir Robert Wade-Gery.

Published Documents and Government Publications

Australia

Andre, Pamela (ed.) (1998), *Documents on Australian Foreign Policy, 1937–1949*, vol. XIV, *Australia and the postwar world: the Commonwealth, Asia and the Pacific 1948–49* (Canberra: Department of Foreign Affairs and Trade).
Hudson, W.J. and Stokes, H.J.W. (eds.) (1983), *Documents on Australian Foreign Policy. 1937 1949*, vol. VI, *July 1942–December 1943* (Canberra: Australian Government Publishing Service).
—— (1989), *Documents on Australian Foreign Policy 1937–1949*, vol. VIII, *1945* (Canberra: Australian Government Publishing Service).
Hudson, W.J. and Way, Wendy (eds.) (1991), *Documents on Australian Foreign Policy 1937–1949*, vol. IX, *January–June 1946* (Canberra: Australian Government Publishing Service).

—— (1993), *Documents on Australian Foreign Policy 1937–1949*, vol. X, *July–December 1946* (Canberra: Australian Government Publishing Service).
Neale, R.G. (ed.) (1976), *Documents on Australian Foreign Policy 1939–1949*, vol. II, *1939* (Canberra: Australian Government Publishing Service).

Britain

Ashton, S.R. and Louis, Wm Roger (eds.) (2004), *East of Suez and the Commonwealth 1964–71* part I, *East of Suez*, part II, *Europe, Rhodesia, Commonwealth*, part III, *Dependent Territories, Africa, Economics, Race*, British Documents on the End of Empire, series A, vol. 5 (London: The Stationery Office for the Institute of Commonwealth Studies).
Goldsworthy, David (ed.) (1994), *The Conservative Government and the End of Empire 1951–1957*, part II, *Politics and Administration*, British Documents on the End of Empire, series A, vol. 3 (London: HMSO for Institute of Commonwealth Studies).
House of Commons (1959), *Third Report from the Select Committee on Estimates*, 252, Session 1958–9 (London: HMSO, 15 July).
—— (1996) Foreign Affairs Committee, First Report, Session 1995–6, *The Future Role of the Commonwealth*, vol. 1, *Report Together with the Proceedings of the Committee* (London: HMSO).
Hyam, Ronald (ed.), *The Labour Government and the End of Empire 1945–1951*, part I, *High Policy and Administration* part IV, *Race Relations and the Commonwealth*, British Documents on the End of Empire, series A, vol. 2 (London: HMSO for Institute of Commonwealth Studies, 1992).
Hyam, Ronald & Louis, Wm Roger (eds.) (2000), *The Conservative Government and the End of Empire 1957–1964*, part 1, *High Policy, Political and Constitutional Change*; part 2, *Economics, International Relations, and the Commonwealth*, British Documents on the End of Empire, series A, vol. 4 (London: The Stationery Office for Institute of Commonwealth Studies).
Report of Inter-Imperial Relations Committee (1926), *Imperial Conference 1926. Summary of proceedings*, HMSO, Cmd. 2768.
Report of the Committee on Representational Services Overseas (1964) (Plowden Report) (HMSO, Cmd. 2276, Miscellaneous No. 5, 1964).
Parry, Clive (ed.) (1965), *A British Digest of International Law Compiled Principally from the Archives of the Foreign Office*, part VII, *Organs of States* (London: Stevens & Sons).
Rathbone, Richard (ed.) (1992), *Ghana*, part I, *1941–52*, part II, *1952–1957*, British Documents on the End of Empire, series B, vol. 1 (London: HMSO for Institute of Commonwealth Studies).
Smith, H.A. (ed.) (1932), *Great Britain and the Law of Nations. A Selection of Documents Illustrating the Views of the Government in the United Kingdom Upon Matters of International Law*, vol. I, *States*, (London: P.S. King & Son).
The Parliamentary Debates, fifth series, *House of Commons, House of Lords*.

Canada

Barry, Donald (ed.) (1990), *Documents on Canadian External Relations*, vol. 18, *1952* (Ottawa: External Affairs and International Trade Canada).
—— (1991), *Documents on Canadian External Relations*, vol. 19, *1953* (Ottawa: External Affairs and International Trade Canada).
Clark, Lovell C. (1970), *Documents on Canadian External Relations*, vol. 3, *1919–1925* (Ottawa: Department of External Affairs).
Documents on Canadian External Relations (1967), vol. 1, *1909–1918* (Ottawa: Queen's Printer).
Donaghy, Greg (ed.) (1996a), *Documents on Canadian External Relations*, vol. 16, *1950* (Ottawa: Department of Foreign Affairs and International Trade).
—— (1996b), *Documents on Canadian External Relations*, vol. 17, *1951* (Ottawa: Department of Foreign Affairs and International Trade).

—— (1997), *Documents on Canadian External Relations*, vol. 20, *1954* (Ottawa: Department of Foreign Affairs and International Trade).
—— (1999), *Documents on Canadian External Relations*, vol. 21, *1955* (Ottawa: Department of Foreign Affairs and International Trade).
—— (2001), *Documents on Canadian External Relations*, vol. 22, *1956–7*, part I (Ottawa: Department of Foreign Affairs and International Trade).
—— (2002), *Documents on Canadian External Relations*, vol. 23, *1956–7*, part II (Ottawa: Department of Foreign Affairs and International Trade).
Hilliker, John F. (ed.) (1980), *Documents on Canadian External Relations*, vol. 9, *1942–3*, (Ottawa: Department of External Affairs).
—— (1987) *Documents on Canadian External Relations*, vol. 10, *1944–1945*, part I (Ottawa: Department of External Affairs).
—— (1990), *Documents on Canadian External Relations*, vol. 11, *1944–1945*, part II (Ottawa: External Affairs and International Trade Canada).
Inglis, Alex I. (ed.) (1971), *Documents on Canadian External Relations*, vol. 4, *1926–30* (Ottawa: Department of External Affairs).
—— (1973), *Documents on Canadian External Relations*, vol. 5, *1931–5* (Ottawa: Department of External Affairs).
King, William Lyon Mackenzie (1983), *The Diaries of William Lyon Mackenzie King* (Toronto: University of Toronto Press); and Ottawa: National Archives of Canada. Also http://king.collectionscanada.ca/EN/default.asp.
Mackay, R.A. (ed.) (1969), *Documents on Canadian External Relations*, vol. 2, *The Paris Peace Conference of 1919* (Ottawa: Department of External Affairs).
Mackenzie, Hector (ed.) (1994), *Documents on Canadian External Relations*, vol. 14, *1948*, (Ottawa: Department of Foreign Affairs and International Trade).
—— (1995), *Documents on Canadian External Relations*, vol. 15, *1949* (Ottawa: Department of Foreign Affairs and International Trade).
Munro, John A. (ed.) (1972), *Documents on Canadian External Relations*, vol. 6, *1936–1939* (Ottawa: Department of External Affairs).
Murray, David R (ed.) (1974), *Documents on Canadian External Relations*, vol. 7, *1939–1941*, part I, (Ottawa: Department of External Affairs).
—— (1976), *Documents on Canadian External Relations*, vol. 8, *1939–1941*, part II (Ottawa: Department of External Affairs).
Page, Donald M. (ed.) (1977), *Documents on Canadian External Relations*, vol. 12, *1946* (Ottawa: Department of External Affairs).
Riddell, Walter A. (ed.) (1962), *Documents on Canadian Foreign Policy 1917–1939* (Toronto: Oxford University Press).
Stevenson, Michael D. (ed.) (2003), *Documents on Canadian External Relations*, vol. 24, part I, *1957–8* (Ottawa: Department of Foreign Affairs and International Trade).

Commonwealth

Mansergh, Nicholas (ed.) (1953a), *Documents and Speeches on British Commonwealth Affairs 1931–1952*, vol. I, (London: Oxford University Press for Royal Institute of International Affairs).
—— (1953b), *Documents and Speeches on British Commonwealth Affairs 1931–1952*, vol. II (London: Oxford University Press for Royal Institute of International Affairs).

Ireland

Crowe, Catriona, Fanning, Ronan, Kennedy, Michael, Keogh, Dermot, O'Halpin, Eunan (eds.) (2004), *Documents on Irish Foreign Policy*, vol. IV, *1932–1936* (Dublin: Royal Irish Academy).
Fanning, Ronan, Kennedy, Michael, Keogh, Dermot, O'Halpin, Eunan (eds.) (1998), *Documents on Irish Foreign Policy*, vol. I, *1919–1922* (Dublin: Royal Irish Academy).

—— (2000), *Documents on Irish Foreign Policy*, vol. II, *1923–1926* (Dublin: Royal Irish Academy).
—— (2002), *Documents on Irish Foreign Policy*, vol. III, *1926–1932* (Dublin: Royal Irish Academy).

Secondary Works

Abdul Rahim, Radziah (2005), 'Consular relations within the Commonwealth: from the negotiation of the Vienna Convention (1963) to the London conference (1972)', PhD thesis, Keele University.
Alexander, Philip (2003), 'From imperial power to regional powers: Commonwealth crises and the second application', in Oliver J. Daddow (ed.), *Harold Wilson and European Integration. Britain's Second Application to join the EEC* (London: Routledge) 188–210.
—— (2006), 'A tale of two Smiths: Labour Party politics and the changing concept of Commonwealth', *Contemporary British History*, vol. 20, no. 3, 303–21.
Amery, L.S. (1927), 'Some aspects of the imperial conference', *Journal of the Royal Institute of International Affairs*, vol. 6, no. 1, 2–24.
Anyaoku, Chief Emeka (1994), 'The Commonwealth and South Africa: making the world safer for diversity', address to the South Africa Club, London, 19 January (London: Commonwealth Secretariat).
Attard, Bernard Paul (1991), 'The Australian High Commissioner's Office. Politics and Anglo-Australian relations 1901–1939', DPhil Thesis, St Antony's College, University of Oxford.
Austin, Dennis (1998), *The Commonwealth and Britain* (London, New York, Andover: Routledge & Kegan Paul for the Royal Institute of International Affairs, Chatham House Papers no. 41).
Ayres, Philip (2003), *Owen Dixon* (Carlton: Miegunyah Press for Melbourne University Press).
Barder, Jane, 'Early British diplomatic representation in Australia', unpublished manuscript.
Beck, Peter J. (2004), 'From Munich to Suez and beyond via Abadan in 1951: taking British policy forward by learning from the past', lecture delivered at 16th annual conference of the British International History Group, University of East Anglia, September.
Beloff, Max (1989), *Imperial Sunset*, vol. 2, *Dream of Commonwealth 1921–42* (London: Macmillan).
Berridge, G.R. (2005), *Diplomacy: Theory and Practice* (London: Palgrave-Macmillan, 3rd ed.).
—— and James, Alan (2003), *A Dictionary of Diplomacy* (Basingstoke: Palgrave, 2nd ed.).
Bissell, Claude (1986), *The Imperial Canadian. Vincent Massey in Office* (Toronto, Buffalo, London: University of Toronto Press).
Bland, Sir Nevile (ed.) (1964), *A Guide to Diplomatic Practice by the late Rt. Hon. Sir Ernest Satow*' (London, New York, Toronto: Longmans, Green, 1957, 4th ed.).
Brown, J.C. Gordon (2000), *Blazes Along the Diplomatic Trail. A Memoir of Four Posts in the Canadian Foreign Service* (Victoria: Trafford Publishing).
Bull, Hedley (1959), 'What is the Commonwealth', *World Politics*, vol. 11, no. 4, 577–87.
Campbell, Gerald (1947), *Of True Experience* (New York).
Carrington, C.E. (1955), 'A new theory of the Commonwealth', *International Affairs*, vol. 31, no. 2, April, 137–48.
Carrington, Lord (1988), *Reflect on Things Past* (London: Collins).
Catterall, Peter (ed.) (2003), *The Macmillan Diaries. The Cabinet Years, 1950–1957* (London: Macmillan).

Chadwick, John (1982), *The Unofficial Commonwealth. The Story of the Commonwealth Foundation 1965–1980* (London: Allen & Unwin).
Clifford, The Honourable Sir Bede (1964), *Proconsul. Being Incidents in the Life and Career of the Honourable Sir Bede Clifford* (London: Evans Brothers).
Colville, John (1986), *The Fringes of Power. Downing Street Diaries*, vol. 1, *1939–1941* (London: Sceptre, first published 1985).
—— (1987), *The Fringes of Power. Downing Street Diaries*, vol. 2, *1941–April 1955* (London: Sceptre, 1st published 1985).
Commonwealth Secretariat (1971), *Diplomatic Service: Formation and Operation. Report on the Commonwealth Seminar held in Singapore 1970* (London: Longman).
—— (1998), *The Commonwealth in Action. South Africa* (London: Commonwealth Secretariat).
Cook, Ramsay (1965), 'A Canadian account of the 1926 imperial conference', *Journal of Commonwealth Political Studies*, vol. 3, 50–63.
Cook, Ramsay & Bélanger, Réal (eds.), *Dictionary of Canadian Biography Online*, http://www.biographi.ca/EN/index.html.
Cross, J.A. (1967), *Whitehall and the Commonwealth. British Departmental Organisation for Commonwealth Relations 1900–1966* (London: Routledge & Kegan Paul).
Dale, (Sir) William (1982), 'Is the Commonwealth an international organisation?', *The International and Comparative Law Quarterly*, vol. 31, no. 3, 451–73.
—— (1983), *The Modern Commonwealth* (London: Butterworths).
—— (1994), *Time Past Time Present. An Autobiography* (London Dublin, Edinburgh: Butterworths).
Dalziel, R.M. (1975), *The Origins of New Zealand Diplomacy. The Agent-General in London 1870–1905* (Wellington: Price Milburn for Victoria University Press).
Dawson, Robert MacGregor (1937), *The Development of Dominion Status 1900–1936* (London: Oxford University Press).
Dean, D.W. (1992), 'Final exit? Britain, Eire, the Commonwealth and the repeal of the external relations act, 1945–1949', *The Journal of Imperial & Commonwealth History*, vol. XX, no. 3, 391–418.
Delvoie, Louis A. (1998), 'Canada and India: a new beginning?', *The Round Table*, no. 345, 51–64.
Denza, Eileen (1976) (1998), *Diplomatic Law. A Commentary on the Vienna Convention on Diplomatic Relations*, (New York: Oceana, 1st ed., Oxford: Clarendon Press, 2nd ed.).
Dilks, David (ed.) (1971), *The Diaries of Sir Alexander Cadogan, 1938–1945* (London: Cassell).
'Diplomatic relations within the Empire' (1930), Record of an informal discussion held on 8 November 1929 by members of the British Empire delegations attending the third biennial conference of the Institute of Pacific Relations at Kyoto, Japan, *International Affairs*, March, vol. 9, no. 2, 202–6.
Dixon, C.W. (1969), 'Memoirs of Sir Charles William Dixon, KCMG, KCVO, OBE', unpublished manuscript.
Donaghy, Greg (2004), '"The most important place in the world": Escott Reid in India, 1952–7' in Greg Donaghy and Stéphane Roussel, *Escott Reid. Diplomat and Scholar* (Montreal and Kingston: McGill-Queen's University Press) 67–84.
Doxey, Margaret (1982), 'Canada and the evolution of the modern Commonwealth', *Behind the Headlines* (Toronto: Canadian Institute of International Affairs) vol. XL, no. 2.
—— (1989) *The Commonwealth Secretariat and the Contemporary Commonwealth* (London: Macmillan).
Durr, Kent (1993), 'South Africa and the Commonwealth—my point of view'. A paper for South African political leaders.
—— (1994), 'South Africa and the Commonwealth', *The Round Table*, no. 330, 169–73.

Du Toit, S.F. (1969), *Home and Abroad* (Cape Town: Nasionale Boekhandel).

Edwards, Cecil (1965), *Bruce of Melbourne. Man of Two Worlds* (London: Heinemann).

Edwards, P.G. (1980), 'The rise and fall of the high commissioner: S.M. Bruce in London, 1933–45, in A.F. Madden and W.H. Morris-Jones, *Australia and Britain. Studies in a Changing Relationship* (London: Frank Cass in association with the Institute of Commonwealth Studies).

—— (1984), *Prime Ministers and Diplomats. The Making of Australian Foreign Policy 1901–1949* (Melbourne: Oxford University Press in association with the Australian Institute of International Affairs).

Egeland, Leif (1977), *Bridges of Understanding. A Personal Record in Teaching, Law, Politics and Diplomacy* (Cape Town and Pretoria: Human and Rousseau).

English, John (1992), *The Worldly Years. The Life of Lester Pearson*, vol. II, *1949–1972* (Toronto: Alfred A. Knopf Canada).

Evans, Graham and Newnham, Richard (1998), *The Penguin Dictionary of International Relations* (London: Penguin).

Falle, Sam (1996), *My Lucky Life in War, Revolution, Peace and Diplomacy* (Lewes: The Book Guild).

Fanning, Ronan (1981/2), 'The response of the London and Belfast governments to the declaration of the Republic of Ireland, 1948–9', *International Affairs* vol. 58, no. 1, 95–114.

Farr, David M.L. (1955), *The Colonial Office and Canada 1867–1887* (Toronto: University of Toronto Press).

—— (1982), 'Sir John Rose' in *Dictionary of Canadian Biography*, vol. XI, *1881–90* (Toronto, Buffalo, London: University of Toronto Press) 766–72.

Fawcett, J.E.S. (1963), *The British Commonwealth in International Law* (London: Stevens and Sons).

Garner, Joe (1978), *The Commonwealth Office 1925–1968* (London: Heinemann).

Gelber, Nancy (1980), *Canada in London. An Unofficial Glimpse of Canada's Sixteen High Commissioners 1880–1980* (Hastings: Hastings Printing for Canada House).

Geldenhuys, Deon (1984), *The Diplomacy of Isolation. South African Foreign Policy Making* (Johannesburg: Macmillan for South African Institute of International Affairs).

Goldstein, Erik (1997), 'The politics of the state visit', *DSP Discussion Papers*, No. 26 (Leicester: Centre for the Study of Diplomacy).

Gordon Walker, Patrick (1962), *The Commonwealth* (London: Secker and Warburg).

Gore-Booth, Lord (ed.) (1979), *Satow's Guide to Diplomatic Practice* (London and New York: Longmans, 5th edition).

Granatstein, J.L. (1981), *A Man of Influence: Norman Robertson and Canadian Statecraft 1929–1968* (Toronto: Deneau).

—— (1982), *The Ottawa Men. The Civil Service Mandarins, 1935–1957* (Toronto: Oxford University Press).

Greenhill, Denis (1992), *More by Accident* (Bishop Wilton: Wilton).

Hall, H. Duncan (1971), *Commonwealth. A History of the British Commonwealth of Nations* (London: Van Nostrand Reinhold).

Hall, Henry L. (1937), *The Colonial Office. A History* (London, New York, Toronto: Longmans Green for Royal Empire Society).

Hancock, W. K. (1937), *Survey of British Commonwealth Affairs*, vol. 1, *Problems of Nationality 1918–1936*, (London: Humphrey Milford, Oxford University Press for Royal Institute of International Affairs).

Hankey, Maurice (1946), *Diplomacy by Conference. Studies in Public Affairs 1920–1946* (London: Ernest Benn).

Harland, Bryce (1992), *On Our Own. New Zealand in the Emerging Tripolar World* (Wellington: Institute of Policy Studies).

Harvey, Heather J. (1952), *Consultation and Co-operation in the Commonwealth* (London: Oxford University Press for Royal Institute of International Affairs).

Hasluck, Paul (1980), *Diplomatic Witness: Australian Foreign Affairs, 1941–1947* (Melbourne: Melbourne University Press).
Heeney, Arnold (1972), *The Things that are Caesar's. Memoirs of a Canadian Public Servant* (Toronto: University of Toronto Press) (ed., Brian D. Heeney).
Hempstone, Smith (1997), *Rogue Ambassador. An African Memoir* (Sewanee: University of the South Press).
Henshaw, Peter (1989), 'South Africa's relations with Britain and the Commonwealth, 1945–1956', PhD thesis, Cambridge University.
—— (1994), 'The Commonwealth and South Africa', in Greg Mills (ed.), *From Pariah to Participant. South Africa's Evolving Foreign Relations, 1990–1994* (Johannesburg: South African Institute of International Affairs) 158–68.
Hillary, Sir Edmund (2000), *View from the Summit* (London: Corgi, 1st published 1999).
Hilliker, John F. (1984), 'Distant ally: Canadian relations with Australia during the Second World War', *Journal of Imperial and Commonwealth History*, vol. 13, no. 1, 46–67.
—— (1990), *Canada's Department of External Affairs*, vol. 1, *The Early Years, 1909–1946* (Montreal and Kingston: McGill-Queen's University Press).
—— and Barry, Donald (1995), *Canada's Department of External Affairs*, vol. II, *Coming of Age, 1946–1968* (Montreal and Kingston: McGill-Queen's University Press).
Hillmer, Norman (1979), 'A British high commissioner for Canada, 1927–8' *The Journal of Imperial and Commonwealth History*, vol. 1, no. 3, 339–56.
—— (1981), 'The Foreign Office, the Dominions and the diplomatic unity of the Empire, 1925–29' in David N. Dilks (ed.), *Retreat from Power: Studies in Britain's Foreign Policy of the Twentieth Century*, vol. 1, *1906–1939* (London: Macmillan) 64–77.
—— (ed.) (1999), *Pearson. The Unlikely Gladiator* (Montreal and Kingston: McGill-Queen's University Press).
Holmes, John (1962), 'The impact on the Commonwealth of the emergence of Africa', *International Organization*, vol. XVI, no. 2, 291–302.
—— (1966), 'The Commonwealth and the United Nations', in W.B. Hamilton *et al.*, *A Decade of the Commonwealth, 1955–1964* (Durham, N.C.: Duke University Press) 349–65.
—— (1979), *The Shaping of the Peace: Canada and the Search for World Order 1943–1957*, vol. 1 (Toronto: University of Toronto Press).
—— (1982), *The Shaping of the Peace: Canada and the Search for World Order 1943–1957*, vol. 2 (Toronto, Buffalo, London: University of Toronto Press).
Horgan, John (1999), 'Irish foreign policy, Northern Ireland, neutrality and the Commonwealth: the historical roots of a current controversy, *Irish Studies in International Affairs*, vol. 10, 135–147.
Horne, Alistair (1989), *Harold Macmillan*, vol. II, *1957–1986* (New York: Viking).
Hudson, W.J. (1986), *Casey* (Melbourne: Oxford University Press).
—— and Sharp, M.P. (1988), *Australian Independence. Colony to Reluctant Kingdom* (Melbourne: Melbourne University Press).
Hunt, Sir David (1975), *On the Spot* (London: Peter Davies).
James, Alan (1980), 'Diplomacy and international society', *International Relations*, vol. VI, no. 6, 931–48.
—— (1986), *Sovereign Statehood. The Basis of International Society* (London, Boston, Sydney: Allen and Unwin).
—— (1992), 'Diplomatic relations and contacts', *The British Year Book of International Law*, vol. 62, *1991* (Oxford, Clarendon Press), 347–87.
—— (1993), 'Diplomacy', *Review of International Studies*, vol. 19, no. 1, 91–100.
—— (2002), *Keeping the Peace in the Cyprus Crisis of 1963–64* (London: Palgrave).
Keith, Arthur Berriedale (1929), *The Sovereignty of the British Dominions* (London, Macmillan).
Keenleyside, H.L. (1981), *Memoirs of Hugh L. Keenleyside*, vol. 1, *Hammer the Golden Day* (Toronto: McLelland and Stewart).

Kirk-Green, A.H.M. (2000), 'Accredited to Africa: British diplomatic representation and African experience, c. 1960–1995', *Diplomacy & Statecraft*, vol. 11, no. 1, 79–128.
Kirkman, W.P. (1966), *Unscrambling an Empire. A Critique of British Colonial Policy 1956–1966* (London: Chatto and Windus).
Lee, J.J. (1990), *Ireland 1912–1985. Politics and Society* (Cambridge: Cambridge University Press).
Lee, Luke T. (1991), *Consular Law and Practice* (Oxford: Oxford University Press, 2nd edition).
Lloyd, Lorna (1997), 'Britain and the transformation from empire to Commonwealth: the significance of the immediate post-war years', *The Round Table*, no. 343, 333–60.
—— (2000), 'What's in a name? The curious tale of the office of high commissioner', *Diplomacy & Statecraft*, vol. 11, no. 1, 47–78.
—— (2001), '"Us and them": the changing nature of Commonwealth diplomacy', *Journal of Commonwealth and Comparative Politics*, vol. 39, no. 3, 9–30.
—— (2003), 'Loosening the apron strings: the Dominions and Britain in the interwar years', *The Round Table*, no. 369, 279–303.
—— (2004–5), '"Family diplomacy": Canada and the Commonwealth office of high commissioner', *International Journal*, vol. LX, no. 1, 111–28.
—— and James, Alan (1997), 'The external representation of the Dominions, 1919–1948: its role in the unravelling of the British Empire', *The British Year Book of International Law, 1996* (Oxford: Clarendon Press) 479–501.
Lowry, Donal (1998), '"A fellowship of disaffection": Irish-South African relations', *circa* 1921–1961, Paper presented at Workshop Conference on 'The Dominion Concept: Inter-State and Domestic Politics in the British Empire', The University of Warwick, July.
—— (2000), 'New Ireland, old empire and the outside world, 1922–49: the strange evolution of a "dictionary republic"', in Michael Cronin and John M. Regan (eds.), *Ireland: the Politics of Independence, 1922–49* (Houndmills and London: Macmillan) 164–216.
MacDonald, Malcolm (1969), *People & Places. Random Reminiscences of the Rt. Hon. Malcolm MacDonald* (London: Collins).
Macnab, Roy (1983), *The Story of South Africa House. South Africa in Britain: the Changing Pattern* (Johannesburg: Jonathan Ball).
Mallaby, George (1965), *From my Level. Unwritten Minutes* (London: Hutchinson).
Mansergh, Nicholas, (1948a), 'Britain and the Dominions: consultation and co-operation in foreign policy', *India Quarterly*, vol. IV, no. 1, 3–12 (in NAC, RG2 18, vol. 107, U-10-11).
—— (1948b), 'The implications of Eire's relationship with the British Commonwealth of Nations', *International Affairs*, vol. 24, no. 1, 1–18.
—— (1948c), 'Postwar strains on the British Commonwealth', *Foreign Affairs*, vol. 27, no. 1, 129–42.
—— (1952), *Survey of British Commonwealth affairs. Problems of External Policy 1931–1939* (London: Oxford University Press for Royal Institute of International Affairs).
—— (1958), *Survey of British Commonwealth Affairs. Problems of Wartime Co-operation and Post-War Change 1939–1952* (London: Oxford University Press for Royal Institute of International Affairs).
—— (1982), *The Commonwealth Experience*, vol. 2, *From British to Multiracial Commonwealth* (London: Weidenfeld and Nicolson, 1st published 1969 as one volume).
Massey, Vincent (1963), *What's Past is Prologue* (London: Macmillan).
McEvoy, Fred (1977), 'Canadian-Irish relations during the Second World War', *The Journal of Imperial and Commonwealth History*, vol. 5, no. 2, 206–26.
McGibbon, Ian (ed.) (1993), *Undiplomatic Dialogue. Letters between Carl Berendsen and Alister McIntosh 1943–52* (Auckland: Auckland University Press in association with Ministry of Foreign Affairs and Trade and the Historical Branch, Department of Internal Affairs).

McIntyre, W. David (1991), *The Significance of the Commonwealth 1965–90* (Christchurch, University of Canterbury Press).
—— (1998), 'Canada and the creation of the Commonwealth Secretariat', *International Journal*, vol. LII, no. 4, 753–77.
—— (1999), 'The strange death of dominion status', *Journal of Imperial and Commonwealth History*, vol. 27, no. 2, 193–212.
—— (2000), 'Britain and the creation of the Commonwealth Secretariat', *The Journal of Imperial and Commonwealth History*, vol. 28, no. 1, 135–58.
—— (2001), *A Guide to the Contemporary Commonwealth* (London: Palgrave).
—— (2002), '"A formula may have to be found". Ireland, India and the headship of the Commonwealth', *The Round Table*, no. 365, 391–413.
McMahon, Deidre (1984), *Republicans and Imperialists. Anglo-Irish Relations in the 1930s* (New Haven and London: Yale University Press).
—— (2000), 'A larger and noisier Southern Ireland: Ireland and the evolution of dominion status in India, Burma and the Commonwealth, 1942–9', in Michael Kennedy and Joseph Morrison Skelly (eds.), *Irish Foreign Policy, 1919–66* (Dublin: Four Courts Press) 155–91.
McNaught, Kenneth (1988), *The Penguin History of Canada* (Harmondsworth: rev. ed.).
Millar, Thomas B. (1962), 'The Commonwealth and the United Nations', *International Organization*, vol. XVI, no. 4, 736–57.
—— (1967), *The Commonwealth and the United Nations* (Sydney: Sydney University Press).
Miller, J.D.B. (1961), 'South Africa's departure', *Journal of Commonwealth Political Studies*, vol. 1, part 1, 56–74.
—— (1966), 'British interests and the Commonwealth', *Journal of Commonwealth Political Studies*, vol. 4, part 3, 180–90.
—— (1974), *Survey of Commonwealth Affairs. Problems of Expansion and Attrition 1953–1969* (London, New York, Ottawa: Oxford University Press for Royal Institute of International Affairs).
Millin, Sarah Gertrude (1950), 'Smuts at eighty', *Foreign Affairs*, vol. 29, no. 1, 130–42.
Mousavizadeh, Nader, Lee, Jonathan and Lu, Robert (1990), 'Bhutto or "bhutto"?', *Harvard International Review*, vol. 12, no. 2, 28.
Muller, Marie (1996), 'Rejoining the world: South Africa and the diplomacy of integration', paper presented at the annual convention of the International Studies Association, San Diego, 16–20 April.
Nicholls, G. Heaton (1961), *South Africa in my Time* (London: Allen and Unwin).
Nicolson, Harold (1952), *King George the Fifth. His Life and Reign* (London: Constable).
Noel-Baker, Philip (1929), *The Present Juridical Status of the Dominions in International Law* (London: Longmans Green).
Nöthling, F.J. (2005), 'A department in its own right' in Tom Wheeler (ed.), (J.B. Shearar trans.), *History of the South African Department of Foreign Affairs, 1927–1993* (Johannesburg: South African Institute of International Affairs) 521–55.
O'Brien, John B. (1988), 'Ireland's departure from the British Commonwealth', *The Round Table*, no. 306, 179–194.
O'Farrell, Patrick (1980), 'Irish-Australian diplomatic relations', *Quadrant*, vol. 34, no. 3, 11–20.
O'Halpin, Eunan (2000), '"Weird prophecies": British intelligence and Anglo-Irish relations, 1932–3', in Michael Kennedy and Joseph Skelly (eds.), *Irish Foreign Policy, 1919–66* (Dublin: Four Courts Press).
Palmer, Gerald E.H. (1934), *Consultation and Co-operation in the British Commonwealth. A Handbook on the Methods and Practice of Communication and Consultation between the Members of the British Commonwealth of Nations* (London: Humphrey Milford, Oxford University Press for Royal Institute of International Affairs).
Parks, John (1997), 'Britain's South African Foreign Policy 1979–1989 Bilateralism and Multilateralism', PhD thesis, Keele University.

Patterson, Henry (2006), *Ireland since 1939. The Persistence of Conflict* (Dublin: Penguin Ireland).
Pearson, Lester B. (1973), *Memoirs 1897–1948. Through Diplomacy to Politics* (London: Victor Gollancz).
Peck, John (1978), *Dublin from Downing Street* (Dublin: Gill and Macmillan).
Penson, Lillian M. (1925), 'The origin of the Crown Agency office', *English Historical Review*, vol. XL, April, 196–206.
Phillips, Horace (1995), *Envoy Extraordinary. A Most Unlikely Ambassador* (London, New York: The Radcliffe Press).
Pimlott, Ben (1996), *The Queen. A Biography of Elizabeth II* (London: HarperCollins).
Redcliffe-Maud, John (1981), *Experiences of an Optimist: Memoirs* (London: Hamish Hamilton).
Reid, Escott (1981), *Envoy to Nehru* (Delhi, Toronto, Oxford: Oxford University Press).
—— (1990), *Radical Mandarin. The Memoirs of Escott Reid* (Toronto, Buffalo, London: University of Toronto Press).
Renwick, (Lord) Robin (1997), *Unconventional Diplomacy in Southern Africa* (London: Macmillan).
Ritchie, Charles (1974), *The Siren Years. Undiplomatic Diaries, 1937–1945* (London: Macmillan).
—— (1981), *Diplomatic Passport. More Undiplomatic Diaries, 1946–1962* (Toronto: Macmillan).
—— (1983), *Storm Signals. More Undiplomatic Diaries, 1962–1971* (Toronto: Macmillan).
Roberts-Wray, Sir Kenneth (1966), *Commonwealth and Colonial Law* (London: Stevens and Sons).
Robinson, H. Basil (1989), *Diefenbaker's World. A Populist in Foreign Affairs* (Toronto, Buffalo, London: University of Toronto Press).
Robinson, Kenneth (1966), 'The intergovernmental machinery of Commonwealth consultation and co-operation' in W.B. Hamilton *et al.*, *A Decade of the Commonwealth, 1955–1964* (Durham, N.C.: Duke University Press) 89–123.
Sanger, Clyde (1995), *Malcolm MacDonald. Bringing an End to Empire* (Montreal and Kingston: McGill-Queen's University Press).
Scott, David (1981), *Ambassador in Black and White. Thirty Years of Changing Africa* (London: Weidenfeld and Nicolson).
—— (2003), *Window into Downing Street* (Spennymoor: The Memoir Club).
Skilling, H. Gordon (1945), *Canadian Representation Abroad: from Agency to Embassy* (Toronto: The Ryerson Press).
Smith, Arnold (with Clyde Sanger) (1981), *Stitches in Time. The Commonwealth in World Politics* (London: André Deutsche).
Sole, Donald, 'This Above All. Reminiscences of a South African Diplomat', unpublished manuscript.
Southern African Research and Documentation Centre (1997), *Mozambique in the Commonwealth* (Maputo).
Stacey, C.P. (1984), *Canada and the Age of Conflict. A History of Canadian External Policies*, vol. 1, *1867–1921* (Toronto, Buffalo, London: University of Toronto Press, 1st published 1977).
—— (1981), *Canada and the Age of Conflict. A History of Canadian External Policies*, vol. 2, *1921–1948. The Mackenzie King Era* (Toronto, Buffalo, London: University of Toronto Press).
Stirling, Alfred (1974), *Lord Bruce: the London Years* (Melbourne: The Hawthorne Press).
Sunderland, David (2004), *Managing the British Empire. The Crown Agents, 1833–1914* (Woodbridge: Boydell and Brewer for Royal Historical Society).
Templeton, Malcolm (1991), 'Introduction' to Malcolm McKinnon (ed.), *New Zealand in World Affairs*, vol. II, *1957–1972* (Wellington: New Zealand Institute of International Affairs).

Tennyson, Brian Douglas (1982), *Canadian Relations with South Africa. A Diplomatic History* (Washington: University Press of America).
The Round Table (2000), 'Pakistan and the Commonwealth' (editorial), no. 354, 157–60.
Thorne, Christopher (1978), *Allies of a Kind. The United States, Britain and the War against Japan, 1941–45* (Oxford: Oxford University Press).
Thorpe, D.R. (1996), *Alec Douglas-Home* (London: Sinclair-Stevenson).
Tothill, F. David (1993), 'The Australian/South African diplomatic connection', lecture to the Pretoria branch of the South African Institute for International Affairs, 9 November.
—— (1995), 'South African-Australian diplomatic relations 1945–1961', Unpublished DLitt et Phil thesis, University of South Africa.
—— (1996), 'Menzies and the South Africans', paper delivered at the Australian Defence Studies Centre conference on the Defence and Foreign Policies of the Menzies' Governments, Australian Defence Force Academy, Canberra, 5 July.
—— (1997), 'The establishment of diplomatic relations. Australia and South Africa', *Diplomatic Studies Programme Newsletter*, no. 3.
—— (1998), 'Further confessions of a South African ambassador', paper presented to the biennial conference of the Australian Historical Association, University of Sydney, 6 July.
—— (2000a), 'Early Australian-South African connections up to the establishment of official relations in 1945', *Australian Journal of International Affairs*, vol. 54, no. 1, 63–77.
—— (2000b), 'A white South African perspective on the diplomatic career', paper delivered to workshop on 'Anthropology of diplomacy: a new subfield?' at the sixth international conference of the European Association of Social Anthropologists, Cracow, Poland, 26–9 July.
—— (2003), 'In the belly of the beast: a personal perspective on apartheid South Africa's diplomacy', *Diplomacy & Statecraft*, vol. 14, no. 1, 1–28.
—— (2004a), 'A visit to New Zealand', *Diplomacy & Statecraft*, vol. 15, no. 1, 163–94.
—— (2004b), 'South African diplomats in Australia, 1949–1961', *Historia*, vol. 49, no. 2, 79–100.
—— (2006), 'A horse designed by a committee: *History of the South African Department of Foreign Affairs 1927–2993*, T.F. Wheeler (ed.), J.B. Shearar, trans., Johannesburg, SIIA, 2005, 778 pp.', paper presented at the 2006 biennial conference of the Australian Historical Association, Canberra, 4 July.
Tyler, J.E. (1967), 'Development of the Imperial Conference, 1887–1914', in S.E. Benians, Sir James Butler and C.E. Carrington (eds.), *The Cambridge History of the British Empire*, vol. III, *The Empire Commonwealth 1870–1919* (Cambridge: Cambridge University Press) 490–537.
van Wyk, A.J. (2005), 'The high commissioner in Britain' in Tom Wheeler (ed.), (J.B. Shearar trans.), *History of the South African Department of Foreign Affairs, 1927–1993* (Johannesburg: South African Institute of International Affairs) 35–63.
Watt, Sir Alan (1972), *Australian Diplomat: the Memoirs of Sir Alan Watt* (Sydney: Angus and Robertson for Australian Institute of International Affairs).
Wheare, K.C. (1960), *The Constitutional Structure of the Commonwealth* (Oxford: Clarendon Press).
Wigley, Philip (1977), *Canada and the Transition to Commonwealth, British-Canadian Relations 1917–1926* (Cambridge: Cambridge University Press).
Wilgress, Dana (1967), *Memoirs* (Toronto: The Ryerson Press).
Williams, E.T. and Nicholls, C.S. (eds.) (1995), *The Dictionary of National Biography 1961–1970* (Oxford: Oxford University Press, 1st published 1981).
Wilson, Robert R. (1957), 'Some questions of legal relations between Commonwealth members', *The American Journal of International Law*, vol. 51, no. 3, 611–7.

Wood, F.L (1958). *The New Zealand People at War: Political and External Affairs* (Official history of New Zealand in the Second World War 1939–1945) (Wellington: Department of Internal Affairs, War History Branch).

Woodard, Gary (2000), 'Ministers and mandarins: the relationships between ministers and secretaries of external affairs 1935–1970', *Australian Journal of International Affairs*, vol. 54, no. 1, 79–95.

Young, William R. (ed.) (1988), *Paul Martin. The London Diaries 1975–1979* (Ottawa, University of Ottawa Press).

Ziegler, Philip (1995), *Wilson, The Authorised Life of Lord Wilson of Rievaulx* (London: Harper Collins, 1st published 1993).

INDEX OF NAMES

This index gives the relevant positions held by individuals who feature in the book and, where pertinent, their national and political affiliations. Where through hereditary succession or the award of an honour the title of a British subject changes during the period when he 'appears' in the book, this is indicated by the use of the terms 'knight' (addressed as 'sir') or, in the case of a peer, his degree of nobility: 'baron' (addressed as 'lord'), 'viscount', 'earl', 'marquess', 'duke', followed by the year of the change. Where a peer's title is different from his surname or a previous courtesy title, this is indicated. (Courtesy titles are held by the eldest sons of earls, marquesses, and dukes.) Thus: Adeane, Michael, knight 1951, baron (Lord Stamfordham) 1972.

INDEX OF SUBJECTS